Praise for Ede
of original zombie fiction

THE BOOK OF ALL FLESH

"This is one anthology that you shouldn't let get buried in your to-read books."

—SCIENCE FICTION CHRONICLE

"Editor James Lowder has done an admirable job of assembling a collection that explores zombies in all their varieties, from traditional to new age, with stories that do more than gross out the reader."

—TANGENT

"As eleven honorable mentions in *The Year's Best Fantasy and Horror* bear out, there's plenty of thoughtful writing amongst the grue."

—CEMETERY DANCE

"Full of excellent stories from 25 different authors. All have their own little spin on what a zombie story should be and all of them entertain . . . definitely pick up this book." **Rating: A**

—GAMES UNPLUGGED

and for the sequel

THE BOOK OF MORE FLESH

"[The] nearly two dozen contributing authors have approached the subject matter with nearly as many distinctive angles of approach. . . . I can conscientiously encourage adventurous readers to seek out *The Book of More Flesh*. Along with supplying a fair amount of amusement and provocation, it conclusively proves that yet some genuine life remains in the living dead."

—LOCUS

"Though these first two volumes contain fewer bankable names than John Skipp and Craig Spector's Book of the Dead anthologies, their literary quality is equal to or better than those seminal works. Zombie fans won't want to miss out."

—HELLNOTES

MORE ZOMBIE TERROR FROM EDEN STUDIOS

<u>ROLEPLAYING</u>

All Flesh Must Be Eaten™
ZOMBIE HORROR ROLEPLAYING GAME

Zombie Master Screen

Enter the Zombie

Pulp Zombies

Fistful o' Zombies

Zombie Smackdown
(Summer 2003)

One of the Living
(Fall 2003)

<u>FICTION</u>

The Book of All Flesh

The Book of More Flesh

The Book of Final Flesh

All Flesh Must Be Eaten

The Book of Final Flesh

EDITED BY JAMES LOWDER

EDEN
STUDIOS INC

Please address questions and comments concerning this book, as well as requests for notices of new publications, by mail to: Eden Studios, 6 Dogwood Lane, Loudonville, NY 12211.

Visit us at at www.edenstudios.net and www.allflesh.com.

FIRST PAPERBACK EDITION

10 9 8 7 6 5 4 3 2 1

Eden Studios publication EDN 8702, April 2003.

ISBN 1-891153-78-1

Printed in Canada.

ACKNOWLEDGMENTS

All works are original to this anthology, and are printed by permission of the author.

Introduction by James Lowder. © 2003 by James Lowder.

"Charnel Blues" by Joe Murphy. © 2003 by Joe Murphy.

"You'll Never Walk Alone" by Scott Nicholson. © 2003 by Scott Nicholson.

"Opiate of the Masses" by Lee Thomas. © 2003 by Lee Thomas.

"Not Quite Ghosts" by Kealan Patrick Burke. © 2003 by Kealan Patrick Burke.

"Relapse" by John Sullivan. © 2003 by John Sullivan.

"Zombies are Forever" by Mark McLaughlin. © 2003 by Mark McLaughlin.

"What Comes After" by Kristine Dikeman. © 2003 by Kristine Dikeman.

"The Blonde" by Sarah A. Hoyt. © 2003 by Sarah A. Hoyt.

"Homelands" by Lucien Soulban. © 2003 by Lucien Soulban.

"Not on the Books" by Roland J. Green. © 2003 by Roland J. Green.

"Dawn Patrol" by Joseph M. Nassise. © 2003 by Joseph M. Nassise.

"Aces Undead" by Pete D. Manison. © 2003 by Pete D. Manison.

"Layabouts" by Scott Reilly. © 2003 by Scott Reilly.

"Provider" by Tim Waggoner. © 2003 by Tim Waggoner.

"If a Job's Worth Doing" by Andy Vetromile. © 2003 by Andy Vetromile.

"The Secret in the Cellar" by Ed Greenwood. © 2003 by Ed Greenwood.

"Familiar Eyes" by Barry Hollander. © 2003 by Barry Hollander.

"Christina's World" by Steve Melisi. © 2003 by Steve Melisi.

"What Dead People are Supposed to Do" by Paul E. Martens. © 2003 by Paul E. Martens.

"So Many Things Left Out" by Paul G. Tremblay. © 2003 by Paul G. Tremblay. Material quoted with permission from *Mark Twain–Howells Letters: The Correspondence of Samuel L. Clemens and William D. Howells, 1872–1910*, edited by Henry Nash Smith and William M. Gibson with Frederick Anderson, Cambridge, MA: The Belknap Press of Harvard University Press. © 1959 by the Mark Twain Company and Mildred and John Howells, 1959, 1962 by the President and Fellows of Harvard College; copyright renewed 1990 by Elinor Lucas Smith.

"Shouting Down the Moon" by Myke Cole. © 2003 by Myke Cole.

"Seven Brains, Ten Minutes" by Christine Morgan. © 2003 by Christine Morgan.

"The Cannibal Zombies of West Los Angeles" by Jonathan Petersen. © 2003 by Jonathan Petersen.

"The Last Supper" by Scott Edelman. © 2003 by Scott Edelman.

TABLE OF CONTENTS

INTRODUCTION

With *The Book of Final Flesh* now safely in your hands, I've broken the zombie horde's three-year-long domination of my office. It's a temporary victory. True, the boxes in which I corralled the story submissions for the trio of anthologies in this series yawn as empty as a grave on Judgment Day. And the next fiction I edit will be tales of pulp adventure or superheroes in action, not zombies. But the living dead still lurk everywhere around me, waiting to regroup. And as I look out over the stack of zombie-related books and comics on the shelves nearby, and the plastic zombies encircling the Coke can on the desk before me, I wonder how it came to this.

I saw my first zombie in about 1973. That was not a particularly good time for the living, what with the political blight known as Watergate fighting it out for time on the nightly news with the tail end of the Vietnam War and the front end of an Arab oil embargo. Being all of ten, I didn't know CREEP from OPEC. I could, however, name all the city-smashing monsters incarcerated alongside Godzilla on Ogasawara Island, and I believed with a zealot's faith that *The Abominable Dr. Phibes* and *The Legend of Hell House* would prove as cool as the ads promised when I finally got old enough to see them. And I knew about zombies.

I'd not yet stumbled upon any zombie fiction, so my understanding of the "living dead" came mostly from radio spots for drive-in double features I was too young to see and from the pages of *Famous Monsters*. Seeing a grainy black-and-white still is not the same as seeing a zombie, though. The shuffling gait is part of their shtick, a visual cue that makes them effective as objects of terror.

I must have made my parents sit through the Japanese monster-bash showing on Channel 56's Creature Feature one too many times, because we were tuned in to Channel 5 when *White Zombie* ran in the Classic Horror slot in the wee hours of that Sunday morning. At first I didn't get it. Bela Lugosi was cool and all, but the movie had nothing to compare with the thunder and chaos of *Destroy All Monsters*. Then came the scene in the mill. Lugosi, in his guise as voodoo-savvy plantation master Murder Legendre, provides a helpful little tour of his sugar plant. We see some shots of the zombies powering the machines, images that make it clear these unfortunates are just as mechanical as the mill's other crude hardware. Then one of the living dead men falls into the works. He's a goner. But he doesn't react as he tumbles to his doom. Neither do his fellow zombies. They keep on working, grinding up the clumsy slave as if he were just so much sugar cane. The zombies have their orders, and those orders don't include *stop if the guy next to you falls into the gears.*

Almost thirty years later, that scene still makes me shiver. It's a fine summation of why zombies are frightening, too: They embody the powerlessness every marginally self-aware person feels at one time or another.

In its classic form, derived from Haitian folklore and ritual, the zombie is slave to another person's will. In its more modern incarnation, popularized by George Romero and a host of cinematic imitators, the zombie is slave to a mindless urge to consume the flesh of the living. There's no reasoning with a zombie, no outrunning it. You either destroy the walking dead or become one of them. They don't care either way, which actually makes it all the worse.

Pondering why the zombie is so horrible—for me, the most frightening of monsters—has taken up a fair amount of my time in the past three decades. I've sat through far more than my share of zombie films. There were the classics (*Dawn of the Dead, I Walked With a Zombie*), the amusing and ironic (*Return of the Living Dead, Dead Alive*), and the just plain awful (*The Video Dead, Raiders of the Living Dead*). There's even a whole group of films that remain entertaining for me despite their obvious flaws as cinema—*Living Dead in Tokyo Bay*, for example, or the Blind Dead series by Spanish film-maker Amando de Ossorio.

I've hunted down whatever zombie-related prose I could find. Several terrific fiction anthologies line my shelves, the most noteworthy being *The Mammoth Book of Zombies* and the two Book of the Dead collections. I have my copy of Seabrook's *The Magic Island*, the 1929 travelogue of Haiti that first introduced the concept of the zombie to the American public, right alongside more recent books by Wade Davies on the sociology and ethnobiology of the Haitian zombie. The latest additions are dozens of pulp stories (reprints only, alas) in which the living dead figure prominently, including tales from the relatively staid pages of *Argosy* and that crazed and sadly short-lived chronicle of master villainy, *Doctor Death.*

It's hardly a surprise, then, that zombies play a role in my own published fiction—how frequently I hadn't realized until I came to work on these anthologies. As an author I've sent undead tromping through the jungles of Chult and along the grim byways of Sithicus, gathered them in a movie theater in the World of Darkness and a godforsaken cave in Victorian-era Afghanistan, even given them control of the city streets in Al Capone's Chicago. In fact, it's easier for me to list the books and stories I've penned that do not involve the living dead in some way than to rattle off the ones in which they appear.

When we started work on *The Book of All Flesh*, Eden and I assumed we would exhaust the topic with that one book. Now, despite the word *final* in the title of this anthology, we know that there are plenty more interesting and inventive zombie-related stories out there, waiting to see print. Some of those unpublished tales are bound to make it onto my desk sooner or later—and hopefully as part of another project from Eden Studios. Working with Alex Jurkat and George Vasilakos on *The Book of All Flesh*, *The Book of More Flesh*, and *The Book of Final Flesh* has been both creatively rewarding and an amazing amount of fun. And that's on top of the pleasure it's been to edit the dozens of terrific authors—veterans and newcomers alike—who provided the content for these anthologies.

So, yes, my workspace and my schedule are clear of the living dead at the moment. (Relatively clear, anyway.) But after the countless hours I've spent watching movies about zombies, reading about them in books and comics, writing about them, and even facing them in games like *All Flesh Must Be Eaten* and *Zombies!!!* and *Resident Evil*, I can safely say that it's only a matter of time before they rise up and reclaim my office. And I'll welcome them when they do. I suppose I should be flattered something thinks there are still brains down here worth shambling after.

—James Lowder
January 2003

CHARNEL BLUES

JOE MURPHY

Where a man with missing fingers
Plays a strange guitar
—Tom Waits, "A Little Rain"

The copper prongs of the homemade prod sparked against the gray flesh of Barbara's throat. She shrieked a long, jagged wail, black lips pulled taut over yellowed teeth.

John nodded, satisfied, and checked the pool table's restraints again. Thick leather straps nailed to a hardwood frame held his wife, naked save for a dirty sheet, flat on her back. He tried to ignore the quiver of her decaying flesh, the charred stench of necrotic tissue that lingered in the beer and urine smell of the Rosie Creek Saloon.

As John moved around the table, Barbara lunged against her straps. She snapped at him so viciously that he flinched, bumping his bad hand. Even through the swathe of bloody bandages, the pain almost brought him to his knees.

Goddamn it all; the words died unspoken in his throat. He wanted to smash in her face for putting him through this hell. Instead, he sucked in a gasp and tried to cradle his hand without dropping the prod.

"I love you, Barb," he murmured, staring at her spastically twitching jaws. "It's not over between us yet, baby."

If she heard, she gave no sign. The rheumy film over her eyes made it impossible to tell if she had focused on him.

The throbbing in his hand gradually diminished. John turned from his wife to the twisted wiring and decapitated remains that had once been a Fender amp. Now it provided juice for the prod. Atop its cabinet sat a half bottle of schnapps. He glazed longingly at it, decided his hand still hurt enough, and carefully set the prod down.

A long, minty pull of schnapps eased the pain from his hand but left his stomach churning. He adjusted a knob on the amp to increase the voltage, picked up the prod, and turned to face his wife.

"We're in this together, babe." His good hand trembled as he again brought the prod to her throat.

Barbara's shriek bubbled into a wheezing cough. A second

quick touch of the prod produced a gagging, high-pitched whimper.

"That's not like you, honey." John shook his head. Tears blurred his eyes. The schnapps left him dizzy. When Barb settled again, he stepped up the voltage. With such jury-rigged equipment and only a smattering of electrical knowledge, he couldn't be sure by how much. But damn it all, he'd done his best for her in life, and he wouldn't fail now—would not fail either of them.

John brushed a sleeve over his forehead, still mindful of the bandage. Even that slight change in altitude made his hand ache. He pulled down the sheet, and then lowered the prod's copper prongs to where he thought they would do the most good. The two heavy-gauge wires touched the sagging skin of her left breast, just below the nipple.

Barbara convulsed upon the green felt, heels slamming into the slate, fingers clenching and unclenching. But her scream!

She shrieked with a vibrant, throaty rasp, a deeply buried trace of her old voice. A voice that had belted out blues and would have left Big Mama Thornton envious, a voice that would have brought sweet tears to Bessie Smith's eyes. . . .

The lights flickered. Thin smoke coiled up from the amplifier.

"Shit!" John muttered, just as the bar plunged into a darkness lit only by daylight through boarded slats over the windows.

"Oh, for Christ's sake!" His sister stomped in from the back room. Tall like John, she wore the usual baby-shit yellow coveralls rural Alaskans favored during deep winter. Dark, unruly hair lay bound, like his, in a ponytail. Long, slender fingers plucked cotton balls from her narrow ears.

Being twins, they shared the same face. On him, he'd always assumed it looked pleasantly masculine. On her—well, some assholes called her horse-faced. But not while he was around.

"You wanna check the generator for me, Elsie?" John sighed and put down the prod. Barbara thumped and rattled on the pool table; after a moment, she went still.

"John . . . ," Elsie started, looking down, away from Barbara. Her thick eyebrows furrowed; chapped lips frowned. "John, what good's it gonna do?"

"You heard the radio." When he shrugged, his bad hand started to throb once more.

"*You* heard it." Elsie shook her head. "What I heard was a raging nutcase. No one ever confirmed—"

"They might not have had time. The station went down." John reached for the schnapps. He took a pull and offered her the bottle.

Elsie waved it away. "Or it might not have worked." Her eyes came up to meet his. Her lower lip quivered. "They might all be dead."

"They might," John admitted. He turned away from her, resting his good hand on the pool table, just beyond Barbara's randomly twitching fingers. "But I have to keep trying, Sis." His voice hardened. Anger wouldn't do any good, he reminded himself. "After all, Barb and I would do the same for you. You know we would."

"That's just it—" Elsie's voice barely rose above a whisper "—I wouldn't want you to."

John stared down at his dead wife's hand. Such a slender, delicate hand. He remembered how she had stroked a guitar with a lover's touch, as she had caressed him in a gentler darkness. Now, her wedding ring glimmered in the gloom, the flesh around it worn until bone peeped through. "Please," he said, blinking back tears. "Just restart the generator."

He heard his sister sigh, then the tromp of her boots as she started for the back room. A ladder led up to a trap door on the roof, where the generator was housed.

She'd get it going, he knew. She'd always done what he needed her to do and he'd always taken care of her. They owned the bar together, performed together. Elsie had even introduced him to Barb.

Good times, and now bad times, more than their share, more than anyone could imagine—at least in this tiny hamlet north of Fairbanks. Man, Barb used to bitch about the winter road closures and isolation.

The dead had arrived before the first set. Elsie had been setting up her drums. He and Barb had been going over an amped-up version of John Lee Hooker's "Boogie Chillun." Old Man Summers had slouched into the bar, typical for a Friday night, until he'd lurched onstage and sunk his teeth into Barb's shoulder.

They'd lost eight of Rosie Creek's sixteen inhabitants that night. The rest succumbed during the next three days. He and Elsie had found and burned them all, one by one.

Barb had held on as long as she could. With a final, pleading gaze, her sky-blue eyes had gone blank and gray even as he clutched her hand. She brought his fingers to her lips . . . a last, cold kiss that left him with stumps.

Now, he and Elsie were the only survivors in Rosie Creek.

Maybe the only survivors in Alaska. Who knew anymore? One by one, the radio stations had dropped into silence.

Only the last broadcast had meant anything. It could have been from Seattle. He'd only caught part of the bulletin—something about the use of electricity to reverse the changes in the recently dead. A radical treatment that wasn't always successful.

Electricity, they'd said, could even treat the mysterious infection that caused the change. Still experimental, still doubtful, but the best anyone had come up with.

The generator coughed to life. Lights flickered and glowed dimly, then brightened. John picked up the prod, lowered the voltage in the amplifier, and returned to his wife.

Elsie tramped back into the room, her heavy footsteps pausing behind him.

"Thanks, Sis," John said without looking up.

"I'm going hunting. See if I can bag a few rabbits before the light goes."

John nodded. "Be careful, then." They had plenty of meat; he'd taken two moose this season. His sister, however, hated the screams and woke up with her own night terrors. She was hoping for a zombie, he knew, or anything she could shoot.

He waited until she was out the door, heard it thump heavily into place, before touching the prod to a spot just below Barbara's ear.

She screamed as long as he held it there. And could he hear a little more of her old voice? Maybe. Bit by bit, note by note, if it had to be that way, he'd bring her back.

Janis Joplin would have sold her soul for a voice like Barb's. John would have snapped up a Devil's deal to bring her back in a heartbeat.

"One more time, baby." He brought the prod to her temple.

✛   ✛   ✛

John jerked awake. A hand clutched his shoulder. He swung, dimly realizing how damn drunk he was. Swung with the wrong hand. It slammed into the table and the pain almost made him puke.

"Jesus, John." Elsie's voice. "You gonna sleep with her now?"

John opened his eyes. Barb gaped back at him with filmy eyes and rot-stained teeth. His head had been resting on the corner pocket of the pool table, barely out of her reach. He straightened, almost fell off the bar stool, and stared up at his sister.

"I'm not sure which of you looks worse," Elsie said.

In the darkness, he could barely see more than her outline. She held her shotgun loosely; a game bag bulged against her hip. The last fading light through the window slats caught her frown, turned her lips black.

"The generator's out again," Elsie growled, starting toward the back room. "And, Christ, it's freezing in here. See if you can get the woodstove going."

John climbed off the stool, staggered, and gripped the pool table with his good hand. Finally he veered toward the stove, a soot-blackened fifty-gallon drum with the bar, pool table, and small stage surrounding it.

Leaning his good hand on the cold metal, he paused. The last strains of Muddy Waters' "I'm Ready" died away in his soul. The last of the words, sweet yet raspy, drifted into silence.

"Was that you?" John murmured, turning to his dead wife. "Were you singing in my dreams?"

The lights flickered on just as he got a fire going. John slammed the stove door and returned to Barbara. Small, prong-shaped burns pocked her gray skin.

He hadn't noticed them before. Had he been looking? Was he giving her the attention she deserved, that any man should give his wife? He'd better put something on them.

Her face turned toward him. No grimace this time, no drawn back gotta-bite-you leer. Unable to help himself, he stroked her hair. Barb always had the most beautiful hair, a sleek, glossy black mane. A patch came off on his fingers, fleshy bits of scalp clinging with congealed blood.

He stared at it a long time, and finally wiped his hand on his jeans.

"Are you ready, babe?" He forced a smile and picked up the prod.

"She might be, but you're not," Elsie said just behind him. His sister took his good arm before he could turn on the prod. "You haven't eaten all day, John. Let's get some food in you."

Eyes still on his wife, John nodded and let himself be pulled into the back room. He blinked in the fluorescent glare as Elsie guided him to the table. Gently she pushed him down in a chair.

Cigarettes burns pocked the table. Its gray enamel was only a shade darker than Barbara's skin.

Elsie wrinkled her nose, sat down beside him, and took his bad hand. "We better change that bandage first."

John nodded. He gazed up at the posters lining the clapboard wall while she unwrapped his hand. B. B. King, Buddy

Guy, Howlin' Wolf all seemed to be frowning down at him—
frowning as if to say that he should treat his woman better.

Elsie gasped. The stubs of his three fingers had turned
black. The half-knuckle length of thumb oozed a dark greenish fluid mixed with equally dark blood.

"Oh god, John." Elsie choked off a sob and bit her lower
lip. Her eyes glimmered moistly.

"It's happening." John heard his voice from far away. He
lifted his hand, not even wincing when he tried to flex what
remained. "I'm turning, Sis. I'll be one of them soon."

"I'll amputate it," Elsie said. She'd stood by him in more
than one bar fight, could handle a switchblade with the best
of them, but her voice was shaky now. "That might stop the
infection."

"No." John rose on legs that seemed miles too long.
Holding his hand out away from him as if it were something
obscene and poisonous, that didn't even belong to him, he
cocked his head toward the bar room. "You got to shock it, Sis.
Use the prod on me."

"John." Elsie's voice was soft, almost pleading. Nevertheless, she followed him back into the bar, waited while he
flicked on the amplifier. Its hum filled the silence; static
crackled over the remaining speaker.

A throaty coughing came from his dead wife. John looked
over and found her face turned their way.

"You see," he said to Elsie. "It *is* working. She's coming
around."

"Yeah," Elsie answered without a trace of belief. "Or she's
laughing at us."

"You know better than that." He scowled and offered her
the prod. "It's ready. Just touch my hand with those prongs.
We'll try shocking each of the stumps. Do the thumb first."

Elsie nodded and took the prod, staring with haunted eyes
at the pointed copper prongs. John sat down on the stool,
held out his hand, and waited. Elsie looked up at him, then
down at his hand. Abruptly she brought the prongs to his
thumb stump.

Agony thrashed through him. Up his arm, into his head,
down to his groin, everywhere—a single intense bolt of pure
pain. He damn near pissed himself. Then he stumbled off the
stool, dropped to his knees, and clutched his wrist.

Elsie whimpered. She was the best though; they didn't
come any tougher. She brought the prod down again. Sparks
flashed where it touched the stub of his first finger. Pain again
seared through him.

John screamed. He fell on his side. His legs jerked. He clutched his hand and tried to get his breath. The prod came down.

John's vision flickered. Elsie above him, tears streaming down her weathered cheeks. The prod looming closer, prongs glinting, the duct tape around its pool cue handle in Elsie's bone-white grip. Again, it touched him.

The bar swirled. Stool legs, Elsie's boots, wooden floor: It all blurred and flowed as the lights danced. Somewhere a voice sobbed. Yet somewhere else, some place he couldn't point to, couldn't glimpse beyond the pain in his goddamn hand, a voice crooned, wordless, soft—accusing.

"I'm sorry," he screamed. "I didn't know, Barb! I didn't know how much it hurt!" The song grew fainter and drifted into darkness.

✛ ✛ ✛

A scream woke him. John rolled onto his side and sat up. Another scream, from the back room. He stumbled up, checked the pool table. Barbara lay still, unmoving, staring at the ceiling.

Grabbing the shotgun from the bar as he staggered past, John thumbed off the safety and ran into the back room. Elsie crouched in the corner, hands wrapped around her head. Her eyes rolled, glancing his way.

"What?" John leveled the shotgun, gazing around the room. Elsie pointed. On the kitchen counter by the sink, her game bag squirmed. Though still closed, the blood-soaked canvas writhed and twisted. A soft scratching of claws came from the bag.

"I'll be damned." John looked at his sister. "Sure you killed 'em?"

"Fuck you, goddamn it," Elsie screeched. "You know I did!"

"It's okay, Sis." John moved closer to the counter and dipped the shotgun barrel low enough to snag the bag's carry strap. Squelchy wet noises came from inside as John carried it back to the bar.

When the bag neared Barbara, she lunged and struggled, teeth snapping empty air as John hurried to the woodstove. He kicked the latch with his boot. The door opened and he gently swung the bag inside. Tiny squeals rang through the flames. He kicked the door closed, put down the shotgun, and latched the door. The stove thumped and rumbled.

When he returned to the back, Elsie was huddled in a chair by the table. She was trying to pour a shot of Yukon Jack and failing miserably. John steadied her fingers with his good hand.

"Animals, too?" Elsie looked up at him with the pathetic hopelessness of a dying child.

"Looks that way." John took a strong pull on the bottle. Elsie managed to get the drink to her lips. They set bottle and glass down at the same time, refusing to meet each other's eyes. Instead, John gazed at his injured hand.

"It doesn't seem quite as bad," he said. "Does it?"

Elsie cocked her head, studying the stumps.

"Some of the blackness might have gone away," she admitted. "And it's not oozing that green stuff."

"Help me with the bandage?"

"No." She gazed up at him, eyes narrowed but without expression. "I want to shock it again."

"But we just—"

"You're not going to leave me alone." Elsie gripped his bad wrist and hauled him to his feet. "Not now—not ever, if I have any say."

"My wife," he heard himself whine. "I've got to get back to her."

"After I'm finished with you," Elsie tugged him toward the bar, half dragging him. "I'll take care of Barbara." She halted, released his arm, and glared at him. "What other choice we got? What else can we do?"

He swallowed, throat still burning from the liquor. After a moment, he nodded. Staring down at the gray, yet not-so-black stumps of his fingers, he entered the bar. He knew how fucking much that damn prod hurt now. How much hell he'd have to go through to have any chance. And Barb . . . he'd already put her through ten times as much.

"Get down on the floor," Elsie ordered. She turned on the amp and picked up the prod. "It will be easier that way."

The quiet hum, the brief static crackle, John barely heard them over his own heart. He did as ordered, first onto his knees, then cross-legged, bad hand cradled in front of him.

Elsie rewarded his quickness by turning to the pool table. With all the detachment of a welding machine, she pushed the prod against Barb's neck.

His dead wife wailed and jerked, heaved and screamed. A perfect D sharp. Her voice was clearer. He could hear even more now of the old Barb. Her scream lingered, echoed in his ears.

"It *is* working!" Elsie looked from Barb to him, a tight smile on her lips. "You were right, John." She brought the prod down and plunged it against his hand.

✛ ✛ ✛

He heard Barb singing in his dreams again. When his eyes blinked open, when he woke and stared up at the ceiling above his bunk, her song didn't stop. Wordless, ethereal, like that fabulous blues riff from Pink Floyd's *Dark Side of the Moon.* Ungodly beautiful, a haunting wonder filled him; it was always that way whenever Barb sang.

Elsie must have done it, he realized. She must have worked on Barb all through the night. He stared down at his bad hand. No blood on the bandages, no green ooze. It didn't hurt nearly so much. The shock treatment worked.

John bolted for the bar. With the lights off, a gray gloom played shadowed stripes through the window slats, streaks across the pool table.

"Elsie?" he called softly. "Sis?"

The singing ended and it damn near broke his heart. John bit his lower lip. His hand throbbed briefly; looking down, he realized he'd clenched his fists.

His sister didn't answer. Where was she?

Warily, John crept closer to the pool table. The darkness made it hard to tell, but something looked different about his wife.

"Barb?" John reached out with his good hand, not quite daring to touch. A blackness had spread over the green felt. Something quivered. John brought his face closer.

It lashed out at him. The stump of an arm brushed the side of his face. John jerked away, barely in time. He stared down, mouth open, already gagging at the stench of corruption.

Barbara had torn off her own hand. Gray light played across her form. Flesh decayed into a lumpy putrescence soaked her sheet, outlining her ribs and thighs, the barely swelling lumps of her breasts.

The handless stump waved listlessly. Barbara's head turned toward him. A pale mush filled her eye sockets and leaked down her cheeks.

John stepped back, fumbled, and found a bar stool. His breath steamed around him. He became acutely conscious of the room's freezing temperature as it sucked away his warmth.

Fire, he thought, but no, that would make the smell unbearable. Something bumped in the darkness beyond the pool table. The hairs on the back of his scalp crawled.

"Elsie?" John looked around. No generator again, no gun either. However, if he opened the door, that might let in enough light. Slowly John stood. He eased around the pool table, keeping his eyes on the floor, not wanting to look again at what remained of his wife.

With a soft cry, he flung the door open. A blast of arctic air froze the sweat on the back of his neck. Light slashed across the room.

Elsie sprawled between the pool table and the woodstove. Her arms twitched. It looked like she was trying to get up on hands and knees. John rushed to her.

"Sis?" He took her shoulder in his good hand, tried to turn her over. Elsie collapsed at his touch. He rolled her onto her side.

"Oh, jeez, no. No!" John jerked away. Elsie's throat gaped open from chin to sternum, no flesh, only bone and gristle and blood.

It wasn't hard to realize what happened. She'd gotten too close to Barb. Ravenous for flesh, Barbara had ripped off her own hand, wrapped that arm around Elsie's neck, and fed.

Briefly, John looked around. Where could he tie Elsie down? The prod worked. He could still save her. A second look at his sister though, another glance at her throat, and his shoulders sagged. He'd thought everything, all the life had gone out of him when Barb died. But he'd still had hope; at least he could bring himself to try.

Nothing remained inside him now. With so much of Elsie's throat gone, he had no chance of bringing her back. Instead, he dragged her out into the cold, the clean, pure cold.

"Gotta burn you, Sis," he murmured. He'd have to climb up to the generator, drain some fuel oil, get it down somehow, pour it on her. . . .

An ache tightened his chest until he couldn't breathe. His knees didn't want to hold him up. A drink first, something to steady him.

John gazed out across the snow-shrouded spruce. Lonely cabins, their smokestacks jutting from snowy roofs, peeked out from between the trees. Beyond them, beneath low, gray clouds, lay the distant peaks of the White Mountains, sunless and remote. Not a soul lived between him and the Arctic Ocean. Nothing moved.

"Dead winter, dead world." He slammed and bolted the door. Then, careful not to look at Barbara, he wandered into the back room. The bottle of Yukon Jack waited on the table. John tumbled into the chair and took a long, deep pull.

He sat in the dull light and poured a shot for Elsie. So many good times, so much great music they'd made together. Man, oh man, they used to raise the roof. Who cared about the endless winter dark with all the laughter and juke-jumping blues.

He'd nearly finished the bottle when his wife began to sing. Softly at first, merging with the memories, a long, slow blues drifted into the cold, still air.

John stared at the shadowed doorway. The tune twisted, slithering up a weird minor scale. He couldn't place the song, didn't dare place it. A blues from the other side, it sang of emptiness and a hunger that lingered forever.

Something thumped outside, hard enough and loud enough that John jerked, knocking over the whiskey. Again the thump, then another, finding the beat, keeping time. His hand began to throb with it.

Elsie'd been a damn fine drummer.

John unwrapped his hand. The wounded stumps had sealed. The flesh was puckered and red now, without any gray or black. Why had the treatment worked on him and not Barbara? She'd only been bitten once.

It must have been this craving the dead had for flesh. Once Barbara had gotten hold of Elsie, the shock treatment stopped working. The decay of death returned with a vengeance.

John rose and shuffled into the bar. He'd reached his own crossroads here. Every bluesman knew that's where the Devil dwelt. John knew the choice he was being offered, too: He could live on in a dead world, or he could give his soul to the band.

He neared the pool table. Was Barbara looking at him? Her lips moved. Her voice, sweet as her soul, breathed out through black lips.

John brought his face closer. His jaw clenched, and he almost gagged. Forcing his eyes closed, he gazed into blue eyes once more, smiled at her full red lips. Distantly, his voice joined hers. When their lips touched, she refused him nothing; he bit down, tasted her spongy putrescence, and swallowed.

"Blues got soul," he whispered, stroking her hair. "You know it's me, babe. You're still in there."

Over by the wrecked amplifier lay his acoustic guitar. He picked it up with his good hand.

John stared at his left hand, his useless hand. After all, without those fingers how could he form chords? A beer bottle glimmered in a gray slat of light. His finger stumps began bleeding again, but what the hell. He still managed to pick up the bottle by sliding his little finger into the neck.

Barb's wordless crooning grew louder. Elsie's steady thumping set the pace—slow, like a beating heart not quite dead.

John sat down on a stool and placed the guitar flat on his lap. Most bluesmen favored an open tuning with a slide, but he was in too much pain. Besides, Muddy played with standard tuning. So he brought the bottle down. Sliding it up the strings produced a tinny moan.

His eyes closed. Barb smiled at him in his mind. He'd loved her, always would love her, but he loved her voice even more. He still had that, and without thinking, matched her note for note.

"One last blues, baby." His guitar and dead wife wailed together. One last charnel blues before that long, dark road.

You'll Never Walk Alone

SCOTT NICHOLSON

Daddy said them that eat human flesh will suffer under Hell.

I ain't figured that out yet, how there can be a place under Hell. Daddy couldn't hardly describe it hisself. It's just a real bad place, hotter than the regular Hell and probably lonelier, too, since Hell's about full up and nobody's a stranger. Been so much sinning the Devil had to build a basement for the gray people.

It was Saturday when we heard about them. I was watching cartoons and eating a bowl of corn flakes. I like cereal with lots of sugar, so when the flakes are done you can drink down that thick milk at the bottom of the bowl. It come up like a commercial, some square-headed man in a suit sitting at a desk, with that beeping sound like when they tell you a bad storm's coming. Daddy was drinking coffee with his boots off, and he said wasn't a cloud in the sky and the wind was lazy as a cut cat. So he figured it was just another thing about the Aye-rabs and who cared if they blew each other to Kingdom Come, except then they showed some of that TV that looks like them cop shows, the camera wiggly so you can't half see what they're trying to show you.

Daddy kept the cartoons turned down low because he said the music hurt his ears, but this time he took the remote from beside my cereal bowl and punched it three or four times with his thumb. The square-headed man was talking faster than they usually do, like a flatlander, acting like he deserved a pat on the head because he was doing such a good job telling about something bad. Then the TV showed somebody in rags moving toward the camera and Daddy said, Lordy, looked like something walked out of one of them suicide bombs, because its face was gray and looked like the meat had melted off the bone.

But the square-headed man said the picture was live from Winston-Salem, that's about two hours from us here in the mountains. The man said it was happening all over, the hospitals was crowded and the governor done called out the National Guard. Then the television switched and it was the president standing at a bunch of microphones, saying something about a new terror threat but how everybody ought to stay calm because you never show fear in the face of the enemy.

Daddy said them damned ragheads must have finally let the bugs out of the bottle. I don't see how bugs could tear up a man's skin that way, to where it looked like he'd stuck his head in a lawn mower and then washed his face with battery acid and grease rags. I saw a dead raccoon once, in the ditch when I was walking home from school, and maggots was squirming in its eye holes and them shiny green dookie flies was swarming around its tail. I reckon that's what kind of bugs Daddy meant, only worse, because these ones get you while you're still breathing.

I was scared then, but it was the kind where you just sort of feel like the ashes in the pan at the bottom of the wood-stove. Where you don't know what to be afraid of. At least when you hear something moving in the dark woods, your hands get sweaty and your heart jumps a mite faster and you know which way to run. But looking at the TV, all I could think of was the time I woke up and Momma wasn't making breakfast, and Momma didn't come home from work, and Momma didn't make supper. A kind of scared that fills you up belly first, and you can't figure it out, and you can't take a stick to it like you can that thing in the dark woods. And then there was the next day when Momma still didn't come home, and that's how I felt about the bugs out of the bottle, because it seems like you can't do nothing to stop it. Then I felt bad because the president would probably say I was showing fear in the face of the enemy, and Daddy voted for the president because it was high time for a change.

I asked Daddy what we was going to do, and he said the Lord would show the way. Said he was loading the shotgun just in case, because the Lord helped those that helped themselves. Said he didn't know whether them things could drive a car or not. If they had to walk all the way from the big city, they probably wouldn't get here for three days. If they come here at all.

Daddy told me to go put up the cows. Said the TV man said they liked living flesh, but you can't trust what the TV says half the time because they want to sell you something. I didn't figure how they could sell anything by scaring people like that. But I was awful glad we lived a mile up a dirt road, in a little notch in the mountains. It was cold for March, maybe too cold for them bugs. But I wasn't too happy about fetching the cows, because they tend to wander in the mornings and not come in 'til dark. Cows like to spend their days all the same. If you do something new, they stomp and stir and start in with the moos, and I was afraid the moos might bring the bugs or them gray people that eat living flesh.

I about told Daddy I was too scared to fetch them by myself, but he might have got mad because of what the president said and all. Besides, he was busy putting on his boots. So I took my hickory stick from by the door and called Shep. He was probably digging for groundhogs up by the creek and couldn't hear me. I walked out to the fields on the north side, where the grass grows slow and we don't put cows except early spring. Some of the trees was starting to get new leaves, but the woods was mostly brown rot and granite stone. That made me feel a little better, because a bug-bit gray person would have a harder time sneaking up on me.

We was down to only four cows because of the long drought and we had to cull some steers last year or else buy hay. Four is easy to round up, because all you got to do is get one of them moving and the rest will follow. Cows in a herd almost always point their heads in the same direction, like they all know they're bound for the same place sooner or later. Most people think cows are dumb but some things they got a lot of sense about. You hardly ever see a cow in a hurry. I figure they don't worry much, and they probably don't know about being scared, except when you take them to the barn in the middle of the day. Then maybe they remember the blood on the walls and the steaming guts and the smell of raw meat and the jingle of the slaughter chains.

By the time I got them penned up, Shep had come in from wherever and gave out a bark like he'd been helping the whole time. I took him into the house with me. I don't ever do that unless it's come a big snow or when icicles hang from his fur. Daddy was dressed and the shotgun was laying on the kitchen table. I gave Shep the last of my cereal milk. Daddy said the TV said the gray people was walking all over, even in the little towns, but said some of the telephone wires was down so nobody could tell much what was going on where.

I asked Daddy if these was like the End Times of the Bible, like what Preacher Danny Lee Aldridge talked about when the sermon was almost over and the time had come to pass the plate. I always got scared about the End Times, even sitting in the church with all the wood and candles and that soft red cloth on the back of the pews. The End Times was the same as Hell to me. But Preacher Aldridge always wrapped up by saying that the way out of Hell was to walk through the House of the Lord, climb them stairs and let the loving light burn ever little shred of sin out of you. All you had to do was ask, but you had to do it alone. Nobody else could do it for you.

So you got to pray to the Lord. I like to pray in church, where there's lots of people and the Lord has to mind every-body at the same time. It's probably wrong, but I get scared when I try to pray all by myself. I used to pray with Momma and Daddy, then just Daddy, and that's okay because I fig-ured Daddy's louder than me and probably has more to talk about. I just get that sharp rock feeling in my belly every time I think about the Lord looking at nobody but me, when I ain't got nothing to hide behind and my stick is out of reach.

But these ain't the End Times, Daddy said, because the gray people don't have horns and the TV didn't say nothing about a dragon coming up out of the sea. But he said since they eat human flesh they're of the Devil, and said their bodies may be walking around but you better believe their souls are roasting under Hell. Especially if they got bit by the Aye-rab bug. I told him the cattle was put up and he said the chick-ens would be okay. You can't catch a chicken even when your legs is working right, much less when you're wobbling around like somebody beat the tar out of you with an ax handle.

He said to get in the truck. I made Shep jump up in the truck bed, then Daddy come out of the house with a loaf of white bread and some cans of sardines. Had the shotgun, too. He got in the truck and started it, and I asked him where we was headed. He said in troubled times you go get closer to the Lord.

I asked him if maybe he thought Momma would be okay. He said it didn't matter none, since the Devil done got her ages ago. Said she was already a gray person before this bug mess even started. Said to waste no prayers on her.

The dirt road was mushy from winter. The road runs by the creek for a while, then crosses a little bridge by the Hodges' place. That's where I always caught the school bus, with Johnny Hodges and his sister Raylene. Smoke was coming out of their chimney and I asked Daddy if we ought to stop and tell them about what the TV said. Daddy said they might be gray people already. I tried to picture Johnny with his face all slopped around, or Raylene with bugs eating her soft places. Mister Hodges didn't go to church and Johnny told me he used to beat them sometimes when he drank too much. I wondered if all the people who didn't go to church had turned gray and started eating human flesh.

We passed a few other houses but didn't see nobody, even at the preacher's place. The church was right there where the gravel turned to paved, set up above the road on a little green hill. The graveyard was tucked away to one side, where barbed wire strung off a pasture. The church was made of brick, the windows up high so that people wouldn't look outside during the preaching. Seeing that white cross jabbed up into the sky made me feel not so scared.

We parked the truck around back. Daddy had me carry the food and he carried the shotgun. Said a Bible and a shotgun was all a man needed. I didn't say nothing about a man needed food. I found a little pack of sugar in the truck's ashtray and I hid it in my pocket. We didn't have no Co'-colas.

They keep the church unlocked in case people want to come in and pray. Daddy said people in the big city lock their churches. If they don't, people might come in and sleep or steal the candleholders and hymn books. But this is the mountains, where people all know each other and get along and you don't need to lock everything. So we went inside. Daddy made Shep stay out, said it would be disrespecting to the Lord. We locked the door from the inside. I thought somebody else might want to come get close to the Lord in these troubled times, but Daddy said they could knock if they wanted in.

We went up to the front where the pulpit is and Daddy said we might as well get down and give thanks for deliverance. I didn't feel delivered yet but Daddy was a lot smarter about the Bible, so I went on my knees and kept my eyes closed while Daddy said O Lord, it's looking mighty dark but the clouds will part and Heaven will knock down them gray people and set things right. I joined in on the amen and said I was hungry.

Daddy opened up the sardines and they stank. I spilled some of the fish juice on the floor. We ate some of the bread. It was gummy and stuck to my teeth. I was tired and tried to lay down in the front pew but it was like sleeping in a rock coffin. I didn't know why people in the big city would want to do such a thing. Daddy started reading from the Bible but the light got bad as the afternoon wore on. The church ain't got electric power.

I asked Daddy how long we was going to stay holed up and he said as long as it took. I wished we had a TV so we could see what was going on. Night finally come, and I was using the bathroom in back when I heard Shep whimpering. I reckon he was lonely out there. Sounded like he was scratching in the dirt out back of the church.

I climbed up on the sink and looked out the little window. Under the moonlight I saw the graveyard, and it looked like somebody had took a shovel to it, tore up the dirt real bad. Something was coming up out of one of the holes, and I reckon that's what Shep was whimpering about.

I went and told Daddy what I seen and he said maybe it was the End Times after all. Shep started barking and I begged Daddy to let me open the door. He said the Lord would take care of Shep, but then I heard him bark again and I was trying to open the door when Daddy knocked me away. Said he'd take a look, stepped outside with the shotgun, and the gun went off and Daddy started cussing goddamn right there on the church steps. Shep started moaning and I ran to the door and Shep was crawling toward the woods on his belly like his back was broke. I thought Daddy had shot him and I started to cry but then I seen somebody coming from the woods. Daddy racked another shell into the chamber and hollered but the person just kept coming. Daddy told me to go in and lock the door but I couldn't. I was too scared to be in that big dark church by myself.

Daddy shot high and the pellets scattered through the tops of the trees and still the person kept coming, walking slow with a limp. Another person came out of the trees, then another. They was all headed in the same direction. Straight toward the church.

One of them bent down and got Shep, and I never heard such a sound from a dog. Daddy was cussing a blue streak and let loose both barrels and one of the people stood still for just a second, and I could see that gray face turned up toward the moon, the eye holes empty. Then his insides tumbled out but he kept on coming for us and Daddy was pushing me back through the door and we got inside and locked it.

Daddy went up front and I could hear him crying. Except for that, the church was quiet. I thought the gray people might try to knock the door down but maybe they got scared away because of it being a church and all. I went up beside Daddy and waited until he was hisself again. He said he was sorry for showing fear in the face of the enemy and said O Lord, give me the strength to do your work. I said Lord, protect Momma wherever she is, and Daddy said it was wrong to ask for selfish things.

Daddy said the End Times was a test for the weak. Said you had to stay strong in the Lord. Said it about fifteen hundred times in a row, over and over, in a whisper, and it made me scared.

I was about asleep when Daddy poked me with the gun. Said come here, Son, over by the window where I can see you good. The moon was coming through the window and I could hear the gray people walking outside. They was going around in circles, all headed in the same direction.

Daddy asked me if I got bit by one of them bugs. I said don't reckon. He said, well, you're looking a little gray, and I told him I didn't feel nary bit gray. He asked me if I was getting hungry and I said a little. He gave me the rest of the bread and said eat it. I took a bite and he said you didn't say thanks to the Lord. Then he thanked the Lord for both of us.

I asked Daddy if Shep had gone to Heaven. He said it depended on whether he was dead before the gray people ate him. Said Shep might have done turned gray hisself and might bite me if he saw me again. I almost asked Daddy to say a prayer for Shep but that sounded like a selfish thing.

I must have finally dozed off because I didn't know where I was when I opened my eyes. Daddy was at the front of the church, in the pulpit where Preacher Aldridge stood of a Sunday. The sun was about up and Daddy had the Bible open and was trying to read in the bad light. Somebody was knocking on the church door.

Daddy said the word was made flesh and dwelt among us. Daddy stopped just like Preacher Aldridge did, like he wanted to catch his breath and make you scared at the same time. Then Daddy got louder and said we beheld His glory, the glory as of the only begotten of the Father, full of grace and truth.

I asked what did that mean and Daddy said the Lord come down among people and nobody saw the signs. Said they treated Him just like any normal person, except then He set off doing miracles and people got scared and nailed Him to the cross. Said it was probably gray people that done it. I asked Daddy if we ought to open the church door and see who was knocking.

Daddy said gray people wasn't fit to set foot in the House of the Lord. I asked what if it's the preacher or the Hodges kids or Opalee Rominger from down the road. Daddy said they're all gray, everybody. Said they was all headed under Hell. Said ever sinner is wicked and blind to their sinning ways. I didn't see how Opalee Rominger could eat living flesh, because she ain't got no teeth.

The knocking stopped and I didn't hear no screams so maybe whoever it was didn't get ate up.

I listened to Daddy read the Bible. The sun come up higher and I wondered about the cows. Did the gray people eat them all? It wasn't like they ain't enough sinners to go around. I didn't for a minute believe that everybody was gray. There had to be others like us. There's a hymn that says you'll never walk alone. I don't reckon the Lord breaks promises like that but I was way too scared to ask. Daddy's eyes were getting bloodshot, like he hadn't slept a wink, and he was whispering to hisself again.

I drank water from the plate that Preacher Aldridge passed around on Sundays. The water tasted like old pennies. Daddy didn't drink nothing. I asked him if he wanted the last can of sardines but he said man can't live by bread alone but by the word of the Lord. I wondered what the Lord's words tasted like. I wondered what people tasted like. I ate the sardines by myself.

That night was quiet, like the gray people had done gone on to wherever they were headed. I woke up in the morning plenty sore and I asked Daddy if we could take a peek out the door. Daddy hadn't moved, only stood up there at the pulpit like he was getting ready to let loose with a sermon. He had the shotgun raised toward Heaven and I don't reckon he heard me. I asked it louder and he said you can't see the gray people because ever sinner is blind. I said I ain't no sinner but he said you're looking mighty gray to me.

I said I ain't gray, and then he made me prove it. Said get on your knees and beg the Lord to forgive you. He pointed the shotgun at me. I didn't know if he would use it or not, but the way his eye twitched I wasn't taking no chances. I got on my knees but I was scared to close my eyes. When you close your eyes and pray it's just you and the Lord. You're blind but the Lord sees everything. I asked Daddy to pray with me.

Daddy set in to asking the Lord to forgive us our sins and trespasses. I wondered if we was trespassing on the church. It belonged to the Lord, and we was here so we wouldn't get ate up. I didn't say nothing to Daddy about it, though. I added an extra loud amen just so Daddy would know for sure that I wasn't gray.

Later I asked Daddy how come ever sinner is gray. He said the Lord decides such things. He said Momma was a sinner and that's why she was gray all along and her soul was already under Hell. I didn't say nothing to that. Sometimes Daddy said I took after my Momma. I wished I'd took after Daddy instead and been able to pray all by myself.

I said it sounded like the gray people was gone. Daddy said you can't trust the Devil's tricks. Said the only way out was through the Lord. I said I was getting hungry again. Daddy said get some sleep and pray.

I woke up lost in the dark and Daddy was screaming his

head off. He was sitting where the moon come through the window and he said look at me, look at my skin. He held up his hands and said I'm gray, I'm gray, I'm gray. Said he was unfit to be in the House of the Lord. He put the shotgun barrel up to the side of his neck and then there was a flash of light and a sound like the world split in half and then something wet slapped against the walls.

I crawled over to him and laid beside him 'til all the warm had leaked out. I was scared and I wanted to pray but without Daddy to help me the Lord would look right into me and that was worse than anything. Then I thought if Daddy was in Heaven now, maybe I could say a prayer to him instead and he could pass along my words to the Lord.

The sun come up finally and Daddy didn't look gray at all. He was white. His belly gurgled and the blood around his neck hole turned brown. I went to the door and unlocked it. Since it was Sunday morning, I figured people would be coming to hear the sermon. With more people in the church, I could pray without being so scared.

I stacked up some of the hymn books and stood on them so I could look out the window. They was back. More gray people were walking by, all headed in the same direction. I figured they were going to that place under Hell, just like Daddy said, and it made me happy that Daddy died before he turned gray.

Time passed real slow and the bread was long gone and nobody come to church. I never figured so many people that I used to pray with would end up turning gray. Like church didn't do them no good at all. I thought of all the prayers I said with them and it made me scared, the kind of scared that fills you up belly first. I wondered what the Lord thought about all them sinners, and what kind of words the Lord said back to them when they prayed.

Daddy's fingers had gone stiff and I about had to break them to get the shotgun away. He'd used up the last shell. The door was unlocked but nobody set foot in the church. I was hoping whoever had knocked the other day might come back, but they didn't.

The gray people didn't come in the church. I figured if they was eating live flesh they would get me sooner or later. Except maybe they was afraid about the church and all, or being in plain sight of the Lord. Or maybe they ain't figured out doors yet. I wondered if you go through doors to get under Hell.

Night come again. Daddy was dead cold. I was real hungry and I asked Daddy to tell the Lord about it, but I reckon Daddy would call that a selfish thing and wouldn't pass it on. I kept trying to pray but I was scared. Preacher Aldridge said you got to do it alone, can't nobody do it for you.

Maybe one of them Aye-rab bugs got in while the door was open. Maybe the gray people ain't ate me yet because I ain't live flesh no more. Only the Lord knows. All I know is I can't stay in this church another minute. Daddy's starting to stink and the Lord's looking right at me.

Like I'm already gray.

I don't feel like I am, but Daddy said ever sinner is blind. And the hunger gnawing at me is the kind of hungry that hurts.

Outside the church, the morning is fresh and cold and smells like broken flowers. I hear footsteps in the wet grass. I turn and walk, and I fit right in like they was saving a place for me. I'm one of them, following the ones ahead and leading the ones behind. We're all headed in the same direction. Maybe this entire world is the place under Hell, and we've been here all along.

I ain't scared no more, just hungry. The hungry runs deep. You can't live by bread alone. Sometimes you need meat instead of words.

I don't have to pray no more, out here where it ain't never dark. Where the Lord don't look at you. Where we're all sinners. Where you're born gray, again and again, and the End Times never end.

Where you never walk alone.

OPIATE OF THE MASSES

LEE THOMAS

Finding raw material for the product became more difficult once the government got into the game. Task forces and
National Guard details torched the crops as soon as they were
discovered and all of the government's high-tech surveillance
toys made it tough on independent businessmen, who were
forced to rely on small networks of spotters. Now, Tico Shapera
didn't know who the first Ra-Ra was that had decided to "bake
the gray" and brew it, but he did know that the pipeline from
Latin America was drying up, while the demand was explod-
ing through the States. So a man with vision, a man such as
Shapera, could make himself a good pile of coin should he be
able to harvest from a reliable, homegrown crop.

But Shapera knew that there was nothing reliable about
this crop, and his Latin compatriots would have supported
that claim had any of them lived.

The South American crops had turned on the cartels, seemingly overnight. Peasant greed had produced colonies too large
to be managed by the poorly prepared wranglers. According to
the news, the entire continent—which had once been so rich
with product, ripe and varied—would be fire bombed, just as
with the offensive that had reduced Cuba to a blistered rock.

Shapera considered that unpleasant situation as Mogg
steered the car to the road's shoulder and slowed to a stop.
Leafy branches shone bright in the bath of headlights and
spread above the windshield like lacy ghosts, only to disappear
when the driver killed the lights.

"Mogg," Shapera said, "get the men on the radio. I want it
made clear that there is to be no shooting unless absolutely
necessary. Have them use the machetes. If they have to shoot,
make sure they use small-caliber sidearms."

Mogg turned in the seat. His head, as big and square as a
bull's, lolled to the side. "He's a priest, sir," Mogg said in a high-
pitched voice that had once amused Shapera. "We shouldn't be
shooting at a priest."

"I'm not talking about the priest," Shapera said. "I'm talking about the crop."

The bullish face pinched with concern. "You think he's got
some in there with him?"

Shapera shook his head as if dealing with a child. Mogg had come into his organization a little under a year ago, after his previous crew, run by a man named Hernandez, had gotten tangled up in a bad harvest. Mogg had proven himself loyal, brutal, and efficient, but he was about as sharp as a ball of Jell-O. "That's why we're here, isn't it? The locals have been talking about this guy for months; they say he can control the crop. I need to see if it's true."

"But he's a priest, sir."

Amazing, thought Shapera. With everything that had happened with the Church before the first rising—the scandals, the mass arrests—it was a wonder priests could avoid being shot on sight. Besides, coming from a thug like Mogg, such ethical musings were the worst sort of hypocrisy. The man's career, his life, mocked the shattered tablets of the Ten Commandments. For a man like him to claim any piety was not only ridiculous, it was infuriating.

Light filled the car, glared off the windshield. The vans carrying Shapera's men eased to a stop behind them. "Get them on the radio," he said, dismissing his driver's perplexed expression. "I don't want any product damaged."

Mogg did as he was told, radioing the information to the squad. A moment after he had given the order, the vans' doors flew open and the men, a dozen shadows against the tree line, disappeared into the wood.

"We'll give them a few minutes to get into position," Shapera said, eyeing the break in the trees ahead.

He lit a cigarette and exhaled the smoke against the closed window, losing himself briefly in the whorls and currents. As he waited, he thought about the stories he'd been told about a priest who delivered sermons to the risen dead. A man who, it was said, could make them calm, could make them listen and obey.

Shapera had made this trip to confirm those stories. He wanted proof of the man's talent; more importantly, he wanted to use the skills or tricks the priest used to command the crop.

"Let's go," he said, now too impatient to sit idly in the car.

Mogg turned his bulk in the driver's seat and reached into the back to retrieve his weapon of choice: an antique Japanese sword.

Shapera opened the door, stepped into the crisp night air, and crushed his cigarette into the gravel. He met Mogg at the front of the car, where his driver stood tense, the narrow sword jutting toward the ground, its point nestled in the gravel. Both men looked at the black cave of the drive.

"It's awfully dark down there," Mogg said.

"And not getting any lighter. Come on."

Some primal anxiety had its claws in Mogg tonight, and Shapera didn't like it. In the past, the thug had faced his enemies, living and dead, with a cold, sharp fury that had bordered on sadistic righteousness. But this evening, Mogg was sullen and unfocused, and Shapera knew it was because of the priest.

"We should have driven up," Mogg suggested in his little girl's voice.

"And let him know we're coming?" Shapera asked. "We need to take him off guard, particularly if he can control the crop. Now come on, and stay quiet. We need to be able to hear what's going on."

Without speaking, they crept down the dark lane. Mogg, a step behind his boss, rested his sword on his beefy shoulder, while Shapera gripped the handle of a small pistol. Noises from the wood—the snapping of twigs, the shuffling of leaves as his men adjusted positions—accompanied their quiet advance.

A loud thrashing rose to his left and Shapera's heart danced into his throat. He threw a look to the tree line and saw only the quilt of night, but he heard a dull thump accompanied by the splintering of twigs. One of his men had brought something down.

At the bend in the road, Shapera lifted his hand to halt Mogg. Before them, thirty yards down the drive, the porch light of the priest's house glowed. A black shape raced toward them, moving far too quickly and with too much purpose to be one of the priest's resurrected congregation.

Shapera's man, Tally Kant, came to a stop before him. Kant had the face of a tough kid, which he was, and though he wasn't old enough to buy beer, he'd been pedaling chemicals for over a decade.

"He's here," Kant said. The kid's round, dark face was twisted with excitement. "He's in the back, but you aren't going to believe what this freak is doing."

Hardly true, Shapera thought. Even before the first rising, he had seen any number of atrocities, from the rape of children to the slow dismemberment of a junkie who had come up short in repaying his debt. Once you accepted the new order of things, little in this world was shocking. "Show me where he is."

Kant escorted them down the lane and along the side of the low ranch-style house. As Shapera eased along the outer wall, he saw that an addition, perhaps a sunroom, had been built on the back of the place; along this extension, windows rose from waist level to the eaves. Approaching the glass, the three pushed against the siding, stopping just short of the windows' span. Light from the interior of the house lapped against the panes and spilled into the yard.

"In there," Kant said, grinning his tough kid's grin.

Shapera leaned forward to peer through the window, his hand gripping the pistol tightly. The sunroom was revealed in a slow sweep of images: a brightly cushioned white rattan couch; matching chairs and cocktail table; a small potted palm; a harbor painting, with vivid blues and stark whites; Mexican tile on the floor; and in the center of the room. . . .

He suppressed a chuckle, and it came out as a cough. "Shit," he said with amusement.

In the room, decorated like a Miami bungalow, more than a half-dozen doughy bodies engaged in a perverse bacchanal. Six of the dead moved awkwardly, like clockwork figures, simulating a variety of sex acts. In a palsied frenzy they thrust, collided, and thrashed clumsily, heads and hips jerking in a squalid dance.

Then Shapera saw the choreographer of this carnal ballet: the priest, the man he had come to find, who was even now entertaining himself at the back of the room.

A silver crucifix dangled from the man's neck as he straddled the face of a fat Hispanic laying face up on a tabletop. The priest's hands rested on the flabby gray-green meat of the corpse's chest. His hips moved forward and back in a slow rhythm. To Shapera, the intercourse looked wrong. The sexual union appeared to be taking place low on the dead man's throat. Then he realized the man's neck had been opened, either in life or in death, to accommodate this particular violation.

"Have a look," he said to Mogg, stepping back into the shadows to allow his driver access to the window.

Mogg did as he was told and leaned forward into the spill of light. Apparently his underdeveloped mind took several seconds to process what he was seeing, because he stared blankly through the glass for a very long time before spinning away, holding his belly in disgust.

"There's your man of God," Shapera said, slapping Mogg on the shoulder.

The big man looked at him with an expression stained by wonderment, confusion, and pain. The shock of disillusionment hissed from the driver's pores like a cloud of steam.

"Let's introduce ourselves," Shapera said. "Tally, get me

five men to clear out the house. And make sure they don't damage the priest."

Kant radioed in the order, then jogged back to the front of the house to manage the attack. Shapera searched the tree line for any signs of movement before turning his attention back to Mogg. The driver stared blankly into the woods.

"Don't take it so hard," Shapera said. "He had a dick before he had God. He was bound to be led by the familiar."

Shapera heard the sound of the door crashing open, and a shrill scream rang out in the house. Most likely the priest. Then, muffled sounds of destruction played through the wall at his back. Shapera returned to his vantage before the window and watched his men work their way through the room, the blades of machetes separating skull from spine. Two of the crop turned and reached for Kant, but the tough kid removed their heads with quick slashes, and their bodies dropped to the floor like sacks of manure. The priest was forced to his knees, the barrel of a pistol pressed to his forehead. Tears rolled down the man's cheeks as his lips moved in panicked protest.

Shapera led Mogg inside. It was a beautifully furnished home, far too opulent for a man of the cloth. How many poor widows had donated their pennies to afford this man his silver coffee service, his mahogany china cabinet, his Caphalon cooking pots? Shapera registered his disgust by knocking a crystal vase from a dining room sconce.

In the festively decorated sunroom, the priest still knelt with the pistol to his head. The bodies of his playmates had been stacked against the wall. Their heads, containing the product, were lined up on the table where, moments before, they had entertained their master. Shapera had his men go outside to secure the perimeter while he and Mogg remained with the blubbering cleric.

"You like the fat ones," Shapera said, noting the bulk of the stacked corpses. The priest lowered his head. "Don't be ashamed," Shapera continued. "I like full-figured *women* myself. Though, they're usually alive when I'm screwing them."

The priest looked up at the intruders, then away. He searched the room slowly before his eyes fell on the table and its display of heads. He crawled forward and began to pet the stubbled cheek of one of the severed heads, caressing the skin with delicate strokes.

"Funny thing about that," Shapera said. "I mean, I was watching a little earlier. Rude, I know. Forgive me. But I couldn't help but notice your party. Your crotch was about an inch from that thing's mouth. Now, if it had been anyone else, he would have chewed them a new asshole, but he let you ride him without so much as a love bite. You want to tell me how you do that?"

"Leave us alone," the priest whispered.

"Technically, there is no more *us*," Shapera corrected. He laughed and shot a glance at Mogg, who looked on with solemn disgust at the kneeling man. "There's only you."

"Raul," the priest said with a voice made cold by shock, his fingers still caressing the pudgy, unshaven cheek. "Goodbye, my boy."

"Yes," Shapera said. "Sad thing, that. But the crop can be unwieldy, and we didn't want to take any chances. I'm sure you understand."

"What do you want?"

"I want to offer you a job, doing something that comes naturally to you."

The priest looked up, his expression lifeless, a perfect mimicry of the heads collected on the table next to him. Suddenly he became conscious of his nudity before these strange, living eyes. Never rising, the scrawny little man pulled his robe from the floor and slid his arms through it.

"My problem is this," Shapera said. "I deal in a product that the kids are calling Baked Gray. It's a narcotic and it's become increasingly popular over the last few years. So popular, in fact, we can't seem to make enough of it. Normally, this would be an enviable position. But my former suppliers are no longer viable, and I am forced to start manufacturing locally."

"I don't know anything about drugs," the priest said.

"You don't have to. I know enough for the both of us." Shapera lifted one of the severed heads and rolled it in his hands as he sat on the edge of the table. "There's about eleven thousand dollars worth of product in here," he explained, tapping the rotting temple with his finger. "The price goes up every day. But the government is randomly exterminating the crop, which means that if we have any ourselves, we have to keep them hidden. I am currently going to great expense to have a parking structure reinforced so that we can keep a crop of about a thousand on hand at any given time. We can replenish their numbers quickly and quietly, but we need someone to keep them under control. Word has it that you are that someone."

The priest looked from Shapera to Mogg and then back at the body-bereft face of Raul. He shook his head. "I won't do it."

Shapera rolled the head he had been toying with, sent it spinning across the table. It teetered on the edge before crashing to the tiled floor. "There's one other option," Shapera said. "Tell me how you do it, and I'll let you get back to your party."

"I can't teach you anything."

"Pity," he said, managing his frustration by looking away and appraising the room. The priest had rich tastes, but likely had enough money already to keep himself in style. A different sort of lure was in order. . . .

"What if I were to give you your pick of the litter? You could have a dozen lovers for your own use, and I promise they wouldn't be processed until you were tired of them."

"They aren't cattle," the priest snapped. "For God's sake, they were human beings."

"They were human once," Shapera noted, "but now they're just a commodity. I use them to get my clients high, and you use them to get off. They're not people—they're just tissue to process or penetrate. Unless, of course, you believe they still have souls floating around in those rotting husks. . . ."

"Didn't you ever ask yourself why this was happening?" the priest asked. "Do you have any idea what has come to pass?"

"Haitian Beetle Virus."

"It's not a virus," the priest said. "It's a plague, sent down by God himself."

"Then you'll have to remind me to drop Him a note of thanks."

"How blind are you?" the priest asked. "Can't you remember back even a dozen years? All of the signs were in place. The Holy Land was a death factory, earthquakes were killing thousands in the Third World, and corporations disintegrated under their own corruption. Our society unwound. And then the virus was discovered, but by that point it had already spread."

"And you see this as biblical prophecy?" Shapera said with a laugh. "Some little jungle children were smoking insects and they didn't burn them up good enough. That hardly sounds like the work of God."

"It is *fire this time*," the priest said, shaking his head.

"Fire?" Shapera asked, slightly annoyed but willing to indulge the man's lunacy. It might even help him recruit the guy if he could get into his head.

"In the time of Noah, God sent a flood to cleanse the world," the priest said, his voice trembling. "But Isaiah 24 tells us that God will use fire at the time of the Apocalypse to purge His Earth. The Bible attributes this final holocaust to God's initiative, but asserts that the flames will be sparked by the hands of men."

"Funny," Shapera said, "I smell smoke, but maybe that's because you're blowing it up my ass." He burst out laughing and slapped Mogg on the shoulder, but the big man was not amused.

Despite Shapera's mocking, the priest continued. "Every day, the United Nations sanctions another strike, identifies another country to be burned. We are being consumed in flame, and you don't even care. You're polluting God's children with drugs, making them sleep when they should be awake and praying for their souls. God is offering man a chance to atone, and you—you and your disgusting business—are perverting His will."

"You're talking to me about perversion?" Shapera asked, his voice sharp with astonishment. "I sell people a few minutes of escape from this fucked up world. You put your dick in these things, and you have the balls to call me disgusting? Fuck you, padre."

"Sir?" Mogg said in an uncomfortable squeak.

Sliding off the table, Shapera walked to the priest and put his foot on the man's shoulder. He slapped at Raul's severed head. It rolled off the table and hit the floor with a crunch before wobbling its way over the tile to rest, face out and staring, against the white weave of the rattan chair.

The priest winced.

"Mogg here seems very distressed by my treatment of you," said Shapera. "Why don't you tell him how long you've been playing nice-nice with dead people? Or, better yet, why don't we go back a few years and you can talk about what you used to do to the living. We've all seen the news, but I'm certain you could describe the incidents more vividly. . . ."

"My indiscretions will be punished," the priest whispered. "Even now, under God's eyes, I'm an abomination. All I can do is pray that my guidance of His flock will earn me understanding, if not redemption. But I never damned any soul except my own."

"Sure you did," Shapera drawled. "You guided them in life, and they did what you told them because you wore the uniform of the righteous. The light from your fucking halo blinded all of them and struck them mute while you led them into greater darkness. Then you shot your load and called it baptism."

"Sir?"

"Shut up, Mogg," he snapped.

With one brutal kick, Shapera sent the priest to his back. He stared at the man and found he wanted nothing more than to put a hole in the deluded freak's head. "You know what I think your trick is? Your parishioners flocked to you in life, seeking hope, and I think some of that desire stayed with them in death. But they aren't running to *you*, Father. They're running to things you represent, the comfort of all those holy fucking lies. Any face could float above that collar, and they'd still be drawn to it."

The man struggled back to his knees and clutched his robe closed. "If that's true, find another priest. You've picked the wrong one." There was an edge in his voice now, just the hint of a growl. But Shapera wasn't concerned with the priest's agitation.

"Maybe," the drug lord said. "But you've been playing puppet master with your congregation long enough to know what strings to pull. You're skilled, and you are going to bring that skill to my organization. Now, you can profit by your service or you can suffer for it."

"God did not choose me to lead his flock to the slaughter— not your slaughter."

"Do you actually believe that there is something holy in what you're doing?"

"That's enough," the priest said in disgust. "I didn't bring you here to negotiate a deal, and I certainly didn't bring you here to judge me."

"What?" Shapera roared. "You think you have control over any of this?"

But he recognized that edge in the priest's voice now, and unease rolled through him. The atmosphere in the room was changing, growing thick and tight around him. Shapera drew his gun and looked toward the windows, to the yard and the trees beyond. Nothing. No sign of the men he'd tasked with securing the perimeter.

When Shapera turned back to the priest, he saw that the shame and sadness had melted from the old man's face. In their place was an expression of confident serenity. No longer trembling, the priest pointed to the wall of glass on the far side of the room.

When Shapera looked at the window this time, he saw movement. A procession of tattered parishioners appeared between the tree trunks, emerging slowly from the darkness as if they were floating up from a foul lake. Moving with a weird fluidity, the congregation crossed the yard in a shuffling advance. Wounds long dried to scabrous pits spoiled their pallid flesh. Some carried bits of black fabric in their clawed hands; fresh blood smeared their cheeks, their mouths, and their teeth.

One wore a machete like a steel sash imbedded diagonally across its torso.

"Jesus," Shapera whispered, the room suddenly pressing in on him, suffocating him. It was a trap. The realization settled like a lump of cold grease in the pit of Shapera's belly.

A young man dressed in black—Tally Kant, the drug lord realized distantly—stumbled into the yard, and Shapera suffered an excruciating flash of hope. If one of his men had survived, others might have, too. But the hope flickered out and died completely when he saw the panic twisting the tough kid's face.

The dead swarmed Kant just as he reached the window. He tried to shatter the glass with his fists, but it had been reinforced and easily absorbed his abuse. Rotting fingers danced over his face, pulled, tore his lip back as if they were removing a pliant mask from his skull. Members of the congregation ripped fabric and flesh; blood struck the window in hot spurts. A woman with a cloud of teased brown hair sucked a palm-sized swatch of Kant's cheek over her lips and began to chew it like a wad of bubble gum.

Shapera leveled his gun at the priest's forehead. "Call them off," he ordered, his voice shaking. "Let us out of here or I'll open your head and feed you to them."

The threat seemed not to register with the priest. "Join my church," he said. "Become part of my congregation, and God will bring you home in the flames."

"Your God doesn't exist!"

"Then believe in me." He gestured to the dead things outside the window. "The evidence of my power is all around you."

"And my power is pointed at your face."

Shapera sighted down the barrel, focusing on the wrinkles between the man's eyes. His finger tightened on the trigger, but the gun flew from his hands. Startled, he watched the metal glint of Mogg's sword arc toward the ceiling, then slice back toward him. Before Shapera could even gasp in surprise, he found the sword point positioned a hairsbreadth from his stomach.

"Living or dead," the priest said, "they believe in me."

His rib cage visible beneath his skin like the slats of a condemned house, the priest stood and ran his hands over his scalp to smooth down the wispy strands. He straightened his robe and cinched it tight. "Bobby here has been coming to my church since he was a boy. Isn't that right, Bobby?"

"Yes, Father," Mogg replied.

The priest looked to the window, casting his serene smile on the flock gathered there. "My devout congregation," he said with rapture and love.

Blank faces pushed up against the pane. Tongues flattened over the surface and teeth clicked on glass. The impatient, damaged horde struggled for position; one row of faces giving way to another and another until the darkness of the woods obscured them.

"Every day there are more of them," the priest said. "Like missionaries, they go into the dark places to bring light, to seek converts, and the congregation grows."

"Converts?" Shapera said distractedly. He needed to keep the sick bastard talking, needed time to figure a way out.

"Look at them, Mr. Shapera. Look at their number. Do you really think all of them came from my living congregation? Alive, they represented any number of faiths; some had no faith at all."

It took a moment for Shapera to take that in, and when he did, the statement made him shake his head in dismay. His assumptions about the priest's powers crumbled, and he found himself asking, "Then how can you control them? If they didn't believe in you or your God when they were alive, what makes them serve you now?"

"Nobody wants to die and have that be the end," the priest said. "And yet death is inevitable. It looms before us, large and hungry. Inevitable. If we cannot escape the inevitable, we must deny it. We must deny the mortal and create the eternal. And so begins the path to God."

"But they didn't believe," Shapera insisted.

"But they wanted to," the priest told him. "They may have spent an entire life defiling my faith, but with death's approach, they couldn't help but seek salvation. Even in their damaged state, they understand the promise of hereafter. They sense that what is left to them now is not the true end. And so they're seeking God's path."

"What does God have to do with any of this? You're talking about the desperation of trapped animals!"

"I'm talking about the perfection of God's design," the priest countered, eyes wild, voice tight with passion. "God gave us fear, and fear gives us faith." He jabbed a finger at the window where his congregation stared on. "Their faith has brought them to me, just as God intended."

The insanity of that statement overwhelmed Shapera's forced calm. "God sent them here to get fucked?" he shouted.

"Hey," Mogg warned, jabbing the sword point into Shapera's belly.

"It's okay, Bobby. His opinion of me means nothing." The priest patted Mogg's shoulder to calm him. Then he turned his attention back to his prisoner. "I've admitted my corruption, Mr. Shapera. I'm a beast of flesh, like you, and I am no less susceptible to desire than any of God's flock. But I am as He made me. Even my filthy weakness serves Him, and through me His will is done. The events of this evening should be proof enough of that."

Shapera looked back to the window where he saw the skinned face of Tally Kant rise up next to the frothy-haired woman who had recently consumed the boy's cheek. More of his men—their wounds moist and leaking, their unblinking eyes searching—joined the gathering beyond the glass.

"Of course, I'm a traditionalist," the priest said. "So every now and again I offer communion. I'll have Bobby call in the rest of your crew once we're finished here, so my children can work their jaws a little. I understand you have three times the men that Raul did. That's good."

Raul? Shapera thought. He glanced at the decapitated head leaning against the leg of the rattan chair. "Raul Hernandez?" he whispered.

"Yes," said the priest. "Bobby used to work for him. He had an even fouler presence than yours, which made his conversion all the more necessary. Still, he did have his good points." The priest ran his hand over Shapera's sweating face and licked his lips. "You've been living well," he laughed, grabbing Shapera's pudgy cheek between his fingers.

Dread blossomed in Shapera. He tried to back away but the heavy table blocked his retreat, and Mogg's sword remained leveled at his belly.

"Oh, don't be that way," the priest said brightly. "If you're right, and this is nothing more than the result of a beetle virus, you'll soon have the opportunity to 'chew me a new asshole,' as you so eloquently put it. But there's only one way to find out, isn't there?"

"I'm coming back for you."

"Bobby," the priest said, waving away the threat with one bony hand, "you know how I like them."

Mogg lifted the blade to the dimple beneath Shapera's Adam's apple. With a thrust of his arm, he punched the point through the drug lord's throat.

Blood bubbled from the gash in Shapera's neck, and he gasped for a breath that would never reach his lungs. Falling to his knees, he looked into the eyes of his driver, pleading with the big man for help.

But Mogg's loyalty had been established long ago.

"Such a sweet boy," the priest said, kissing Mogg on the cheek. "I'll make sure Helen and the girls are particularly nice to you this evening."

Shapera struggled to hold onto consciousness. Through the spinning lens of his pain he saw the priest turn to him. "As for you," he heard the priest say. "I'm expecting you to be particularly nice to me."

I'll bite your nuts off, Shapera thought as he collapsed onto his face. Similar threats rolled through his mind, fading and surging with the slowing beats of his heart. He clung to the hate, wanted it to fill his mind so that he would not pray. He wanted no time to call on God's mercy, because here, in this place, prayers were damning.

"Hurry back," the priest said to Tico Shapera, who finally lay still on the cold tile. "We don't have much time before the fire comes. Not much time at all."

NOT QUITE GHOSTS

KEALAN PATRICK BURKE

God was scraping His heels against the carpet of the sky as Angela turned up the lapels of her raincoat and bowed her head against the promise of rain. The promise quickly became a threat as His heel punched through the steel-colored clouds and a torrent of rain hissed down on top of the unsuspecting and woefully unprepared people waiting at the Lincoln Street bus stop.

Angela felt no satisfaction that she'd been right in predicting the rain or that the strange looks she'd earned from the shirtless teenagers milling around the stop dressed in loose shorts were now pointed skyward. It was July and she was sweating beneath the thick folds of her raincoat, but she'd been right. As usual.

An old man grabbed her elbow, not forcefully but hard enough for her to gasp in surprise as she turned to face him, her lime-green eyes meeting his milky blue ones. He was stooped as if already boarding the bus, one gnarled hand absently massaging his lower back, the other slipping from Angela's arm now that he'd caught her attention.

Her smile flickered on but the weight of it could not be sustained by the absence of sincerity. "Yes?"

"Excuse me, ma'am," he said, looking genuinely apologetic. "How did you know?"

"About the rain?" She shrugged.

He gave no indication that he had seen or heard. "How did you know it was coming?"

She stared at him for a moment and wondered if she should tell him. Perhaps it would be best not to. "I don't know," she lied and turned away.

The bus hissed and snorted its way to a halt, the door flapping open with a labored wheeze.

She was sorry for the lie and could sense him juggling with indecision at her back, wondering whether or not to accept her brusque termination of their exchange.

Eventually she boarded the bus, his eyes heavy on the back of her neck, and she knew he recognized her for what she was. Hoping he wouldn't choose to sit beside her when she found a seat, she ducked her head and tried to let the grumbling of the passengers, the *chink* and *clack* of the driver's ticket machine, and the drumming of the rain on the roof of the bus occupy her mind.

She took a seat at the back and kept her head low, her dark, sopping hair hanging in her face.

After a few minutes the bus swung away from the stop and plunged like a steel leviathan into traffic.

A peek over the headrest in front of her showed no sign of the old man anywhere. She sighed and rubbed her eyes.

The window rattled beside her as the rain tapped invisible fingers against the glass.

She had known there would be rain.

Just as she had known the old man would attempt to talk to her.

And that he was one of the dead ones.

Charlotte, what have you done?

Brett Reed made a ragged ball out of his saturated sweatshirt and tossed it into the waiting mouth of the dryer. He was still wondering where the hell the rain had come from, forcing the cancellation of the tennis lesson he was due to teach, when the little girl stepped out of the washing machine, next to where he had been about to poke the dryer into action.

"Jesus!" He staggered back, curls of black hair poking through the hand he clamped against his damp chest.

The girl straightened, her legs horribly warped and twisted as if by some disease ignorance and half a proper education had kept from Brett's awareness.

She was naked, her chest yawning wide in a bloodless and pitch-dark vertical eye. Her almost-white hair had been cropped short, seemingly by a blunt scissors and with little affection. Beneath the alabaster brow, milky, leaking white eyes stared at Brett.

"Where is she?" the girl hissed and Brett shook his head, perplexed and frightened all at once, inspired to flee but paralyzed by amazement at what the deceptively benign washer had birthed. The child's face was crisscrossed with angry red scratches that looked fresh and drew the eye away from the perverse exposure of her chest cavity.

"Who are you?" he stammered and felt the wall behind him for his tennis racquet.

"Where is she?" the girl repeated and twitched as if shocked by a sudden current from the machine at her back.

"I don't know who you're talking about."

Her face crackled into a toothless smile. "Yes, you do. She loved you."

Brett frowned and felt his stomach tighten, sending bile shooting up his throat.

"She loves you, but you did some nasty things to her, didn't you?"

The child wobbled forward and Brett was compelled to abandon his search for a weapon. Watching the child—who to all intents and purposes should be dead—closing the distance between them, he reluctantly acknowledged the fact that nothing would save him from this waking nightmare. He couldn't possibly fight something that God hadn't created.

The child stopped, smiled. *Crackle.* She cocked her head and stared up at a point in the corner of the room, somewhere above where Brett's bladder was at that moment giving up the ghost.

God, please help me, he thought. *I'm a fucking addict and I've made some bad calls, but I'll make it up to you if you please, please,* please *make this thing go away.*

"I hate her, you know," the child continued and Brett flinched, his shoulder blades attempting to force their way through the wall as if this bizarre scenario nullified their obligation to stay within their owner's body.

The child looked back at him. The motion was accompanied by the sound of shells being crushed underfoot as the ragged bones in her neck ground together.

"After you made me, she hurt me. It was awful."

"Wh-who?"

The corners of the girl's mouth drew downward in synch with her brow. "Why are you pretending you don't know?"

Brett swallowed, his voice close to breaking. "Because I don't. I don't know who *you* are. I don't know who '*she*' is. I don't have a fucking clue what's happening here."

"You put your dirty thing into her, so you *must* know her," she said.

"What?" To hear this coming from the mouth of a child, or whatever the hell this thing was, spun the volume up on his fear.

"You put your dirty, filthy thing into her."

"Into who?"

The girl stepped closer, swaying on her broken feet, the bones rolling beneath mottled greenish blue skin. "Into *her.*"

The sob escaped, forced outward by the weight of desperation buoying to the top of his throat. "I don't understand."

This time when she smiled, it was almost human. "Don't

worry. I didn't understand either, until she used a clothes hangar to teach me. Did she try to make *you* understand?"

He slid to the floor and lowered his head, welcoming the darkness when he covered his weeping eyes with his hands. *It's not real. I'm not seeing her.* He repeated this over and over and over again, sometimes aloud but more often in his head, where nothing could touch him.

"Not to worry," the girl croaked, and this time her voice sounded awfully close. "I'll help you understand everything."

Brett, braving a peek through the safety of his fingers, only saw her eyes before there was nothing left to hide behind.

✢ ✢ ✢

"Jason?"

Charlotte trotted up the dark stairs, drawn like a moth to the amber glow from the room at the top of the steps. She felt a mild sense of panic leave scratch marks on her heart as she eased the door open fully. She expected to see the most horrible thing imaginable—nothing.

Her fears evaporated at the sight of her husband standing at the window, staring out at the rain, the room filled with the distant swish of traffic sailing through the wet streets below.

"I thought you might have left," she said, shrugging off her coat and draping it over the arm of the floral-patterned sofa. Ordinarily, she might have been concerned about dampening the fabric, but not now. Not today. Not when she was in danger of losing Jason.

"All the way home I imagined what it would be like to come back and find you gone," she continued when he didn't respond. She stopped a few feet from his back, wanting to touch him but afraid he might recoil from her. These days, everything seemed to push him further away. The thin curtain that hung between her love for him and her grief at having lost him was rapidly coming loose from the rail.

"How long?" he said coldly, not turning around to look at her.

She hugged herself and stared at his back. "How long what?"

His shoulders shook. Laughter? Tears? She silently pleaded for him to turn around, to face her, just so she could see his eyes.

"How long has it been?"

Again her hands floated toward the black shirt, underneath which lay the skin she yearned to feel beneath her fingers. "I don't know what you mean."

"Yes, you do, Charlotte. I want you to tell me."

She sighed and let her hand fall away, imagining how the two of them would have looked to anyone else.

"Almost three weeks."

This time she heard the slightest chuckle, devoid of mirth and colder than the rain still trickling down her face.

"Why am I here?" he said. "*How* am I here?"

Tears welled in her eyes. She touched him, watched him flinch.

"Because I need you to be here."

✛ ✛ ✛

Scott ran.

The street swept beneath him, his feet a blur, the puddles reaching up to soak his jeans, and he ran, wheezing, cursing until his lungs filled with molten lava.

But stopping was not an option.

Not so long as *she* was behind him.

He rounded the corner of the alley and collided with an elderly woman who squawked in surprise and fell heavily to the pavement, her plastic sack vomiting groceries out onto the road. Scott muttered an apology as he leaped over a rolling tin of canned peaches.

He ignored the enraged yells and cries of disgust from the people no doubt moving to form a protective huddle around the fallen woman.

Fine, let them, he thought. They *aren't running from a fucking corpse.*

A quick glance over his shoulder made his heart lurch and his stomach hurt.

She was there—still behind him, still gaining—and he wondered how fast she was capable of going, if there was any point in running from something that didn't need to use its feet to move.

But the fact that Tracy had come back for him wasn't the worst of it. Oh no.

The fact that he had slit her throat and almost decapitated that bastard she'd been blowing when he'd come home from work early should have put the whole mess to bed. But now here she was, floating two feet over the pavement like a ghost but proving herself all too tangible by thumping against people who shrieked and fled and thanked God it wasn't them she was after. He imagined them crossing themselves and soon moving on, muttering about the return of those long buried and how the world was going to hell.

Tracy filled his head with whispers, deadly promises and obscene threats, perhaps attempting to drive him mad. Madness was an eventuality he felt drawing as close as the reanimated parody of his dead girlfriend, hung like a puppet from God's fingernails and gliding toward him through the rain.

Another look over his shoulder and she was near enough to grab him.

With a strangled cry, he turned and raced down an alley much the same as the last, plumes of steam billowing upward toward a sky the color of steel, the concrete hollowed and filled with rainwater. She swooped into the entrance. Her long black hair was knotted but dry, despite the deluge hammering down from above. Her head lolled on a ravaged neck, black marble eyes fixed on her murderer.

"What are you running for?" a guttural voice asked and Scott slipped attempting to come to a full stop. He went down in a puddle and gasped at the cold against his skin.

He looked up at the man towering over him and paled. "You!"

To anyone else, the guy with the baseball cap might have appeared normal, unless you looked closer, peered beneath that chiseled jaw and saw the tendrils of flesh dangling from the dark hole where his throat had been hacked open.

"Oh, shit," Scott moaned and backpedaled away from the grinning form of his dead girlfriend's lover. A cold breeze stopped him and he deigned not to look.

"Caught," she said as if it were nothing more than an innocent game of tag.

"I'm sorry," he whimpered and raised his arms over his face, anticipating a blow.

"Oh, there's no need to apologize," the man with the baseball cap croaked. "You did us a favor."

"What?"

"We've come to return it," Tracy whispered and grabbed a handful of his hair. Scott screamed as he was dragged to his feet. Rainwater blinded him, pounded against his widened eyes, reducing the clues to his fate to mere blurs. He felt the wind breathing down on him as he was lifted higher and higher and higher still, until the air grew cold. Tears ran and mingled with the rain.

"Please, Tracy, I'm sorry," he moaned, his voice strangled with sobs. He blinked and saw they had risen above the buildings. He shut his eyes, sobbed, his adrenaline fueling the stuttering engine of self-preservation and fooling him into thinking he might make it out of this alive.

"Now, now. Don't worry," Tracy gurgled. "David will catch you."

Scott almost allowed himself to be comforted, until he realized what she was saying. She meant to drop him from this height. How could her dead lover possibly. . . ?

Her hands were gone. He fell. The ground rushed up to meet him. And as he drew in a breath to scream, he saw her lover waiting below and it registered in Scott's horrified, dying mind that David was not holding his arms out to catch him, as Tracy had promised. Instead, his mouth was open and growing wider.

And wider still. . . .

There would not be time enough to scream.

✢   ✢   ✢

Angela slid the key into the lock and paused.

He's in there. She nodded imperceptibly, as if the prompt had come from somewhere other than a dark, whispering knot in the center of her own mind. Sucking a long breath in through her teeth, she opened the door.

The hallway was dark and she proceeded slowly through it, her eyes probing the corners for leering faces. *He got in. But how?* She had made sure her apartment was locked up tight before leaving it this morning. How could he have gotten in?

Fool, another part of her whispered. *You know doors don't stop them. They're not ghosts but they're much more than just walking corpses, too. You know that.*

She could feel electricity tingling beneath her skin as she reached the kitchen and gave a quick glance upward toward the cracked ceiling, where she half expected to see him hiding. Nothing but stains.

Angela put her purse down on the kitchen table and hurried to the phone in the living room, thinking: *If he's here, will he let me make it?*

A shaky sigh escaped her as her hand found the receiver. She dialed. Immediately a shadow crossed the walls. But she couldn't turn. Couldn't look at what might have crossed the room, what might have thrown its cold shadow against the walls as it passed the narrow wedge of light peering in through the partially drawn curtains. She sensed the room shrinking away from her, a cold lump twisting in her throat, then gagged, as a stench of rotting meat embraced her, invading her mouth and crawling deeper down. The room was small. The rank odor filled it quickly, bringing tears to her eyes. Then something tugged at her hair.

"*You bitch,*" an all too familiar voice said. "*Daddy wants a word with you.*"

She closed her eyes and tried to ignore the feeling of his uncut nails hoisting up her skirt, her raincoat, leaving cold tracks like snail trails on the backs of her legs. Her lower lip quivered and she sank her teeth into it. "Go away." The curtains shifted, setting off a skirmish between shadows and light for dominance on the wall to her right.

The fingers scratched their way toward her inner thigh. "*Remember what my pal Tommy said when they asked him if he had any final words? He had a little mantra. Remember? Just before they threw the switch?*"

The phone continued to ring in her ear, the receiver trembling in her white-knuckled grip. Her lip began to bleed. "Please," she whispered. The nails became fingertips, scratching against the soft flesh of her buttocks.

"*He said, 'Never Deny the Guy the Pie.' Remember that? And you've been denying me the pie for a long time, haven't you?*"

She could feel the weight of him behind her, his foul breath against the nape of her neck.

A click from the phone. "Hello?"

The hands were ripped away. Angela jolted, winced, wondered if the wounds were deep enough to bleed. The room exhaled, returned to its natural state, but she knew he was there, like a magician who had apparently vanished into thin air but was merely hidden by mirrors. "It's Angela," she said into the phone.

"What do you want?" Charlotte asked with barely concealed impatience.

"I want to know how you did it."

"Did what?"

"Don't play the fool with me. You know exactly what I'm talking about. Daddy was here. I want to know how you did it and what the hell you thought you were doing. Was it the mirror? *His* mirror?"

Silence, but for a faint crackling on the line.

"Charlotte, take a look out your window. Can you tell the dead from the living anymore?"

Charlotte cleared her throat. "It's because you're a sensitive, isn't it? An easy explanation. You're seeing all of them. I only see the ones I want to see."

Angela chuckled dryly. "Is he the man you married? Did bringing him back also bring back all the love and happiness you had hoped? Will he be happy living again with his all-important looks rotten and ruined?"

"I don't have to listen to this," Charlotte said, her voice now matching her sister's with its uneven, quavering tone. "He's home and that's all that matters."

Angela closed her eyes and forced herself to be calm. "So you pretend he's your darling husband, even though he's some monstrous *thing*. They're not quite ghosts, Charlotte. That's why you can touch them. They're corpses, brought back from the dead by foolishness. How far does this need to go before you acknowledge it as a mistake, an error spawned from your grief and loss? And if you manage to convince yourself everything is fine and dandy, what about me? What about your sister? Do you think I'll survive with the decaying flesh of our bastard father sprouting from the walls at every turn?"

Charlotte said nothing.

"Jason may not hurt you. He may, in fact, be incapable of hurting you because he's one of the gentler ones. But Daddy isn't. Daddy died and—"

"No," Charlotte interrupted. "Daddy didn't die. You killed him, remember?"

Angela's fingers tightened on the receiver. "He deserved it. Or doesn't that matter because he gave you everything and stole everything from me? The man was a cold-hearted, child-molesting psychopath who dabbled in things no man should know. But even now, you'd use one of his evil toys to satisfy yourself. Spoiled little Charlotte."

"I'm hanging up."

"Fine. Have my death on your conscience then, as long as your world fits the insane picture in your head. But remember that your world may bring the end of everyone else's." Angela slammed down the phone.

Almost immediately an intense wave of cold air flooded over her, cementing her feet to the floor.

"I'm going to get me some of that fine pie, Angie, and you're going to love every minute of it."

Angela moaned as the hands returned, pushing her forward roughly. A cloak of darkness swept around her as he chuckled into her ear, and the room withdrew once more. But not before she was granted a glimpse of rotten, purple flesh sliding from the arm that curled around her throat.

This time she had no doubt there'd be blood.

✛ ✛ ✛

"Where's Scott?" Jason asked. He was still staring out at the city, watching a veil of twilight descended quickly over the buildings, forced down by the weight of rain.

Charlotte switched on the lamp beside her armchair and sighed. "He left here a few nights ago in a blinding rage. I think he finally realized what his precious girlfriend has been up to behind his back. I imagine she gave him a sob story and they're away somewhere patching things up. Silly child."

"Has he seen me yet?"

Charlotte gave a short, unconvincing laugh. "Of course he has. You're his father."

"Has he seen me like *this*?"

Charlotte's forced mirth dwindled to nothing. *Please look at me*, she thought. *Please. Just a glimpse.* "No."

"And what do you see in *me* as I am now?" His voice was flat, emotionless. Empty.

She considered his words, but they were overruled by the recollection of what her sister had said earlier: *"Is he the man you married? Did bringing him back also bring back all the love and happiness you had hoped? Will he be happy living again with his all-important looks rotten and ruined?"*

Yes, she told herself. *Yes, I damn well will be happy, and he will be happy, too, once he remembers.*

Remembers what? A sneering shadow in her mind countered. *Remembers your affair? How he walked in on you getting it from your tennis instructor? That was a magic moment, wasn't it? Coming home and finding him watching the video was even better. Should have a golden memories photo album for that one, don't you think? Pregnant? Not a problem. A clothes hanger right through the fetus' chest did the trick, leaving Tennis Boy sans worry and your husband with a heart attack.*

Stop it, she almost said aloud, and clenched her teeth, willing away the pessimistic shade. "Honey, please look at me." Jason said nothing, continued to stare at the darkening street.

Yes, I'm sorry for the affair, but he paid our debts, dragged us out of the hole Jason had dug. If not for him, we wouldn't have been able to keep our nice home, have our two cars and—

A dead man in your living room.

—everything we've ever needed. I'm sorry, yes. But I'd do it all over again if I had to.

"Honey?"

His shoulders might have shifted; Charlotte couldn't be sure, but now it was incidental. The crawling horror that was steadily forming a shawl over her spine made her consider the awful truth that maybe, just maybe, she had made a mistake in bringing him back. What possible good would his return serve if he refused to look at her? It would only remind her of how he might have been had the affair not killed him.

"I can't look at you," he said finally, in the same dead tone.

She got to her feet, hands clasped to her breast, radiating need. "Why?"

His shoulders shook again, and she felt a twinge of sorrow in her stomach. "Honey, why?"

As she drew closer, she realized he was not weeping. He was laughing. The soft, dry rustling of his mirth drifted over his shoulder and she stopped dead, watching the pale slope of his bloodless neck as he slowly shook his head.

"I can't look at you, Charlotte dear," he said in a voice made watery by amusement, "because they stitched my eyes shut."

" 'They'?"

There was no time for panic, only dazed amazement as she looked from his trembling form to the reflection in the window. What she saw superimposed over the fading city forced her mouth open and tore out a scream.

"Yes, dear," he answered, nodding once. "Those who make us what we are."

"Nooo," she cried, gripping the sides of her face, dragging her nails through the skin as he turned toward her. Patches of purple and black mottled his stark white skin. The stitches in his eyes had ripped just enough for her to see the oozing, tarlike blackness rolling beneath the lids.

"Oh, don't do that," he said with a crooked smile. "Don't damage your face. I need it. I mean, I can't very well go outside looking like this, can I?"

✛   ✛   ✛

Angela was lost amid moving tunnels and—

They said the light was supposed to be white not red not red not red . . .

—shifting shadows whispering feverishly in her ear.

She was dimly aware of her father working over her dead body—

Cutting, slicing, chewing, licking, tasting, eating . . .

—but it was as if she were watching the depravity being bestowed upon another.

She was free, free to pick her destination from the myriad tunnels, each drawing her in a different direction so that even her spirit rent apart under the magnetic pull of indecision.

Eventually, she chose a scarlet rectangular doorway. It looked familiar—

Charlotte used daddy's mirror to bring them back . . .

—and as she neared it, she felt the warmth radiating,

burning, searing, scorching, and she screamed, jumped, tripped, fell, sprawled across the doorway and emerged in a room of a different color, where the shadows stood still and a stairs led to a light—

The right light right color saving light . . .

—at the top of the stairs.

Home. A brief smile flickered across her blistering, smoking features, but was singed away by realization. She looked behind her and saw herself. Charlotte's mirror—

Fashioned from the ground-up bones of the dead and the skin of the living. Part of Daddy's collection . . .

—stood propped against the wall.

I'm not home not home not home. I've come through the mirror to join the dead but walking, angry hungry dead . . .

She tried to weep, but the tears recoiled from her scorched flesh.

She tried to scream, but the flames she'd never seen had cauterized her throat.

So in her mind, she screamed and screamed, and begged and cried. And after a while, she began to ascend the stairs.

There's no Heaven up here. No Heaven at all. Only death and hunger. And I can feel it all . . .

She reached the top of the stairs and pushed the door open fully. The light to which her hope had drawn her was daylight.

Daylight. Charlotte's house. She used Daddy's mirror, Daddy's doorway . . .

Outside, pale shapes shambled past the window.

She stood and watched them, felt the tremble leave her charred body, thought, *I must go with them, wherever they're going. I can't be alone, please don't leave me alone. I'm frightened and hurt and alone. And hungry . . .*

She staggered across the kitchen and flung the door wide—

So very hungry.

—and watched a legion of her brethren stalk forth through the streets of a new world. A world ripe for the harvest.

Relapse

JOHN SULLIVAN

It was the smell that woke me. Like fresh bacon ready for the pan. *Yes,* I thought. *Hungry. Breakfast. Good.*

Then the noise broke through my waking fog and it dawned on me, first that I'd slept through the alarm, and second that the heartrate monitor on my nightstand was in panic mode. I turned over and watched the flatline rolling by like old man river under the blinking *000.*

I tried telling myself I'd just been tossing in my sleep and I'd rubbed the pickup off my chest. But it was right where it belonged. *Ah, damn.* I was dead again. And the tantalizing smell? Yeah, that would be people's brains.

As always, it took a second to really hit me and then there was that rush of dread. I looked around, afraid I'd find the half-eaten remains of some unlucky girl I'd brought home from a bar last night. But my bedroom was no messier than usual. Of course it wasn't. What was I thinking?

I shut off the alarms and switched on the tube to check "Matt and Claire in the Morning!" Then I stumbled into the bathroom to see just how bad it was. I looked like hell. Slack-jawed stare, deep bags under my eyes, blood pooling in strange places. I'd been dead a few hours at least.

Claire's voice drifted in from the bedroom: ". . . primarily to the north of the city, though victims of previous outbreaks across our viewing area are at increased risk of relapse. Metro authorities have asked us to remind viewers that sufferers of Romero's Syndrome can be revived with proper medical treatment. Despite their dangerous tendencies, they're to be harmed only in self-defense and only as a last resort. So just stay out of their way and call for qualified help. Matt."

Matt sounded especially chirpy this morning. "That's right Claire. And with thunderstorms rolling in by afternoon, the best thing to do is just stay inside today unless you absolutely have to go out."

When I shambled out of the bathroom they were running live shots from the traffic chopper, which was stationed over some clogged suburban intersection. Dozens of the walking dead were making a banquet out of the morning commute and getting run down by minivans. Idiots. I switched it off.

I'm actually one of the lucky ones, if you can call it that. I got it in the first big outbreak, back in Philly in '99. I was a senior in college and I was right next to the campus medical center when some zombie came out of nowhere and took me down. I was pretty chewed up by the time the security guards got him off me, but he hadn't gotten to any of the important stuff. The ER crew pumped me full of tPA, the "golden hour" stuff they give stroke victims. Then they shocked my heart and I was back up. I was dead ten minutes, max.

I can still relapse, like anybody else with the disease, but I keep more mental function than most. A lot of zombies can't think about much more than how a little fresh brain would really hit the spot. With me, it's more like I've gone three days on nothing but processed sugar and no sleep.

But I still needed to get to the hospital before any long-term damage set in. They know me at Bay General. I've got their Zombie Center on a speed dial button, big for clumsy fingers. I pushed it and heard the quick burst of touchtones. Then the phone cheerfully said, "All circuits are currently busy. Please hang up and try your call again later."

I tried a couple more times, but it was no good. That's the problem with emergencies. Everybody freaks at once. I'd have to get there myself.

I dressed for the office: long sleeves, overcoat, as little exposed skin as possible. This would be tricky enough already. The more I looked like someone on his way to a cubicle somewhere, and the less like a flesh-starved dead guy, the better. Next came the briefcase where I keep copies of my medical records for an emergency. Proper accessorizing counts.

I made it out of my apartment and staggered down the hall, past closed doors redolent of fresh brains beyond. I practiced saying "Bay General Hospital" while I waited for the elevator.

The doors finally opened on an empty car. More good luck. I got in and punched *L*. My luck held down to the eighth floor. Then the doors slid open and there she stood. We'd traded polite smiles a few times, in the lobby or the hallways. When it happened in the mailroom I'd noted which box she opened and checked the label after she'd left. *S. Buening, #802.* I kept wondering what the *S* stood for.

I turned into the corner as she bopped in wearing jogging shorts and punched for the lobby. It took me a couple floors to figure out why she was going jogging now, of all times. Finally I realized that she didn't know. I guess some people don't switch on their TVs the moment they wake up. I almost turned around to warn her, but caught myself. That wouldn't help much. If Matt and Claire were right about the epicenter, then she'd be okay.

So I stood very still and hoped she wouldn't notice me. I could see her blurry reflection in the button panel, shifting from the ball of one foot to the other to stretch out her calves. Her brain smelled really nice.

As we were passing five, she glanced at me in my trench-coat and briefcase, and checked her watch.

"You're going to be late."

I gave a noncommittal grunt.

"I swear I'm not gloating," she said. "I work rotating shifts. Afternoon today."

"Mmm." Four. Just a little longer.

She laughed. "Rough night? You're Brian, right? Up on twelve? I'm Susan."

Had she checked my mailbox, too? She stepped closer and held out her hand. Why did this have to happen now? I nodded, but she shifted around to get a better look at me. Suddenly she shrieked and leaped back into the far corner of the car.

I held out my medic alert bracelet, like that was going to reassure her or something. "It's okay," I tried to say. "I'm going to the hospital."

She blasted me with pepper spray.

I stood there trying to sigh while pepper spray dripped down my cheeks. I was dead, for Christ's sake. But she wasn't thinking. She just cringed in the corner, clawing at the wood panels and screaming. All I could do was keep still and not make things worse. I felt lower than dirt.

She was still shrieking when the doors dinged and slid open for the lobby. She darted out, and her screams brought the janitor. He shouted in Spanish and whacked me with his mop as I retreated toward the revolving door. Those really aren't made with zombies in mind, by the way.

I finally made it out to the sidewalk and the janitor didn't follow. I headed for the corner to hail a cab. It was maybe a three-minute ride past the park to Bay General. I'd chosen this building for a reason.

It was a beautiful day. The sky was clear and a warm breeze swept between the buildings. Only a handful of people on the street. A cab slid up to the curb, the passenger window already whirring down.

"Where you go today, sir?" said the driver through a thick accent. A handheld dispatch radio squawked in his lap.

"Bay General Hospital," I said, just like I'd practiced.

"Come again, sir?"

I should have printed it up on a card, I realized. Let them think I couldn't speak or something. Well, next time.

"Bay General Hospital." I moved toward the back door. But he leaned over and peered at me with suspicion. Then he wailed and hurled his radio at me. It caught me in the chest and I scrabbled to catch it. He was leaning down, reaching under the seat. I tried to give back his radio, but he came up with the biggest pistol I'd ever seen.

I shouted, "Don't shoot!" But he was screaming and I could see the terror in his eyes. The gun went off with a shattering roar, and I was spun around. I slumped against the car, gripping the window frame to pull myself up. I was leaking fluids from my side. This wasn't good.

The driver saw me climbing up over the edge of the passenger door and tried to fire again, but he had to cock the hammer first and he dropped the gun trying. In a panic he bailed out and ran down the street, screaming for help.

Things were getting out of hand fast. The gunshot wound was one more thing they'd have to patch up before they could revive me. I wasn't used to having holes blown in me by terrified cabbies. And I wasn't thinking all that clearly to begin with. It may not have been the best move, but at the moment it was all I could come up with. I fumbled for the door handle, climbed into the driver's seat, and took off into the intersection.

I think I ran a red light, but somehow I didn't hit anything and even managed to wheel the cab around and aim it in the right direction down Parkside Avenue. A couple more blocks up and I'd reach the park itself. Then a right at the far end and I'd be there.

Driving turned out to be more complicated than I'd thought. My body was numb, and I couldn't steer very well. I roared down the street, weaving in and out of my lane. Everything outside seemed to be rushing by way too fast. I saw the buildings on my right give way to the green of the park.

Then I heard a horn and something cut me off. I went for the brake. Again I must have hit it too hard, because suddenly the car was fishtailing. I watched a huge shape cross in front of me and rocket across the sidewalk. Then the cab bounced over the curb and went airborne. At last it slammed into a wall of green, and I smashed against the wheel and the windshield.

I was beginning to think it was a good thing I was dead. Otherwise, half the things that had happened to me this morning would have killed me.

I'd gone down the embankment into the park, I realized. I

saw what had cut me off. A Japanese pickup, coated in chrome and lightbars, and jacked up enough to see through second-story windows. It was a miracle he hadn't rolled the thing.

The pickup's door flew open and a man climbed out, looking around wildly.

"Yeah, God damn!" he whooped. "You all right in there?"

I managed to get the door partly open and crawled out onto the ground.

"Ah, shit!" the man said. He circled back to his truck as I got to my feet, and returned with an aluminum crossbow. His T-shirt read *God Hates Zombies.*

This was just what I needed. An outbreak always brought the vigilantes out of the woodwork. Half of them were church fanatics who figured if God wanted us dead we must have done something to deserve it and we should stay that way.

The rest, like this guy, kept their shotguns and crossbows handy just for days like this. After the first outbreaks there had been a rash of really dumb laws and high-profile test cases. So far, at least, the courts had drawn a sharp line between the living and the dead. Alive, we had the same rights as anyone else. We couldn't be rounded up on general principles, or charged for things we'd done while we were incapacitated. But a dead body, especially one intent on eating everyone in sight, was another matter. Today, this jerk could slaughter me and get frowned at instead of sent up.

He cocked his crossbow and looked me over. He didn't even bother to hide the thing because I was supposed to be too stupid to know what it was.

"Yeah," he said, pointing to his forehead with his free hand. "Come get some, you fag zombie bastard."

Like I'd want to eat his pea brain in the first place.

When I heard the shouting and scattered gunshots from the direction of the ponds, I realized the guy had been on the way to a party. They'd be herding the dead with their pickups and maybe some blowtorches. Once they had them bunched up, they'd start shooting. The cops would show, but not until it was too late to do anything. Then there would be some hand-wringing in the newspapers, and a backlash of letters saying we got what we deserved. Except when it was all over, a whole lot of people wouldn't be coming back.

I could see Mr. Survivalist getting worked up, ready to go. "Maybe you want a little crossbow action with your brains, huh?"

He pointed it at me, and I dove to the side as he fired. The razorpoint slashed my arm, but by now that was nothing. I retreated up the bank toward the street while he recocked the crossbow. I was worried about his back-up weapon. Zombies tend to cluster. He'd have a gun in the truck. But mostly I needed to get out of the park before his friends caught me up in their little trap.

I saw motion beyond the pickup and for a second I thought they had me. But then they came around the truck. They weren't his friends, but mine. Sort of.

Five of them stumbled toward us, spreading out to flank him. He was focused on me instead of checking his back, and one almost grabbed him before he realized what was going on. They'd already cut him off from the truck.

He was almost surrounded. The only way out was past me. But, of course, he didn't know that.

He started screaming "Help me!" and waving the crossbow around like a club. He was sinking into panic. He'd be meat in seconds.

I hated the son of a bitch, but did he really deserve to be torn apart and eaten? I remembered support groups full of people who weren't as lucky as me. Some of them had actually eaten people before they'd been caught and revived. I could still hear the wracking guilt in their voices. More of them than I could count had ended up killing themselves. Always the same way: gunshot to the head. It was the only method they knew they could trust.

One of them caught the crossbow and wrenched it from the guy's hands. I wasn't really sure who I was trying to save then, but I turned and staggered straight into the melee. I grabbed him and pulled him backward. For a second I really had to fight the urge to take a bite out of his scalp.

Then I threw him behind me, up the bank as hard as I could. "Run!" I snarled.

He sprawled on the grass at the edge of the sidewalk as I laid into my fellow sufferers. They weren't interested in eating me, but they wanted to get past me more than anything. If they couldn't get around me, they'd settle for going through.

I shoved one down the bank, caught another by the wrist as she tried to push by me, and swung her around into the others. I was falling back, on the sidewalk now. I heard people screaming and sirens in the distance. Crossbow boy was sprinting across the street, getting up speed. He'd make it, at least. There didn't seem to be anybody else near enough for my comrades to feed on, so I broke off and staggered down the street, toward Bay General.

The sirens were getting closer. A police zombie unit was

better than what my friend with the crossbow had planned for me, but not by much. They could still kill us in self-defense and, when you were dealing with zombies, self-defense was pretty much a given. This was not where I wanted to be right now.

I'd gotten maybe twenty feet when a little hatchback roared up and screeched to a stop with its tires smoking. A figure leaned over to open the passenger door.

Instinctively I turned to flee, but I heard a woman's voice shout, "Get in!"

I turned around and saw Susan. "Get in!" she shouted again. It took me a second to work through my astonishment. Then I staggered over and fell inside. She peeled out even before I got the door closed. Behind us, the police vans surged into the cluster of the dead, riot cops pouring out to mop them up. I sat there leaking while she drove like a maniac toward the end of the park. I don't remember much after that.

When I woke up, everything hurt. That was a good sign. The upside of being dead is that you're a lot less delicate. They can fix all kinds of things before they revive you. I lay there, eyes closed, breathing, and tried to remember the important things in my life. There aren't that many, but they all seemed to be there. Apparently there wasn't any serious brain damage.

"You're going to be okay," someone said. I opened my eyes to find her sitting there beside the bed. Susan.

"You found me."

"I remembered you said you were going to the hospital, so I came looking. After I calmed down I felt so horrible. You needed help and I just freaked."

"It's okay," I said. "I'm not easy to—"

"But I'm an EMT. I'm not supposed to panic like that. How are you feeling?"

"Thirsty," I said, realizing it as I spoke.

"You lost a lot of fluids. Mostly on my seats."

If she could handle this, I realized, she could handle just about anything. "I'll clean them for you later."

"Damn right you will. I have to run. Busy day out there. I'll check back on you. You like Mondo Thai?"

"Place around the corner from us? Sure."

"All right. Pass on the dinner cart when it comes around and I'll fix you up."

It occurred to me how handy it would be to have an EMT around, but it wasn't that simple.

"Wait."

She stopped in the doorway and looked back at me.

"You know I've . . . got this thing."

"Duh. And?"

"I'm just . . . I mean it's not going to go away."

"Right now I'm just curious to find out if you're as well-mannered when you're breathing," she said. "Plenty of time to deal with the rest down the road."

She grinned. "Besides, a girl likes to be appreciated for her mind."

She disappeared into the hall while I sat there with my jaw hanging open. Then I started to laugh. It hurt like hell so I laughed some more, because I knew that I was alive.

Zombies are Forever

MARK McLAUGHLIN

"So, what'll it be?" asked the bartender, a bald, muscular man with pockmarks and a scar over his right eye.

On the party side of the bar stood a handsome man with thick black hair and a wry smile. His eyes were large, black, and alert—almost childlike. His skin was pink and smooth, without even a single wrinkle. He wore a black tuxedo with a white rosebud pinned to the lapel. "Carrot juice," he said, "if you have it. Tomato juice, if you don't."

"Sorry, no carrot juice. Bugs Bunny drank the last of it." The bartender started shaking a small can of tomato juice. "How about a Bloody Mary?"

The handsome man wrinkled his boyish nose. "Why ruin some perfectly good tomato juice with alcohol?"

The bartender laughed. "Isn't it time for church, choir boy?" He poured the tomato juice into a plastic cup and set it on the bar. "Here ya go. On the house. Are you even old enough to be in here?"

The handsome man put a five-dollar bill in the tip jar and took his drink. "I don't know. Do you serve forty-year-olds?"

"Forty!" The bartender looked the man up and down. "Hell, I'd have guessed twenty-two, twenty-three tops. What's your secret?"

"Clean living." The man in the tuxedo turned back toward the party and walked over to the buffet table. He leaned slightly over a huge silver bowl of jumbo shrimp on ice and sniffed—once, twice. A little off. He picked up a radish from a vegetable tray and munched on that.

He studied the other partygoers. Politicians, tycoons, all sorts of folks with too much money and too many bad habits. They all looked so tired . . . so unhealthy. There were plenty of beautiful trophy wives wandering about, but theirs was an artificial beauty. Their sagging flesh had either been pulled tight or plumped up with implants.

A pink-cheeked, sixtyish woman walked up to him. She wore a pinstriped suit, high heels, no make-up, and a white rosebud pinned to her bun of steel-gray hair. "Good evening, Pi," she said softly. "How are you enjoying the festivities?"

"For a birthday party, it's rather depressing," he said.

"These people all look so sickly. Nice suit, Omicron. Where's the guest of honor?"

"Senator Phelps is in a private meeting right now, but he should be here shortly." She glanced at her wristwatch. "We'd better start heading toward the balcony. It's almost time to meet our new friend."

Pi smiled briefly. Omicron always used such charming euphemisms.

As they moved through the party, Pi noticed that many of the older men turned to give Omicron the eye. And rightly so. She was lovely and perfectly fit. She didn't need make-up to enhance her stunning patrician features. One could tell just by looking at her that she was a strong, confident woman.

Pi was proud of her, but he was a little peeved at the men. He didn't like it when guys ogled his mother.

The balcony doors at the south end of the room were locked, but Omicron had the key. She opened them, and Pi walked through. Omicron untied the curtains of the French doors so that they covered the glass. Then she passed through, locking the way shut behind her.

Out on the balcony, a woman stepped from the shadows behind a large potted plant. She wore a hooded cloak of blue velvet. The hood was up, so that all Pi could see of her face was the tip of her nose and the gleam of her eyes. "You're right on time," she said. Her voice was raspy, like that of a chain smoker.

Omicron smiled. "Of course we are. Hello, Olive."

"Can I see some identification?" the woman asked.

Pi handed her a small leather case containing his badge. He noticed that she was wearing long gloves.

Olive opened the case and looked inside. "Unhip."

"Excuse me?" Pi said.

"United Nations Health Investigations Program. The initials spell out *unhip*—that's funny." She handed back the case.

"Just a coincidence, I'm sure," Omicron said. "You have the papers we discussed. . . ?"

"Yes, and photographs, too." Olive reached behind the potted plant and picked up a black leather valise. "There's enough evidence here to have Dr. Loki put away forever."

"Let's hope so." Pi took the valise from the woman.

"We'll be leaving now," Omicron said. "Will you be rejoining the party?"

Olive laughed, though it sounded more like the crunch of autumn leaves underfoot. "I didn't come in that way. Parties are a thing of the past for me." So saying, she threw back the hood of her cloak. At one time, she had been a very beautiful woman. Certainly the left side of her face was beautiful. But the right—that was a horrid mass of livid yellow scars and orange lumps. She pulled off her gloves, revealing hands and arms streaked with yellow and orange. Her palms and fingertips looked like they had been coated with lime-green paint. She hurried toward the wall, kicked off her shoes, and jumped.

Pi gasped. For a split-second, he'd thought she was jumping off the balcony. But, no—she was, in fact, flinging herself *onto* the wall. She stuck to it by her hands and the tips of her toes. Then she quickly scuttered away along the vertical surface. The only sound to be heard was a faint squelching sound, oddly reminiscent of suction cups.

"Could I borrow your handkerchief?" Omicron said.

Pi handed her a square of white silk from the breast pocket of the tuxedo. "Catching a cold?"

Omicron walked over to the wall and used the cloth to wipe a bit of slime from its surface. She then folded the handkerchief neatly and handed it back to her son. "Silly boy. I've never been sick a day in my life. You know that. Give that little keepsake to the lab folks."

She opened the balcony doors, and the duo returned to the party. They only stayed long enough to grab some more radishes and carrot sticks from the buffet table. On the way out, they walked by the table of Senator Phelps, a tall, stocky man with a deep tan. Omicron nodded to the politician and he gave her a smile and a wink.

"Nice fellow, that senator," Omicron said to her son as they walked out of the building, into the cool autumn night. "He asked me out to dinner while we were arranging tonight's social call."

"Oooh, is he going to be my new daddy?" Pi said with a laugh. He tucked the valise under his arm, since its thin leather handle was starting to dig into his hand.

"I've yet to meet the man who could replace your father. He was the—" Suddenly she stopped. "Over there." She pointed across the lawn.

Three figures emerged from a group of trees and rushed toward them. The figures moved quickly, hunched down so that their hands touched the ground as they scrambled forward. Their yellow and orange skin gleamed in the moonlight. One of them gave voice to a raspy howl, revealing a mouthful of jagged yellow teeth.

Omicron and Pi both reached into their jackets, pulled out

lightweight gas masks, and slipped them on. Omicron removed her high heels. She flipped the silver buckles on the shoes, which were, in fact, safety catches. She then pressed small, flat buttons on the sides of the heels, releasing a spray of fine mist toward the creatures.

The gas should have paralyzed their assailants on the spot. But they kept coming, so Pi handed the valise to his mother and rushed forward. He grabbed the foremost creature by the arm and swung it in a circle, back at the other two.

Suddenly, a thin young man rushed out from behind a nearby parked car. He wore a black fedora with what looked like a raven feather tucked in the hatband. He took the feather and flung it like a dart at Omicron.

Pi pushed one of the creatures into the path of the projectile. The monstrous thing squealed as the feather pierced its shoulder. Its flesh began to bubble, releasing billows of steam. The bubbling spread from the shoulder to the entire body, reducing it to a pile of bones mired in thick, reddish mush. Frightened, the other two creatures ran back into the woods.

Omicron pulled out her gun. The thin man jumped into the car and drove off.

"Shoot out his tires," Pi said.

His mother fired several silent shots at the car. But it just kept racing down the road.

"That ought to do the trick," she said.

"But you missed!"

Omicron shook her head. "This gun isn't loaded with bullets. It's got magnetic tracers instead. They'll broadcast a signal that we can trace back to Dr. Loki."

Pi frowned. "But what if Brimley had jumped you?"

"Brimley? Jump me? That pipsqueak wouldn't dare. He's just a coward—that's why he only attacks from a distance. No, I knew he'd run the moment he saw a gun." Omicron pointed to the feather, which now rested on the skeleton's shoulder blade. "Another souvenir for the lab folks. We'd better give them a call."

The next day, Pi and Omicron visited the office of their supervisor, Gamma. The cluttered room was filled with filing cabinets and piles of newspapers and videotapes. In one corner was a cardboard box housing a pregnant cat asleep on a pillow.

It was against department policy to bring in pets, but Gamma was a widower with only cats for company, so nobody complained. Besides, he was the head of the department.

"You two did some fine work last night," Gamma said. He was a heavyset man with wavy white hair and thick glasses. "So did the lab folks. They had that mess in the yard cleaned up before any of the senator's guests started for their cars. I looked over the evidence in the valise. This thing is bigger than any of us would have dreamed."

"Well, then," Omicron said, "don't keep us in suspense. Give us the lowdown."

"I think today's the day." Gamma sat on the floor by the cardboard box and stroked his cat's belly. "This will be Lulu's eighth litter. At this rate I'm going to have to buy a bigger house! Or maybe just move out into the country, so the cats can wander around. They'd like that."

"That's great," Omicron said, "but I was talking about the case."

"Oh, sorry." Gamma sighed. "It's hard to concentrate when the little ones are on the way. Well, Balthazar Loki is still bent on world domination. No big surprise there. I mean, what else is an evil genius billionaire going to do—open a hardware store? That woman you met with last night—Olive Mylove—used to be his chief assistant. She's an expert in biochemistry, and with her expertise she helped him to develop two deadly compounds.

"They call the first compound Gecko Juice. Silly name, but what the stuff does—not so silly. It's made with DNA from three different types of Brazilian rainforest lizards. These lizards have incredible powers of regeneration. Hack off a leg and it grows back in a week. Olive and Dr. Loki spliced DNA from those lizards with that of a fast-growing slime mold.

"If some of that Gecko Juice comes in contact with a human, that nasty genetic cocktail gradually combines with the person's DNA and grows over them and into them. Eventually it kills them. After a day or two the new DNA completely saturates the body, just as mold works its way through anything rotten, and brings it back to—well, not life, but a damned active form of death. The flesh becomes more reptilian, and so does the brain. The person becomes a sort of reptilian zombie. The body is still rotting, and the mold lives off the dead tissue—eating the host zombie from the inside. But if the host eats something living, the mold lives off of that instead. If the zombie gets enough nourishment, the lizard regeneration factor kicks in: The stuff actually strengthens the body and repairs a fair bit of damage. So, basically, the more these zombies eat, the stronger they get. If they're starved, they'll eventually shrivel away to dust.

"Also, they have a unique mutant power. Their hands and feet can exude a tarlike adhesive substance that gives them remarkable climbing abilities. You saw Olive in action with that. I guess the poor gal got some Gecko Juice on her in the lab. It hasn't killed her yet, but in about a week she'll be . . . you know. One of them."

"But I touched one of those creatures," Pi said. "Does that mean—?"

"No, don't worry. You're not going to turn into a zombie. Their skin is dead and dry; no Gecko Juice there. But if one of them bit somebody, and some of their active DNA got into the bloodstream—that's a one-way ticket to Zombieville. Omicron, the paralysis gas in your pretty heels didn't work because zombies don't breathe. Like the slime mold that animates them, they have no use for lungs." Gamma tickled his cat under the chin. "Isn't Lulu a real cutie pie? Have you ever seen a cuter cat in your entire life?"

"Adorable," Omicron agreed. "So what about the other compound?"

"Dr. Loki gave that stuff the delightful name of Piranha Spit," Gamma said. "They stumbled across that formula while they were making Gecko Juice. It's a super-activated form of slime mold that eats away flesh, living or dead, in record time. He lets his flunky Brimley use it to get rid of his enemies. You got a lively demonstration of Spit last night. By the way, I found out something interesting about Brimley while going through those papers. He's Dr. Loki's son."

Pi scowled. "What about those tracers that Omicron fired at the car? Do we have a fix on Dr. Loki's headquarters?"

"Yes," Gamma said. "But I can't tell you where it is. You two won't be going after him."

"What?" Omicron cried. "I thought this was our case!"

"It was. But now it's time to call in the big guns: the military." Their supervisor gave them an apologetic shrug. "One of the documents in that valise mentioned Project WILD—World Insurrection of the Living Dead. We've recently received reports of zombie outbreaks in China and Australia. Sounds like Dr. Loki is giving his plan some test runs before going global with it. We're here to protect the health of the planet—and in this case, that's going to take troops. But you two collected some valuable information, and I'll see that you're commended for that. Next week I'm sending you on a new assignment in

Morocco. You did your part to help defeat Dr. Loki, so please—go celebrate. I know you two don't drink, but in this case, I think you should crack open a bottle of champagne. That's what I'll be doing after Lulu has her babies!"

In the elevator on their way out, Pi said, "I think Gamma's about ready for retirement."

Omicron gave him a hard look. "Why? Because he likes kittens? Gamma is brilliant man. A fine leader. He just gets a little . . . over-enthusiastic about cats. That's all." Then she grinned. "And after all, Lulu is sooo cuuute!"

Mother and son went down the street to a quaint little coffeehouse called Bean There, Done That. Coffee was their beverage of choice when it came to celebrating.

Pi ordered a cup of French Roast and Omicron decided to go all-out and have a latte. They sat in a booth under a painting of Elvis on velvet.

"I know I should feel happier," Omicron said, "but still, I'm a little disappointed. I wanted to be there when Dr. Loki was defeated. You and I have been chasing him for ten years. Before that, your father and I chased him for twenty years. I still sometimes wonder about the way your father died. . . . Was Dr. Loki responsible?"

"I don't think so," Pi said. "He slipped in the bathroom and hit his head on the tub."

"Yes, but maybe your father was distracted, thinking about what to do about Dr. Loki, and . . . and . . ." Her voice trailed away. Then she said, "Listen to me. I've completely demonized Dr. Loki in my mind. Ridiculous. He's only a man. An evil, filthy-rich megalomaniac—but a man just the same."

"I know what you mean," Pi said. "Everywhere I go, I think I see him. Like that man by the counter, looking at the big cookies. I keep thinking, 'Is that Dr. Loki?'"

Omicron glanced toward the cookie display case and gasped. "Keep your voice down," she whispered. "That really *is* Dr. Loki." She turned away from the counter but continued to watch the billionaire in the mirror of her compact. There was no make-up in the silver case. Instead, it held a small communications device. She pressed a small red button, sending a distress signal to headquarters.

Pi picked up a menu sheet and pretended to read, watching Dr. Loki over the top of it. "What's he doing in here?"

"Looks like he's buying some big cookies. They're putting his order in a sack. It's 'to go.' I've signaled headquarters. We've got to stay on his trail, so when they find us, they'll find him, too. Hey, what's he doing? Is he coming over here?"

Dr. Loki was a tall, silver-haired man with black eyebrows and almond-shaped blue eyes. He walked up to their table and waved the "to go" sack in front of them. "Hello, Margaret. Hello, Perry. Want some cookies? I followed you here from your secret headquarters. I hope you don't mind. Actually, I've known the location of your headquarters for years—not much of a secret, I'm afraid. Would you like to come with me and see *my* secret headquarters? My car is right outside."

"I suppose we don't have a choice," Omicron said.

"Of course you do." the billionaire replied. "I'm not pointing a gun at you. Brimley isn't here pointing a feather at you. Now come along, please. Aren't you even the least bit interested in my latest diabolical plan?"

✛ ✛ ✛

They sat in the back of Dr. Loki's limousine, eating big cookies. Brimley was driving with one hand and holding his big cookie with the other. He was still wearing his black fedora, with a fresh feather tucked in the hatband.

"I do wish you'd drive with both hands, Son," Dr. Loki said. "Put down that cookie."

"It'll get crumbs everywhere," the young henchman said.

"So what? We have one of those handheld vacuum thingies at the garage." Dr. Loki sighed with exasperation. "I don't want to get in a crash, okay? Now, put down the cookie. You can eat it later."

He turned to Omicron. "Children. They need guidance every minute. I do admire how well you and Perry work together."

"You have a funny way of showing your admiration," she said. "You sent Brimley and some of your zombies to exterminate us the other night."

"Oh, I knew they wouldn't kill you," the billionaire said. "You're much too clever for that. I just wanted to distract you so that Brimley could get that valise back. I was very disappointed that he failed." He turned toward his son. "*Very* disappointed."

"Yeah, Dad, I heard you," Brimley said.

"Well, that was very civil of you, not really wanting to kill us. I guess." Omicron crossed her arms. "But why this great show of kindness all of a sudden? You're not trying to make me switch sides again, are you? You try that every five years. When a woman says 'No,' she means 'No.'"

Dr. Loki laughed. "Ah, you know me so well. Yes, my dear woman, I'm afraid I am. But this time I have a different sort of alliance in mind. Look what we have here. You, me, two fine young lads. Rather like a family. You and I have known each other for—what, about thirty years now? Isn't it time we got married?"

"You've got to be joking!" Pi cried.

Now it was Omicron's turn to laugh. "I can't believe what I'm hearing! Me, marry *you*? You've been trying to ruin the world's health and enslave the masses for years! Right now you're trying to turn people into zombies! Plus, if the smell of this car is any indication, you smoke. I could never love a smoker."

Dr. Loki thought for a moment. "I would be willing to give up the cigarettes. Ah! We've arrived."

Pi looked out the window. They were in the parking lot of Yummy Cream Doughnut's corporate headquarters. "So you're in the doughnut business now?"

Omicron shook her head. "I don't approve of doughnuts, either. All that sugar."

A few minutes later, they were in the building's main lobby. Dr. Loki led them down a hallway lined with offices, through another small hallway cluttered with cardboard boxes, to an elevator with an *Out Of Order* sign on it.

Brimley took off the sign and pressed the *Down* button. "Dad likes classical music," he noted.

No one said anything.

He gestured toward Omicron. "I was hoping you liked classical music, too. Maybe you two have that in common."

Again, no one responded.

The henchman shrugged. "Well, excuse me for trying to make small talk."

The elevator doors opened and they entered. Brimley flipped up a panel above the floor buttons, revealing a small keyboard. He pressed several of the multicolored buttons in rapid succession. The elevator began to descend.

"By the way, we found those tracers you fired at the car Brimley used last night," Dr. Loki said. "That vehicle is currently parked outside of a Presbyterian church."

"Earlier, you claimed you knew the location of our headquarters," Omicron said. "Why haven't you destroyed the place?"

The doctor smiled. "Because my greatest spy has ready access to that building. Top clearance."

"You don't mean Gamma!" Pi exclaimed.

"No, his cat Lulu. Gamma's veterinarian has been on my payroll for years. Gamma brings Lulu to work whenever she's sick or pregnant. And she always wears a lovely pink flea collar installed with an equally lovely listening device." Dr. Loki tapped Omicron's purse. "Oh, and that compact you were using in the coffeehouse—a homing device, perhaps? You never wear make-up, my dear."

"A squadron will be invading this cover operation any minute now," Pi said. "So you might as well give up."

The elevator doors opened and Dr. Loki led them out, down a long white hallway. "A squadron, you say? That's fine with me," he said. "Right now all the friendly Yummy Cream Doughnut employees are driving home, and their offices are being filled with reptilian zombies. Your people have quite a surprise in store for them. And even if they get past the zombies, they'll never be able to get down here." He pulled a small metal box out of his pocket. Then he lifted its lid and pressed a button. A thunderous roar echoed behind them. "That elevator shaft is well and truly 'Out Of Order' now."

The hall soon ended in stainless steel double doors with a row of multicolored buttons above one of the handles. The doctor stabbed a finger repeatedly at the buttons, and a loud *clack* sounded. He then pulled open the doors and ushered the group through.

They now stood on a railed metal platform high above a cavernous work area. On the floor below hulked dozens of huge cages, each containing a group of the orange and yellow zombies. Metal tunnels led from the backs of the cages to the far wall, and presumably beyond. Workers in lab coats moved between the cages, throwing red chunks from buckets to the zombies. They reminded Pi of zoo keepers throwing meat to the lions. Some of the zombie keepers were almost as homely as the creatures they were feeding.

"It really is quite a chore, keeping them supplied with the sort of nourishment they crave," Dr. Loki said. "They'll rot to nothing if they don't get fresh meat regularly. Fortunately, the world above us is teeming with homeless people, druggies, prostitutes, all sorts of walking tragedies. Project WILD will help to clean up the streets."

"I see. Dr. Loki, the great humanitarian." Omicron stared at the billionaire with contempt.

The doctor stepped up to a dais in the center of the platform. There he stood before a large control panel with several view screens. "See those tunnels behind the cages? They connect with the city's sewer system. They're closed off now, but I can open the way for my hungry darlings just by pressing a few buttons. I think you'd better agree to join forces with me,

Margaret. It's really for the best. I can release zombies to routes leading to various sections of the city. They'll be swarming out of manholes everywhere. The people they don't devour will soon become zombies, too. Now, let's see . . ." He pointed down toward the work area. "That cage leads to the park. That one heads straight for a hospital zone. . . ."

"Get away from those buttons," Pi said, rushing toward the doctor.

"Not so fast!" Dr. Loki pulled out a gun. "I have a lot of state-of-the-art toys, but this old thing works pretty well, too."

Omicron slipped to the side behind Brimley, twisting the thin henchman's arm behind his back. She then put one of her own arms around his neck. "Come on now, Balthazar. You don't want me to snap your son's neck."

"I see we're at an impasse." Dr. Loki sighed wearily. "What shall I do now? I think the park could use a bit of color. . . ." So saying, he pressed several buttons on the control panel. Below, a metal squeal sounded and a tunnel gate began to open behind one of the cages.

The squealing became louder, almost deafening—and then stopped entirely. The zombies remained in their cage.

"I don't understand," Dr. Loki said. "Why didn't it open?" He stared down at the cage.

Pi heard a faint, familiar squelching sound. He glanced up.

Olive Mylove clung to the wall six feet above him. She wore filthy jeans and a ripped sweater. She was almost completely transformed by the compound. Only one eye and part of her forehead appeared to be human.

She jumped down to the platform. Dr. Loki fired his gun, hitting her in the chest and shoulder. She didn't even flinch.

"Nice try," she said, "but I'm already more dead than alive. Now it's my turn." She removed Brimley's hat, pulled the feather from the band, and flung it with deadly accuracy at the doctor's throat.

The billionaire screamed as the voracious slime mold devoured his flesh. His head lolled to one side, and then his neckbones gave way as the tissue connecting them dissolved. His head fell off, hit the floor, and began to roll.

Straight toward Omicron and Brimley.

Omicron let go of the young man and scrambled back. Brimley was too terrified to move. Dr. Loki's head wobbled unsteadily toward them both. Then Olive grabbed the head by the hair, and the henchman breathed a sigh of relief.

Olive sneered at Brimley. "Oh, I would never get between

a father and his son," she said. "I was just making certain you had him all to yourself." With that, she tossed the grisly prize to the henchman. "Here. Play catch with daddy."

Brimley caught the unpleasant lump without thinking, streaking both his hands with bubbling gore. The pestilence spread quickly—to his wrists, his arms, and onward until his entire body was consumed.

Soon Dr. Loki and his son were both nothing more than steaming piles of bones and human sludge.

"Thank you, Olive," Pi said. "You saved our lives. How did you get down here?"

"I know a secret way through the sewers," she said. "I jammed all the tunnel gates so that the zombies couldn't get loose. I came back while I was still *me* to deal with Dr. Loki and his brat."

"Can we do anything to help you?" Omicron asked. "Is there some kind of cure? An antidote?"

Olive let loose with a hard, rasping bark of a laugh. "This isn't something you can undo. Once a zombie, always a zombie. Zombies are forever. Now that I'm going to become one, the only answer is complete destruction of the body. For me—" she pointed down toward the work area "—and for them. Even the people feeding them. Most of them have been bitten. And even the ones who haven't been bitten—they're traitors to the human race. They don't deserve to live."

Olive shambled to the dais and pressed some buttons on the control panel. A section of the wall opened up, revealing another white hallway.

"Dr. Loki's secret escape passage," Olive said. "He always tried to plan for every contingency. That will lead you to the bottom level of a nearby parking garage. You might as well take his sports car. Cherry red. Beautiful." She picked something up from the dais and threw it to Pi. He caught it in midair: a metal ring with car keys on it.

"But we can't just leave you to—to—" Pi wasn't sure how to finish the sentence.

"To destroy myself?" Olive whispered hoarsely. "I assure you, oblivion is the best thing for me right now. I believe in reincarnation. I'll try to come back as something simple and helpful. Maybe a bee. A wonderful bee that only wants to make sweet honey." She nodded toward the exit. "What are you waiting for?"

"How are you going to . . . end this?" Omicron said. "I think we should know."

Olive smiled. "Yes, I suppose you should. You'll need to

file a report, I'm sure. It's a two-part solution. The first part is *this*." She pushed some buttons on the control panel. Down below, cage doors opened into the work area. The zombies rushed out and attacked their keepers, tearing into them with ravenous zeal.

Olive stroked the panel next to a large, square black button. "In a few minutes, I'll push this particular button exactly three times. That will activate the sprinklers."

Pi and Omicron both looked up. Metal pipes crisscrossed the chamber's expansive ceiling, with a nozzle at every intersection.

"Can you guess what's in those pipes?" Olive asked.

Pi looked at the pile of bones and slush that had once been Dr. Loki—and nodded. Omicron nodded, too.

"Good." Olive said. "Now, go."

Without another word, Pi and Omicron stepped over the threshold of the escape route. The wall panel slid shut behind them.

For a moment, mother and son stood in silence, lost in thought.

"So," Omicron said at last, "Dr. Loki is dead."

"Are you happy now?" Pi asked. "You even got to see him die. And next week, we're off to Morocco. Business as usual."

"Sure, I'm happy. It's strange, though. . . . I had no idea he wanted to marry me. Do you think he actually loved me?"

"Does it matter? You could never have returned his love."

"I know that," she said with a sad smile. "But I suppose it's flattering. He was a handsome man. And smart. Rich, too. Pity he was so evil. . . ."

They walked down the white hallway, toward the parking garage. Pi jangled the car keys in front of his mother. "Here you go. A souvenir."

"Oh, thanks." Omicron took them for his hand. "You know, maybe it's time for me to start dating. After all, Dr. Loki seemed to think I was hot stuff."

"Dating? But your work—a lot of guys might have a problem with that."

"There is one man who has asked me out a few times. I've always turned him down, but maybe that was a mistake. He's very sweet . . . about my age. And he doesn't have a problem with my career."

"So who's—" Pi stopped walking and stared at Omicron. "Hey, wait a minute. Are you talking about Gamma?"

"As a matter of fact, I am." Omicron smiled and shrugged. "He's goofy about cats, but he's very nice and I always like talking with him. He could never replace your father, but he's charming in his own way. I think I'll have dinner with him after we get back from Morocco. Is that okay with you?"

"Wow. I didn't see that coming." Pi took a deep breath. "Sure. I just want you to be happy. And Gamma is a great guy. He treats Lulu like a queen, so I bet he'll spoil you rotten. Flowers and mushy stuff."

Omicron nodded. "Probably. But a little mush can be nice." She cocked her head to one side. "You know, maybe you should start dating, too. I wouldn't mind being a grandmother someday. . . ."

Pi rolled his eyes, a blush rising to his cheeks. "Oh, Mother!"

What Comes After

KRISTINE DIKEMAN

Reade glanced up as the cruiser rolled past the outermost barricade, into the countryside proper. It was a perfect, clear September day, a crisp taste of fall on the breeze, but the blue sky stretching above the car only made him feel vulnerable and exposed. The National Guard had done a good job of cleaning up, but the wrecks and burned-out cars scattered along the gravel shoulder on both sides of the road made him nervous. They provided ample cover for anyone—anything—waiting, like a wolf in a fairy tale, to gobble up unlucky passersby.

In the road ahead, a deep, raw gouge cut into the blacktop where the bulldozer had moved the battered wreck of the school bus onto the shoulder. The bus was back upright; it was filthy with mud and soot, one side horribly crumpled. It sat on its deflated tires in a drift of debris: gravel, slivers of chrome, bits of plastic, paper, and broken glass, lots of broken glass. "Crash dandruff," Sheriff Howell used to call it. All the little bits of crap that accumulated, as if by magic, whenever there was a wreck.

Reade turned his face away from the bus as the car passed by, tried not to look at the smashed windows and the emergency exit door torn almost off its hinges, streaks of clotted blood and gore spattered across the sooty yellow paint. He put his foot on the gas, willed the car to take him away from this place, this bad place—*crime scene, call it what it is; it's a crime scene*—and saw a child's sneaker, a black high top, close to the road's edge. The dirty laces stirred and flapped idly as the cruiser shot past.

Goddamn those guardsmen anyway, he thought. *Why the hell couldn't they have picked that up?*

He knew his anger was irrational. The soldiers had done their best—done things he didn't like to think about—but the heat of indignation helped push back the queasy feeling in his stomach. With the wreck getting smaller in the rearview mirror, Reade remembered how Sheriff Howell had sneered when the Guard had shown up.

"Weekend warriors, Georgie," Howell had said, hitching his belt buckle up over his gut and reaching for his spit cup. "Soft boys in suits, pretending to be soldiers."

But they had turned out to be more, even Howell had admitted later. How much more had been made clear the night the innermost security fence had given way. The dead, pale and gray in the glare of emergency lights, had poured through the breach by the dozens. Reade remembered the look of calm control on the face of the Guard captain as he fired the flame thrower into the vanguard of the zombie mob. They had gone up like kindling, their burning bodies lighting up the night.

The Ransom place was coming up on his left. The windows and doors were still tightly boarded up and, except for the overgrowth of weeds and high grass, the house looked in good shape. John Ransom and his wife had moved into town one week before martial law had been declared. Reade had come out and helped John board up windows, drain the pipes, and get the house ready to stand empty. While they'd nailed sheets of plywood into the window frames, Ransom's wife Lorraine, her face ashen, had silently carried boxes of clothes out to their minivan. The previous day, a zombie had come up behind her son Jason as he was picking tomatoes. Jason had been plucked himself, there one second, gone the next.

"I saw them things on the news, Georgie," John Ransom had said, pulling another ten-penny nail from the jar on the porch and setting it against the plywood. "But I threw that fat fool boss of yours off my land when he told us to come into town. And now my boy is a monster, and his mother's heart is broken. . . ."

A sudden movement in front of him jolted Reade from his reverie. Adrenaline surged through him as the cruiser slowed.

A dead raccoon moved across the road before him in a crabwise shuffle, the track of the tire that killed it clearly visible on its flattened midsection. The animal glared up, eyes shining, teeth bared, misshapen body tensed to spring. Reade veered as the car reached it, closed his eyes as the thing crunched under the left front wheel. All the while he told himself that it was not possible for him to hear the *pop* of its brain pan under the tire. He looked in the rearview mirror and saw the dark stain on the road twitch and quiver, teeth spilling out as the ruined jaws snapped mechanically.

He had almost reached his destination. And just beyond it, the cemetery.

The house was almost completely hidden by a high chain link fence, like the perimeter fence that encircled the town. As he pulled up to the gate and put the cruiser in park, Reade saw that the electricity was off. He took an enormous key ring from his pocket and searched until he found a key with a little piece of white tape and the words *Buren Fence* in Howell's fussy printing. Reade checked the rearview mirror, then the sides, put his hand on the door handle, and took a few quick deep breaths, like a swimmer preparing for a race.

There's no need for this nonsense, he thought. The Guard had sanitized the graveyard; there hadn't been a sighting in days. But when he touched the door handle, he flashed back to Bob Kerrigan, the town's mayor, being yanked out of his Ford pickup.

"I'll just be a minute, Georgie," Bob had said. "I left something on the kitchen ta—" And then the stinking, putrescent arm reached in and grabbed Bob by his hair and yanked him backward out of the truck, and he was gone. Reade had sat, frozen, and listened to the screams getting fainter and the slurping sounds getting louder. *Who's gonna sign the paychecks now?* he had thought foolishly. And then he saw the keys dangling in the Ford's ignition and next thing he was tearing down the road back to town, to the shocked and unbelieving townspeople, to the sheriff's black fury.

"You were supposed to look after him." Howell had thundered. "I can't run this whole goddamned town by myself, you know!" And Reade had stood, head down, miserable, overwhelmed. Out of his depths. That's what his mother had called it whenever he got himself into a situation he couldn't possibly handle.

Now he fought to keep his breathing under control until the familiar panicky feeling receded. He climbed out of the car and unlocked the gate, keys jangling in his hand only a little. He suppressed the urge to glance behind him, slid back into the cruiser, and pulled the car into the driveway. As he re-locked the gate, he tried to keep his back straight and his hands steady. He turned slowly when he heard the front door open. Sheriff Howell's star was a ponderous weight on his chest, the gun awkward and heavy on his hip. Reade wondered for a bleak moment if he looked as ridiculous as he felt.

Mrs. Buren stepped out on the porch. "Hello there, Georgie," she said. "I'm glad you're here."

"Hello, Mrs. Buren."

Her dress was clean and freshly ironed, her hair set in a familiar tight bun. She looked like what she was—a retired small town schoolteacher—and Reade could feel something in his chest loosen a little. She had deep circles under her eyes, and in the unforgiving light of midmorning he could see the lines around her mouth had deepened considerably since he'd seen her last. But her eyes were focused and clear, none of that glazed, faraway look he had seen so much of lately.

She's made of sterner stuff than that, he thought, and felt an unexpected surge of affection for this woman who had terrorized his childhood. She had been the strictest teacher he'd ever known, with high, exacting standards. He had barely kept his head above water in her classes—been "out of his depths" there more often than not. Now she smiled at him, and Reade realized she had been assessing him, too, checking to see what kind of stuff *he* was made from. That smile, so open and genuine, meant she had not found him wanting. He was surprised and a little amused to find that her approval— so hard to win in the past—still meant a great deal to him.

"Well now, Georgie," she said. "Come on into the house, why don't you. I've made tea."

He came up the steps, and as he reached her she slipped her arm under his, like a lady being escorted to a fancy dinner. She gave off a fragrance of lavender and spray starch. Reade felt disoriented; in the jumbled memory of his childhood, Mrs. Buren was a towering presence. This faded, delicate old woman barely came up to his chin.

Mrs. Buren pointed him to an overstuffed wing chair. "Pardon me, dear, while I put pot to kettle," she said, and went into the kitchen. The tea things were already set out on a small rolling table: crustless sandwiches, china cups, silver spoons. The room was immaculate. There were ceramic figurines on the mantle, a grandfather clock ticking calmly in the corner, an assortment of pictures in antique frames arranged on a lace doily across the piano. He settled into the chair more deeply, closed his eyes, thought how it was nice to sit in a room without boards on the windows or bloodstains on the floor.

"It's a comfortable chair, isn't it?" asked Mrs. Buren as she stepped back into the room. Reade jumped up and took the silver tray with the steaming teapot from her, set it down next to the little trolley. She picked up a cup and poured him out some tea. "That was my husband's favorite chair. That young captain from the National Guard liked it, too. He made himself right at home here." Mrs. Buren frowned. "He certainly enjoyed giving me orders. He forbade me to set foot out of this house until you arrived. There's no milk, but will you take sugar?"

"No, thank you, ma'am." Reade took the teacup and saucer, and balanced them on his knee, mindful of the faded Oriental rug. "I imagine those fellows from the Guard just wanted to keep you safe, Mrs. Buren. They caught h—uh, they got a lot of criticism for even letting you stay out here in the first place, after martial law was declared."

Mrs. Buren gave a small, tight smile of satisfaction as she poured his tea. "Martial *rule*, Georgie, depends for its existence upon public necessity. Necessity creates it, justifies it, and limits its endurance. The captain and I had quite a few interesting discussions on the subject. In the end, he saw the sense of my staying here."

"Yes, ma'am." Reade took a sip of tea to hide his smile. He remembered the Guard captain sitting with Sheriff Howell in his office, a map of the county spread out across the battered oak desk between them.

"*You* tell the old bag she has to move out," the captain had said. "Every time I mention to her that she's living next to a graveyard, that fuckin' *dead people* are digging their way out of the ground at the rate of about two per day, she gets this stuck-up look on her face and starts in arguing with me. 'The civil law cannot be displaced, young man. And let us call things by their right name—it is not martial *law*, but martial *rule*.'"

The sheriff had tipped Reade a sly wink as he commiserated with the captain on the frustration of dealing with an old lady so well-versed in the intricacies of the law. But after the guardsman had left, Howell's laughter had rung through the office.

"He's a fair shot with a flame thrower, Georgie, but he's no match for that old biddy. I'd sooner face a roomful of the dead than cross her m'self," Howell had said, wiping tears from his eyes. And Reade had laughed, too, though secretly he felt sorry for the captain, who was clearly used to people jumping up when he yelled frog. Unfortunately for him, Mrs. Buren was also used to giving orders, and it would take more than the end of the world to change that.

Now she passed Reade a plate of sandwiches. "Once those young men learned to respect my privacy, and not help themselves to things they shouldn't, the time passed quickly enough. Some of them turned out to be quite useful. I was almost sorry to see them go."

Reade looked over one of the dainty sandwiches. The bread was the same government issue whole meal everyone in town had been eating for weeks, though this had the crusts neatly trimmed. The filling was a single leaf of lettuce and a thin slice of pink meat. He took a small bite and chewed carefully. Spam.

"It's the Guard's leaving that's brought me out here, Mrs. Buren," he said, and took another sip of tea. It had a strong, smoky flavor.

She leaned back in her chair. "You want me to come into town."

"I do." Reade set down his teacup and looked her in the eye, hoping he sounded more authoritative than he felt.

"I'm afraid you've wasted your time, Georgie." She looked at him more closely. "I should be calling you *Sheriff* Reade, shouldn't I? You are the sheriff now. And with the mayor gone, as well, you're all the town has by way of an authority figure. Poor Bobby Kerrigan. He was such a good student, and a fine mayor. You were there when he was killed, weren't you?"

Reade struggled to keep his voice steady. Getting angry now wouldn't accomplish anything. "You know I was." *But I'm not ten anymore*, he thought. *I won't let you get the upper hand on me all that easy.* "And since I am the sheriff now, I may as well say what I've come to say. I need you to pack up some things and come into town. All of this is far from over. Your house is completely isolated. The idea of you staying here alone is just crazy."

To his surprise, Mrs. Buren's face quickly went dark with anger. "That is an inflammatory and imprudent thing to say, Georgie. I thought I taught you better than to speak so carelessly."

Reade flushed. "I'm sorry, Mrs. Buren. Of course I didn't mean—I meant to say, now that the Guard has left, I've had to make a decision. I'm responsible . . ." He hated the way the tone of her voice shot him back across the years, turning him into a frightened, floundering child again.

To his relief Mrs. Buren smiled at him, her anger gone as quickly as it had come. "Of course you are. You just spoke without thinking. I know you're doing your best, all on your own. The guardsmen certainly cleared out in a hurry. Drink your tea, dear, before it gets cold."

Reade took another sip. They were both silent for a moment, then Mrs. Buren stood up and pushed the tea trolley back. "This house has been in my family a long time. Since things are getting back to normal, I don't see why—"

Reade stood up, too. "Nothing is normal. Now that the National Guard has left, it's even more important to be careful. I can't guarantee your safety all alone out here. Everyone else has moved into town—" He sat down heavily, feeling drained. He pointed to her chair, and Mrs. Buren sat down.

"No one can predict what will happen," he said, "or what won't happen. Like the graveyard out here. Everyone thought it was going to be a real mess. No one could figure out why they hadn't—why you hadn't been . . . hurt right away. Plenty

of other graveyards in town gave up their dead, all the church-
yards, even the old potter's field. No one gave any thought to
how stony hard the ground was out this way. So they rushed
all those guardsmen here, and it turned out to be a kind of
turkey shoot, with the dead coming up so slow, it was actually
pretty easy—"

Mrs. Buren looked away. Red spots of color bloomed on
her cheeks.

Reade cursed himself and started again. "That's a dumb
way to describe it, and I'm sorry. I know some of the people in
that graveyard belonged to your family." He hesitated. "At
least your husband wasn't there."

"There were quite a few of my people out there," she said,
a little hoarsely. "But I was spared that, at least."

Mrs. Buren's husband had died in the Korean War, his
body never recovered. Reade hated that he knew that. He
could point to any person still alive in town and say where
their dead relatives were buried, or at least where they should
be buried. It was an awful thing to know more about the dead
of his town than the living.

"Mrs. Buren, not all the dead come out of graves we know
about. We put men on shifts to watch the cemeteries, but
there are family plots all over the place—on farms, old estates.
Unmarked graves. Not all of them registered with the county.
And then there's the other ones, hidden bodies that nobody
knew about—"

She looked up sharply, and for the first time he saw a
trace of fear in her expression. Reade was encouraged; perhaps he could convince her yet.

"Hidden bodies?" she said. "What are you talking about?"

"Do you remember Jennifer Collins?"

"Remember?" she said, her eyes wide. "Oh, oh, no. . . ."

"I know she was a favorite of yours."

"A teacher should never have favorites, but I truly thought
I could help that poor girl." Mrs. Buren lowered her eyes to the
floor. "Growing up without a father can have such an enormous impact on a child. And then, last year, that man she
was living with ran off, abandoned her and their little boy. It
was like a curse, passed down the generations. She turned
out to be no better than her mother. What a waste," she said,
her anger flaring up again. Reade wondered what she thought
had been wasted: Jenny's life or her own time.

"She killed the boy's father."

"Oh, Georgie, what an awful thing!"

"Everybody knows he slapped her around, and I guess he

went too far. Maybe she was scared for the baby. She killed him and hid his body in the privy out behind their mobile home. That must have been tough, shifting a big man like him, but she managed it. . . ."

I shouldn't be telling her all this, he thought, but he found he couldn't stop. In his mind he saw Jenny Collins' little boy, barely a toddler, blue pajamas covered with blood and slime. The baby had launched itself at Reade, right across the shattered, stinking remains of its father. Sheriff Howell had pushed Reade aside and the baby had battened itself onto Howell's leg, a feral animal in footie pajamas. Howell had actually given out a startled laugh—until the child's tiny teeth pierced his skin. Then he screamed. Reade had been the one to pull the boy from Howell's leg. When he'd finally torn it away, the baby still had a goodly chunk of shin in its mouth and its round cheeks were filthy with blood. Its squirming body had been so horribly *cold*.

He didn't want to talk about it. But all the awful things Reade had seen and done in the past months were building up in him, filling him up like poisoned water in a well. If he didn't speak, he'd drown. . . .

"One night the body of Jenny's husband woke up. It got Jenny, and the little boy, and about a dozen other people down in the trailer park. Then they rose up and set off on a rampage, and there was hell to pay. We lost a lot of people. As for Jenny and the baby—well, Sheriff Howell actually burst out laughing—"

"Jenny was punished." Mrs. Buren's voice was a whisper, but the venom in it shocked Reade out of his recitation. "Her sin came back to her. It was no better than she deserved, but the baby, that innocent child—he never even had a chance. He deserved a chance. . . ."

Mrs. Buren put her hand in front of her face, shooing away the rest of Reade's words like flies, and the sheriff cursed his own selfish stupidity. He got down on one knee in front of her, almost like a suitor, and gently pulled her hands away from her face.

"You have to listen to me," he said. "I *can't* let you stay out here by yourself. They sanitized that graveyard out there, but there could be unmarked graves. There could be bodies we don't know about, making their way up. That soil is stony, and that makes it hard going for them, but there's something in it, something that makes the older dead ones more . . . preserved than normal. We had one come out of the church graveyard that was over a hundred years old, and it did a lot of harm before we could stop it. It doesn't matter how long ago they died. If there's even a scrap of bone and muscle left, it hungers, and if the head is intact, it'll hunt."

Mrs. Buren pulled her hands out of Reade's, stood up again, and walked to the window. "You don't have to tell me these things. My people certainly are out there. We heard them at night, scratching their way up. Out there in the moonlight, the bones clicking against the earth reminded me of castanets. My husband and I took a trip to Spain once. That was just after we were married. Really, I think that was the happiest time of my life." She stopped for a moment and looked down at the floor.

"Two weeks after the soldiers arrived, I woke early and walked out to the fence to take in a breath of morning air. And standing on the other side to greet me was my dear cousin, Annabelle. She was just fifteen when she died. I was twelve, and hadn't been allowed to go her funeral. Influenza, they said. But now I know the truth. She was there at the fence to greet me. And so was her unborn baby."

"My God. . . ." Reade sank back in the chair. Had he really thought of this house as safe? Had he worried about frightening this woman? It was a miracle she was still sane.

"She stood there, her arms wrapped around her stomach, cradling her poor little bastard, her tattered burial gown swaying in the breeze. They buried her in white. That's funny, don't you think? She tunneled out of that hard ground, and the baby burrowed out of her. It yowled at me from her torn belly, with its horrible little puckered-up face. It was hungry."

Mrs. Buren walked back across to the tea tray and picked up her cup. "I think she killed herself. Or perhaps she simply died from the mortification of it. Either way, it was her shame that killed her. But the truth comes out. It comes up. Secret things don't stay secret forever. Like that soldier that ran away. Sooner or later, he'll be found."

One of the guardsmen had gone AWOL just before his unit had been reassigned, taken some food and his gun and left the house during the night. The captain had come to see Reade about it the day they shipped out, as worried as he was angry and embarrassed. Reade had promised to keep an eye out, told the captain he'd keep in touch. On the desk between them was Sheriff Howell's revolver and badge. And down the hall, the zombie that had once been Sheriff Howell raged and shrieked, throwing itself against the cell bars.

"Do you want me to do it?" the captain had asked, and Reade had said no, no thank you; he would manage.

Mrs. Buren saw the concerned look on the sheriff's face and gave a shrill laugh. It was an unpleasant, brittle sound. "You think your old teacher is going to go crazy out here, don't you? Oh, Georgie Reade! That is funny!" And through her laughter, Reade saw that black anger bubbling up again.

"Lots of people have had problems coping," he said. He thought of Lorraine Ransom, with her pale face and empty eyes. The night they burned her son's body, she threw herself on the pyre. Reade had caught a glimpse of her, cradling her zombie boy in her arms, just before the flames roared up to consume them.

He ran a hand through his unwashed hair and slumped down in the chair, suddenly feeling very tired. "I haven't been sleeping so well lately," he said in response to the concern he thought he saw in his host's eyes. "I can't catch the knack of sleeping more than an hour at a time anymore."

"You'll sleep now, dear. For a while, I think." Mrs. Buren's voice sounded as if it came from some great distance. Reade looked up at her, and it took a moment for him to realize he was on his knees again. There was one more brief moment of lucidity before he pitched forward onto the carpet and darkness took him.

He woke up slowly, head pounding, a taste in his mouth like century-old grit. Masses of dull silver duct tape secured his wrists to the armrests of a heavy, straight-backed wooden chair. His legs were strapped solidly to the chair's legs in the same fashion. Dim light filtered in from the high rectangular windows set close to the ceiling. He was in the basement. The cinderblock wall before him had been whitewashed recently, the red earth floor around him neatly swept. The air was thick with the terribly familiar stench of dead flesh, cut with a strong smell of disinfectant. The Oriental carpet from the living room was piled in an untidy heap next to the chair. *That's how she got me down here*, he thought. *She wrapped me up in the rug and dragged me down the stairs.*

To his right stood a small table covered with a blood-stained tea towel. On the towel rested a roll of duct tape and a copy of *Gray's Anatomy*, with a small boning knife laid across the pages to hold the book open at a color illustration of a dissected biceps.

"You're awake, Georgie. That's good. I was worried I let your head hit the steps one time too many." Mrs. Buren stepped in front of him. Her hair was disheveled. Smudges of earth and something dark stained the front of her dress. Behind them, Reade could hear movement.

He cleared his throat and tried to speak. "Mrs. Buren." It came out as a harsh whisper. "Whatever it is you've done, we can talk about it. Please, just cut me loose."

"I'm sorry," she said, and her eyes were oh, so far away. "But I can't leave this house. He needs me. And we need you."

"Did one of the soldiers hurt you? Did you do something to them? If they hurt you, whatever you did was self-defense." He forced himself to try and think clearly, past the steady throbbing in his head. He could feel blood trickling through his hair. But his gun was still strapped to his hip.

Mrs. Buren looked at him with pity. "You don't understand, Georgie. I've done so much wrong. I've sinned, and suffered for it, as sinners should. But now I've been given another chance." She reached out and tipped his chair back on one leg, spinning Reade in neat pirouette away from the wall to face the basement's other occupants.

The soldier was taped to his chair in the same manner as Reade. Large sections of flesh had been neatly stripped away from the meaty parts of his arms, thighs, and chest, leaving precise rectangular holes. His heart peeked out from a dark mass of rotting viscera and coagulated blood. The arms and seat of his chair were black with gore. Reade knew that the dead didn't bleed that way; the soldier had still been alive when the flesh was stripped off him. He had crossed over and risen up—that was clear from the gray, grainy texture of his skin and the feral way his teeth gripped the wad of duct tape securing his head and neck—but he posed no threat now. His head was gone from the bridge of his nose up, the skull scooped clean of it contents.

Just behind the soldier was a mattress piled high with quilts and blankets. In the center, hands and feet trussed with more tape, huddled a zombie child. Reade thought it might have been about five when it died. Its flesh had the hard, desiccated look of a body that had been underground for some time. Next to the mattress lay a stinking pile of rags, bits of bone, and chunks of dried flesh. Farther back, close to the wall, two holes—one large, one small—gaped in the cellar floor, with stony earth heaped around their edges.

Mrs. Buren nodded toward the pile of rags, bones, and flesh, all that remained of a brutally demolished corpse. "She came here after my husband died. Horrible woman. She said the child was my John's, that John was going to leave me and marry her, that she would be a truer wife to him, because she had given him a son. She said she wanted money, or she'd tell. So I gave her some tea, just like the tea I gave you, only stronger. Much stronger. And I gave the boy some lemonade. Then I brought them down here and buried them. I waited for someone to come looking. But no one ever did."

Reade tried to speak and found he couldn't. The shock of it all was too great.

"We've lived here together, the three of us, all these years. They were my secret. And then the dead began to rise. I came down here every night. I waited, and I prayed. And one night, when those awful men were off in town, I heard a noise, no louder than a mouse scratching for food. But oh, it made my heart light. He was finally coming up, coming back to me."

She gestured at the pile of flesh. "I didn't regret killing her—that slut, that whore. But the child, that had been wrong. Bastard or not, he was all that was left of my dear husband. Killing him was a terrible mistake, one I regretted bitterly. But when I heard them coming up I knew I've been given a second chance."

"The Guard," Reade managed in a gasp.

"They searched the cellar the day they came. 'Securing the perimeter,' they called it. That was before the boy came back to me, so the guardsmen didn't find anything. But one of them did help himself to a jar of my best preserves. I pretended to be angry about that and made them put a lock on the cellar, and then took the key. They had a good laugh at the foolish old lady, but they kept out after that, just to keep me quiet." She chuckled at her own cleverness. "By day, I watched those men destroy what was left of my kin. At night, I came down here and listened. And when the time was right, when I knew they were ready to break through, I told one of them."

She pointed to the remains of the soldier.

"He was the greediest—I've always been good at spotting the weak ones, the greedy ones. I told him they were here, and I needed help destroying them, because they were a secret. I offered him money if he'd come down when the others were out in my garden, swilling beer, smoking God knows what to celebrate their last night. And he came down. He took care of that—" she jerked her thumb again at the pile "—and then I took care of him. He turned out to be very useful. He lasted much longer than I'd expected."

She smiled down at the boy, her face radiant with affection, and in a distant corner of his mind Reade thought he had never seen her look so happy. She stepped over to the soldier's corpse and tore a dangling strip of flesh from his shoulder, then dropped it in front of the child. Its head came up immediately, and cellar dirt trickled from the empty eye sockets. It wriggled forward toward the flesh, sniffed it with its ruined and rotted nose, and moaned in disappointment.

"But now my little boy doesn't want him any more, do you dear?" The child moaned again, and she made a little shushing sound. Then she leaned forward and gently squeezed Reade's biceps, testing its firmness. Reade remembered that moment on the porch, her sharp look of assessment, her sudden smile of approval. It'd had nothing to do with how he carried his badge.

"Mrs. Buren," Reade said as calmly as he could manage, "don't do this. . . ."

He struggled for breath, hunted for the words that would reach this woman. But even as he spoke them, he knew that they were wrong. He was, once more, out of his depths. "He is not a child anymore," Reade sputtered. "He—it is a monster. For God's sake, think about what you're doing. Please, I don't want to die this way!"

She stepped past him to the table. "But you won't die, Georgie. At least not right away. I've learned a great deal about how much to take, and from where. I'm sure you'll last much longer than the soldier. And I'll be here to help you, dear."

She glanced at the anatomy book, just as Reade had seen her consult her lesson plans at the start of a class. Then she gave a short nod, picked up the knife, and stepped toward him. Reade moaned. The zombie boy mewled with excitement. Mrs. Buren smiled.

"If you're ready, Georgie, I think we will begin."

THE BLONDE

SARAH A. HOYT

It rained for the three days we rode, slow and solemn, in wedding cortege, from the city of Sintra in southern Portugal to the capital in Coimbra.

It rained as if the sky sweated. The low gray clouds hung over us like God's own anguish. Of that anguish stinking rain dripped, more than fog but less than a proper rain, casting a pall over this, most strange of all weddings.

I rode beside the groom, my lord, the king Don Pedro, my friend, my childhood companion. He looked feverish and laughed too often, too joyously, too falsely. His laughter made the noblemen turn pale and look frightened, and some of the glittering ladies whimper. The peasants, lining the road, watching us pass, looked silent, expectant.

As the procession wound, like a fat black snake, along the muddy roads under the stinking rain, the peasants' dark eyes looked on with the knowing, confident gaze of believers who understood punishment awaited this heretical union.

And I thought of Inez. The bride. She who was carried in her velvet-draped coffin at the back of the cortege. I thought of her golden hair, her mobile, smiling lips.

I thought of her, whose death I'd instigated. She—whom my lord had loved with maddening passion. She—who'd been my obsession and my bane, the haven of all my secret desires.

She—who'd come between me and my lord. She—whose love had all but destroyed kingdom and king, and my belief in good and loyalty.

Though my father was only the royal accountant—by the grace of the lord's father that was the king Don Afonso IV of Portugal—I was raised with the prince and with him learned riding and falconing and the arts of the great ones, as well as writing and reading and the necessary tools of my estate.

With him I'd been friends. With him I'd played through the vast, resounding halls of his ancestors. With him I'd laughed and wenched and studied and rhymed.

I'd loved him, as much as man can love another in this corrupt world. I'd loved him as a brother, or yet as another reflection of my own self—a heart extruded from my own chest and beating beside my own.

My prince was easy to love, easy to obey, easy to follow. His golden falcon eyes showed clear understanding and intent sight. His shoulders were broad, his hands strong and sword-callused, and he rode his horse as if he were part centaur and the horse's body and his united by a single spark of life. Only his mouth was soft, heart-shaped, and seemingly set in infinite sadness.

And Inez . . . she'd been just as fascinating, as strong. Even now, many years dead, she remained with us.

Her presence loomed large over the cortege, and through the slow, sweating rain I saw her hair, shining like moonlight, spilled like a golden harvest. I saw her eyes, sparkling summer skies. And I heard her laughter, her silver laughter that had captured my master as surely as a spider web's delicate threads will imprison the hapless fly.

At the memory of her, I felt again the dread, unconfessed love that had bound me to her as certainly as a bird to the snake that spies it. I'd loved her and hated her, and hated myself for loving her, who was my lord's bane and my lord's love.

Their romance was like that, you see, and not like the troubadours will say, a meeting of equals, a love of innocents.

Oh, it was never innocent. Inez de Castro—come to the Portuguese court as companion and maid to our Queen Beatrice, of blessed memory—was never an innocent.

Her presence was a cursed, light-robbing, mind-devouring, body-withering rapaciousness, as cruel and mindless as a falcon's claws. She struck all, left and right, with no regard, and if she had a master or a love, it must have been Satan himself.

Only he could have tamed her.

The first time we saw her, we had no such presentiment, no warning of what was about to befall us.

Almost twelve years ago, my lord was but a prince. His father, Don Afonso IV, held the throne and the responsibility of keeping our small country safe against our envious neighbors of Castile and Navarre and Lion. And the king had contracted to marry the prince Don Pedro to the princess of Castile, as a way of keeping peace between the two countries.

Such a marriage, as others before it, was political, meant to pour oil on the troubled waters of politics and, with a thread of love and shared descendance, quiet the striving neighbors.

Yet, Castile's ambassadors had given us such reports of the princess that they'd inflamed the hearts of every one of us. Dona Beatrice, a modest and beautiful maiden, with the patience of an angel and the mind of a poet, had been described to us in such terms that the prince, and I, and every man in the prince's entourage was half in love with her.

I knew that I would lose my lord's company, that our wild rides through the untamed woods would be at an end. But I rejoiced that I would lose him to a worthier companion, a more intimate, more sacred union.

That spring, we rode three days out from Coimbra, not at the pace of a funeral procession, but as young men will ride half inflamed by desire and love. All ten of us wore our best apparel and sang merry songs, and told stories of war and crusade.

My prince often rode ahead, as I strove in vain to catch up with him. The others, pages and counselors, rode behind, at a pace. And Don Pedro rode on and on, laughing, till he'd stop and, in some green grove, wait till we caught up with him.

I was always the first to catch up, and together, side by side, we'd wait for the others. I was glad to be his second, the best man after his excellence.

That was how the two of us came to be alone at the bridge over the Coa, the river between the two countries.

It was a sparkling spring day, cool and brilliant, one of those days when it seems as though the world has just emerged new-scrubbed and fresh from the Creator's hands. Sun dazzled the clear water of the shallow, broad river and shone upon the dew-drops that dotted the dark green needles of the pine trees that climbed the banks on either side.

From the other side, far away, a single thread of smoke rose, evoking a peasant fireside. The birds' song twined the gurgle of the current in melody sweeter than any troubadour's creation.

The bridge that crossed the river was gray stone, shiny with age, polished by countless winters. Its clean lines spoke of antique Roman construction.

On the other side of the bridge stood the lace-bedecked Castillian assemblage: maids and nurses, and the men of war that protected such a noble cortege. The maids and nurses would pass through, but the men of war must stay on the other side.

From now on, the princess would be our responsibility, and my chest expanded with pride at the thought.

Yet, at first glance I could not tell who the princess might be. Oh, the maids and the nurses rode in closed carriages, but in the center of it all, on twin white horses, stood two women who, by the deference and care paid them, might both be the princess. But they were as different from each other as perfumed night and blazing day.

One was a dark woman with an amiable, round face and the body of one who would bear strong children. She was flushed from what must have been a rebellious decision of riding those horses, and she looked pretty, in a bland way, the way a man could tame and accommodate to.

The other one. . . . The other one was blond, her hair pure sun pleated into two braids, framing a face more intriguing than beautiful. And yet, I lie, for she was beautiful in her fascination and incomparably fascinating in her dazzling strength.

On that face would no man meet rest when, weary from war and affairs of state, he came to find her by her hearth.

No, her eyes—the deep, dark blue of a summer sky—would be more whip than soothing caress, more a sting of spurs than a whisper of peace. Her face—oval and gifted with features too strong to be called lovely—could shape pleasure or pain or eager excitement with such intensity that no man would think of anything else. Only of her. Of her only. And her body, barely contained within a loose, gauzy gown, suggested milk and honey—from her rounded breasts to the limber shape of her long legs, one on either side of the horse.

She rode like a man and seemed neither aware of her offense against modesty nor mindful of her maidenhead.

We rode halfway onto the bridge, and the armed men closed about their charges, as though we—regally dressed and better mounted—could be highwaymen. But the two women remained. They looked up at us and smiled. The darker one smiled and looked down, but the blonde smiled and beckoned us with her blue eyes. Thus had Eve smiled, proffering to Adam the sinful fruit.

I forced my mind to think, I forced my lips to work, and I managed to say, in a whisper that I didn't mean to use, "There they are. Those must be them."

My voice caught in my throat, tight and small, and it seemed to me that my heart flamed and caught at the sight of the blonde's wanton beauty.

My prince sighed and his voice trembled as he asked, all eagerness, his heart pumping madly in his voice, "The blonde?"

"No, the brunette, sir," answered an older counselor, one of those who had been our teachers in history and the arts of war. He'd just caught up with us, and his voice poured into our moment of solitude like cold water over a blazing fire.

In that moment my prince looked at me, and I at him. His golden eyes looked dimmed, lost. It was just a moment, but I knew it then. His heart was given. Given already, and he couldn't call it back. Given to the blonde.

He spurred his horse and rode to meet the two maidens. I followed, but neither of them looked at me. They had eyes only for the prince.

The whole ride back to the capital in Coimbra, he rode entranced by the smile of the succubus, by her pretty promises and vacuous double-entendres.

Strangely, this seemed not to bother the princess. Dona Beatrice smiled at seeing her fiancé thus enamored of her friend, and accepted with gratitude the meager attentions we gave her to make up for his desertion.

As we neared Coimbra on the third day, and while my prince made a fool of himself singing his poetry to the Castellian strumpet, Dona Beatrice caught my attention, held my arm and said, "Don't resent her, Fernao. She can't help it. Inez has always been like that. Men love her and offer her their hearts, their minds, and all their will. She doesn't mean it, but it happens anyway."

Oh, perhaps it happened anyway. But that time it was meant and intended. Maybe she'd fallen for him as hard as he had for her. I can't say, and I can't tell.

Left outside of their love, like a pup kicked away from his master's fire, I could only watch it. To my jealous eyes, it looked uncommonly like she cared nothing for him—and he the noblest and most perfect of princes—but only for the benefits and advancement she could get from him.

Still, for the next seven years she was quiet enough. She played the bawd that could be bought with jewels and benefits, nothing more.

My prince, recalling his position, paid perfunctory court to his wife, enough to conceive an heir. On the bawd, whom he had set up in her own house with her own court, he begat six children—three boys and three girls, all possessed of their mother's fatal beauty, all gifted with their father's clear understanding.

But the poison was there. I saw it grow. Little by little, my master—who had been the keenest mind in all Christendom, gifted in Latin, practiced in Greek, in poetry bedazzling the poets, in accounting penetrating the darkest confusions of lawyers—my master, I said, lost interest in all. Little by little he stopped spending time at court, and spent more and more time at his bawd's call, at her benighted service.

Even hunting, which had formerly been his passion, now could not stir him from her fireside. His athlete's body, once limber and agile, became slow and soft with his rest. And his love for her consumed him, like a flame will consume the candle it feeds on.

But he saw only the light.

Watching him languish, I felt cowed, like a dog tied up in the courtyard, unable to follow his master at the hunt.

My body still longed for her, and she—Inez, the temptress—made sure to give me a look now, and then a word, and sometimes a touch of her velvet fingers, to keep me wanting, to keep me panting, like a dog after the stag it cannot catch.

Oh, my lord still hunted with his courtiers, now and then, but more often than not she went with us and they disappeared, both in mad cavalcade, and ended up in some shady spot, no doubt enjoying the pleasures of solitude. And we, the groomsmen and me, and the dogs, were left to find what prey we could and take it back with muted rejoicing. I could no longer follow him, much less catch up to him. I was no longer his closest counselor.

After six years, my master's wife died, leaving her son behind and departing—angel of patience that she had been—with no curse for her husband and her betraying friend.

Her departure put a pall upon my days, because nothing now would stop my prince from marrying his bawd. And in that marriage I'd lose both friend and the unquenchable hope that one day Inez's tantalizing laughter would echo for my sake. That she would one day turn to me as the attainable husband, who'd erase the mark of her infamy. That she'd some day be mine.

Still, I could have endured the prospect of their marrying. It wasn't for jealousy alone that I betrayed. It was not in me the bend of the traitor, the easy fall of those whose thought folds in secret upon their own actions.

No, I wouldn't have betrayed my lord. And I wouldn't have wished her dead and gone. Though she was a temptress, she was beautiful, and there is in beauty that which stays the hand that would destroy it.

There were the children, too. Their mother was a bawd, but their father was my prince. The oldest, Don Joao, showed much of his father's character, his easy way. I'd become his friend, his storyteller, and in a few years I'd have been his advisor, as close in his favor as I'd been in his father's, once. He, too, more than his legitimate brother, showed the marks of a perfect prince. His golden beauty was matched, measure by measure, with clear intelligence and a daring arm for battle. His father's planned marriage wouldn't make him legitimate, and yet, such is the memory of the people, in a way it would—and, should his brother die, he would have reigned.

He would be a great one, and who was I to strike the blow that would deprive him of both mother and position?

I resolved to brood in silence and suffer in quiet solitude.

But fate had other plans. The dark fate that had brought Inez de Castro like a curse upon the kingdom of Portugal was not done tormenting me.

His oldest bastard son was seven when my prince gave signs of reviving. Perhaps only I saw it. Perhaps it took old brotherly love and accustomed friendship to see it.

His falcon eyes became intent once more. His face lost the half-sleeping look that it had acquired in the bawd's care. He went riding more, and, day and night, in the courtyard of the farm he shared with Inez, he'd gather his men together. Day and night, from early dawn till midnight sounded, we would practice war. His arms strengthened again with plying the sword, and he laughed at our coarse jests and was one of us again.

Those days I felt happy, contented. I'd regained my brother, my companion. As men of war, together, we could forget the golden temptress. We could be young again.

The confines of the seven-foot-tall stone walls, the broad facade of the building forming one side of the yard, resounded with the harsh clang of metal on metal, and male laughter, and the sound of horses' hooves.

His intensity, his joy was like an antic fever, not different from his love but directed this time to the more fitting arts of war.

I thought then that the poison had left him. I thought it had done its worst and would now subside. I thought this mad passion for war and swords and horses and strategy—when no war threatened our borders—was a purging of her soft venom, a clearing of his pent-up energies. The fighting, the energy, the tireless days with swords and lances cleansed my own mind of Inez and of thoughts of her touch on my roughened skin.

It was only when I caught a glimpse of her, in some hall, bent over her needlework, her golden hair framing her face, a contented smile upon her lips, that I thought perhaps . . . perhaps when he left her, she would find consolation in my humble love.

But it doesn't matter what I thought. Fate spelled out crookedly the lines upon which all of us wrote our destinies.

It was a winter day; I remember it well. The rain fell hard upon the courtyard, washed the flagstones with unrelenting whipping. Above, the sky crisscrossed by the lash of lightning foretold disturbance upon the Earth.

On such a day even my prince would not demand that we practice fighting in the courtyard. We'd tilted at dummies earlier in the day, but now I and the men of his company sat in the vast hall, drinking the fine sparkling wine of the region and talking.

Our prince was not with us but—a capital sign, I thought—also not with her. He was in his study, with his papers—hopefully, I thought, minding the kingdom's finances and the sorry state of his own lands. His father, the king Don Afonso, of blessed memory, was getting no younger.

She was in the hall with her maids, her children, her needlework. And I hoped she was tamed. I hoped she was humbled.

And so when he called me to him and asked me, with intent eyes and falconlike attention, if I'd do him a service and take a letter not far away, I thought he meant something for his father, whose palace was only two hours ride distant.

But the letter he gave me, sealed with his seal, was not to his father. It was intended, my prince told me—looking at the fire, not at my face—for someone who would wait in a ruined farm, six hours ride from this abode. He told me to deliver the letter and ask no questions, and come back quickly.

It was his not meeting my eyes that undid me, his manner, like a sly cur edging around the fire, meaning to steal the ham's bone. I feared what he might mean. My mind misgave me. I feared he'd read my lust for Inez in my eyes. How many times had I not heard of a man's being made the unwitting messenger for his own death sentence. How could I be sure the message I carried said more than *Kill the bearer*?

I rode from the prince, as commanded, but at the nearest village I sought out an inn and took a room under an assumed name. In that room, with candle carefully plied, I opened the letter without disturbing the seal.

My prince should have known I could do that. After all, in our wild younger days we'd thus intercepted the love secrets from all the ladies in the court.

But he trusted me. Perhaps she trusted me, too.

Opening the letter he'd told me to deliver unopened, I found it was addressed to certain noblemen in Castile, noblemen connected to the bawd's house. Her family, the Castros, was a large and powerful and power-hungry family, and lovely Inez had brothers aplenty. All of them power greedy and honor hungry.

In the letter, my prince committed himself—the hair rose at the back of my neck as I read this—to sending help to the rebels and to striving to place himself upon the throne of Castile, to which he had a very tenuous claim through his mother.

Castile was larger than Portugal and as much more powerful as the wolf is than the mewling pup. Should we meddle in its affairs and attempt to replace their strong king with our besotted prince . . .

I looked at the letter, but the words swam before my eyes. While the rain whipped at the window of the farmhouse, I saw blood, I saw our kingdom defeated. In that fell moment, in that narrow inn's room, staring at whitewashed walls and lumpy bed, listening to rain lash at the window, I saw my prince dead and laid upon his bier.

Worse, even if he won, what would be his prize? What would be his position but puppet of the bloody-minded Castros, through their beautiful sister?

I saw my prince in his bier, and I heard the bawd's golden laughter spilling through the air like a curse.

In that moment, I thought not of how that golden laughter could spill like sun over a cloudy day. I thought not of the fevered quickening of my blood at her sight. I thought of him, my lord, my blood brother. Whose life I must save.

I called for ink and copied the letter, then I resealed it. I took it where my prince had instructed me, and gave it to the cloaked man who, by his height and golden hair, was a Castro.

Then I took my copy—I, whose every breath since I'd been aware of breathing had been devoted to my prince's service—I took my copy to the old king.

I rode into the king's summer palace by stealth of night. Wrapped in a cloak, I used passageways only one who'd grown up in the palace would know.

I found the king in his study. It was the work of a minute to reassure him that I—emerging as I had from a long-forgotten passageway—had no ill intent. Then I told him the story of the planned rebellion that could but end in his son's death or, worse, in his ruin.

The king read the letter and looked at me, as if in my eyes he could read the confusing turmoil of my divided loyalties. He had dark, piercing eyes, quite unlike his son's and yet just as penetrating. When he stared, I thought he'd see my sin and mistake my jealousy for the whole motive.

But he ran his fingers through his white beard and sighed. Wrapped in an old, frayed cloak, he looked not kingly at all. He was a quiet man, serious, declining steadily toward the grave, but with the kind of upright build, the kind of stubborn dignity that doesn't allow for a show of weakness.

"Thank you," he said. "Thank you, Fernao, for your service to your prince."

I stared at him and it took me a while to understand him. I'd thought he would condemn me. For even if I saved my country, I had betrayed my prince.

But the king, his eyes sad and serious, his hand playing absently with the letter in his hand, spoke in an even and slow voice: "You've done your prince a service this day, such as we all wish our retainers would do for us."

Such as all wished. And yet I'd betrayed my prince.

Mingled shame and pride warring in my chest, mingled bitterness and contentment fighting for my mind, I rode back and used the weather as a blind for my delay.

My prince was so trusting that he didn't even question such a long delay, rather called for wine and wenches to warm me, and joked and laughed as he hadn't since we were both young.

Now I perceived in his fevered excitement equal parts of fear and shame. He knew the danger he brought upon his country, knew that a prince should not behave so. But he could no more resist the bawd's blandishment than a horse can resist the spurs. Could I have resisted, had I been him? Could I have resisted the touch of her hand, the clear light of her blue eyes?

The war training went on, the mad training, and for months nothing happened. I thought that the king had remedied it all with diplomacy and that my treason, my moment of duplicity, would never be known.

Then, in spring—a sunny, smiling day—my prince called for a hunt. For once, Inez was left behind, perhaps because this was a crazed, intense hunt, searching the stag in groves and scarps, bringing it to bay in bloody mercilessness.

When we came back at night, laden with prey and singing victory songs, the farm was quiet. Too quiet. Too dark. No tapers burned in the yard. No light shone within.

Opening the gates, we entered the courtyard.

There she lay. Beautiful Inez of the singing laughter. She would laugh no more. Her body lay on its stomach in the courtyard, her neck poised on a stool that had been split, end to end, as if by the stroke of an ax. And her head, having rolled a little off, rested face up, staring at the sky with a vacant expression. Yet her lips, her broad, generous lips, now pale and bloodless, seemed to have curled up in a final smile.

My prince flung himself upon the remains, tumbling from his horse more than descending.

With shameless grief, he beat his chest and called, "Inez, Inez." His clothes smeared in her blood, he crawled on the broad flagstones of the yard, and kissed her bloodless lips, and tried to unbend her stiff body into an embrace. Tearing his hair and clothes, and rending my heart with his sobs, he shed tears as no woman had ever shed at tragedy, and howled as no beast ever had at pain, and swore to Heaven and the minions of Hell that he would take revenge on her murderers.

We carried him to his rooms by force, and by force made him swallow enough wine to make him quiescent and quiet, and make him bend his raging grief into no more than the tearful weeping of a drunkard.

Then did we find the women of the house—aye, and the children, too—hidden in a cellar at the back.

They told us how the king and his advisors had ridden into the yard, and taken the lady by force, and told her she was condemned by treason to the kingdom of Portugal, and then and there executed swift, cruel justice.

The prince cried for hours. Vengeance he wanted, and for vengeance he thirsted, as a man longs for food who's fasted for forty days, as a man longs for water who's battled all day in the heat of the sun.

Clutching his children to him and smearing their blond hair, their bright clothes with their mother's blood, he swore to their staring eyes, their pale, scared faces, that this would be avenged and everyone from his father, the king, to the least of the counselors who had decreed Inez's death, would pay for this widowing of Pedro's bed.

And I, in a corner of the room, hiding, stared on his grief and shed tears for his tears, and half hoped he would find me out, kill me now. The other half of me knew I'd done what I had to, and hoped he would live long and forget the woman's poison and become the great king he could be.

That night, overnight, silver threads twined my lord's hair.

That night, while a thunderstorm echoed in the valley and crackled over the pine trees of the nearby forest, the children's old nurse found me drinking in the kitchen and muttered to me that Inez's death had come too late. Inez and my lord had been married by an authority greater than the Church and less forgiving.

A witch, the nurse said—and crossed herself in saying— the blond Inez had been. And by witch's rites, she and my lord had been married one dark midnight. They'd been bound to each other such that even death could not part them. Now must he go to her or she to him would call, always, till her corrupt form drove him to madness.

And yet, such had Inez's attraction—her beckoning—been that the nurse cried for her while talking of her evil. And, patting her reddened eyes with a sodden kerchief, the nurse said, "She was beautiful, master. So beautiful." Setting her lips in a wistful smile, she added, "A loving mother, too. Whatever else she be."

With those words, the good woman looked as if she'd like to expunge all evil from Inez's memory and let the blonde sleep in peace.

But I went to bed and dreamed of horrors that made me wake in the morning, sweat-soaked and yet cold, in tumbled bed.

I could remember naught of those dreams but the bawd's laughter echoing, as golden as her hair, into the mute spaces of my sleep.

Did my prince hear the same laughter? I don't know. Sometimes, in the months that followed, he woke in the middle of the night and made us all—his entire court—stay awake with him and sing to him, and talk till the day dawned.

But he never said anything bad about Inez. If he spoke of her at all, it was with the sad, slow reverence of a lover parted from his loved one. Yet he never talked as if she were dead, even as he tore up the country and almost destroyed his throne to avenge her. Only as if she'd gone ahead to a pleasant location where, shortly, he'd join her.

You know of the civil war. No use dwelling on that. With the noblemen loyal to him, my master took to the hills and made war on his father, raging again and again over the country, flinging himself at his father's defenses—hoping for death, I think, rather than for vengeance.

His was a dark mood in those years and he cared not what damage he inflicted on the small farms, the little villages caught in his path. I saw my prince sully himself with innocent blood. And I fought beside him—what else could I do? I'd betrayed him once, and I'd not do it again. For his sake, I'd sacrificed the blonde with the golden laughter, the only woman I'd ever loved. I could not lose his friendship, also.

Then came peace, imposed upon the two warring noblemen by the merchants of the kingdom who'd formed their own army and threatened to destroy both their lords should they not find an end to their differences.

Peace it was, an uneasy peace negotiated by trembling priests. But the prince . . . ah, the prince. He never again regained his joy. His eyes had turned inward as if, in his soul, he sought for the ghost of his beloved.

His father, Afonso IV, died but a few months after that contrived peace, grieved at heart, bitter in mind.

My prince ascended to the throne and, swift and cruel, condemned to death those who had advised that Inez be killed.

The death, too, happened in such a way as had never been seen in this small, mild kingdom, not since Roman atrocities. One of the counselors was eviscerated while still alive. Another's heart was pulled out through his mouth and burned before his still-living eyes. The king himself served as executioner, tainting his majesty with their blood.

I stood and watched this, knowing I, too, deserved the like death, but lacking the courage to effect it. I stood beside him. I poured water over his bloodstained hands. I talked to him as though everything were normal and he'd done no more than what he was duty-bound to do.

And his fever grew. His eyes filled with longing. A week ago the prince had her corpse brought out from the tomb and clad in wedding raiments, and commanded us all, all of us, to trek from Sintra, where she was buried, to the largest church in Coimbra for the marriage.

Their secret, dark marriage—if it had happened—was not enough. It might have bound their souls eternally. But my king, or the dream visitation of the blonde, wanted more. Something demanded he be bound to Inez before God and man.

He told me it was because the people should know her as their queen and the court should acknowledge her as their better.

In my heart, I wondered if he thought holy rights could wash away the unhallowed ritual that linked them. I wondered if, perhaps, he thought that sacraments could lay Inez to rest. And I hoped they might.

The church was decorated in black and gold, feast and funeral mingling in macabre dance. When we arrived there and dismounted, the coffin was carried into the church and set before the altar, and I thought that was it, he would marry her remains while they were in the coffin, and with them contrive this strange union.

That none dared protest showed how much my master frightened his court, how much his mad excitement daunted us all.

His eyes burned like ill-quenched coals, where the red will peek through the black. His face was haggard, his beard wild. For the three days of the cortege, he had drunk little, eaten less, and he had not slept.

He always talked, to one or the other of us, usually to me, and the talk was always of her—her excellency, her greatness, the gifts of her mind, and her beauty. Her beauty.

As he spoke, she seemed to rise again before my eyes, and I remembered her grace, her smile, her laughter.

And now and then, like a man possessed, the king would make the attendant priests open the coffin and he would kiss her moldering lips and talk to her—talk to her—as a man will talk to his beloved, asking if she was comfortable, and if she liked the cortege, and if the music pleased her.

And he inclined his head as if, I'd swear, he heard her response from the still air.

My gorge rose and icy fingers of dread played upon my spine when I smelled her corruption upon his clothes. What madness was this, or did he truly talk to her spirit? And if he did, what did she know—in that place beyond time where she now dwelled? What did she know of me, of what I'd done? And what did she want of him, of me—our bodies, our hearts, our souls?

Thus we'd come to the cathedral, where all the tapers burned in festive light, and where the high noblemen of Portugal filed into the pews in cowed horror, and looked on while my prince had the coffin opened and the ghastly remains propped up beside him.

She'd been dressed in a gold and white gown, and her head, somehow, affixed to her shoulders. Around the worm-eaten ruin of her face, her hair remained, golden and as shining as it had been in all its glory. It dazzled in the cathedral like a twin of the sun, touching off a cold light to the stone of the walls, the dark pews, the carved, gilded altar. I'd have sworn that the statues of the saints cowered in their niches and sought to escape this horrible sight.

And it seemed that the remains of her lips smiled.

Even her children were frightened. I tried to calm the young Don Joao, while his father, with mad, joyful laughter, commanded the bishop to proceed with the rites of marriage.

Oh, that the bishop consented to it. But how could he not? It was his king that ordered it, and the pope, his other master, was far away in Rome, while King Don Pedro was here, and King Don Pedro had just killed a man by pulling his heart out through his mouth.

The words were said, resounding like ill omens off the cold walls of the cathedral. The smell of rotting flesh pervaded all and no light came through the windows, except the gray and dank luminosity that filtered through the drizzle outside. We might as well have been in a tomb, all of us.

When her answer was called for, the king listened intently, then smiled, as though having heard the "yes" whispered by those half-rotted lips. And the bishop married them.

The king took his crown off and set it on that moldering head. And, with the help of two maids, he turned the corpse so it faced the pews, then drew his sword.

"Kiss your queen's hand," he said.

He stood beside her rotting body, and held his sword, glimmering in candlelight, and grinned at us the insane rictus of a madman. "Kiss her hand, and I shall know you to be true. The one of you who doesn't pay her homage shall sleep in Hell tonight."

Oh, how the fire burned in his mad eyes.

One by one we filed, by rank and order—dukes and counts and barons, all of them kissing the corpse's hand and filing aside, then bowing to the madman and his dead bride.

When my turn came, I looked into my lord's eyes, looked into those eyes sunk in cavernous circles, and thought not of her but of him.

Oh, I'd loved her madly, but she was gone. And he was here. And perhaps I'd done the right thing, after all. Perhaps once the ceremony was done, once the dark rite that had bound them had been washed by the binds of the holy Church, the poison would be gone from his mind. And maybe my master would quiet down, like a patient who, having reached the peek of a fever, will defeat it and subside into quiet sleep. Perhaps he would be well once her dread remains had been entombed in the brand new tomb he'd had sculpted for her and which waited—open—in the corner of this same cathedral.

Perhaps all Inez needed was to sleep in hallowed ground and to be called a queen in her death.

I picked up the hand, that hand for whose touch I had so longed in my solitary, fevered dreams. Only a few shreds of gray flesh clung to the skeleton, but his ring still adorned her finger.

Clasping the frail bones, I fancied that they were warm, that they moved. I thought that the rotted lips smiled wider and not altogether benevolently. Ghosts of blue eyes seemed to stare at me from her empty orbits.

I took the hand to my lips, trembling at the horror, gagging from the stink and struggling to keep nausea at bay.

It was then, when my lips touched the dead flesh, that I heard her laughter. Unmistakable, of course, unmistakable. Only a woman in the world, only one woman, ever, could laugh like that—golden laughter like a clash of cymbals.

I looked up, startled, certain that this must be someone else's corpse and Inez still alive somewhere, still alive and still malevolent. Still knowing how I desired her. Still wishing to use my desire as she used my king's love, as a sword drawn at both our chests, as a weapon suspended over both of us.

But no one else looked disturbed. No one else seemed to have heard her laughter. The man who'd kissed her hand before me stood a little to the side, his expression the same frozen look of respectful horror he'd worn through the whole ordeal. And the people behind me looked just as they had, apprehensive but quiet.

Only the prince gave signs of having heard. His eyebrows arched, his lips curved in wry amusement. He inclined his head toward her.

"Fernao Dias?" He looked puzzled and tilted his head toward the dead lips. "Are you sure my pet? Fernao has been loyal." He graced me with a surprised look. "Fernao is my own counselor and has been loyal always. I've known him from the cradle. I'd have sworn by his loyalty."

His head still inclined, he listened on. He sighed, a sigh like it would break his chest. "If you are sure," he said. "You would know better."

He looked at me. There were tears in his eyes, but not so much that they would fall, rather like insufficient water poured on a smoldering fire. Beneath the tears, the fire still burned and, beneath the grief and shock, I read hatred in my master's eyes.

She had told him. She had revealed my treason. Perhaps my jealousy. I told myself I'd betrayed him—I'd betrayed her—for the country and not out of jealousy. But in that moment, while my lord's mad gaze shone by the light of candles, while Inez's smell of corruption mingled with the scent of burning wax, while her ghostly eyes glimmered from her empty sockets, I knew that jealousy had been at least half of it.

Had I not been jealous of his regard for her, had I not been jealous of her love for him, I would have talked him out of waging war on Castile. Or I'd have destroyed the letter to the

Castros and taken off, a fugitive, across the wild mountain country. Had I not been in love with her, I would have talked to her and made her see that she would win nothing by her scheme, except the death of her patron, the destitution of her children.

But love makes fools of us all. Love had made a murderer of me.

Looking at my king's anger-filled eyes, his betrayal-wounded, pain-mad eyes, I scrambled out of line, away from the king's sword, from his reach.

I ran to the rear of the church while, behind me, a few brave souls tried to restrain the king in what they thought was his fury at my breach.

But now I know he's no more insane than any of them. Or no madder than I. I can see and hear what he sees and hears. And I know there's no way out of this for him.

I must die for my sin, for my forsaken love. For the blonde.

I've taken refuge behind the great stone tomb of some forgotten king.

I've drawn my sword and, like a Roman fool, I'll presently fall upon it, to save my noble lord spattering himself with the blood of a friend. But I know that even death will bring me no escape.

Peering around the tomb's edge, I see that the noblemen still restrain the king, encircling him on all sides and raising a great clamor as they wrestle with his still-formidable strength.

Not one of them notices as Inez's corpse trembles, as though wakening.

And none of them sees or hears as she turns, a shadow of an amused smile upon her putrid lips, a glint of ghostly eyes in her vacant orbits.

She still moves gracefully, as no dead thing should move. And, while the noblemen fight, while the noblewomen watch them in concern, it is as though we were alone in the church—Inez and I.

The light of the candles glints off her golden hair, and the silk of her dress shines soft and white, as she walks toward me.

My legs seem to have turned to water. I cannot run. And even if I could, I lack the will to escape her. My fear and my love meet in my heart. I dread and I desire her more than ever.

My end will meet me here. At the hands of the blonde.

HOMELANDS

LUCIEN SOULBAN

Shanghai burned, God's judgment against the Asian Sodom rendered. . . .

A gaily painted river of umbrellas and parasols drifted down Bubbling Well Road in a slow, lethargic ballet. Beneath the cloth canopy bustled yellow palanquins, leather sedan chairs, and bamboo rickshaws. British and American colonists streamed past, heading for the already crammed docks along the Bund, a picturesque stretch of road bordering Whangpu River. Most maintained an air of refined panic, fleeing as fast as propriety allowed. Such was the price of "civilizing" China: the facade of control. Others moved swiftly, gentility be damned.

Cedric Halston watched the crowd surge past white European-style colonial villas, a few of which coughed a steady pillar of black smoke from soot-blasted windows. A lanky six-footer and topped with an original tan Stetson, Halston held a commanding view over people's crowns, and he didn't much like the vista. He wanted to fire a gun, if only to move this herd even faster, though admittedly, he was an impatient man. Instead, he kept one hand tight on his holstered Army revolver and used the other hand to brush aside locks of black hair latched to his sweating face. His hands, rough and callused, bore the marks of his days in the Union's Dead Walker unit. Still, no Nevada heat could prepare him for the Shanghai humidity, which made walls perspire and plagued civilized folk with "unmentionables" like ringworm. The burning houses didn't help settle the heat either, and instead sent a frantic twinkle in his gray eyes.

A scream broke Halston's reverie. The skittish crowd moved and swelled, continuing the first cry with their own panicked shrieks.

"Move!" Halston shouted, gun drawn.

Two Sikh policemen, the red-turbaned Bulwan and Sohan, their shag beards and waxed mustaches framing grave faces, fell in at Halston's elbows, helping him push through the crowd. The mob surged forward, but Halston and his two escorts straight-armed their way through. Bulwan fired his rifle skyward once, splitting the herd like frightened sheep.

The trio burst into a narrow adjoining alley where a Brit spun and shrieked like a wild Moroccan dervish. A dead body, bloodied, lay at his feet. Halston raised his revolver and aimed; Bulwan and Sohan followed his lead with their rifles, hoping he'd venture the first shot—and thus take responsibility—for killing the Britisher. Halston paused, his breath suspended in the raucous, naked moment, waiting . . .

Waiting . . .

Finally, a rip appeared across the man's stomach. The clothing and flesh beneath parted, opened as though by the will of God. Blood sprayed out in a fan of crimson, painting *something* in the air. A lengthy red cord of internal organs unraveled from the Brit's wound. The man shrieked before his throat puckered inward and a fistful of flesh vanished in a ragged bite, betraying a floating set of teeth.

Halston fired at the unseen attacker. Bulwan and Sohan followed suit, their shots thudding into solid air that bled black ichor.

The Brit collapsed. His attacker fell atop him a second later, pressing down on him and creasing his clothes with its flour-sack bulk. Whatever it was, it was no longer moving. The dark-skinned and impassive Sohan walked over and emptied a bullet into the skull of the Brit and, after running one hand over the other, fired another into what he assumed to be the assailant's skull, punctuating both reports by reloading his single-shot carbine. Dismayed outcry moved through the crowd, but Halston swept his gun across the mob, parts of which lurched backward.

"Don't you folks have somewhere to be?"

Reluctantly, the onlookers moved down the street, but a few shot Halston poisoned looks.

"Well, *sahib*," Bulwan said. "Things aren't very tiptop."

"Not tiptop, indeed," Halston said.

The crowd drifted past, their contempt for Halston unspoken, but naked in their stares. Halston knew their thoughts: *Bloody indolent Americans. Damn Yank refugees.* That's what they thought of all Americans these days.

Now that America was no more.

✛ ✛ ✛

"The Admiralty's blockaded the bay," Commissioner Lexington said, running his fingers through the frayed bush of white hair that rested above an equally impressive snowy hedge of eyebrows. He clipped his words in proper British military style. "They'll sink any ship leaving the docks."

"Tell that to them," Halston said, staring out the window of the Cathay Hotel. The docks below were lost beneath a sea of black hats, bonnets, and coolie caps, and a forest of arms waving wads of money at stevedores and captains, anyone who'd smuggle them aboard the next ship. It was like the Frisco evacuation all over again—parents holding up children, blindly offering them up for a chance at salvation; captains indenturing those who couldn't pay the suddenly exorbitant price for a passage. Halston fought the momentary onslaught of panic's echo, saw himself lost, looking for a ship.

He didn't want to lose everything again.

"They're frightened," Lexington said. "They remember the Admiralty's handling of that outbreak in Port Sudan and what."

"Well, if the city keeps burning, the Admiralty won't have to fire a single volley," Halston said.

"No," Lexington admitted, easing himself back into the velvet chair.

"Railways?"

"Blockaded by the blasted Chinese. Devils don't want our problem spilling into their districts."

"And the fire?"

"Spreading across the International Settlement and French Concession."

"It'll handle some of the dead meat. What about the Chinese districts?"

"Unaffected—for now. The flames haven't leaped across Soochow or Sillawei Creeks yet."

Halston shrugged. "It's sparing them a tarring, but the creeks are just funneling the fires and driving the dead meat here."

"Mr. Halston," Lexington said curtly, "we hired you for your experience in these matters. To handle them before they became inconvenient. They're now inconvenient. We were told you were the best the Americas had to offer."

"Don't get upset." Halston said. "I can handle any problem involving the walking dead. It's just I never met any invisible ones before."

"Perhaps the work of one of your infamous zombie masters? I should think we'd do well to round up all the Negroes."

"Don't waste your time."

"What then?"

"Leave Bulwan and Sohan with me. They're good. So far, it looks like the unseen zombies can't turn others invisible or even Lazarus them with a bite. That's all to the good. It means we don't have an epidemic. I'll figure out who's turning them invisible and nip this problem in the bud."

"Very well. We'll relocate to the Astor House Hotel in Hongkew and hold the bridges for as long as we can. If we have to raise anchor, we'll do so without you."

"I thought the Admiralty blockaded the city."

"Balderdash," Lexington said. "Not for us."

✝ ✝ ✝

"Bulwan, Sohan," Halston said, elbowing his way down the hotel's crowded marble stairs. "You're with me."

"Are we killing more dead-*wallah*, *sahib*?" Bulwan asked. He fell into step behind Halston. Sohan followed, shouldering his rifle quietly.

Halston nodded. The crowds thinned farther down the street, and the dusk sun shone through rips in the rising smoke. Those who hadn't made it this far now sought refuge where fate dictated.

"We need ammunition," Halston said, checking his belt. Eight bullets, not counting the pills in his guns. "Lexington said he couldn't spare any."

"Of course he did. I'm thinking you're going to Lauza Police Station?" Bulwan asked. "They are pulling out, across the Garden Bridge. And many people are stealing ammunition for themselves."

Halston sighed. "What do you suggest, Bulwan?"

"The Sûreté."

"Frenchies got their own problems."

"Yes, *sahib*," Bulwan said, "but they are employing Chinese detectives, from the Green Gang."

Halston nodded. The French hired local scofflaws from the Big Eight Mob, which ran Shanghai's underworld. The Sûreté turned a blind eye to their pirating, so long as they didn't prey on Europeans. In return, the Mob provided a ready source of agents and even gave the Frenchies access to their arsenal.

Yes, the Sûreté would have ammunition—for a price.

✝ ✝ ✝

South of Nanking Road rested Foochow Road, the rapidly beating heart of Shanghai's entertainment district. Teahouses and pagoda-roofed businesses lined the street in a parade of bright colors. Adjoining the street were dozens of thin alleys called *li*, which were low on respectability and high on discretion. Tonight, however, the once-lively avenue lay forsaken. A few spilt sedan chairs testified to some panicked moments, but otherwise, the streets bore no witnesses. Fortunately, fire hadn't consumed any buildings here; instead, the blazes remained west of Thibet Road, turning the horizon into a burning crown.

Halston walked down Foochow Road with Bulwan and Sohan flanking him. Down each *li*, Halston saw the same scene: empty alleys and red Chinese lanterns burning above doorways. He stopped, sniffing the air.

"Smell that?"

"I am smelling many things, *sahib*," Bulwan said with a grin. "Fires, dead bodies, you."

"Funny. I thought the Brits trained you boys better?"

"They did," Bulwan responded. "But you are not being British."

Sohan grinned ever so briefly.

"Trust me, *sahib*. Not being British is a good thing," Bulwan said before sniffing the air. There was a sharp reek to it. "Opium," he noted.

"And lots of it," Halston said. The smell normally pervaded the alleys, but tonight, the vapors clung to the road's cobblestones.

Flickering red lanterns adorned the doorways of the colorfully named "sing-song" houses and nail sheds, where prostitutes plied their trade. Lanterns also capped the summits of the opium dens' doors, proclaiming they were still open for customers. Halston walked to the closest *li* and inhaled the smoke tendrils from the nearest lantern. His vision swooned, everything suddenly slippery.

"*Sahib*?" Bulwan asked. His voice echoed in the empty cavern of Halston's skull.

Halston shook his head, trying to jar the molasses cobwebs loose. "They're burning opium in the lanterns," he said, looking up and down the *li*. "Som' bitch. They all are."

"*Sahib*!" Bulwan cried, his gaze fixed on something a dozen yards away on the cobblestone street. Sohan aimed his rifle down the road.

Then Halston heard it—a low groan, part breathless exhalation, part effort. A sigh plundered of emotion. Zombie.

The groan grew louder, but the street remained empty. Halston's heart skipped a beat.

"Damn," Halston said. "Shoulder your rifles. Pull out those toothpicks of yours."

Bulwan and Sohan shot Halston strange looks, but followed his example as he pulled an eighteen-inch bayonet blade by the makeshift handle from his thigh sheath. Most veterans of the old Union forces were shy about using bayonets, but

Halston recognized their usefulness in facing zombies; they threaded dead meat eyeballs and skewered brains easier than needle through silk. The invisible ones, though, would take more skill.

The two Sikhs unsheathed their ceremonial *khirpan* blades from their red sashes before drawing in, shoulder to shoulder, with Halston. The groaning bounced off walls and down alleys with a queer, rising tone. Halston estimated the dead man was within ten yards now and closing. He wanted to run, regroup, but he could be running into other zombies for all he knew.

The irregular swish of fabric and the sound of dragging feet grew more pronounced, shifting to Halston's left, then the right. Five yards or so now. An old, familiar fear awoke in Halston's guts.

"Shit," Halston said. "The bastard's weaving all over the place."

The groaning hit a steady, incessant pitch. Then, the stumbling rush of feet. It was three yards away now, close enough that Halston smelled the deep, pungent rot of earth and gangrene. An anxious Bulwan stepped forward, swinging his *khirpan.*

"Stop!" Halston said, but the command came too late.

Bulwan imbedded his blade deep into unseen flesh. At the same instant, Halston heard a second clatter of footfalls right beside the Sikh. The snarls and steps weren't echoes in the street. Two invisible things stalked them.

Before Bulwan could react, the second attacker hammered his shoulders with meaty fists. Bulwan's collar bone snapped, and the Sikh let loose a shriek. The zombie lifted the screaming soldier into the air, the broken clavicle a blind man's knife dancing in and out of his wound. At his partner's peril, Sohan rushed in, but the dead thing dropped Bulwan and backhanded him. The blow sent Sohan flying back several feet.

Halston reached out blindly and locked his fingers when they came in contact with what he figured to be the zombie's arm. He pictured his adversary in his mind and lashed out with his bayonet. The blow was perfectly aimed, the steel driving into the soft underside of the zombie's rotting jaw and up through the roof of its mouth. Halston's bayonet seemed to disappear, to vanish into the night air. But he knew he had struck true when the thing in his grip spasmed, then went slack. And when Halston pulled the blade back, its surface was thick and shiny with black ooze.

The first zombie, pig stuck with Bulwan's blade, thrashed

on the ground and moaned. Halston kicked at the sound, catching the zombie full in the ribs, if he interpreted the noise of splintering bones correctly. Anger had motivated the blow, not fear. Halston could see by the feeble movements of the half-exposed *khirpan* that the dead thing was floundering, helpless. But he was furious with himself for the way the fight had gone, for getting Bulwan hurt, for feeling defenseless—and afraid. He almost kicked the zombie again, but controlled his temper long enough to pull his revolver. Four shots cracked the air, splattering the ground black.

✛   ✛   ✛

The doors to Saint James' Church burst open on the receiving end of Halston's brogan. His grip was full of splintering plank, on which Sohan and he carried Bulwan. A few startled cries echoed through the church, but most folks hunched or lay in the pews, serene or deathly calm. Some even slept.

An Anglican minister moved forward, his balding pate wet with Shanghai heat, his jowls bouncing with each step. His blue eyes puffed out like those of a strangled fish.

"We need help," Halston said, setting Bulwan down. The Sikh gritted his teeth against the jostling. The minister stared blankly at the three men.

"He's been wounded," Halston snapped.

A shadow of disdain crossed the minister's face, the same look Brits gave Chinese commoners when they accidentally brushed against them. The same look Americans received for begging alongside Chinese hobos. Halston didn't have time for intolerance. Pulling his revolver, he leveled it straight at the clergyman's forehead.

"Administer aid to him," Halston said, cocking the hammer. "Now."

"There's no need for that. . . ."

Halston turned to see a nun step through the crowd. His gun inched down, but he kept the hammer eager.

The nun stood a couple heads shorter than Halston; her black habit stretched over a well-fed body. She spoke with a New England accent, but Halston barely noticed. He was more interested in her eyes, which swam in a mist of opium languor. In fact, the bite of opium hung over the whole church, overwhelming even the smell of stale sweat. Before Halston could comment, the nun swished past him to tend to Bulwan.

Halston finally holstered his firearm, then gestured for Sohan to take watch at a broken stained glass window.

"Your friend should remain here a while," the nun said, satisfied with her examination.

"Can I talk to you, Sister—privately?" Halston said.

The minister, fish eyes struggling to focus on the stranger, interposed himself between them. "That would be improper," he slurred.

Halston ignored the clergyman. "Just us Americans."

The nun paused, on the brink of deferring to the minister's authority, but moved off with Halston anyway. The minister tried following them, but a sharp click drew his attention to the stained glass window. Sohan's gaze was still directed outside, but the rifle on his lap was primed and aimed conspicuously at the minister. The fish-eyed man took the point.

"Where you from?" Halston asked once they'd moved behind a pillar near the confessionals. He loomed over the nun, pressed close and lowered his voice to a rumble.

"Boston," she said, no more frightened of him than she was of her needy charges. "I made it out on the last boat."

"A lot of misery got spread around in those final days."

"It was as bad in Boston as it got anywhere."

Halston nodded and stepped back. His intimidation tactics wouldn't work on her. "In case you haven't heard, there are zombies on the loose. You saw firsthand what they can do; why isn't anyone keeping watch at the windows?"

"Oh, I'd heard, but we're safe here. This is God's house," she said, not entirely convinced or convincing.

"I've seen dead meat cross themselves before entering a church and tearing apart everyone inside."

The nun looked away.

"Listen," Halston said. "You know what'll happen if they bust down that door."

"But they won't!" she snapped. Her eyes were suddenly clear; anger or defiance had burned away the opium dreams.

"I'm figuring that out," Halston said. "I'm just not sure what it's got to do with opium."

The nun bit her tongue and offered nothing but a stare.

"Every opium den and nail shack on Foochow is burning the stuff like incense on Chinese New Year. Now I find this church reeking of it. The dead meat we tangled with came past here, but they left you alone. That's got to be why."

"Yes," the nun finally admitted. "Minister Parsons gave us the opium. He said it would calm folks—and keep the zombies away, if we burned enough of it."

Halston nodded. "How long you been chasing dragons? It doesn't affect you like the others. You're used to it."

"I don't want to remember everything I've seen," she said. "It's easier to believe in God that way."

Halston moved out from behind the column and stalked up to the minister. "Father," he said, draping his arm around the shorter man's shoulders, "who told you about the opium keeping the dead meat at bay?"

Minister Parsons blinked with a bovine slowness. "A Chinaman."

"What Chinaman?"

"I don't know his name." Parsons' words dragged across his tongue.

"Did he sell you the opium?" Halston asked.

The minister nodded.

"Some Chinaman you don't know tells you opium keeps zombies away, and you believe him?" Halston said. "Either you're a fool for trusting him, or for thinking I'd believe you."

He drove one hand into Parsons' pockets, searching. The minister squirmed, but Halston grabbed him in a headlock. Some of the parishioners moved to help Parsons. They sat down again when Sohan stood and leveled his rifle at them.

"You're supposed to protect us," a Brit cried out to Sohan. He pointed one trembling finger at Halston. "From riffraff like him!"

"Actually," Halston announced, "Sohan's been deputized by the Shanghai Municipal Council to help me however necessary. Ah, here we go. . . ."

He pulled a tin from the minister's pocket. It was decorated with faux gold leaf, with painted poppy plants and flower vines framing the rim. Raised black lettering identified the brand as *Persephone's Odyssey.* Below it was the stenciled logo of Nichols and Company.

"Thanks, *padre,*" Halston said. "If you hadn't lied, I wouldn't have known who you were protecting."

✛ ✛ ✛

Avenue Edouard VII was a thin no man's land separating the International Settlement from the more liberal French Concession. Escaping the law in Shanghai often meant crossing this or any of the dozens of similarly situated streets, where extraterritoriality rendered nations immune from each other's laws. Many Americans, however, had no such consideration in these sour times. Without a country to call home, they were subject to Chinese law until they could buy another passport or citizen certificate. Many came to Shanghai because local European counsels sold nationalities like a saloon sold whiskey. Business was booming and havens could be had, if you could afford to pay. Most Americans could not. They worked, like Halston, as mercenaries or found some cobble-stoned patch of street from which to beg, huddled shoulder-to-elbow with native Chinese beggars. The Europeans hated the Americans for that. No sin could be as great as shattering the facade of white man's superiority.

Conditions were especially hard on women. They inden-tured themselves to ship captains for a ticket out of the embargoed zone and across the Pacific. The captains, in turn, sold their markers to labor contractors, dance hall propri-etors, and bordello madams.

Halston and Sohan crossed the empty Avenue Edouard VII and made their way toward the brightly lit windows of the sing-song house known as the Delightful Flower Gardens. A gold pagoda-style roof topped the two-story building, while red strips of paper fluttered from the eaves, tastefully announcing the services offered within. The muted sound of piano music haunted the air like the fragrance from plucked flower petals.

Halston remembered seeing the club and its financial backer, one Detective Sun, mentioned in the local mosquito press, tabloids notorious for their stinging gossip. Sun Chen was a nasty piece of work, a hoodlum who headed the Sûreté's Chinese Detective Division.

Approaching the door, Halston smelled the opium. He motioned for Sohan to stand watch outside, and entered the building's dark interior. No use dragging Sohan along. The Chinese uniformly disliked Sikh policeman for their heavy-handed methods. Sohan would only hinder negotiations.

Blue- and tan-robed ghosts drifted through the opium mists. Some cast sidelong glances Halston's way, but few really cared enough to notice. Halston moved through rooms covered in silk curtains, past low blackwood tables and red benches and the occasional jade painting. Clients lay on their sides, cradled by satin cushions and the blessed lethargy of the poppy, while hostesses glided among them with serene purpose.

Halston caught the elbow of an Asian beauty bathed in green silk. "Sun Chen" was all he said.

With an unreadable, porcelain expression, the daydream-ing ghost glanced to a darkened archway, then drifted away. Halston walked through the silk curtains and into a private room commanded by a carved and lacquered red table, around which sat four robed gentleman, each with a prostitute on his

arm. The men's cuffs had been rolled up, exposing their fore-
arms in a manner most Chinese considered vulgar. That alone
marked them as individuals of dubious integrity.

"I'm looking for ammunition," Halston said. ".50 caliber
centerfires and .44s."

One gentleman with slight features stretched across an
oval, milky white face, leaned forward, smiling. "*Chinois* or
Russian." His voice betrayed an odd French lilt, an unusual
Franglais.

"You have Russian?"

"*Oui.*" The man shrugged as if the answer were obvious.
"It's more expensive, but—"

"And the Chinese ammo?"

"From Kiangnan Arsenal. The best."

Halston scowled. The Chinese, desperate to bridge the gap
between Europe's military might and their own, had hired
thousands of dispossessed Americans to head the foundries
and gunsmith shops at places like Kiangnan. Another betrayal
of the West's vaunted superiority.

"Price?" Halston asked.

"Money means little to men like us, Monsieur Halston."

"You think you know me, Monsieur Sun?"

Sun laughed. "Not many cowboys like you in Shanghai.
You're the Brit's Number One Boy."

The words stung. "I'm nobody's 'boy'!"

Sun sat back. "All Americans are *boys* now. No better than
us *pauvre Chinois*—or the slaves who revolted against you."

Halston held his tongue. He needed Sun's help. "What's
your price?"

"I heard you were quite the zombie killer in *les États-Unis.*"

"And?"

"And, I want to know how you make them."

Halston blinked, stunned. "Make them?"

"*Oui*—alcohol, opium, *les filles*, weapons . . . zombies.
Even you Americans are commodities these days. Only, those
of you who know how to create zombies can make a fortune.
Sell yourself or sell what you know."

"I don't know how they're made," Halston said, "and I sure
as hell wouldn't tell you if I did. Damn things are dangerous.
They spread faster than crabs in a whorehouse."

"*Mais non,*" Sun said with a face-splitting smile. "Not anymore. Not if you know how to control the infection."

"Opium?"

Sun sipped his tea.

"How is it everybody knows about the opium?"

"Not everybody," a Chinaman at the table said. Everybody laughed, except Halston.

"Monsieur Halston," Sun said, "if you cannot help us, we cannot help you."

Halston might have argued, had he been in any position to do so. "Then you can't help me," he said at last. "But before I go, I got one question. Just between us. No bullshit."

Sun motioned Halston to continue.

"How does every nail shed and saltwater sister in Shanghai know about the opium?"

Sun sighed. "Monsieur Halston. . . . Very well, but no tricks, *oui*? You have no ambassador to protect you, and the British care little about your fate."

"My word."

"They know because somebody wants them to know. Somebody is creating a . . . as you say, monopoly, *oui*? For opium consumption. This brand above all others."

Halston showed Sun the tin he found on Parsons. "The locals are being told that only this brand will save them."

"It *will* save them. This Persephone's Odyssey is very effective for keeping at bay the zombies now plaguing Shanghai. Very fortunate for Nichols and Company, eh? But it is a tricky business. Politics prevent the other opium sellers from properly displaying their displeasure with the situation. And many of these other sellers are our friends. . . ." Sun paused and let that last comment hang in the air. Then he added, "Are you going to visit this Nichols, perhaps?"

"No choice now."

Sun muttered something to the girl next to him. She left the room, returning a moment later with a box of Russian .44 bullets on a wooden platter.

"What's this for?" Halston asked.

Detective Sun shrugged and smiled. "Good for business."

Halston took the box. He had no problem playing six-shot messenger.

✛ ✛ ✛

The night sky released its burden in a thick downpour that doused the fires and turned the wet cobblestone streets into something reptilian.

Halston walked up to the Nichols estate alone. By the light of the windows, he could see refugees in makeshift tents crowded on the lawn. As Halston reached the gates, a tall man, his face sliced by a mean grimace, stepped forward. The slight bow of his legs revealed him as a born rider, and though he was dressed like a gent, he looked like he would be equally comfortable in jeans and a duster.

"Can I help you, son?" the man asked, his accent deeply Southern.

"I'm here to see Nichols."

"And you are?"

"The law," Halston said. "I'm with the Shanghai Municipal Council."

"Then you ain't the law here. We're nationals of Mexico City, subject to their laws, not Britain's."

Protected within a bowl of mountains and ruled by the iron general Porfirio Díaz, Mexico City had escaped the Americas' fate. It boasted the only functioning government on the continent, but remained besieged by dead meat trying to penetrate the enclosed basin. Rumor had it, though, that Díaz was turning the tide, thanks to the help of a zombie master of African and Indian parentage working for him.

Mexico's citizens were protected by the so-called Extrality Laws. Halston had no authority here. He cursed Sun Chen for not warning him about that.

"Fine," Halston said. "Then may I *please* speak with Nichols?"

"That's better," the man replied. "Sure you can."

The Nichols' estate was massive and covered with manicured lawns and broad-canopied plane trees. The refugees stared as Halston and his escort walked by. The grime on their fine clothes and the hollow expressions on their faces betrayed the strain of this unaccustomed hardship.

"Who are they?" Halston asked.

"Guests of Mrs. Nichols."

"*Mrs.* Nichols?"

"Mr. Nichols died during the evacuation of New York. Mrs. Nichols has been his estate's proprietor since."

They reached the front steps of the three-story mansion, which appeared from this vantage more Greek monument than home. On the porch, four impressive Doric columns supported a triangular and ornately carved overhang, while the straight-faced marble walls accommodated inset windows. A disheveled gentleman waited near one of those windows, his tan suit stained with grass and his bowler a touch battered.

The double doors opened and a fifty-something gentleman stepped out, clutching a bag to his chest. He looked broken, but muttered a string of British-dappled "thank you"s to the middle-aged woman escorting him out. A born and bred socialite, her dusty hair bled more toward the white than straw, and her skin resembled nothing so much as freckled alabaster. She wore tasseled boots that ran to the knees, black Kentucky jeans, and a dark blue Bolero-style jacket over a ruffled white blouse. She appraised Halston with a glance.

"Curran, dear," she asked Halston's escort, "who is this?"

Halston offered his name, but didn't bother to mention his sponsors.

"Ah. And whereabouts are you from?"

"Nevada," Halston said. "And you're Mrs. Nichols?"

"I am. What brings you here?"

Halston shot the waiting gentleman a sidelong look. Mrs. Nichols smiled and turned to the gentleman. As she did, Halston got a look at the papers he was holding. From the stamps and seals, he figured them for property deeds.

"Forgive me, Mr. Pennworth," Nichols said, "but I must attend to this matter. I shan't be a moment." She looked at Halston and invited him in with a restrained sweep of the arm. "In private, then?"

"If it's all the same," Halston noted, "I'd prefer to stay outside."

Nichols offered a civil smile, then turned to Pennworth. "Mr. Pennworth," she said, "why don't you go inside. The servants will bring you tea and cucumber sandwiches."

Pennworth thanked her profusely, with the eagerness of someone who hadn't eaten in some time, and vanished behind closed doors.

"To what do I owe the honor, Mr. Halston?" Nichols asked, stepping down to the manicured lawn.

Halston followed, his eyes slowly taking in the buildings surrounding the estate. He appeared impressed by the architecture, but was actually gauging which had the best sightlines. "Opium," he offered at last. "I'm here about opium."

"You don't strike me as the type."

"I'm not," Halston said. "I'm just wondering why your particular brand seems to affect dead meat."

Nichols studied Halston briefly before dismissing Curran, who had trailed them at a discreet distance, with a nod.

"Coincidence?" she asked after the servant had gone.

"Awfully lucrative coincidence."

"Opium distribution isn't illegal, Mr. Halston."

"Nope, but if it could be proved a merchant was creating a problem one of their products was solving—well, I don't think any treaty would shield someone like that. Do you?"

Nichols remained quiet a moment. "Mr. Halston," she said, as if examining the name for a watermark. "Are you the same

Halston who works for the Shanghai Municipal Council? Rumor has it that you served with the Dead Walkers."

"I am, and I did. Are you avoiding my question?"

"Not at all." Nichols turned and walked slowly across the lawn, toward the back of the mansion. Before he followed, Halston again glanced at the roofs of the neighboring buildings.

"Please, indulge me a moment," Nichols said when Halston caught up. "Where'd you evacuate from?"

"Frisco."

"New York," she replied to a question never asked. "My husband and I were separated during the evacuation. He bought his way aboard another ship—one later scuttled by the British when they discovered it carried infected passengers."

"Sorry. But it's no sadder than the other stories I've heard."

"My husband could have prevented a lot of that sadness, had he been given more time. He served in a field hospital outside New York during the uprising, you see. He used a cornucopia of drugs—including opium cordials—to treat emotionally distressed patients. That's how he discovered that zombies disliked the . . . taste of these patients. They killed them, but never ate them.

"Unfortunately, his discovery came too late—for him and America. We had to evacuate, but dear Henry told me everything before we parted. The key was opium. So, when I arrived here, I continued his research, eventually buying some Indian poppy fields belonging to Jardine, Matheson, and Company. They were abandoning the business as beneath them," Nichols concluded. "So they had no problem selling to an American."

Nichols led Halston to a brick shed with a padlocked door. She opened the padlock and door, revealing stairs leading down into the rough and dark earth.

"It's called a *tykhana*," Nichols said. "I borrowed the idea from India's Mughals. It's a cooling room, intended to stave off the summer heat."

Halston caught the smell of rotted flesh wafting up from the depths, even as he heard the sound of rushing feet behind him. He reached for his gun, but it had not cleared its holster when a shot rang out. Halston didn't even flinch. He knew he was not the target.

A dozen steps from Halston and the shed, Curran collapsed, a coin-sized hole punched in his ribs. On a rooftop across the street, Sohan reloaded his carbine and turned his sights on Nichols. Halston, however, already covered her with his revolver.

"You were going to feed me to the things down there."

Nichols, saddened by the accusation, offered a melancholy smile. "No. We just wanted to speak with you—as Americans—and show you everything we're doing. But we thought you might injure one of the zombies," she said. "They're caged. Curran was only going to take your gun."

Nichols moved toward her servant, but Halston motioned her back with his revolver. "He's done for. If you don't want to join him, you best explain yourself—and fast."

"Do you know the legend of Persephone, Mr. Halston? No, I doubt it. Hades kidnapped Persephone. Her tormented mother, Demeter, created the poppy to—"

"I'm not here to listen to folktales. How'd you turn them invisible?"

Nichols sighed. "During my research, I discovered a Hermetic ritual. By soaking poppy seeds in wine for fifteen days, then drinking the wine for five days while otherwise fasting, you can make yourself invisible at will."

"And you got the dead meat to do that? I thought they hated the taste of the poppies."

"Of opium, Mr. Halston. There's a difference."

"Okay. You can step away from the door," Halston said. "We'll let the Brits handle you, extrat or no extrat."

"Don't! I beg you—reconsider. You're resourceful and you're American. That's why I want you in my employ."

"I won't ask again," Halston said, drawing back the hammer on his gun. "Close the door."

Nichols nodded, her countenance infinitely wounded, and moved to shut the door. Suddenly, distant thunder rippled across the silent night and reverberated through Shanghai's shallow canyons. For a second, Halston thought Sohan had fired another shot, but the noise was too deep. A rumble broke the stillness again, tripping over its own echoes, followed by the clap of another volley.

"Dear Lord," Nichols gasped. "They've begun."

"That's cannon fire!" Halston said. "The bastards! They don't have to do this!"

The first shells whined through the air with certain and deadly aim, and the stables at the Shanghai Race Club evaporated in a fiery blossom. The thunder was steady now, as the Royal Navy's battleships—two new Royal Sovereigns in the pack—competed to unleash their full horror upon Chinese soil.

The ground shook with each titan footfall of cannon fire. Two apartment buildings across the street from the Nichols' estate vanished, a well-placed shot ripping through their foundations. The structures collapsed like they'd been of built of matchsticks, then exploded into flame.

Halston watched, momentarily stunned, before he waved at Sohan to escape. Then another whine rang in Halston's ears with a peculiar timbre that rose in pitch. He recognized the sound as the herald of an incoming shell, and grabbed Nichols' arm in a most unceremonious fashion. He pushed her through the door and followed, more leaping than running. An explosion up on the lawn collapsed the *tykhana*'s entrance. Halston's world went bright white from pain as he tumbled down the stairs.

Into the hungry dark.

Halston hit the floor hard, and blood filled his mouth. Nichols grunted from the pain, and tried moving, but Halston leveled his gun on her, fully intending to reunite her with her husband.

"They did this—the people you serve." Nichols' eyes glittered in the dark. Another blast shook the ground and rained debris inside the *tykhana*.

"The blasted Brits didn't unleash this chaos on Shanghai," Halston said, spitting blood. "You did, by creating the dead meat!"

"Perhaps. But the Brits have had a taste of their own bitter medicines now, haven't they?"

"Then all this . . . just for revenge?"

"No, Mr. Halston. This was both a lesson and a test. The British don't know what it means to be homeless . . . refugees. In fact, they derive no small pleasure from our misery. They keep us cowed and humiliated. And they've done nothing but remind us of how they saved us during the exodus."

Halston stood. "I was right the first time. This *is* about revenge. The Brits kill your husband, and you—" Another explosion shook the earth, interrupting him.

"Hardly. There are other considerations." Nichols retrieved a lantern still suspended from a wall hook. She lit it, casting long shadows down the corridor. "I'm consolidating power, for all Americans."

"Through opium."

"An opium monopoly won't last. Not if the Society for the Suppression of the Opium Trade has its way in London. No, I'm purchasing a homeland—here in Shanghai. In twelve years, land prices have soared from fifty pounds an acre to twenty thousand pounds. The chief buyers were Europeans, who then rented the property for profits of ten thousand percent, Mr. Halston. Ten thousand. That's what I'm after. Once I purchase Shanghai's available property, we can build a homeland for Americans. The Chinese have already promised us recognition as a sovereign nation, if we help them modernize."

"You think folks will just sell you their land?"

"But they *are* selling. Those refugees on my lawn—they're landowners who believe Shanghai is overrun by dead meat and figure that's a problem even the Admiralty's shells can't solve. They're more than willing to sell their estates, on my terms, and return to Europe. I already own a quarter of Shanghai."

"Then what?" Halston asked. "You run everything as some 'madame dictator'?"

"No. I only want to see my people returned home. What I have planned will take longer than my years can offer. I need men, like yourself, to help build a temporary homeland here, in Shanghai, where we will consolidate our forces. Afterward, we'll use our revenues from opium, property leases, and the sale of our technical expertise to retake the Americas. Díaz has already offered us Mexico City as a base of operations for military actions directed at retaking the continent. And we can succeed, now that we know how to corral the dead meat."

Halston tried saying something, but the complexity of it all stunned him to silence. And in that momentary quiet, he heard low groans floating through the *tykhana* like echowinged ravens. The sound battered Halston's heart.

"The zombies," Nichols said with surprising calm. "They're loose. The siege must have damaged their pens. But—"

"The stairs to the lawn are blocked," Halston interrupted. "Is there another way out of here?"

Another explosion drowned out her first response. "Yes," she repeated. "But it's through the kennels."

Halston sighed, then motioned with the barrel of his gun for Nichols to lead the way. Their footsteps clattered off the walls. It was dark and cool, the stone path veering away into the shadows, no matter where they held the lantern.

Nichols hesitated, tried to speak, but Halston nudged her forward. They advanced cautiously, with Nichols' back to a wall. The moaning grew louder between the explosions; Nichols almost stumbled into an intersecting corridor, then stopped.

"You'll find the kennels ahead," she said. "To the left."

Halston listened intently. Slow feet dragged against the floor. Reacting on instinct, he pulled Nichols back, even as something grabbed his shirt. Halston whirled and fired.

The muzzle flash punched snapshot images in the corridor, but the shot itself only struck rock. Halston continued firing, felling one zombie, but there was another. He fired twice, blindly. His second shot caught something that grunted and sprayed the walls with a wet splatter of gore.

Silence, then another explosion above.

Halston reloaded one pistol and pulled a matching revolver holstered in the small of his back. He grabbed Nichols, pulling her down the left corridor. They reached another turn. The area beyond was rank with decay.

"The kennels," Nichols said flatly.

Halston moved quickly, pushing Nichols forward. Around the corner, the corridor emptied into a large room with metal cages lining the walls. Some cages were still closed, but the bombardment had broken three open. Halston left Nichols, who pushed herself flat against the nearest wall. He held his ground, waiting for the telltale sounds of the living dead.

And then they came at him, all at once, in a mad, stumbling rush.

Halston backed up, unleashing his own thunder, loud enough in the enclosed room to drown out the rumble of cannon fire overhead. Something dropped at his feet with a thud and grabbed his boot. Halston fired down once, to finish the thing off, then emptied his guns in a slow, steady sweep. But even after the shooting was done, one of the dead things remained. It clamped cold hands on either side of his face.

With the calm of one finally dead himself, Halston dropped the revolvers and pulled his bayonet. He stabbed, sometimes punching air, sometimes threading meat. Finally, he struck upward through soft flesh. The invisible zombie shuddered, then dropped to the floor.

Halston listened, but the only noise, a snarling hiss, came from the back of the shadow-draped chamber. Halston quietly reloaded his revolvers and motioned for Nichols to join him. She did, staying by Halston's side. Cage by cage, the pair advanced, until finally, they reached the last pen.

The zombie's cage was open, but the dead meat—still quite visible—wasn't going anywhere. Iron braces secured the thing to a wooden table. Its legs and arms had been amputated, leaving four gory stumps. Halston raised his pistol. That's when he felt the Colt derringer pressed against his temple.

"Our buck zombie," Nichols said. "I'd be foolish to let something like an infected stallion remain unfettered, not when his bite can create more zombies. By killing the others, you did us a service; we'll need the room down here for the refugees and supplies. But this one is still important to my plans. I'm certain you'll understand that I cannot allow him destroyed. Holster your weapons, please."

Halston nodded and did as he was told. "Your stallion's pulling back from you. Afraid of its torturer?"

"My clothes are treated with opium," she noted. "None of the zombies would have bitten me."

He snorted. No wonder she hadn't fought him when he made her lead the way through the tunnels. "Now what?"

Nichols sighed. "That's up to you. You know what your countrymen have endured—the brothels, the factories, the slums. Do you believe that's a fair alternative to what I'm offering? Do you believe we'll be anything more than second-class citizens, anywhere we go, so long as we are without our own country? We can do it without your help, of course, but I'd prefer not to kill a fellow American.

"What do you say, Mr. Halston?" Nichols asked, the derringer steady on his temple.

✣   ✣   ✣

Shanghai burned, God's judgment against the Asian Sodom rendered. . . .

The British cannon fire continued, leveling the city with a cascade of hammer blows that sent a steady rain of dust plumes falling from the *tykhana*'s ceiling.

"I loved that house," Nichols noted, then set off through the room crowded with refugees, food stocks, and water barrels.

"How long will the Brits keep this up?" a woman asked.

"Till there's nothing left standing," Nichols said. "After that, we go up and rebuild." She tapped the metal strongbox filled with land deeds. "On our own terms."

Nichols slipped between the huddled refugees, offering blankets to some and a reassuring hand to others. She finally reached one corner of the room where two men sat.

"Saint James' Church has a strong cellar," Nichols said. "I'm sure your Sikh friend is safe there."

"Bulwan," Halston said sourly. "His name's Bulwan."

Nichols glanced at Sohan before asking Halston, "You believe you can trust this . . . gentleman?"

"With my life. Besides, way I figure it, they're both in the same boat as us with the Brits and all," Halston said. "And at least I know where I stand with Bulwan and Sohan."

Nichols nodded. "You are doing the right thing."

"I hope so," Halston replied, feeling more cold and numb than he'd ever felt before. "I hope this homeland of ours is worth the price we paid for it."

"That's for our descendants to decide, Mr. Halston. Such considerations are no longer our luxury."

NOT ON THE BOOKS

ROLAND J. GREEN

THE WESTERN CARIBBEAN. MAY, 1917

First Officer David Peck of the S. S. *Matthew Glendunning* contemplated the ship's deck log for a moment. He wiped sooty sweat out of his eyes and focused them on the entry in Captain Pahlen's hand, made at the beginning of the present four-to-eight watch.

> *Chiefie says the six stokers we signed on in French Guinea are bothering the rest of the black gang. They keep to themselves, don't seem to eat or drink much, and hardly talk at all. When they do talk, it's in what might be Creole French but could be something else.*

Peck wiped his eyes again. The Caribbean weather was almost a flat calm, with what little wind there was blowing from astern, just hard enough to keep the ship half-hidden in a cloud of her own smoke. The wretched coal they had to make do with these days didn't help.

Glendunning had been ten years under the Falkirk Lines banner when the war broke out. Since then she'd been even harder worked and worse kept, tramping around South America and the Gulf of Mexico. When the Royal Navy was buying all the good steam coal, a twelve-knot cargo-passenger liner was doing well to make nine knots with all laundry aloft.

Peck refused to contemplate the crime of altering the log, even when he thought Captain Pahlen was starting at shadows. The mysterious stokers were as likely as not backwoods Haitians trying to work a passage home, without enough English to learn that the *Glendunning* was going nowhere near Port-au-Prince. Was the captain maybe just covering his tracks, in case the stokers refused duty when they learned the truth?

The stokers would find a passage home from Kingston soon enough, even if they had to take an island schooner. They would be no problem for David Peck. His problem right now was whether his relief would appear in time for him to bathe before dinner.

✛   ✛   ✛

In a stifling cabin in the forward passenger quarters below the bridge, a man who called himself Lieutenant Ribode of the *Chasseurs Caribes* held an important conversation without speaking a word.

Master, We hunger.

The voudun *boko* recognized the voice in his mind. It was the one he'd allowed the name Clef, or "Key," because some of that one's human wits had survived his coming into the service of Ribode and those whom he served in turn. Clef could see solutions to many problems. Why, then, was he calling his master now?

You should not hunger.

You should be down here. Then you know why We hunger. This is not a place even for Us.

They should be feeding you something that you can eat.

Heh, heh, heh.

The laughter was unmistakable, and the *boko* thought he heard the other five servants he'd seen aboard also laughing. He hoped they were not laughing out loud; laughter might seem strange, in a coal-fired stoke hold in the tropics. But he decided no one would suspect anything, because no one would hear them over the hiss of steam and the clang of metal.

The *boko* drew his thoughts so deeply into his mind that not even Clef could hear them, then snatched his uniform from the hook in the corner and pulled it on. With the old ceremonial sword, it not only honored Ogun the Warrior but would help deceive Europeans.

He picked up the sword, holding it as if to make a sacrifice, even if the blade could hardly cut sugar cane. Then he grinned.

I command you to feed on one of yourselves. Five of you are enough for the Lady's work. Begin now!

Ribode had already read from their thoughts the name of the one the servants saw as the weakest or liked the least. He barely needed to put that name into their minds before he heard a soundless scream of terror from the doomed one.

He sat down again, holding the sword across his knees, ready to wait an hour. By then they would surely be done.

He did not fear the servants being seen or suspected, either. They could see in the dark of a stoke hold much better than any living man, the noise of the engines could drown out screams as thoroughly as laughter, and a well-stoked boiler's furnace was perfect for hiding odd bits of flesh and bone.

✢ ✢ ✢

Peck took the midnight-to-four watch that night, then arranged to take the next day's noon-to-four shift. He could at least hope for a proper bath, then dinner with the passengers, *and* have all night in.

It was past six bells before Peck had to change his plans. The signal for that change was the chief engineer coming into the wheelhouse and asking Peck out on to the bridge's port wing for a discreet conversation.

"The captain's sleepin'?"

"You might say that."

"Aye, and I'll do it, if ye inseest."

Peck frowned. Chief McKenzie's Aberdeen brogue deepened when he was uneasy. After a shipwreck in 1911 and a torpedoing in 1915, it took a good deal to make him that way.

"Weel, they're not on the books, so it's likely no great matter. But one of those Guinea Frog stokers who canna speak a Christian tongue is gane." He nodded as Peck raised eyebrows. "Aye, we've searched, and asked his friends, if ye want to call them that. But nae sign of the fella."

Peck frowned. "We passed close enough to Martinique that he might have swum for it." Then he remembered that they'd passed the French island in daylight, or at least in a rainy dawn, where anybody going overboard risked being seen. "I'll have the bosun question the morning watches. But he's either ashore or in a shark's belly by now."

"Aye. There's still talk of the uncanny, and that's nae a good thing, even wi' out the war and a'. I'll no have any of the mystery lads on the gun, at least."

Peck doubted if all the witch doctors in the Caribbean could make the ship's ancient twelve-pounder dangerous to anybody, except by accident. Besides, the last German surface raider had left the Caribbean years ago, and the U-boats hadn't reached this far from home.

But he did what he could to ease the men's fears, by listening to the bosun's questioning. He also took pains to remind them that any lubber of a French Guineaman could think up more stupid ways to kill himself aboard ship than a man could count without taking off his shoes.

The first officer doubted that he was convincing anyone, but at this point in the war it was enough that they didn't call him a liar to his face. That had happened on his last ship, and several times to Captain Pahlen. Every time it occurred, it pushed the captain further toward thinking that the sea he'd followed for thirty years was going to Hell and that Heaven lay in a bottle.

The meeting with the men went on so long that Peck's dinner plans went over the side with the garbage. But today the wind was over the port bow and the funnel smoke no longer shrouded the bridge. Peck only had to change his shirt, instead of wishing he could have himself and his clothes towed behind the ship for an hour or so.

It seemed to Peck that *Glendunning*'s Clydebank builders hadn't been able to decide whether the officer's mess room was off the cabin passengers' dining salon or the reverse. The bulkheads and furnishings between them formed a meandering line, and when you thought you were in one, you were certain to find yourself three paces inside the other.

Tonight there was no mistaking the passengers' side. Both Madame Lebrun and Lieutenant Ribode were seated on opposite sides of one table. The only other diners were the two Dutch copra buyers on their way from Surinam, who were as usual too busy stuffing themselves to make polite, or any other sort of conversation. Peck decided that it was impossible to offend the Dutchmen, so he would choose his own company.

In spite of his nearly black skin, Ribode spoke excellent French, although with a Creole accent. The lady spoke both French and Spanish, as well as English at least as good as the chief engineer's.

Madame Lebrun was bound for the Dominican Republic in the company of a husband half again her age and also half again the size of David Peck. The one time Peck had seen the man, he looked as if he juggled anvils to work up the appetite he displayed at breakfast. But Monsieur Lebrun also seemed to be a martyr to seasickness, and seldom left the their cabin.

As Peck took a seat with the passengers, the steward brought coffee, one of the few things the galley did well. Ribode had emptied his first cup and was sipping at the second before he turned conversational.

"How fares our voyage?"

They discussed the weather and how even American weather reports were hard to come by, now that the United States had entered the war. Peck was careful with his replies, but no one asked him a question that they could not have answered themselves by reading the newspapers.

"Indeed, one hopes the weather will remain *convenable*," Madame Lebrun said. "For my husband's sake, at least. He has not yet recovered from his *mal de mer*." She turned a warm smile on both of the men at the table.

Ribode didn't twitch a muscle or even take a deep breath. Yet Peck still had the sense that somewhere in those last words lurked a message from the lady. Likely enough, it was one of the oldest and simplest messages between a man and a woman.

If Madame Lebrun was thinking of an assignation with the commandant, black as he was, Peck knew that he should be offended. He had also been in the Caribbean too long to wish to interfere. A tramp passenger-cargo ship crossing the Caribbean in a war-torn world was neither a convent nor a even a dockside club with a color bar.

Of course, the Lebruns could be spies. They were strange ones, to be sure, and if one believed the papers, the Germans had more agents abroad than they had soldiers on the Western Front. But what would spies be seeking aboard an aging steamer with a cargo of copra, lumber, and baled jute bags?

Perhaps Ribode was their target; he wore no uniform that Peck recognized, but then the uniform-recognition manuals were never accurate or up to date. Or perhaps one of the Dutchmen or one of the mysterious stokers was a high-ranking Allied officer in a truly ingenious disguise. Peck could not help smiling, then laughing, at the idea.

"Is it something amusing that you might share?" Ribode asked.

Peck spoke without hesitation. "Yes. How well do you speak the local dialects of French?"

"Some well, some less well. Why?"

"As an Allied officer, you have the authority to interrogate our crew on a matter that affects the safety of this ship."

He normally wouldn't have asked anything of the sort from the lieutenant. The main crew wouldn't take being questioned by a black too kindly. But few of the men Ribode would be interrogating were much lighter than he was. And Peck himself didn't care if the man was pea green with a purple tail, if he learned what was going on.

"So long as the interrogation takes place with the captain's permission, of course," Peck added.

"Of course," Ribode said. "But putting the mind to hard labor is best done when the body has a full stomach"

Peck wondered if this was an effort to delay him or merely a sign that his companions were hungry enough to have an appetite for the cook's notorious "masterpieces."

The soup arrived first, and after a cautious spoonful, Peck smiled again. Nobody asked him why, not after they also sampled it. For once, the soup did not taste as if made by boiling a chicken two weeks dead.

✛   ✛   ✛

In his cabin, Ribode was having another of those conversations without words, that none but a *boko* and his servants could hear. Clef's voice in his mind was insistent:

The Lady waits. Why?

She waits on the one who comes for her, he replied. *He has not yet come. She does not wait for her own pleasure.*

The *boko* sensed amusement—or was it rebellion?—in Clef's thoughts.

Perhaps the Lady did wait for a new pleasure, to be taken with that young Peck. Her other partner had to be given youth, but not him. He still had it by nature. In the *boko*'s unnaturally long life, he had seen the Lady many times wresting every possible opportunity from seeming human.

What wish you?

Not Clef this time, but the one named only Chevre—"Goat"—for the way his hair stuck up on either side of his head like the horns of a goat—or of the Christian Satan.

Were he being honest, Ribode would have answered that he wished the Lady would finish the night's business and return to those who would surely be waiting for her. But that would be telling the servants more than it was fit for them to hear.

I wish you content yourself with the ship's fare this night. I can explain one stoker missing. Not two.

We still hunger. Our work is still great.

Ribode tried to edge his reply with just the right amount of anger and righteous indignation:

The Lady is greater than any of us, and we must give of ourselves that she may do her work.

That was quite true, but the servants did not seem ready to be bound by that truth tonight.

✛ ✛ ✛

After dinner, Madame Lebrun insisted that Peck accompany her to her cabin. Once below decks, she undid her collar and unbuttoned the top two buttons of her shirtwaist. The skin revealed was as fine as Peck had expected and belonged to a woman no more than thirty. He suspected a touch of Spanish blood a few generations back to produce skin of that particular hue.

What made Peck's breath catch in his throat was the ugly bruise that ran from the hollow of her throat down to disappear under the shirtwaist. Peck's imagination followed it all the way to where it ended, over her collarbone or on her left breast. He had begun to dream of seeing that breast tonight, with no barrier of garments or interruptions of ship's business.

His nanny had been of an Evangelical bent, given to reading him all kinds of tales of men who came to bad ends through pursuing wicked women instead of waiting for virtuous ones. This had not made Peck the muscular Christian she had expected, but it had taught him the perils of women too good to be true, as well as a tolerance for those too true to be good.

"Do you need some liniment and a dressing for that bruise, or salts for your husband?"

"It does not hurt much anymore, and I do not think he knew what he was doing when he struck me."

Her words were much milder than the look in her vast, dark eyes. If that bruise had ever been worse, the blow that made it would have broken bones. It was perilous to come between a wife and her husband, even if he seemed to be something of a brute. It also seemed to be, at the moment, the duty of a Christian gentleman, or at least of one David Peck.

"As you wish. I could arrange for you to have a cabin to yourself—with a lock on the door, if you wish—until we dock in Kingston. I have friends there, both on the police force and with a room to spare. If you decide to bring the matter before the law, I can help."

"I shall surely think upon it. In the meantime, do you have any sleeping powder that I could give my husband? Then, if I decide to take you up on your offer, I can move my clothes to the other cabin and he will not notice until morning."

Peck normally carried packets of Epsom salts and bicarbonate of soda, for when his own stomach made an uproar. He also carried packets of a mild sleeping draught, for dealing with Captain Pahlen far flown with rum. Now he tore open two packets and mixed the contents in a large teacup.

"Fill this with water and have your husband empty it. He will sleep like a babe."

The look in Madame Lebrun's eyes alarmed Peck a little, and he realized that a husband who slept soundly enough for his wife to move out without waking him also slept soundly enough for her to do other things, too. It was not the best of ideas for Monsieur Lebrun to be altogether helpless.

"And," the first officer added, "I'll have a steward look in on him from time to time during the night."

The lady gave Peck an open-mouthed kiss that left his lips and face glowing. When she turned away, his heart hammered as if he'd just run a mile at his school-champion pace. His mind spun out a plan by which he could take her up on her none-too-subtle offer:

If Captain Pahlen is sober enough to stand watch tonight, and I don't need to ask Derrick to take an extra turn—it will be glorious. . . .

Then Peck recalled the look in her eyes, when she thought her husband would be helpless, and his passion cooled just a little.

Glorious, yes—if there is nothing hiding behind the lady's kiss.

✛ ✛ ✛

Peck saw to the movement of Madame Lebrun's necessities, then returned to the bridge. He found that Captain Pahlen was not only standing his watch, but was almost sober. The ship would be safe in Pahlen's hands for the next few hours.

The first officer still prepared carefully for his visit to Madame Lebrun, taking his loaded Colt .32 from his strongbox and adding extra cartridges to his pockets. He was glad the pistol was small and easily hidden. It would be a bad joke on everybody to visit a willing woman with some monstrous piece of iron-mongery like the captain's Webley service revolver.

Madame Lebrun's new quarters were in the after cabins, in a deckhouse jutting out from the poop deck. The cabin roof ran flush with the poop, with portholes on either side. A skylight ran half the length of the cabin, but adjacent to it, to brighten the passageway there.

Prudence had led Peck to carry his Colt. Now it led him to advance like a schoolboy approaching the maids' quarters, skulking and crawling until he could look out from under the starboard lifeboat into the cabin window. The best way to deal with even the most improbable trap was not to fall into it.

Madame Lebrun had the faded green baize curtains open, and Peck could see that her glossy, dark hair was down. A hint of shapely shoulders peeped from under her tresses. He crept closer—and his breath stopped as a resounding *clang* echoed overhead. He flattened himself on the deck until he saw that the lady wasn't moving, then looked about.

Two sailors were working on the twelve-pounder bolted to the poop, testing the training gear. They had the tompion out and the cover off, and wrenches and prybars littered the deck. One sailor, who wielded a wrench the size of a battle-ax, had a revolver tucked into his belt.

Devil of a time to pick for work on the gun, Peck thought. Then he remembered what Chiefie had said about the mysterious stokers, how he didn't want them near the gun. That would explain the revolver; the sailors were doing double duty, as mechanics and guards.

Suspicion hung thicker tonight on the *Glendunning* than coal dust in her stoke hold. Peck almost turned around and skulked back the way he'd come, but that thought vanished the moment he looked again through the cabin porthole. Madame Lebrun had not only let her hair fall, she'd flung aside her shoes and stockings, as well as every garment above the waist. A light sheen of sweat covered her creamy skin, and the sway and curve of her breasts cried out for a great poet's verse—or at least a lusty man's hands.

Peck was a man, not a poet. In the next moment, he knew how lusty he could be. In the moment after that, his ardor died, as his eyes pierced the fog of desire and he saw her neck and shoulder. Not a trace showed of the bruising that had elicited his sympathy earlier. Had it been some kind of paint or makeup that she had wiped off after it had served its purpose? And what, precisely, was that purpose?

How am I going to manage this? Peck thought. *I should go down and just ask her. As politely as possible, of course—*

The need for politeness vanished as a heavy blow thundered against the door to the lady's cabin. The lock started from its screws, and a crack ran down the varnished wood.

Madame Lebrun screamed and raised both hands, but not to cover herself. She held them out toward the door in a commanding gesture. Peck remembered seeing an actress playing Titania in *A Midsummer Night's Dream* make a similar gesture, directed at the actor playing Bottom. Whoever was breaking into the cabin now seemed likely to make as big an ass of himself, with no help from a fairy queen's spells.

The door burst off its hinges and flew across the cabin, knocking the lady backward against the bulkhead just below Peck. The massive form of Monsieur Lebrun followed it. In his left hand he brandished a knife that seemed to Peck as big as a cavalry saber.

The first officer could have sworn the man was frothing at the lips, like a rabid dog. He could also have sworn at himself. Had the sleeping draught been too weak to subdue a man the size of Lebrun? Or had he only feigned swallowing it and bided his time until he was alone and could arm himself?

Madame Lebrun screamed as she rolled out from under the door, a moment before the knife split the wood. She had splinters in her skin, and her skirt hung in tatters around her legs, but she managed somehow to scramble to the nearest corner and raise her hands again.

To Peck, her eyes seemed to glow. Her voice turned from a scream to a murmur. Neither slowed her husband. He snatched the knife out of the door and flung himself at his wife, the knife thrusting ahead like the point of a lance.

Glowing blue smoke wrapped itself around Monsieur Lebrun, slowing, but not stopping his advance. Two steps more, and the knife drove deep between Madame Lebrun's ribs. It pierced vulnerable flesh; she screamed like a mad thing and blood spurted around the steel. In the next moment, Peck had drawn his revolver and emptied it through the porthole at Monsieur Lebrun.

The porthole's heavy, weatherproof glass deflected a wildly aimed first shot. The second and third bullets cracked the glass. The last three shattered the porthole and went home into the murderous brute, who seemed unable to draw the knife from his wife's side. The coils of smoke, still tightening around him, prevented Lebrun from pulling the blade free. Even as the bullets struck him, he struggled against the strange constraints with a madman's strength and cursed in a language that Peck refused to believe belonged on a human tongue.

All the cursing ended in a bubbling gasp and a spray of blood as the bullet wounds at last drove Monsieur Lebrun to the floor. He rolled over on his side, groped for the hilt of the knife, then thudded down on his back.

Peck had a mad moment of trying to push himself through the porthole, but only succeeded in cutting his face and hands on the glass. The smoke drifted away from Madame Lebrun. Her eyes were dulled, and she had both hands clasped over the knife in her side. She whimpered like a dying kitten.

From madness, Peck's thoughts turned to sensible action. He retreated from the shattered porthole and sprinted for the door that gave on to the passageway.

✢ ✢ ✢

Boko Ribode was below, in the stokers' quarters, when the Lady called.

Help me!

He replied with his first thoughts: *You are the Lady. How can you need help?*

He sensed the pain in her chest. A sharper pain ripped through his head from her anger.

The fool I was keeping stabbed me!

It did not make sense, that this should be a danger to the Lady, but if the wound was painful—

He was already running as her explanation seared through his skull, making him stop and clap his hands to his temples. *The handsome young officer shot the fool! Lebrun is dead. I can take no strength from him.*

The *boko* was about to ask if she needed to take strength from another that badly, to survive the wound, then remembered that she was probably still in her human form. The Lady would need strength from elsewhere to survive long enough to transform into her true shape.

He hoped that Dambala was close. He also hoped that the sacred iron dagger he had in his belt would be enough to hold Peck for the Lady's appetite, if she could not bring the young man down herself.

He ran faster, brushing past crewmen who stopped to stare, then turned to stare again at the five soot-caked and hollow-eyed stokers who shambled after the nearly naked Negro officer.

✢   ✢   ✢

Peck knelt on the cabin floor, in the pools of blood rapidly spreading from Monsieur Lebrun and his wife. The man had stabbed her only once, without hitting a vital organ or any of the major blood vessels. A wound like that could still take a life slowly and horribly, as infection ate the woman alive from the inside.

If it's as bad as that, I'll put her out of her pain myself and jump overboard. . . .

Peck carefully drew his pistol, discovered that his spare cartridges hadn't fallen out of his pocket, and started reloading the Colt. Fortunately, he hadn't put in even a single round when footsteps thudded in the passageway and he turned to face Lieutenant Ribode. Had the gun been loaded, he might have shot the man by sheer reflex.

Peck backed away, pistol still drawn. Ribode was naked except for a pair of shorts, and he had either a huge tattoo or some sort of chalk marking on his chest. He was staring at Madame Lebrun, and she was staring back in a way that suddenly made Peck less afraid *for* her than *of* her.

Then she sprang up and hurled herself at Ribode. He flew back through the doorway, almost into the faces of a band of stokers who clustered in the passageway. The remnants of her skirt and her undergarments parted company with her as she moved. Peck saw that every part of her was equally fine.

She put her mouth to Ribode's chest, and he stiffened as that strange blue smoke wreathed them both. The stokers stepped back, but did not turn away. Peck could have sworn that their eyes glowed now much like the woman's had earlier.

The knife slipped from between the lady's ribs and clattered to the deck. The woman staggered, then let Ribode's limp form follow the knife down. As she turned toward Peck, her wound was already closing. Soon, nothing but a faint patch of discolored skin told of where it had been.

Ribode's eyes held no life as the woman stepped over him. Then, still naked, she ran into the passageway. The stokers parted before her, falling back in fear and awe as she leaped straight upward toward the skylight, like a salmon at a waterfall. The glass did not shatter—it vanished into sparkling dust—and Madame Lebrun soared up and onto the deck above, unharmed and still unclad. Only few smears of dried blood marred her otherwise perfect flesh.

Peck knew from the shouts up on deck exactly when the sailors saw her. He would have dashed into the passageway, except that now the stokers crowded forward into the cabin, hands outstretched menacingly.

"Back!" Peck shouted.

He repeated the command, and stronger ones besides, in several languages. He also finished loading his revolver, despite the shaking of his hands. The last thing he wanted was a brawl with a band of mutinous stokers, but he would stand up to them, if it came to that.

But the stokers ignored the first officer and fell on Ribode's body, ready opened before them, like a pack of starving dogs on a sirloin of beef. They had sharper teeth and nails than the run of humanity, and in moments their faces and hands were so bloody that they seemed to be wearing red masks and gloves. Peck thought of sharks in a feeding frenzy, found that his hands had stopped shaking, then aimed at the nearest of the flesh-eating ghouls.

One shot flung the ghoul backward. This was enough to clear an escape route for Peck, since the other ghouls were caught up in quarreling over Ribode's body, now half-reduced to a skeleton. Peck charged out of the cabin; he would have walked through a boiler's firebox to get clear of the stokers.

From above, the lady screamed again. This time Peck thought he heard triumph, not pain, in the sound. More shouts followed, now mixed with curses and obscenities. Then Chiefie's voice called out.

"Load!"

Peck could not have dashed out on deck faster if the ghouls had been at his heels. Indeed, the stokers left the cabin

and came down the passageway a moment after the first officer, now that Ribode's corpse had been exhausted. They
lurched and staggered, dripping blood and gnawing on bits of
human flesh. But Peck was unaware of his peril. By the time
the ghouls had entered the passageway, he had climbed the
ladder to the poop deck and was close enough to touch
Madame Lebrun—or the being who had used that name.

He would rather have touched a cobra, given a choice. But
he did not want to back away. Standing close to her, he kept
the gun's crew from firing, for fear of hitting him. He understood without knowing why that shooting at the lady was not
a good idea.

"Git the bliddy hell oot o' there!" Chiefie screamed, then
his English deserted him and he started screaming in Scottish
Gaelic.

"Madame?" Peck asked, with a politeness that sounded
eerie even to his own ears. She looked ready to kiss him. He
wasn't sure if he could keep from screaming if she did.

"Lasirenn, Lady of the Sea, is grateful to you. Even a goddess can need time to change form and wield magic against
such a one as Lebrun." Her grin was lewd. "Such vitality as he
had—it is a blade with two edges.

"But you bought me the time I needed. Alas, I cannot
reward you as a young man should be rewarded. But you are
also a sailor, and I say that you will sail the seas all your life
without harm."

Before Peck could decide if she'd really said what he
thought he'd heard, she leaped over the side. Peck ran to the
railing, and in that same moment Chiefie jerked the lanyard.
The first officer wondered if he was clear of the gun's line of
sight. He felt the wind from the passing of the twelve-pound
shell, but the target was elsewhere on the poop deck. The
ghouls had emerged from the passageway, and the first shell
tore into them with a gruesome *splat*. And while the shell had
missed Peck, the flying bits of ghoul did not.

Peck barely noticed. He was gaping at the great swell rising
up from seemingly infinite depths, lifting the ship. On a crown
of foam rode two figures, one a regal-looking Negro clad only in
tattoos and an enormous snake with glittering red eyes, and
the other—call it a mermaid. Certainly she had a fish's tail,
glowing in red and gold, blue and green, but from the waist
up, she was Madame Lebrun in all her splendor, wearing only
a chain of golden seashells, and as far beyond the world as
her companion.

The two figures vanished, and Peck felt one of the ghouls

gripping his arm. As it fumbled for his throat, he whirled and set to with fists, knees, and feet. His pistol joined the fight as soon as he had room to draw it, in the same moment that another shell whistled overhead.

✣ ✣ ✣

Chiefie hadn't ordered the second shot. It was the gun layer's whim, and he missed the figures in the water. The recoiling gun flew off its mount, smashing his right knee and crippling him for life. Meanwhile, the rest of the *Matthew Glendunning*'s crew dealt with the ghouls—the *zombies*, to use the Caribbean term—with pistols, iron bars, wrenches, and Captain Pahlen's duck gun.

Then they threw the remains overboard, fumigated the stokers' quarters, and bolted its door for the rest of the voyage.

Captain Pahlen, Chiefie, and Peck composed a log entry that said the Lebruns had died as the result of a jealous quarrel. Apparently engaged in some criminal scheme with Ribode, six stokers had mutinied, killing one of their own and the lieutenant. In an unrelated incident, the gun crew had fired two shots at a suspected German submarine.

Matthew Glendunning survived the First World War and was scrapped at Birkenhead in 1925.

David Peck was never shipwrecked, sick, or injured at sea, and died at the age of eighty-seven at the Sailor's Rest in Halifax, Nova Scotia.

Dawn Patrol

JOSEPH M. NASSISE

POISON GAS ATTACK ADDS TO GERMAN RANKS

Lieutenant Michael Baines read the morning's headline and snorted in disgust. *What else is new?* he thought wearily, wondering why the newsies even bothered printing the damn newspapers anymore.

It certainly wasn't for morale, with headlines like that.

He left the paper unread on the table where Masters, his aide, had dropped it earlier, pulled on his thin leather flying gloves, and stepped outside his tent into the brisk morning air. The sun was just rising, barely visible through the smoke and dust that seemed to be the only constants in this hellish landscape.

Despite the early hour, the home of the 94th Aero Squadron, Air Service, American Expeditionary Forces, was anything but quiet. The mechanics had taken that morning's aircraft out of the hangers and had them facing forward down the airfield. They were being prepped for the dawn patrol. Reports had come in during the night that the Germans had increased their flights in the sector. The enlisted men were already up, manning the machine gun pits that were scattered throughout the airfield, ready to protect the Allied aircraft on the ground in case of a German attack. If the enlisted men were up, so too then were the men of the hospital company, ready to drag the wounded to the hospital tents and the dead to the fire pits. The din of men at work filled the air around the flier.

For the second time that morning, Baines snorted in disgust at the remembered headline. *"Germans"? Hell, they'd stopped being Germans long ago. Aside from the High Command, there couldn't have been more than a handful of opposition troops still breathing at this point. An army of the ravenous dead didn't care about nationalism; all they wanted was their next meal.*

The last three years had been brutal. While the Allied powers had managed to hang onto the small stretch of ground won at the end of the Somme offensive, it had been held by only the thinnest of margins. Even now America continued to increase its support of the beleaguered French and British armies, sending fresh troops to fill the gaps being carved in the Western Front. As the death toll mounted and the ranks of the opposition swelled, Baines' countrymen continued to arrive, knowing that doing anything else could mean certain doom for everything from the English Channel to Moscow.

Baines himself had been involved in the war from the beginning, when the 94th had been activated at Villeneuve, in March of '18. Back then they had been flying French Nieuport 28s under the command of Luffberry and then Huffer. Not long after that came Rickenbacker and the Spad S.XIIIs.

Baines jammed a cigarette into his mouth and removed a battered silver lighter from his pocket. It had been a present from Rickenbacker after a particularly hairy dogfight. *Those were the days,* he thought wistfully, turning the lighter over in his hands and holding it up so that he could read the inscription in the thin morning light. *A Gentleman and a Flier,* it read.

Instead of cheering him, the sight of the inscription made Baines shake his head in near despair. Rickenbacker was gone and Marr with him. *At least they died in fires on the ground,* he thought grimly, *so they couldn't rise up to fight against us, as so many of the others have. Undead, like that bastard von Richtofen. . . .*

A glance at his watch told him that it was just after five. Another hour and there would be enough light in the sky to fly. Then the real day's work would begin.

It was time to get some breakfast.

The mess hall was set up in the old farmhouse. Jenkins, Smith, and Samuels were already there, waiting for the day's briefing.

Not that today's mission had changed much from yesterday's, or the day's before that.

The aerodrome at Toul was only twelve miles from the front lines. Nancy lay fifteen miles to the east, Lunéville twelve miles beyond that. The highway from Toul to Nancy to Lunéville ran parallel to the enemy lines and within easy shelling distance of their guns. This made it very difficult for Allied command to move troops or supplies up to the front in support of the men stationed there. It was the job of the 94th to patrol that stretch of highway and do what they could to keep it cleared, so that the infantry would not be cut off by a sudden forward assault.

Baines joined his men as they were sitting down to a breakfast of eggs and ham, courtesy of the good citizens of

Toul. As had been his habit since he had transferred in to command this unit two weeks ago, he ignored the food on the table before him and settled down instead with a cup of strong coffee. The men were discussing the opposition.

"Have you heard the latest?" asked Samuels. "A French flier who'd been presumed killed far behind the lines wandered back into headquarters today, nearly dead from dehydration and hunger, raving about Allied prisoners of war being fed to the German shock troops. He claimed to have seen giant camps established just for this purpose, that this feeding program is what is allowing the High Command to keep the zombies under control."

Jenkins scoffed. "He expected them to believe that? Be serious! Everyone knows it's that new gas they're using, the one our scientists can't figure out. The gas lets the commanders direct the zombies through mind-control. You know it as well as I do. How else can you explain the way the officers retain control or the fact that shock troops only attack us?"

The argument went round and round, as it did most every morning. Understanding how the Germans maintained control of their unnatural troops was an issue of the highest priority, for with understanding might come a change in the current climate of the war. Baines kept quiet throughout the discourse, nodding noncommittally over his coffee, until the subject of von Richtofen came up.

"What about you, Lieutenant?" Smith asked, keen on drawing the new commander into the conversation. "Why do you think the Baron came back from the dead with all his senses intact? Why isn't he a rampaging freak like so many of the others?"

Baines looked over at his squadron mate, his face a mask of seriousness. "That's top secret, Smith. I could tell you, but then I'd have to kill you. And if I did that, you'd come back as one of those monsters and wouldn't remember what I said anyway, so it really isn't worth all the effort, is it?"

The stricken look on Smith's face caused Baines to crack a smile, and the rest of the squadron joined in.

None of them noticed that the smile quickly left Baines' face or that he was no longer laughing with them. Mention of von Richtofen had soured the last of his good feelings for the day.

After breakfast, while the men were enjoying their coffees, a runner arrived with news that a telephone call had come in from Nancy. Several opposition machines had been observed in the air, headed in the direction of the aerodrome.

"Time to earn our pay, boys," Baines said as he led the way out of the mess hall and to the field.

The entire squadron flew Spad S.XIIIs, and while Baines missed his old Nieuport 28, he had to admit that the Spad was a nice substitute. Introduced in the fall of 1917, the Spad had a maximum range of two hours flying time and a ceiling of just under twenty-two thousand feet. Armed with two synchronized Vickers machine guns mounted in front of the pilot, it had quickly become the favorite of the fliers attached to the American Expeditionary Force. Rickenbacker had flown one until his death. Baines had switched to the same type of aircraft in tribute to his lost comrade.

Baines' mechanic had his bird in the lead position and wasted no time getting the propeller spinning after the lieutenant climbed aboard. Being the careful type, Baines spent a few extra moments before taking off to be certain everything was in proper condition.

He checked the tachometer first, noting that the engine appeared to be running normally as he opened the throttle then closed it back down again to an idle. His gaze swept over the fuel pump and quantity gauges. Next he moved to the physical controls. Waggling the control column, he tested the aileron and elevator movements, taking them through their full range. The rudder was a bit stiff, but he attributed that to the cold air and didn't give it another thought. A quick tap of the finger on the altimeter, a brush of his hands over the petrol cocks and magneto switches, and he was ready to go.

Baines lowered his goggles and gave his mechanic the thumbs up.

When the same signal was received from the rest of the pilots, the mechanic turned to Baines and swept his arm forward in a wide arc.

Baines advanced the throttle, watching as the propeller's flickering dissolved into a darkened haze. The Spad came to life, awkward at first as it tentatively moved onto the grassy field. The engine surged into a throaty roar, and the machine picked up speed and its forward motion smoothed out. The creaking and groaning of the undercarriage finally ceased as the Spad eased itself off the ground and into the chill air. Just a few short minutes later, the entire flight of four aircraft was up and headed east, following the roadway.

Baines flew low over the Allied lines, hoping the presence of his aircraft would provide some small measure of encouragement for the men fighting in the trenches below. A dark cloud of smoke rose from an area a hundred yards behind the

Allied positions, the stench of burning flesh wafting through the air along with it. The corpse fires were already busy this morning.

He couldn't imagine the horror the infantry had to face on a daily basis. How the Germans had gone so horribly wrong in creating that hideous gas was anyone's guess. He had heard so much about it; having to see its effect on what used to be your comrades had to be terrible. How much worse it must be to sit there, mere yards from the newly risen opposition forces, knowing that they saw you as that evening's dinner. It was more stress than he thought he would be able to bear.

Once when he was laid up in the hospital at Reims, Baines listened to the survivors of the battle of Soissons recount their experiences. The opposition had made assault after assault, charging out of that venomous green gas and through No Man's Land as fast as their rotting forms could carry them. The long miles of barbed wire became heavy with bodies and still they came, stepping over the reanimated carcasses of their comrades to rush the trenches and drag off those Allied soldiers unlucky enough to be near the break in the lines. The Allied troops fell back to the secondary and then tertiary trenches before the attack had been repelled.

While that was bad enough, the descriptions of the Allied dead waking up later the same night in the abandoned trenches and crawling under the wire to assault their former comrades was far worse. Baines remembered vividly the look on one private's face as he talked about the horror he felt bayoneting the man who he had just spent the last forty-five days huddled with in a foxhole, and of his shame at then having to burn the body in the bonfires to keep his friend from rising a third time.

Remembering it now made Baines shudder in fear.

As they neared the outskirts of town Baines started to climb, the possibility of being jumped at so low an altitude by the opposition's pilots outweighing his desire to boost the ground troops' morale. The haze was thick, the cloud cover fairly low, and Baines wanted some clear sky beneath their wings before they were forced to engage the enemy.

They were flying nearly half an hour when they crossed over into the opposition's territory. The observation balloon first appeared as a small, dark smudge against the blue-green earth below. Baines had the flight in formation at six thousand feet, with his plane in the lead, followed by Samuels and Smith flying parallel. Jenkins brought up the rear. Together, they formed an aerial diamond. They had been moving in and out of the partial cloud cover. When they emerged suddenly into the weak sunshine, Baines assessed the situation.

The balloon was one of the Caquot styles, a long, teardrop-shaped cylinder with three stabilizing fins. It was below them at an altitude of roughly twenty-five hundred feet, high enough that it provided a good opportunity for them to take it by surprise and get out again before the protective shield of anti-aircraft guns, machine guns, and the ever-present fighter screen could be brought to bear against them.

Baines craned his neck around from side to side, huddled against the rushing wind, searching the sky below for the fighter cover that he knew had to be nearby. The opposition never sent balloons aloft without fighters.

They had to be here.

And they were.

Both aircraft, Pfalzes by the look of them, were a few hundred feet below and to the south of the balloon, drifting lazily along as if they didn't have a care in the world.

Baines waggled his wings, getting the attention of his fellow pilots. He pointed downward at the balloon and then tapped the side of his head with two fingers. He pointed at the escort aircraft circling below and then at his men.

They understood. It would be their job to take on the opposition's aircraft while Baines went after the balloon.

They all circled back around, staying in the cloud cover until they could bring their planes into position, with the sun at their backs. Then, as a group, they fell into a rushing power-glide designed to bring them up on the enemy as swiftly as possible.

Baines watched the balloon grow larger and larger in his field of vision, his comrades forgotten as he focused on his attack. He covered more than half the distance to the other craft before the crew noticed his presence. He could see them floating beneath the wide bulk of the balloon in their wicker basket, frantically calling the ground crew on the field phone. Those on the ground were equally desperate, rushing to the mechanical winch in the hopes of getting the balloon and its crew pulled down out of the sky before Baines could reach his target.

With his Vickers guns thundering in his ears, Baines closed in. Even in the weak sunlight he could see the incendiary tracers arcing away from his aircraft and slashing into the balloon's fabric. Before he got too close, he pushed hard on the stick and banked his Spad, sending it around the edge of the balloon just as a bright arc of color danced along its surface. Seconds later, the sky around him was filled with the glare and heat of an explosion, as the gas inside the balloon ignited.

He looked back to see the observers jump out of the plummeting basket, taking their chances on surviving the fall rather than burning up with their craft. He roared in exultation as he watched the flaming balloon crash to the ground atop the moving forms of the ground crew.

That's four more of the bastards that won't rise again, by God!

For the first time since he began his dive, Baines noted the whine and crack of machine gun bullets coming from the troops below. He pulled back on the stick, taking his Spad up and out of reach of the weapons trying to claim his carcass for their masters.

When he was safely at altitude, he surveyed his chariot, finding a good number of holes in the fabric of his wings and several splinters gouged out of the leather-wrapped wood of the cockpit frame, but nothing that would suggest he needed to return to the airfield.

Satisfied, Baines looked down once more. Only one German biplane occupied the sky and even he wouldn't be up for long. A thick stream of black smoke poured from the German's engine, and Samuels doggedly hung on the Pfalz's tail, firing as he chased it around the sky. As Baines watched, the enemy aircraft suddenly collapsed on itself, falling away in pieces in a graceless ballet of destruction.

The flight regrouped, smiles on the faces of the younger pilots. Even the veteran Baines couldn't help but feel that this was going to be a good day. Both the balloon and the two Pfalzes had been downed in full view of the other pilots in the squadron, so there should be no quibbling with headquarters about credit for the kills. That made for a rather auspicious beginning.

They spent the next forty-five minutes edging their way farther into opposition territory, without a sign of another aircraft. The cloud cover had retreated a few thousand feet and Baines took advantage of it, hiding their aircraft up among its lowest reaches.

It was from this lofty position that they first spotted the damaged aircraft making its unsteady way across the sky below.

It was a lone Fokker Dr.1 triplane, painted a bright cherry red. A thin stream of black smoke was leaking out of the engine, and the pilot seemed to be having trouble keeping the plane on a straight path. His attention surely was focused on maintaining control of his aircraft.

There was only one Fokker Dr.1 triplane in the opposition forces that was painted bright red.

Manfred von Richthofen's.

When von Richthofen arose after dying at the hands of the Australian machine gunner Buie, he requisitioned another fighter identical to the one in which he had lost his life, had it painted the same blood-red color as his previous aircraft, and took to the skies the very next day. Unlike the troops resurrected in the trenches, von Richtofen retained full control of his senses and still possessed his uncanny ability to pilot his aircraft through seemingly unbeatable odds. At this point in his career, his victories numbered close to two hundred. To make matters worse, he'd somehow passed the secret of his mental stability on to the men under his command, until the entire Jagdgeschwader was filled with the undead.

To find von Richtofen in a disabled aircraft, flying all alone, was an opportunity that would never come again. Baines realized that it was also too good to be true.

Flush from their earlier victories and excited at the chance to down the legendary ace, the less-experienced pilots reacted without thinking. As if of one mind, they banked over and swept downward at the Fokker, leaving Baines to yell futilely at them from the cockpit of his own fighter.

The lieutenant had no choice but to follow them down.

He watched as the Allied aircraft closed in on the Fokker, their Vickers winking in the sunlight. They opened up as they moved within range. The opposition pilot continued to ignore them, a large mistake, and it wasn't long before Baines' squadron-mates blasted the plane right out of the sky.

It was at that point that the other side launched their carefully planned surprise.

From the west, out of the sunlight, came seven Albatross D.III fighters, their guns primed and firing before the others even knew they were there. Samuels was taken down in that first pass. One moment his Spad was there. The next it was not, replaced by a cloud of inky black smoke and small pieces of fluttering debris. Smith followed suit only moments later, though he did manage to take one of the Albatrosses with him.

From there it became a tenacious duel in the sky, the opposition forces swarming around the two remaining Allied planes in a deadly dance of death and destruction. Baines and Jenkins managed to give a good accounting of themselves,

together taking three more of the enemy aircraft out of the
fight in a dazzling display of marksmanship.

Baines had just begun to think that they might survive
this encounter when both of his Vickers jammed. One minute
they were roaring steadily, the next, nothing. Suddenly furious and more than a little bit frightened, he clawed at the
charging handles, trying to clear the mechanisms.

Once.

Twice.

Three times.

Nothing.

Knowing he would be no good in the middle of a dogfight
without operational guns, Baines broke away from the scrum
and climbed higher. With a little time, he might be able to fix
the problem.

The opposition let him go, choosing to gang up on Jenkins
instead.

From his higher altitude Baines watched the enemy aircraft make short work of his lone surviving subordinate.

Jenkins' Spad dipped and headed for the ground in an
uncontrolled spin, a clear sign that a well-placed bullet had
ended the pilot's life. Baines could watch no more.

When he turned his gaze away from the destruction
below, Baines recoiled in surprise to find a previously unnoticed aircraft sitting directly off his right wing tip. It was one
of the new Fokker D.VIIIs, the "Flying Razor Blades," as the
British pilots were wont to call them. The single-wing aircraft
was the current pride of the opposition's air corps and one of
the most deadly planes in the skies. It could outmaneuver,
outshoot, and outfly anything the Allies could put in the air.
This particular D.VIII was painted a bright red, the black Iron
Crosses on the wings and fuselage stark and menacing
against the brilliant background.

The aircraft was so close that Baines could see the opposition pilot clearly, right down to the scars on the man's right
cheek. Unfortunately, he recognized the airman, for Manfred
von Richthofen had gained quite a reputation in life, a reputation that had only grown in the years following his spectac-
ular death.

Instantly Baines understood the true nature of the trap to
which his squadron had just fallen victim. As he had first suspected, the triplane his fellow pilots had exuberantly chased
had been a decoy, intended to look like von Richthofen in
trouble, designed to pull the younger pilots into the fray. The
flight of Albatrosses that had dropped out of the clouds to the

rear of the Allied planes had been there to whittle down the Allied fliers, leaving Baines isolated and alone.

Ripe for picking by von Richthofen himself.

Baines did not wait around to see what the opposition ace intended to do next. He stood his aircraft on its beam and whipped around in a turn that came close to pulling off the wings.

Too good a pilot to be taken in so easily, von Richthofen chased Baines into the tight turn, so that the two aircraft were spinning around each other in a vertical helix. Looking directly "up" from his cockpit, Baines could see straight into the German's plane, where the other man was looking "down" at him in return. They flew that way for several moments, arcing around each other in opposite directions, their heads hunched against the chill wind and the centrifugal forces created by the movement, their craft getting closer to the ground with each revolution.

A sudden change in the sound of his engine let Baines know he had a bigger problem than the presence of the opposition's most deadly ace. It was barely discernible at first, just the slightest change in tone and pitch, but he was too experienced a flier to mistake its full meaning. His eyes swept over the gauges, where he immediately noted the change in fuel pressure. One of the attacks by the Albatrosses must have damaged his fuel line, something he hadn't noticed before now. He was about to pay the price for his negligence.

There was no way he could continue this battle in an aircraft with jammed guns and a faltering engine, and he knew it. He waited another moment, watching, until his opponent looked away for a split second to check on his own aircraft's controls, then broke out of the spin. Praying that von Richtofen would take the bait, he headed east in a straight line.

Like a cat with a mouse, the German had been waiting for precisely this sort of move, and he pounced—just as Baines had hoped he would. As von Richthofen's Spandau machine guns began hammering Baines' aircraft to pieces, the American launched his own surprise.

With a sudden turn, Baines arced his Spad over into what first appeared to be an Immelmann turn. As von Richthofen altered course to intercept his arc, Baines turned again, steering directly into von Richthofen's path.

The German reacted quickly, shoving his stick over in an attempt to get out of the way, but even his unnatural reflexes were not quick enough. The edge of the Spad's upper wing struck the top of the Fokker's as it passed beneath. Cloth, leather, and wood flew in all directions as the two aircraft collided and then tumbled uncontrollably away from each other.

There was nothing more for Baines to do now but surrender gracefully. He watched as the ground grew larger in his vision and swiftly came up to greet him.

✢ ✢ ✢

Baines awoke to find himself still strapped into the wreckage of his biplane. A large rat sat on his chest and gnawed the exposed flesh of his right cheek.

He twisted his head to the side and swung one arm across his chest, dislodging the audacious creature and sending others of its kind scattering through the debris. Ignoring for the moment the bite marks on his cheek, he raised his head and assessed his situation.

It was dusk. True night was less than an hour away. He lay half in and half out of the wreckage, his legs pinned inside the cockpit by a heavy weight, most likely the ruined crossbars of the forward fuselage. The smell of airplane fuel was strong, and the damp condition of his left sleeve and the lower half of his flight coveralls let him know that he had been soaked in the spill. The bulk of the aircraft rose over him on his right, one wing jutting into the air like that of a downed angel. It appeared his aircraft had gone down somewhere in the middle of No Man's Land; the ground around him was torn up and muddied, with shell holes and barbed wire stretching as far as he could see. Somewhere behind his aircraft he could hear the not-so-distant sound of artillery and small arms fire.

Off to his left, about a hundred yards away, lay the wreck of another plane.

Even in the dimming light, the bright red of its canvas was easy to see.

The sight was enough to spur Baines into action.

With both hands he traced his legs down into the darkness of the wreck, until he could feel the heavy crossbeam that kept him trapped in the cockpit. By simultaneously pushing with his legs and pulling with his hands, he managed to raise the obstruction just enough to free his legs and work them clear an inch at a time. It was hard going, but knowing his enemy could possibly be doing the same thing such a short distance away kept him at it until he was free.

By the time he had crawled from the downed Spad, the sun had set and the moon had risen, casting a strange, silvery luminescence over the landscape. The sound of gunfire had been replaced by a weird calm.

Free of the wreckage, Baines discovered that his left leg was broken just below the knee. The bone of his shattered shin gleamed in the moonlight.

Just about any other man would have given up at this point, but Baines did not. Gritting his teeth against the distasteful task, he shoved the bone back into place and used strips torn from his gasoline-soaked coveralls to lash his lower leg against a piece of wood scavenged from a broken wing spar.

After resting briefly, he levered himself to his feet with another piece of wreckage, this time serving as a crutch. Once up, he discovered he could move, though not quickly and not very well.

It took him more than an hour of slow hobbling, but at last he approached the remains of von Richtofen's aircraft.

The German ace was sprawled on the ground, with his upper body protruding from his ruined plane at an angle that left little doubt as to the condition of his spine. His left arm was also broken, with the bones at the elbow jutting through his torn flesh. Von Richtofen stared over his right shoulder and watched Baines approach.

The American stood over the downed German flier, neither man saying anything—Baines because he chose not to, von Richtofen because his dislocated jaw and lacerated throat prevented him from doing so.

After a long moment, Baines reached into the pocket of his coveralls and removed a small piece of metal. He gazed at it for a time and then squeezed it tightly in his fist.

"November 16, 1918. You ambushed a squadron of Allied fliers outside of Toulon." Baines voice shook with emotion. "You scored three kills that day—numbers 137, 138, and 139. I know, because I looked them up later to be certain."

The Baron shrugged his shoulders, as if to say, "So what?"

"I was there. I watched as you gunned down my squadron mates. I watched as their planes fell out of the sky, little more than burning piles of debris when you were finished with them. I watched as you turned your aircraft toward mine, intent on getting yourself another kill."

Baines knelt down beside von Richtofen. Holding the object in his left hand, Baines used his teeth to pull his leather flying glove off his right and let it drop, forgotten, to the ground beside him. With exaggerated care, he opened his hand so the other man could see what he held. The small, misshapen piece of metal lying on his palm was still identifiable as a spent bullet, its once-sleek form now crumpled and crushed.

At the sight of it, von Richtofen's eyes widened in understanding.

In a hissing whisper full of hatred, Baines continued: "For whatever reason, I managed to escape that day. I even managed to land what was left of my aircraft in a grassy field on the Allied side of the lines. The soft landing did me no good, though. I choked to death on my own blood before making it out of the cockpit, a bullet from your guns still lodged in my chest. Ten hours later an errant German artillery shell covered that forgotten little meadow in a haze of green gas—and I awoke to this hellish new existence."

Baines propped up von Richtofen's shattered arm and placed the bullet into his hand. Then, carefully, he curled the ace's broken fingers around it to hold it tight.

"It only took me a few hours wandering alone in the countryside to learn the secret. Imagine my surprise when I discovered that I was like you, one of the few who were strong enough to control the hunger." He laughed bitterly. "I discovered that my desire to see this day come was enough to give me mastery over it. I could forget the hunger and keep my thoughts focused on the only thing of any importance—my hatred for you, and for what you had done. Not only to me, but to my friends and to my countrymen. I've despised you with every fiber of my being. And that's been enough."

Baines settled down on the ground next to the Baron, his back leaning against what was left of the D.VIII, his boots propped up on von Richtofen's chest. "I spent months tracking you from the sidelines, biding my time, hiding among the living. Waiting for my chance to even the score. And now, at last, it's time to collect my due."

Reaching once more into the pocket of his coveralls, Baines took out that old gift from Rickenbacker—his silver lighter.

A torrent of unintelligible noise poured out of von Richtofen's mouth at the sight, and his good arm began flailing against the wooden framework that kept him pinned to the ground, but it was no use. Despite the fact that he didn't feel any pain from his injuries, the ace's body was too damaged to generate sufficient leverage to free himself.

"It's ironic isn't it, Manfred? Your love for Germany kept you going long after you should have died, giving you the chance to end my natural life. My hatred of you now gives me the chance to end your unnatural one. I'd say the score is even, wouldn't you?"

Baines casually flicked his lighter.

With relentless hunger—a hunger that both pilots recognized too well—the flames engulfed Baines' hand and leaped to his gasoline-soaked clothes, then spread from him to his helpless enemy.

Baines watched with a dead man's eyes as the flames consumed von Richtofen, until the fire finally took his sight and he could see no more.

Even then, the smile of satisfaction never left his face.

ACES UNDEAD

PETE D. MANISON

You thought you died in the battle, but you were wrong. The Androssi have a new trick in store for you. When you wake up alone and naked on the radiant red slab in one of their prison camps out in the Belt, you don't know what that trick is, don't even necessarily know that there *is* a trick.

But there probably is.

So you slowly rise into a crouch, looking this way and that with rapid turns of your head, the way your ancestors used to do when they thought a sabertooth tiger might be on the prowl. With the Androssi, it might be anything. Once they set fire to a nebula just to make a political statement. And then there was the erection virus. Yes, your adversary in this war can be inventive.

Did they get the rest of my squadron? you wonder as you slide off the edge of the red slab and stand up. The world spins left, then right, like there's a drunken Captain Ahab at the wheel and he's just spotted two Moby Dicks, one at ten o'clock and the other at two, and he can't make up his mind. Then he does, and you feel all right again, except of course for the searing pain behind your eyes, but you must remember your spacecraft did explode a few seconds ago. It looked nuclear, and, in any case, there's the decompression to consider. . . .

You realize then how cold you feel, how stiff your joints are. You touch your elbow and your fingers recoil from cold metal.

You look down.

No, wait—you really shouldn't look. Didn't they ever teach you about not looking down?

Oh, go ahead—*look* down. Yeah, you see it. Your elbows and knees—in fact, *all* your joints—have been replaced by metal ones. And your flesh, it radiates no warmth when you touch it. You raise one hand in front of your face. The hand is a bluish gray and the joints are copper colored and oily. You flex the hand. It works smoothly—perfectly, truth be told. This is something you should think about, but you have other things on your mind.

Speaking of which. . . .

That's it, over there in that jar—the one with the alien

hieroglyphics on it and the wires coming out through the top. Your mind. Well, your *brain*, anyway. But you have to wonder: If your brain's in that jar, what's inside your head?

Don't ask. You'd really rather not know, and I wish you'd start trusting me on this sort of thing.

"Robert," you mutter. It's coming back to you, but there's so much new stuff hitting you at the same time it's hard for anything to get in. "Robert," you say again, more forcefully. "Robert Morris."

And, yes, you have successfully remembered your own name. Don't laugh. That's pretty good for a man with his brain in a jar.

Then your captors come in.

The Androssi have been at war with humanity since shortly after the two spacefaring nations made first contact. The funny thing is, if you study the Androssi even a little bit you find that they have never had a single war in their entire history. They hadn't thought of such a simple idea as killing each other to take what they wanted.

They learned it from us.

Then they decided to eradicate us to prevent anyone else from learning the secret.

Which is pretty silly, if you think about it for a second. But that's the Androssi—silly to the, well, cartilage. Like the time they made that fake planet. Nothing but a gigantic inflatable sphere painted with tiny forests and cities and interplanetary ballistic missile silos. Did we nail *that* balloon with everything we had.

But it's not fun and games this time. They've hit your mothership hard, dropping megamegs all up and down its spine, and you've watched the five thousand scurrying men as they barfed up their lungs and farted out their intestines, and then you've seen the light of God come right through the bulk-head and into your face.

Wait. You're dead. You're stone cold dead, and your joints have been replaced because of rigor mortis. The Androssi must not know that rigor wears off after a day or so, which tells you how little they understand of human anatomy, which ought to tell you something else. And maybe that message is getting through after all, because you're starting to get really scared.

"Robert Morris," you say as the first Androssi enters the cell and walks toward you. "Terraforce Alpha. Serial number XXK-1711."

The sight of the Androssi makes your hair stand on end.

He's browner than most of them, and the three tentacles growing out of his mouth look very thickly muscled and strong.

Oh, and he has a cybernetic implant in his throat.

"Come with me," he says. His speech synthesizer turns out something like "Clumsy knee," but you can read the body language well enough to figure out what he wants.

He follows you closely. He doesn't have a burner on him, but he is carrying a small box in his middle tentacle. It has flashing lights on it. The box, not the tentacle.

And now you near a hatch. No, don't!

You always have to look.

Yes, those are human body parts the aliens are handling: legs and arms and even a few torsos. They are fitting the limbs together with more of those metal joints, stripping the excess flesh off them with instruments that resemble lobster claws and then passing the limbs down along some kind of assembly line. They look up when they hear you.

Hey, I don't blame you. I'd run for it, too. Fuck this party. These guys got no tunes, no munchies, and you would've noticed that they don't smell too good either, except that you haven't been breathing since before all of this began.

You run past your keeper and back the way the two of you came. He waves the box at you and you feel a strange compulsion to turn around and go back toward him, but you manage to slip around the corner, out of his line of sight, and the impulse goes away.

You're in a connecting tube between two large spherical structures hanging in space. The portholes come every few feet, and you stop at one to look. No, they're not structures. They're asteroids. And then you see Jupiter, a bright, steady presence in the background, and you realize where you are.

Asteroid prison camp. Forced labor mine. Where the Androssi take all the humans they capture in battle. Once you're this far out, baby, you're never coming home, no matter what their ambassadors say. Why do you think they have three faces?

You've heard all the talk, about how they're harvesting our solar system and using our own captured military and civilian populations to do the work. But you've also heard other rumors—rumors of torture and mutilation and experimentation. You never believed any of them—until now.

You get up then and you run for it. You're an ace fighter pilot. That's the only thing you need to remember. There has to be a way off this rock, and you're going to find it. There—the light of an approaching ship, growing brighter by the second. Head where it's going. Yeah, that's right. Through that hatchway. But why is it open so conveniently? You don't have time for questions—run!

Now into that long crawlspace. It's got rungs set too far apart for a human, but luckily there's so little gravity it doesn't matter. You just glide up it, and when you come out the other end you're in a space about the size of a barn. It's full of fighter craft that look like they're ready to launch.

And . . . nice. Some of them are Earth ships. The Androssi must have captured them or reconstructed them or maybe even copied them. Hey, you *can* fly out of here!

The ship you saw coming in is just taxiing off the pad. You grab a fighter and blast out of there so fast the incoming ship can't maneuver quickly enough to turn and block you. By the time you clear the bay doors, you're at full thrust and picking up speed fast. The station fires lasers, or you assume they do, since there's no way to tell unless one hits you.

Ouch.

Yeah, like that. You've lost one of your weapons clusters and two of your maneuvering thrusters. You laugh, taking the stick firmly down and to the right. Back in space at last. You love it and you know you do. And your flying is beautiful—as good as it ever was when you were alive. You use every trick you know. You pull out all the stops.

Down and out. Cut power, then lateral dart. Fire. Reverse thrust. Fire again. Now spin and drag the beam.

You got the turrets, but now they've launched fighters. You run off a quick scan while you switch weapons systems over to dogfight mode. The scan comes back: Androssi fighter craft, negative lifeforms. They've sent drones after you, the cowards. It's not like the Androssi, but you shrug it off and go with the maneuvers, balancing every move they make, then stinging them hard with an unexpected rear turret attack as you flash by.

Two fighters down, but they've sent half a dozen in all. You hit it, to gain some distance and separation. They think you're running. Ha! When three start to break one way and one the other, you stop, rotate 180 degrees, and punch it again. The loner is dead in your sights, but the computer lock fails at just the wrong instant. Go ahead—target manually. You practiced it enough in college when you were playing video games instead of studying.

There. Sweet. Now . . . wait for him. Yes! What superb reflexes you have.

You apply thrust to the right, which brings your ship along a curved path as you fire but straightens it out again when you stop. The other three are on you, so you drop a mine and do another burn. The two end guys break. The third hits the mine, and the shrapnel takes out all three.

And you, or nearly so.

Yeah, you're hit—hit bad. The controls respond sluggishly and power's dropping. You look down. There's a hole in you, all the way through your chest and abdominal cavity.

You keep flying. They don't assign wimps to flight duty. So you've got no guts. You make your own glory out here, any way you can, and as you steer your ship back toward the Androssi's prison asteroid, you know how your own daily dose of glory can be obtained today.

Uh-oh. Looks like they've sent out another wave of fighters. Well, that's just as good. Besides, you weren't really going to ram a prison asteroid, were you? What were you thinking? Oh, I forgot, your brain is still back in that jar.

And here come the fighters.

That's it! Show 'em what you got, flyboy. Left, right, stop, go. *Go!*

Awww. You was robbed. There go your engines. Duck and cover! There goes your fuel tank.

You're on fire.

But you never let go of that stick.

What a fine specimen you are.

✛ ✛ ✛

"What a fine specimen you are," says your Androssi captor. He's holding the flight recorder from your ship, and you know at once you've been had. It was all a setup. They brought you back to life, created a digital analog of your brain, and sent you out in a rigged ship against impossible odds. And you performed so *brilliantly* that they now know a little bit more about human beings.

You try to move, but find that you can't. They've got you in a restraint web this time.

But wait.

You burned. You *know* you burned. Yet now, when you look down, you see that everything seems to be just as it was before: Your flesh is gray and cold, and your metal joints are shiny with oil, and your brain is still in that same jar.

Wait again. You never had that mole before. And weren't you male?

"Oh, God," you say.

Brain tissue rarely survives a battle in space. In fact, it almost never does. But often there are bodies left adrift. So many bodies.

You remember then the room with all the limbs in it, where they were assembling human bodies. If *your* brain was the one in ten thousand that survived, then that makes it a pretty valuable thing to them. They can run any number of tests and experiments. They can copy your mind to reanimate a whole army of aces undead.

"Nooo!" you groan, tearing through the restraint web and flinging yourself toward the jar. Your feet trip you up, and you fall right into it. There's a bright light. Something hot pushes you back.

Force field. Your brain is undamaged.

"You motherfuckers," you say, which wouldn't ordinarily be considered polite conversation except that, with the Androssi, it happens to be literally true.

Suddenly you remember something else, like all of this has happened before or something. Maybe a lot of times before.

One of the Androssi comes up to you now. It's the same one as before, you think, and he's got that little flashing box. He holds it out toward you, extending his middle tentacle so far it looks like he ought to fall over. The light from the box flashes in your eyes. You feel one of the other tentacles reach inside your head and pull out some part of you that clicks when it moves.

There now, not to worry. He's just calibrating you for the next run. And then he'll give you a memory wipe, and none of this will have even happened to you at all. It'll all be new—except for the joints, which they do recycle when they can—and you'll probably never again come this close to knowing what use it is to which they are putting you.

Just do me one favor, will you? Try to hang on to this much: Next time, when I say don't look, don't look.

LAYABOUTS

SCOTT REILLY

A body lay sprawled in the road as I drove to work this evening. I swerved to avoid it, but I may have run over an outstretched hand. Fortunately, it was unlikely my car sustained any damage.

I called the hotline to report the incident. The operator said they would send a truck, but I doubted that they'd even follow up on the matter. We both knew the body had probably left the scene by then.

I really couldn't blame them. Cadaver Control was undermanned as it was. And night was coming. They were busiest at night.

When my beeper sounded I knew that, on my last day of work, I would be, too.

✛ ✛ ✛

Cars in the opposing lane of the narrow route through Valley Forge Park sped by me to my left. Up ahead was the fiery scene of an apparent car accident and the flashing blue and red lights of police cruisers. The vehicles in my lane were being turned around. A roadblock.

I stopped next to the state trooper directing the turnaround and rolled down my window.

"Sorry, sir," he said, "but there's a bit of a situation ahead." The air filtration mask hanging at the ready around the trooper's neck gave me a pretty good indication as to the situation. "I'm going to have to ask you to turn back the way you came and find another route."

I flashed him my badge.

"Zuit Suit?" he asked. I gave him an unappreciative scowl about the nickname, though he didn't notice. He had turned his attention to the car accident past the roadblock. "Must've been the deputy who called you guys, 'cause I doubt it was one of us."

"Our field office got a report of a potential sighting," I said. He looked back at me, and I nodded at the heap of mangled metal and the fire that had begun to billow black clouds of smoke into the late evening sky. "Just here to see that it's nothing you guys can't handle."

It was the trooper's turn to give a disapproving scowl.

Without waiting for him to wave me through, I drove past and pulled in next to a parked police cruiser, its door stamped *Montgomery County Sheriff*. The cruiser on its other side surely bore the markings of the Pennsylvania State Police.

I debated whether I should give Samantha a call. A quick one, to let her know I might be getting back late from work tomorrow morning. She had probably just arrived at the nearby Phoenixville Hospital to start what we jokingly called "the early graveyard shift," eight to four in the morning.

I decided against it and got out. If I did call, it would only serve to worry her. Especially since the reason I was likely to be late was the same reason we'd agreed that I would resign my job.

A silhouette framed by fire approached me, a massive man-shape that walked with a slight limp. I tensed and brought my hand to my shoulder-holstered handgun.

"Deputy Mathis," the figure said in a low, gravelly voice. "I was first on the scene and called it in."

"Agent Erschild," I said, relieved this tower of a man was a fellow law enforcement officer and nothing more. Nothing worse.

"You're earlier than I expected," the deputy said. His cool hand swallowed mine when we shook. I could detect the faint and all-too-familiar stench of rotting flesh on his uniform. I also noticed bloodstains.

"You okay?" I asked.

He brushed at the front of the beige shirt pulled taut across his bulky form. "Got bitten. No big deal, but I plan to head to the hospital anyway."

Judging by the amount of blood around his right shoulder, the deputy was probably trying to be some sort of tough guy and downplay his injury. Regardless of the severity of his wound, he'd be treated at the zombie trauma ward and could very well be attended to by Samantha.

"What do you know about the situation?" I asked.

"A dozen or so layabouts on the road over there. Likely the cause of this mess." He pointed down the road, fifty yards past the block and thirty yards from us. Two state troopers stood at opposite sides of a jumbled wreck consisting of four civilian cars. I could just make out another police car on the other side of the fire, blocking traffic from that end. Body parts littered the road. There were a couple other bodies, more or less intact, scattered among the pieces.

The two troopers stationed on our side of the wreck, across the double-lane strip of asphalt from each other, were securing the scene. They faced away from the carnage, shot-guns aimed in the direction of the woods that lined both sides of the road.

Night was falling, visibility diminishing by the moment. The troopers cast occasional glances over their shoulders into the blazing accident scene.

"Those two—" the deputy motioned toward the troopers "—said there might be at least two or three walkabouts in the woods." He cracked a smile.

One of the troopers spun and fired three shots into some-thing that belly-crawled along the ground. His target moved less, but moaned more. He fired another three shots into it before turning back to the woods.

I shook my head. "They said there *might* be walkabouts?"

Which was absurd. If there had been walkabouts around, either the troopers or the zombies would have been in pieces by this point, plain and simple.

The deputy remained smiling and shrugged.

He followed me to the trunk of my car. I didn't have much in the way of gear—certainly not everything I needed—but I had to make do.

I grabbed the jacket. It was the only part of the suit I had with me, but the black, high-gloss jacket was a far cry from having no protection. Light as a feather, tough as hell. And nothing soaks through.

I put it on and assembled the rest of my equipment. In the absence of appropriate headgear I wore a ski mask and a pair of green safety goggles. Goofy, I know, but it was better than nothing. I hoped things wouldn't get that messy.

I pulled out my favorite weapon, affectionately known as the Slammer. It looked like a baseball bat but was longer and wider, and slightly flattened along its length. It was made of lightweight steel, but weighted at the end. A sharp blade ran along the perimeter of its flattened edge. Sort of a cross between a bat and a sword.

In addition to my handgun and the Slammer, a shotgun and a pair of machetes rounded out my limited arsenal. I donned a throat mike and pocketed some extra ammunition.

"Too bad I can't stay and join the fun," the deputy said. "If not for the hospital . . ."

Witnessing a gear-up seems to make the gung-ho types think fighting zombies is fun. So it was just as well that he was leaving; one less person to complicate matters.

"I'll need to talk to you later," the deputy added. "After you deal with this little distraction."

"For your report or something?"

"Or something."

It figured. Gung-ho types also try to fish for an in with the agency, hoping to grease the tracks to becoming an agent.

I left him drumming his fingers on his cruiser's trunk.

The trooper I'd seen do the shooting earlier approached me as I neared the flaming wreckage. He was dressed in a full-body, police-grade zombie protective suit. Not as good as ZUIT-issue, but definitely better than what I had at the moment.

"Agent Erschild," I said.

He looked me over through the glass eyepieces of his air filtration mask.

"You ZUIT?" he asked.

I nodded.

He shrugged, no doubt skeptical of what I was wearing. "I'm Chen," he said. "That's Walters." He pointed to the trooper to the left of the fire.

"The deputy said you ID'd two or three walkabouts."

"Yeah. Saw them dragging people from the cars." He patted his shotgun and spread his arms to indicate his suit. "We were prepared for them, though. But the damnedest thing—they all left as soon as Walters and I arrived."

I gave him a doubtful look.

"I'm not shitting you or anything," Chen said.

"The deputy couldn't confirm your story."

"I don't see how. He was—"

Two shots in quick succession, followed by a scream, cut through the night. Walters, flailing, was being dragged by the hair into the darkness of the woods. The hulking form that had grabbed him was already in the shadows, so I couldn't make out much of its detail.

I sprinted toward his screams, Chen alongside me.

Before we even reached the burning wreck, the screaming had died out. Probably also the case for its source.

Chen fired wildly into the brush where the other trooper had disappeared.

"Walters!" he yelled and reached for more shotgun shells.

"Calm down," I said.

I holstered my handgun and unslung the shotgun. With only Chen to worry about, I could be more liberal with my application of firepower.

Using the high-intensity flashlight mounted under the shotgun's barrel, I swept a beam over the area where I'd last seen Walters. The light penetrated deeper into the darkness than the fire's flickering orange glow, but still no trooper.

A sudden shift in the wind's direction enshrouded us in a nauseating stench. The acrid smell of burning flesh and rotting corpses seared my nose hairs. My stomach convulsed in a pre-vomit shudder. The stench permeated the air and filled my lungs. A taste not unlike that of raw liver dipped in charcoal had me scraping my tongue against my upper teeth. I found myself sorely missing my own air filtration mask, regardless of my heightened tolerance for the smell.

Chen fell to his knees, yanked off his mask, and spewed his stomach contents onto the road top in a series of violent heaves. Case in point as to how ineffective most masks are after long-term or concentrated exposure.

The wind's direction changed again, granting us slight relief from the smell.

Chen drove his fist into the ground. "How can I help?" he asked, his mask back on.

"Head back to the roadblock."

We lucked out by not being attacked during his vomiting. The two of us sticking around would stretch that luck to its limit.

"You going in alone?"

"Hell no. I'm just bringing you out. Then we wait until reinforcements arrive."

"You're just going to leave Walters with those things?"

Motion to my left; I swept the shotgun-mounted flashlight to the area. Nothing.

"Hate to break it to you," I said as I searched the darkness, "but he's dead. If you don't want to be next, then I'd suggest you leave."

For a moment he may have thought I was bluffing, that if he charged into the woods after his friend I'd follow to back him up and save his life if necessary. Perhaps he thought I was a hero. He may have even thought that as a federal agent it was my duty.

A cold, hard stare, with the firelight and shadows dancing upon my grim scowl must have convinced him otherwise. It wasn't my job to save the suicidally stupid. And make no mistake: I wasn't a hero. Not with a wife and kid at home. The resignation letter folded up in my back pocket was proof of where my obligations lay.

Leaves rustled and I fired a shotgun blast toward the source. I wasn't expecting to hit anything, just giving the trooper incentive to move.

I saw him head in the desired direction. Then I heard sounds I always dreaded hearing at a site: the moans of the undead. The gurgling, primal, hungry, hollow, lusting moan-groans only the undead can muster.

A layabout slid along the ground in Chen's path, pulling itself with its arms, its limp legs dragged behind it. The thing's back was bare of flesh; the bones of its spine and rib cage were exposed. It lurched for Chen. Despite being well out of its range and capable of easily running around it, he stopped and fired five shots into the thing.

The vindictive fool.

Two walkabouts emerged from the fire, the remnants of their flesh cindered, falling off in sizzling black chunks.

Chen took aim at the larger of the two and opened fire. The walkabout staggered as each round drilled through its chest, but it continued its steady advance.

"Keep going," I said, rushing toward him.

In my periphery, I saw two dark, airborne masses. I ducked, dodging one, but the other got caught up between my feet. I crashed to the ground, dropped the shotgun, and came down hard on my left elbow.

I looked down at my right foot and saw what had tripped me. A severed leg, still oozing blood, had been thrown from the outlying darkness. I glanced over to the projectile I'd managed to dodge, watched it roll to a stop near the fire.

The head of Trooper Walters stared at me with eyes wide, mouth agape, his expression a mixture of horror and surprise. The opening at the top of his skull indicated the zombies had already had their fill of him.

More shots, as Chen tried to stop the advances of the two walkabouts.

I scrambled for my shotgun and fired at another layabout crawling from the fire. The shot obliterated most of its head. A second shot shredded its neck, and it moved no more.

A high-pitched cry. At first I thought it was Chen, but it came from farther away. The state trooper at the roadblock.

The road I drove in on was now deserted, the only lights coming from the police cruisers. Word must have gotten out to avoid the area. A news radio station's commercial flashed through my head: *We provide updates of zombie hotspots on the fives to keep you alive. . . .*

The roadblock was unmanned. The young trooper was likely dead and the hulking deputy had probably left already.

Another cry. This time it was Chen. He'd focused his attention on the two walkabouts that had emerged from the fire and forgotten about the first one, the layabout dragging itself. It had slithered up and taken a bite out of his calf.

He reflexively dropped his gun and reached for the wound. The zombie grabbed Chen's arm and pulled him down, then ripped his arm from its socket.

Then the other two walkabouts were on him. The largest one ripped the top off his skull with a powerful hand and tossed it aside. With both hands it grabbed the sides of Chen's head and pulled the trooper toward its face. It proceeded to gobble brain as if it were eating watermelon from the rind.

The underbrush alongside the road rustled. Twigs and branches snapped. All at once a wall of zombies emerged from the darkness. The flickering light from the fire made horrid faces more horrid.

Some crawled, some limped, some shambled. And damn, some walked.

A handful of layabouts weren't much trouble, but a dozen could be.

I counted at least three dozen zombies.

Worse yet, most of them were walkabouts. "Two or three of them" my ass.

Curiously, they encircled me instead of charging in an out-and-out onslaught of brain-lust. The heaviest concentration separated me from the roadblock, cutting me off from any working vehicles. This sizable contingent of active corpses, in various stages of rot and decay, surrounded me. Arms extended, jaws opening and closing in expectant fulfillment of their unnatural appetites, they should have had nothing but the thought of eating my brain on their minds. But, for some reason, they didn't rush me.

I didn't have time to worry about my good fortune, though. With each breath I risked vomiting. So I loaded two shells into the shotgun to replace the two I'd expended. I felt the reassuring weight of the Slammer against my back. I double-checked the machetes sheathed on each thigh and the handgun in its shoulder holster.

As the zombie horde drew closer, I had but one thought: *This was gonna get messy.*

✧ ✧ ✧

Layabout had originally been a descriptive term, not a formal classification. When layabouts first made their appearance, some two years ago, there was no need for classification.

In those early days, the occasional dead body would show up in an inappropriate place—sprawled on an elementary school playground, half under someone's car, two or three piled on top of each other in the middle of an isolated road.

Around the country, sightings for the first few months were so sparse that the corpses were believed to be part of some sort of coordinated prank.

There was no reason to suspect the dead bodies capable of independent movement. No reason to even think *zombies*, because the corpses never seemed to move. Then again, no one had any reason to examine them too closely. The local authorities simply stuck them back in the ground.

Then scattered reports began to surface in the media about people seeing dead bodies moving in the night. Their movements were described as slow. Some crawled, some dragged themselves, and a few managed short periods of shuffled walking. That sort of thing. Before long, the term *zombie* was bandied about. By then, sightings of the risen dead had become almost commonplace.

Panic was, quite naturally, the primary worldwide reaction. But it soon became clear that with reasonable precautions came reasonable safety. No one had been directly harmed by the zombies, much less killed. Overall, the menace seemed slight. The panic peaked and soon tapered off.

The undead were more of a nuisance than anything. Like vermin, the population of which grew to epidemic proportions.

Still, they were all just a rather lethargic bunch. Quite frankly, most of their time was spent laying about. Hence the nickname, which gained widespread use within that first year.

The government established the Zombie Uprising Investigation and Termination Agency, whose agents, by virtue of their specialized uniforms and their acronym, were dubbed "Zuit Suits." The purpose of the agency was to investigate the origin and nature of the zombies and to lend assistance to local agencies—Cadaver Controls—in troublesome situations.

It wasn't until the start of the second year that it became clear how bad the situation was going to get. That's when the world became aware of a new type of zombie.

These new zombies were, to put it mildly, more *active* than their layabout kin. They walked. Some could even run.

Walkabouts had emerged.

Their emergence also marked a change in those zombies still classifiable as layabouts. The once-aimless layabouts had developed a purpose, one shared insatiably and unrelentingly by the walkabouts.

That purpose, of course, was the consumption of living human brains.

✛ ✛ ✛

The first shotgun blast tore the head off a saggy-faced walkabout and its one-eyed neighbor.

I had one way out of the situation and that was to head for the cars and the main road. But damned if the layabouts and walkabouts weren't stacked even deeper in that direction.

As ridiculous as it sounded, I couldn't help but think of this as an ambush.

I continued pumping buckshot into the undead vermin. They were fifteen feet away and closing. Decapitation was the surest way of re-killing the zombies, so all my shots were headshots.

The fire from the accident was dying down, and night was wrapping itself around me like a noose. Without the fire, my field of vision was quickly becoming limited to what the moonlight and the conical beam from my flashlight revealed.

"Hey, pardner. You got your ears on?"

For a horrible second I thought the distinctly Texan drawl of Hank Boone, my partner, came from one of the zombies. With relief I realized that his voice came from my earpiece.

"Got 'em on for now," I replied. "Very soon they'll be tasty appetizers."

"You starting the party without us?"

I fired another shot that exploded the head of a more recently deceased body. Brain and shards of skull splattered me. The smell of decay hit me like an anvil to the stomach, and I ripped the ski mask and goggles off my face in time to vomit my dinner. I let loose with another shotgun blast while still hunched over.

The next pull of the trigger produced a dull *thump*. Empty, and no time to reload.

"Shit! Could use some help here," I said, reaching for my handgun.

"ETA two minutes," Hank said, his voice hard and serious. "Sitrep?"

The taste of bile was still thick in my mouth. I spit and began firing three-round bursts of hollow points from my Beretta 93R. I was popping heads left and right, but there were still too many of them.

I gave Hank a quick situation report: "Eighteen still active. Too many of them walkabouts."

Bony fingers scratched at my shoulder. I spun and emptied the last six rounds of my clip into a grotesquely swollen face. More splatter. More stench. I steeled myself against the urge to puke again.

In one fluid motion, I reloaded and continued firing. They

were now five feet away. Things were just about to become close quarters.

Over the clatter of my own gunfire I didn't know if Hank had replied to my last message. But the team had better arrive soon if they were going to make a difference. I communicated the gravity of my situation with the unofficial agency battle cry, a phrase that should bring my support to me as fast as they could manage:

"Slammin' time."

My handgun clicked empty, and I tossed it to the ground even as I unsheathed the Slammer.

Just in time.

Rotten hands were almost on me when I tightened my grip on the Slammer's handle, raised the weapon to the starless sky, and brought it down onto the mud-caked skull of an obese walkabout. The Slammer's blade sliced clear through the head and into the thing's neck.

I planted a boot on its chest and pushed off to free the weapon. They were grabbing at me by then. I swung baseball-style, decapitated two of them, and lodged the blade into the chest of a third. I had a machete out to sever its head before it had a chance to pull the Slammer from me.

This was one fine mess I'd gotten myself into, pun and all. Samantha's voice filled my mind, asking me how, with a newborn daughter, I could jeopardize my life each day. All the protests I'd made, all the reasons I'd given, fell away now. I realized the wisdom in what she'd said and wished I'd heeded her sooner.

Freeing the Slammer once again, I slashed off hands, arms, legs, and heads. Anything within range.

They still came at me. A crawling layabout grabbed at my calf and readied to bite me. I crushed its skull with a blow from the Slammer's blunt side.

Then one did bite me. I felt its teeth dig into my left shoulder, but thanks to the near impenetrability of the jacket, the walkabout was unable to break skin.

I shoved away the maggot-ridden corpse, its jaws still chomping, and slammed its chest. Its internal organs slid out of the wide, bloodless gash.

"Get clear!"

It was Hank's voice, this time in person. The team had arrived.

"Get clear!" he repeated.

Easier said than done.

I sliced the groping hands from a layabout that looked like

it had been someone's grandmother. I finished it off with a clean beheading.

If the team was prepared, I stood a chance.

I dared a deep breath. The circle was thinnest toward the treeline on this side of the road, directly behind me—the least logical path of escape. So I took a quick step in that direction and launched myself into the air.

I tackled two zombies, the three of us falling into a tangle on the ground. I elbowed one of them off me and scrambled to my feet, but not quickly enough. The other one pulled me down before I could react.

It rolled over onto me, straddling my chest. The zombie's long, dark hair dangled into my face in stinking clumps. Its still-fleshy hands clamped down on my throat.

By my side I felt the Slammer, took it by its handle, and swung at the walkabout, caving in its face and knocking the thing over.

"Clear!" I yelled hoarsely, even as another zombie jumped at me.

Fully automatic gunfire erupted, peppering the remaining layabouts and walkabouts with lead. The zombie that had just jumped at me was caught in the first volley. Its head exploded like a jelly-filled balloon. Dead flesh and rotting innards rained down on me.

Silence followed, broken after a moment by the distinct report of a sniper rifle. Someone on the perimeter was taking a shot at something that had escaped the firestorm.

Two people, fully suited, rushed in and lifted me off the ground by my arms. They dragged me from the pile of swiss-cheesed zombie parts.

My pants were soaked through with zombie muck. Slimy chunks coated my face and neck. The smell of rot and decay was not just on me, but also absorbing into me—my clothes, my hair, my skin. Breathing sparingly, through my mouth, was no longer enough to combat the smell.

I heaved. And heaved again. When there was nothing left, I dry heaved. Then everything went dark.

✛ ✛ ✛

When I came to I was on my back, naked, wrapped in a blanket. I recognized the interior of the team's renovated ambulance. As I sat up, I clutched my abdomen, and winced again at the movement of my left shoulder and elbow. The ambulance's back doors were open, and I could see I was still at the scene.

"Dang, man," Hank said as he approached the ambulance. "You got some stank on you." He had his head turned to the side and his nose scrunched.

"No worse than you on one of your better days," I said, and laughed weakly.

My stomach was sore as hell. I'd been stripped and power washed, but that wasn't doing much for the smell. I touched the top of my head with a shaky hand and felt nothing but skin. They'd shaved me bald.

"That's fifteen bucks for the haircut."

"Oh, I'll pay you back all right." I hopped out through the double doors and found my legs unsteady. I supported myself against the ambulance for a moment before being able to stand on my own. It wasn't lost on me how close I'd come to dying. How close I'd come to leaving Samantha and baby Jessica alone. She was right in wanting me to leave my job.

"What'd I miss?" I asked.

"You been out fifteen minutes. I cleaned you up as best I could. Alpha and Bravo teams canvassed the area for walkabouts. Took down a whole load of 'em. Both teams are on their way back now. Locals should be here soon to take care of this mess."

"Erschild, Boone, you guys are going to want to see this." ZUIT Agent Nguyen called for the two of us from the deputy's police cruiser. The sight of the car surprised me. Hadn't the deputy left for the hospital?

Hank followed a step behind me in the event my legs didn't remain steady.

On the ground at the rear of the cruiser was the brain-eaten corpse of a young state trooper, the one who had first tried to turn me away from the scene. Two hollow holes stared up at us from where eyes should've been.

"I found him dangling from the trunk," Nguyen said. "The trunk lid had been shut over his right arm."

I looked to the body and saw that the arm was mangled at the elbow. Someone had been trying to shove him in, but got interrupted. Or had left him there as a pointer.

"And I found these—" Nguyen held out a gloved right hand; two eyeballs were balanced on his palm "—resting on top of the trunk. Like some kind of message."

Hank and I edged closer to the already opened trunk. Nguyen lit its dark interior with a flashlight. The bright light revealed another corpse, this one naked. And brain-eaten, of course.

"Picture ID left in the trunk was for a Deputy Sheriff Victor

Mathis," Nguyen continued. "Wasn't that the guy who called in the initial sighting? Victim's face matches the pic."

I frowned. It may have matched the pic, but this was not the guy who introduced himself to me as Deputy Mathis. I thought back to the deputy with his bloody, ill-fitting clothes, his cool hand, the faint scent of death on him. . . .

"What's a doin' pardner? You look like you've seen a ghost."

"Not quite a ghost," I said, "but dead just the same. And I didn't just see it. I spoke to it and it spoke back. It was impersonating Mathis."

"What the hell are you talking about?" Nguyen prompted.

"*Hell* might just be what's broken out, sir. If I'm right, we're up against something horribly new: talkabouts."

Hank gaped. "Goddamn zombies that talk?"

Things were gonna get a whole lot messier.

"Look alive, guys," Agent Blevin said, coming up behind us. "Just got off the horn with command. There's activity at a nearby hospital. We're to join another team already en route."

"What hospital?" I asked.

Blevin hesitated. "Phoenixville."

Samantha.

"The zombie pretending to be Mathis said something about going to a hospital," I said, turning toward the equipment van. "This is no coincidence."

Hank took a hold of my arm.

"Kyle, you're in no condition for this," he said. "Especially if this is some sort of new—"

I shook off his hand.

"My wife might be in danger. You know I can't sit on the sidelines."

"Then what about this?"

From the chest pocket of his uniform, Hank pulled a Ziploc containing a folded sheet of paper. The paper was slightly stained, but I recognized it as my resignation letter. He must've found it when they stripped me.

I snatched the baggie from his hand. Of all the reasons I'd given Sam why I should stay on the job, I'd somehow missed the most important: I was protecting her and Jessica, too. I hoped she would see that now. If not . . .

Forgive me, Sam.

I pulled out the letter and shredded it.

"Let's go," I said. "We've got work to do."

PROVIDER

TIM WAGGONER

"Looks like we got a flopper over there," Kenny said.

Robert nodded. He put Smoky Joe into low gear and pressed on the brake. The truck juddered to a stop—damn thing was overdue for a tune-up—in front of 3298 Chestnut Avenue. There was a large oak tree in the yard. Its branches stretched out over the street and its leaves, while still green, were tinted gold, red, and brown. Not quite ready to start drifting to the ground yet, but almost. Fall was Robert's favorite time of the year. It made him think of beginnings, much more so than January first. There was the first day of school and the start of football season, of course. And given the way stores advertised, it was the unofficial start of the Christmas season, too.

At least, that's the way it had been, back when the word *dead* meant a corpse that didn't move, didn't walk, didn't try to sink its teeth into the living.

Robert put Smoky Joe in park, but he didn't turn off the ignition. They needed to leave the truck running so the furnace would keep burning. If it went out, it was a bitch to get started again, and if the temperature in the back got too low, the furnace wouldn't be able to do its job effectively. He opened the door and stepped down to the street. He removed his gloves from the pocket of his coveralls and put them on while he waited for Kenny to join him.

Kenny walked around the front of the truck. He never walked around the back if he could avoid it, and Robert couldn't say as he blamed the man. Kenny already had his gloves on, his clear plastic face mask, too.

"I can't believe you still wear that goddamn thing. You've been on the job six months now."

"Five," Kenny corrected. "And I don't care if I'm still doing this stinking job five *years* from now, I'm gonna wear my mask—and I don't give a shit what anyone says about it." Kenny's breath caused condensation to mist the inside of the mask around his mouth.

Robert thought the breath-fog made him look kind of stupid, but he didn't remark on it. No one commented on basic biological processes anymore, whatever they were, not even burping or farting. They were signs that you were alive, and no one made fun of that.

Kenny was a skinny middle-aged man with a scraggly white mustache and wispy white hair that brushed the tops of his shoulders. He had long, tapering fingers—hidden by his work gloves at the moment—that constantly trembled. Robert didn't know if that was due to stress or whether Kenny had a drug or alcohol problem. Though these days the real problem for users was getting hold of recreational chemicals.

Greasy black smoke curled forth from the chimney pipe atop the truck, and flecks of ash drifted through the air. In addition, a nauseating odor somewhat like a backed-up sewer filtered through the neighborhood. Not so many years ago, people would've complained like hell about the pollutants and the stench Smoky Joe pumped out. But that was in the old world. Today, there weren't any such things as environmental protection laws. Well, not unless you counted the kind of work people like Robert and Kenny did.

"Let's go take a look," Robert said.

Kenny grunted assent, though he didn't look too pleased.

They walked up to the oak tree and examined the flopper bound to the trunk. He was held fast against the bark by strong rope, but whoever had put him out hadn't slipped a muzzle on him. The thing gnashed black teeth at them, straining forward, eager to bite off a hunk of flesh. Robert looked into the corpse's eyes but they might as well have been made out of glass for all the emotion they displayed. They were fish eyes, dead eyes.

"Fresh one," Robert commented. No visible wounds, no sign of rot. "Probably died of a heart attack or a stroke last night."

"I don't give a shit what killed him," Kenny said. His voice had a strained edge to it, as if he were on the verge of hysteria. He always sounded like this when they had to deal with a flopper. "I hate it when they tie them up like this."

The preferred method of preparing someone for pick-up was to put a plastic muzzle over his mouth so he couldn't bite, then to bind his wrists, ankles, and legs with plastic ties. Prepackaged kits were readily available and free to any resident. Robert and Kenny had a bunch stashed under the seat of their truck. They'd handed out four kits so far today during their rounds.

"Some people can't bring themselves to truss up their friends and family like a bag of trash," Robert said. Though once they Went Bad, as the euphemism went, that's exactly what they were. A scene from an old Monty Python comedy flashed through his mind then, Eric Idle pulling a wooden cart through the muddy streets of a medieval village, ringing a bell and shouting, "Bring out your dead!" He wondered how long it had been since he'd seen a movie. Years, he supposed.

"And treating them like *this* is any better?" Kenny nodded toward the flopper, who was straining more vigorously against his bonds. He started making a high-pitched keening sound in the back of his throat. It was the sound deaders made when they were hungry—and they were always hungry. Luckily, deaders weren't any stronger than the living, and no matter how hard the flopper struggled, he wasn't going to get out of those ropes. Whoever had tied him up had done a good job of it.

He looked to be—to have been—in his early thirties, black hair, clean-shaven, and thin. Then again, most everybody was thin these days, since food wasn't nearly as plentiful as it used to be. He was dressed in a blue suit, white shirt, maroon tie, and polished black shoes. Sometimes relatives dressed them up, like they used to do when the dead stayed still and were buried in boxes beneath the ground.

"Why couldn't they have done us a favor and bashed his skull in?" Kenny asked. Robert noticed his hands were trembling again, so hard it looked as if he might vibrate right out of his work gloves. Rumor had it that before he'd gone to work as a pick-up man, Kenny had a girlfriend who'd Gone Bad, and he'd had to put her down. Robert had never asked—it wasn't the kind of thing you *could* ask—but if it were true, he wondered why Kenny would do this kind of work. As a way of expunging his guilt, maybe? Or perhaps he was one of those people who was drawn to that which terrified him, like a moth to the flame.

"It's not easy to desecrate the body of a loved one, even when you know it is going to Go Bad soon," Robert said. The only sure ways to kill a deader were to destroy the brain or burn the damn thing to ash. Not too many folks could bring themselves to do either to the remains of someone they cared about.

Kenny didn't respond. He glared at the deader, fear and disgust mingling in his gaze. "Fucking zombie," he muttered.

Robert didn't respond. Instead, he turned and walked back to Smoky Joe. He opened the toolbox bolted to the side of the truck and pulled out a rusty crowbar. He walked back to the oak tree, his thick work boots thump-thump-thumping on the ground.

"Oh, man," Kenny whined. "Can't we use the gun?"

"He's an easy target. No need to waste the ammo." He held out the crowbar to Kenny. "Would you like to do the honors this time?"

"Hell, no. I got the last one."

Kenny hadn't gotten the last one, but Robert decided not to make an issue of it. "Better step back then."

Too bad this fellow's family didn't truss him up right, Robert thought. If they had, then Kenny and he could've popped the flopper into Smoky Joe's furnace without having to "kill" him. Ah, well. Every job had its shitty side, he supposed.

He glanced at the house. The blinds were closed, and he didn't see anyone peeking out. Good. It was easier when relatives weren't watching. Robert took aim and swung the bar at the deader's head. Metal struck hair, flesh, and bone with the same sickening sound as a sledge hammer smashing a watermelon. The deader jerked and shuddered with the first blow, but it took three more before the flopper finally stopped moving.

When he was finished, Robert lowered the crowbar. His arm was tired and he was breathing heavily. He needed to get more exercise. He wiped the crowbar off in the grass, then held it out to Kenny.

"No way am I touching that fucking thing, man."

Robert was starting to lose his patience. "You're a pick-up man, damn it. Do your job."

Kenny looked as if he might protest further, but in the end he grabbed the crowbar and headed back to the truck.

"Get a knife out of the toolbox while you're at it, will you?" Robert called over his shoulder. "These knots look pretty tight, and I don't feel like messing with them."

"Yeah, yeah," Kenny muttered.

Robert looked down, saw that the front of his coveralls was splattered with blood. He checked his gloves, saw a few more splatters. Despite razzing Kenny for wearing his face mask, Robert now wished he'd taken the time to put his on. No one was really sure why the dead came back, or why their bite could make someone living Go Bad. He'd heard lots of theories over the years—a genetic weapon cooked up by one government or another, microbes brought back by a space probe, even a mutation of the AIDS virus. But whatever the root cause, they did know one thing: It was infectious as hell, and if you weren't careful, you could Go Bad, too.

He removed his right glove, reached nervously up to touch his face . . . and found it dry.

Robert let out a breath he hadn't known he was holding. Looked like he was going to stay human another day. He put his glove back on, grabbed hold of the corpse under the armpits, and began dragging it toward Smoky Joe.

✢ ✢ ✢

Come lunchtime, Robert and Kenny sat at a wooden bench in the park. Smoky Joe was parked nearby, engine idling, furnace chugging away, doing its best to reduce Blue Suit to a sooty smear. It wouldn't take long.

Joe was expensive to operate, especially these days, when fuel was difficult to come by. But the town council thought Joe was worth it. The truck might not be as efficient as gathering deaders in the back of a pickup and taking them outside of town to burn en masse—something the hunting patrols did whenever there wasn't enough fuel to run Joe—but the old truck was more psychologically comforting. Joe was like a slice of life from the time before, when cities and towns were able to provide trash service, recycling, and yard waste pick-up. That's why they'd given the truck a nickname, to make it friendlier. The kids in the town had even come up with a song which began "Here comes old Smoky Joe, huff-puffing down the street. . . ."

Robert knew they couldn't keep the truck going forever. The fuel would run out eventually, and so would replacement parts. But as long as Joe still rolled, Robert intended to be behind the wheel, huff-puffing along.

Both men had brought their food in plastic grocery bags; they could be re-used more often than paper ones. Kenny had a hunk of coarse bread, an apple, a bit of cheese, and a bottle of water. Robert had the same, with the addition of a small piece of jerky.

Kenny made a face as Robert bit into the dried beef. "I don't see how you can eat that with the truck so close. I can barely choke down my food as it is, what with that smell in the air. But there's no way I could keep down any meat."

Robert shrugged. "Man's got to keep his strength up. Besides, it doesn't have much taste anyway." He held out the rest of the jerky. "Want to try it?"

Kenny paled and held up a hand. "Hell, no!"

"Suit yourself." Robert took another bite and chewed methodically. He liked eating lunch in the park. Not only was it pleasant—though since the place hadn't been kept up for years, the grounds had become overgrown with weeds and bushes—it was safe. At least, relatively so. There weren't as many roaming deaders as there used to be, thanks to the efforts of the hunting squads that patrolled the town day and night, executing any deaders they saw. The pick-up men helped, too, disposing of the deaders the patrols left in their wake, along with those put out at the curb by individual residents. But if you were going to be out in the open for any length of time, it was only smart to pick a place where you could see around you in all directions, so you could spot a deader before it got too close. They usually moved slow enough that you could avoid them if you saw them in time. *If.*

Robert looked at a nearby swing set. There were two regular swings, and one baby swing.

Kenny noticed where he was looking. "Thinking about your kid?"

Robert nodded. "It'd be nice to be able to take him to a park so he could swing, go down the slide, play in the sandbox. . . ."

"Maybe someday. They have to find a cure eventually, right? Then it'll be safe for kids to play outside again."

"Sure." But Robert didn't believe it. Supposedly there was some semblance of a government in D.C. again, but since there were no network broadcasts anymore, just a few local radio channels that transmitted infrequently, news was hard to come by. If there was a government again, he guessed they probably were working on a cure, but that didn't mean they'd ever find one. Maybe whatever it was that brought the dead back *couldn't* be cured, not by science anyway.

"How's he doing? Your kid, I mean. What's his name again—Bobbie?"

"Yeah. He's fine. Just started crawling last week."

Kenny frowned. "I thought he was already crawling. I remember when we first started working together, you said—"

"Walking," Robert interrupted. "I meant he just started walking."

Kenny looked at him for a long moment, his expression unreadable. Finally he said, "Sure, man," and turned his attention back to his lunch. After several minutes, he said, "There's gonna be a dance in the basement of the Methodist church Saturday afternoon." Not at night; nothing took place at night anymore. "You think you 'n' Emily might come?"

"I doubt it," Robert said. "Emily doesn't like to go out much. She doesn't feel safe outside the house, you know?"

"Yeah. Too bad. Should be a good time."

They continued to eat in silence, and when they were finished, they climbed back in Smoky Joe and resumed their rounds.

✛ ✛ ✛

It was closing in on dusk by the time Robert turned onto Mapleview, the street where he lived. It felt as if his bike were harder to pedal than usual, and he made a mental note to put some air in the tires before he left for work tomorrow. He had a small bag of groceries in the basket attached to the handlebars—nothing vital: a couple light bulbs, some more jerky, a Mason jar full of moonshine—and he cursed himself for taking the time to stop at the general store set up in the city building. He should've waited until his day off to go shopping. Now, he was still outside with the sun dipping toward the horizon. Deaders, while active twenty-four hours a day, were harder to see at night, and therefore that much more dangerous.

He pedaled harder, passing houses with boarded-up windows and lawns wild with tall grass. Deaders could break through glass, and lawnmowers needed gasoline, which no one would dare waste on something so frivolous as cutting grass. As he rolled by the houses, he wondered how many of them were still occupied. He realized he had no idea. People tended not to leave their houses anymore, unless they absolutely had to. He hadn't seen some of his neighbors for months, a few not for years. The only ones he knew for sure were gone were those he had picked up during his rounds and fed to Joe's furnace.

He turned into his driveway, stopped, and got off. He carried the bike up the front walk and onto the porch. His windows, too, were boarded up, and not for the first time he thought what a depressing sight they were to come home to—like his house had long ago been abandoned, and he a ghost come to haunt it.

He unlocked the door, carried the bike and his groceries inside, then closed and locked the door quickly. No one let doors stay open and unlocked for longer than they had to, not anymore. He propped the bike against the wall next, then moved through the gloom to the dining room. He lit the oil lamp that sat in the middle of the dining table, and turned the flame low. Deaders were attracted to light, probably because they knew that light meant live folks were about. Robert was confident deaders couldn't break into his home, but he didn't want to take a chance, so he made sure to keep the lights to a minimum at night.

He walked into the kitchen and put the plastic grocery bag—the same one he had carried his lunch in—on the counter. He heard a soft, high-pitched sound, not unlike the one that had issued from the throat of Blue Suit that morn-ing. But it was muffled and he was able to ignore it. He opened a cupboard, took down a plastic jug of water, and poured himself a glass. Water was distributed at the high school once a week, and going to fetch his share was one of the few times Robert drove his car.

He got a baggie of dried peaches, took them, some jerky, and his water into the living room. He set his dinner, such as it was, onto the coffee table. Then he walked to the entertain-ment center and turned on the battery-powered stereo. First he tried to see if any of the few remaining radio stations were broadcasting, but none was. He switched the stereo to CD and put in a David Sanborn album. He kept the volume low, of course, and returned to the couch to eat his supper.

He listened to the music, closing his eyes to concentrate on the sound of Sanborn's sax more fully. He wondered if the musician were still alive, wondered if he were playing some-where right now, knew there was no way he'd ever know. He considered breaking out the 'shine he'd picked up today, maybe getting a little mellow before bedtime, but the thought of alcohol—especially the paint stripper that passed for booze these days—didn't sound good just then, so he just sat and listened to Sanborn play.

As the music continued, he became aware of another sound intruding—that soft keening, almost like the sound a cat might make, but higher, more . . . human. He tried to shut it out, even risked turning up the volume on the stereo, but no matter what he did, he couldn't ignore it. Finally, he switched off the stereo in frustration, which in the end was probably a good thing, since it would extend the life of the bat-teries. He walked into the kitchen and stopped at the base-ment door. He hesitated for a moment, then put his ear against the wood and listened.

At first, he didn't hear anything, and he began to hope that maybe tonight he'd be able to pretend there was nothing in the basement. But then the keening started again, louder this time. That meant they were closer to the door.

He went into the kitchen, fetched a flashlight from a drawer, and returned to the door. There was a small panel set at eye level, and he undid the latch and slowly opened it. He took a step back—he *always* did—even though there wasn't any need. Before he'd installed the panel, he'd removed the basement stairs. There was no way they could get to the door, not unless they stacked boxes to climb on. There were all sorts of boxes down there, junk he and Emily had never gotten around to unpacking when they'd moved. But he wasn't especially worried; deaders' bodies still worked, after a fashion, but their brains stayed dead. They retained enough instinct to hunt for food and to hide from the patrols, but that was about it.

Still, taking a step back didn't hurt, did it?

He waited a moment, and when greenish gray-skinned hands did not thrust through the open panel, he stepped forward, clicked on the flashlight, and shone it through the opening. As always, his nostrils detected a faint odor that reminded him of a reptile house at the zoo. It was the stink of seasoned deaders, ones that had been around for a while and kept in an enclosed space. It was the stink of his family.

Emily stood directly beneath the door, looking up at him. Her dead eyes didn't reflect the flashlight's illumination. She wore the tatters of a flower-print dress he had gotten her for one birthday or another; he couldn't recall which one. Once or twice he'd tried tossing down different outfits for her to put on, knowing it was foolish but unable to help himself. She ignored them, of course. Her mold-colored flesh was dry and tight against her bones, and she had lost several fingers on each hand over the years. They'd snapped off, like dried twigs. For some strange reason her blond hair had retained its color, though it was now tangled and matted. Her face . . . he didn't like to look at her face for too long.

She reached her hands up toward him and took a couple feeble swipes. Sometimes he fantasized that she was beckoning to him, that in some dim recess of her rotted brain, she recognized him, missed him. Wanted them to be together again, as husband and wife. But he knew better. If Emily got hold of him, she'd tear into his flesh like a starved rottweiler.

Her keening grew louder, and though he wasn't certain her dead eyes could actually see him, he had no doubt she knew he was there. More, that she knew his presence meant it was feeding time. Scattered on the floor around her were small bones and clumps of fur, evidence of past meals.

He heard a second, softer keening in the darkness behind her, and he knew he shouldn't do it, but he shone the flashlight in its direction. A small green-gray thing lay on the basement floor, tiny arms and legs flailing, mouth opening and closing like that of a fish gasping on dry land. His son, Robert Anthony Tollinger, Jr. His son who had never known human life, who'd been miscarried during the seventh month of his wife's pregnancy and who'd actually Gone Bad inside her womb. Bobbie, as Robert had come to think of him, hadn't been able to do any real damage without teeth, but he had been connected to Emily by his umbilical cord. Through that conduit, or by some other means, he had managed to infect his mother before her body expelled him.

There had been no hospital to take Emily to at the time. There was a makeshift one operating in the city building now, but Robert knew that the lone doctor who practiced there wouldn't have been able to do anything for Emily, even if he had set up shop before she changed. There was no cure, no way to halt or reverse the process once it had started.

Robert had been a pick-up man then, though he'd been new to the job, not much more experienced than Kenny. He'd known what he was supposed to do. But like so many others, he couldn't bring himself to do it. Instead, he'd used the hours before they Went Bad to take them down to the basement, bring down some furniture and some toys for Bobbie, even though he knew damn well they'd never be used. Then he dismantled the stairs, tossed the wood into a corner of the basement, and hauled himself out. He locked the door, but he didn't barricade it, even though that would have been the sensible thing to do. It would've been too much like he was putting them in a cage, as if they were nothing more than animals. He installed the panel opening right away, finishing it just as his wife and unborn child began to stir. That had been three years ago.

He knew keeping his family like this made him a hypocrite, and worse, that it prolonged their travesty of an existence. Or rather non-existence. He often lay awake at night, wondering if, on some level, they were aware of what they had become, of what they had once been, what they had lost. And if so, somewhere within the dead lumps of flesh that used to be their minds, did they suffer? Did they long for release?

If so, it was a release he was too weak to grant them. He needed them if he was to keep his sanity in the nightmare the world had become. Providing for his family's needs gave him a purpose in life beyond driving a traveling crematorium. Not much of a purpose, maybe, but it was something.

He turned away from the door, switched off the flashlight, and stuck it handle first in the back pocket of his worn jeans. He walked into the kitchen and opened the refrigerator. There was no light inside because there was no electricity. There hadn't been any for years. He didn't use his fridge to keep things cold, though. He used it because it sealed tight when it shut, holding in the odors of the provender he gathered for his wife and child.

The stench was rank, worse than what he had to put up with on the job. But he didn't care; he'd gotten used to it by now. He reached into the fridge and pulled out a plastic garbage bag. Inside were the remains of a dog he had found two days ago on his bike ride home from work. Deaders preferred human flesh above anything else, but when they couldn't get it—and people had gotten pretty damn good at learning how to avoid getting munched since the plague, or whatever it was, first struck—they turned to animals. Some deader or other had taken a few bites out of the dog, but not many. Either the deader had been satisfied with what he had taken or, more likely, something had scared him off. Perhaps a hunting patrol cruising the streets.

At any rate, Robert had picked up the dog, which had been relatively fresh then, put it in his bike basket, and brought it home. He hadn't given it right away to his family, though. He didn't like to feed them too often. It made them more active and restless, Emily especially. Besides, dog was a treat. Most dogs were wild now, and hard to catch. Normally he fed his family squirrel or rabbit caught in snares he'd rigged in the backyard, though even they weren't as easy to come by as they once had been.

He took the dog to the basement door, feeling something squirm through the plastic. Maggots, most likely; the dog *had* lain out for a while before he'd picked it up. While he'd seen and done too many things since the world changed to be squeamish, he'd rather not touch maggots if he didn't have to. So he left the dog in the bag, though he did untie it. He squeezed the animal, bag and all, through the panel opening. It was a tight fit, but he managed to get it through.

He heard the *rustle-thud* of the bag hitting something, and then another, louder *thud*. He realized with horror that the dog had struck Emily and knocked her down. He shone the flashlight through the opening and confirmed his guess. Emily lay on the ground, arms and legs waving in the air like a turtle that had rolled onto its back. Her nostrils flared, and she turned her head toward the plastic-wrapped dog. Quick as a crab, she righted herself and scuttled over to her prize. As she began tearing at the plastic, Robert was amazed anew at how fast normally slow and awkward deaders could move when they were starved and within striking distance of meat.

She pulled the dog out of the bag, lowered her head to its maggot-covered body, and took a bite. As she chewed, worms fell from her lips, pattering to the basement floor like fat, white raindrops. The baby, scenting meat, shrieked loudly, the sound so near to that of a living infant as to bring tears to Robert's eyes.

Emily looked at the baby as if she'd never seen him before and couldn't quite figure out what he was. Then she bit off another hunk of dog and crawled on hands and knees toward little Robbie, Jr. Once she reached the baby, she chewed for a moment, then lowered her face to the baby's and kissed his mouth.

Back when there had been TV to watch, Robert had seen a documentary on human evolution that claimed kissing began when mothers chewed up food to feed their infants. He wondered if Emily was following a basic maternal instinct so deeply hardwired into her genes that not even death could alter it.

The sight should've sickened him, but it didn't. Yes, it was an obscene mockery of a mother's tenderness, but it still touched him. He'd never had the chance to hold his son, not alive at any rate. He knew Bobbie wasn't a living being, that his movements were due to whatever force—mystic curse or perverted science—animated his dead flesh. But he wished he could touch his boy, just once. Wished he could be a father to Bobbie, a *real* father, and not just a man who threw down dead animals for him to eat. Food he could provide, no problem. But if his wife and son still had any emotional needs—and didn't their keening cries always seem to hold a touch of sadness and loneliness mixed in with the hunger?—there was nothing he could do for them.

He'd tried talking to them on and off over the years, but the sound of his voice always enraged them. They only grew calm when they were fed—or, in Bobbie's case, on those rare occasions when his mother remembered he existed and touched him, sometimes even cradling him in her arms and stroking the dry, dead flesh of his forehead. Robert had often wondered if he would be able to soothe them with his touch, had even contemplated making the attempt once or twice, but he knew he'd never survive it.

He'd even considered going down and letting them have him, purposefully allowing himself to become infected. That way, at least, the three of them would be together. But he knew from his time on the job that if a human body was savaged badly enough by deaders—especially if the heart and brain were damaged or, for that matter, devoured completely—it wouldn't return to life. He'd thought about opening the basement door and then committing suicide elsewhere in the house, maybe by slitting his wrists, so his body would remain intact. But once he changed, how could he be assured that he'd remember his wife and son in the basement—and if he did, that he'd still want to join them? More likely he'd try to get outside and go hunt for live meat. And even if by some miracle he found his way to the basement, there would be no one to bring them food. They wouldn't starve, but they would remain hungry. Forever.

No, there was no way they could be together again, not as a family. He could keep Emily and Bobbie trapped in the basement and feed them like animals, but that was all. It would have to do.

He turned off the flashlight, closed the panel and latched it. There was enough meat on the dog to keep them busy—and quiet—for a while, maybe all the way until morning. That was good. He didn't think he could stand to listen to their plaintive, lonely keening anymore tonight.

✢ ✢ ✢

The next morning he biked to the city building to find out whether they were going to send Smoky Joe out again. He hoped Joe was going to stay in the garage; he didn't feel like dealing with any deaders today. No such luck. The hunting squads had been especially busy last night, and during their patrol, they'd counted a half-dozen more bodies put out by townsfolk for Joe to pick up.

Kenny was already there, looking a bit more nervous than usual, but Robert was in too much of a funk to care why, so he didn't ask. They fired Joe up and chugged out of the garage, heading for the first house on the list the hunters had given them. They had an easy morning of it. The first two deaders they stopped for had been killed by whoever put them out—one by a bullet through the brain, another by a brick or a large rock to the head—and they had no problem tossing them into Joe's furnace.

The third stop was different. Not because of the deader; she was inanimate, too, and so petite that either of them could have carried her, one-handed, to the truck. No, the problem occurred when Kenny, who had been silent all morning, finally decided to speak.

"We're partners, right?"

They stood behind Joe, watching the petite woman burn. She was so tiny, Robert didn't think it would take long for her to fall away to ash.

"We work together, if that's what you mean," he replied, not taking his eyes off the flames.

"Yeah, right, but I mean we look out for each other and stuff. You know, like you wouldn't let a deader take a bite out of me, and I wouldn't let one get at you. Right?"

Robert nodded, wondering where Kenny was going with this. "Sure."

"Well, see, the thing is, I got a problem."

Robert glanced sideways at him. Kenny had taken his gloves off and tucked them in the pockets of his coveralls. He had his mask off, too, and beads of sweat had erupted on his forehead, were beginning to trickle down the sides of his face. Maybe the sweat was due to the heat from Joe's furnace, but Robert didn't think so. Kenny was trembling all over. His hands were the worst; they were vibrating so fast they actually blurred a little.

"You probably heard that my girlfriend Went Bad and I . . . took care of her."

Robert didn't say anything, but he turned to face Kenny.

"I had to do it, right? I mean, I know that's what she would've wanted me to do, but afterward . . . shit, I kept having these *dreams,* you know? Really fucked-up ones. So I started drinking." A nervous chuckle. "I mean, I always drank. Who doesn't, right? But I started in big-time, mostly at night, so I could sleep. If I drink enough, I don't dream."

Kenny fell silent, and they watched the flames for a while. Robert decided to let the man continue in his own time.

"I hate this job. Hate it like fucking poison. But it pays well. Damn well ought to, shit we have to do. I mean, who the hell in their right mind would do this kind of work?" A pause. "No offense."

Robert nodded for him to go on.

"Five ration slips a week is pretty good pay these days. It's more than just about anyone else gets, except for the hunters and the doctor at the city building."

"But five slips aren't enough for you anymore, are they?"

Kenny shook his head. "I guess my body's soaked up too much alcohol for it to work on me the same way. That, or maybe the 'shiners aren't making their stuff as strong as they used to. I use most of my slips for booze, hardly eat much anymore, but I can't seem to get drunk enough to get to sleep. Even when I do, I never sleep through the night. Those dreams . . ."

"Why are you telling me this?" Robert asked softly.

Kenny shrugged—a little too nonchalantly, Robert thought.

"I figure you might be able to help me." A nervous smile. "I know about your secret. I mean, you don't have to be a fucking genius to put it together. Your wife and kid never leave the house. Half the time you can't remember how old your boy is. They're deaders, ain't they? And you've got them stashed in your house somewhere. The garage, maybe, or the basement. Because you're just like all these poor sons of bitches." He made a sweeping gesture to take in the neighborhood. "You can't stand to say goodbye to your loved ones either. The only difference is, you're around deaders all the time, and you ain't afraid of them. You know how to handle them, so while no one else has the balls to keep their family members once they've Gone Bad, you do."

Kenny stopped, a smug expression on his face, as if he were proud of his deductive prowess.

Robert felt a cold twisting in his gut, but he worked to keep his voice level. "So you know. What are you going to do about it?"

"Nothing, *partner.* Not as long as you give me three of your ration slips every week. Otherwise, I'll tell the hunting squad about Emily and little Bobbie, and they'll be over at your house before you can finish singing the first stanza of 'Smoky Joe.'"

Robert said nothing.

"Look, I know this makes me a real prick, but I can't help it, man. I *need* those slips! I gotta get me some sleep!"

A few more seconds went by before Robert finally said, "All right."

"Really? You mean it?" Kenny sounded surprised, as if he hadn't expected his threat to work.

"Yes. But make it two slips a week."

"Uh-uh, no way." He sounded emboldened now. "It's three or bye-bye family."

"All right. Three. But I don't have any on me. You'll have to wait until we get paid."

"That's only a couple more days. I can wait. But if you stiff me, you'll regret it."

"Don't worry. I'll pay. Now let's get back to work. We have at least two more stops to make today, and if we don't keep burning deaders, neither one of us is going to get paid."

Kenny smirked. His expression was easy for Robert to read: He figured he had his partner by the balls now, and he was no longer low man on this team. "What do you mean, *we*? I'll ride along, but I ain't getting out. I'm never gonna touch another fucking deader as long as I live. You do the burning from now on, got it?"

"Got it. Let's go."

Another smirk, and Kenny turned and headed for Joe's

cab. That's when Robert punched him in the back of the neck. Kenny collapsed like a marionette whose strings had been severed, and once he was down, it was an easy matter for Robert to keep him there. He was, after all, thin and weak from malnutrition. Robert clamped his hands around Kenny's neck and squeezed. Kenny kicked his feet and slapped his hands on the asphalt, but Robert kept squeezing until his partner's struggles lessened and finally stopped altogether.

When it was finished, he climbed off Kenny's corpse and stood looking down at it.

Robert wasn't worried that any of the residents of this neighborhood had seen, and even if they had, who would they report it to? There were no police anymore, just the hunting squads—and pick-up men like him. Of course, he'd have to make up a story for his bosses at the city building. He supposed he could always tell them Kenny had said he'd had enough of the job and quit in the middle of today's route, but if no one ever saw him again, they might get suspicious. No, better to say that Kenny got careless, let a deader bite him, and had to be put down. He wouldn't be the first pick-up man who'd ended up that way.

That decided, the only thing left to do was feed Kenny's body to Joe.

Robert bent down, intending to do just that, but as he reached toward Kenny, he hesitated. It seemed an awful waste to just toss him into the fire. He could still be useful.

✛ ✛ ✛

Robert walked into the kitchen, a heavy plastic bag clutched in his hand. Their keening was especially loud today; it had been almost a week since he had last fed them.

"Hold on, it's coming."

He got the flashlight and opened the basement door panel, taking his usual step back and waiting a moment before moving forward again and shining the light inside. There was Emily, hands clawing the air, and little Bobbie, wailing and writhing on the floor behind her. But now there was a third deader in the basement, much fresher than the other two and wearing a pair of coveralls. He stared up at the light with a blank, unseeing gaze, mouth opening and closing hungrily.

Robert smiled. "I really appreciate you helping me out like this, partner. It means a lot to me."

The male moaned as if in response to those words, but Robert knew the thing was just hungry. He lifted his latest find—a possum he'd managed to hit while out in Joe earlier that day—and stuffed it through the opening. The possum struck the floor, and Emily and Kenny fell on it like starving dogs.

Bobbie screamed for his share, and this time it was Kenny who took a mouthful over to the baby, feeding the boy with a gentle kiss.

Robert felt no jealousy. Not only had he provided food for his wife and child, he'd found a way to be down there with them, if only through a surrogate. Still, they were truly a family again, in every way, and that was all that mattered.

Robert watched them for a while longer, then closed the panel and put the flashlight away. Time for bed; he had to get up early for work tomorrow. Not only did he have a new partner to break in, he had a family to feed.

IF A JOB'S WORTH DOING

ANDY VETROMILE

Vince grunted like a pregnant woman, but pulled instead of pushing. It seemed like that was all he was doing tonight, grunting and pulling, shifting and twisting, and now his labor bore fruit as the car's trunk gave birth to a large plastic sack. The bulky load fell heavily to the dirt, and Vince wiped a sleeve across his forehead before retrieving the shovel with a latex-gloved hand. It was a chilly night, but his efforts were keeping him warm.

"More fat bastards per capita in the Mob than anywhere else in the world, Arnold, and I gotta get you," he told the sack as he stepped over it. No mean feat; the bag was like a hurdle in a steeplechase.

Vince had known he was in for it when Pellacini called him into the office and told him to take out Gallo.

"'Jelly Belly' Gallo?" he'd asked. "Boss, the guy's gotta weigh four-fifty, easy."

"And all of it a traitorous bag a' shit," Pellacini confirmed. "I want him gone. Make sure he knows why."

"Hell, what do you need me for? Feed him another dozen doughnuts, wait a couple hours, he'll kill himself lifting the coffeepot," Vince had protested. He was a professional, and this felt more like work for the janitor, but the boss had shaken his head slowly with an evil smile and that was that. "Fine. I'll take him to the gym; that ought to do it. I'll trick him into walking up a flight of stairs."

The job hadn't been much more difficult than that, but the aftermath was turning out to be as unpleasant as Vince had suspected. Shaking his head, he reached under a heavy tin can half-buried in the earth and withdrew a map, checking it with a penlight he had tucked behind his thick ear. The diagram was crude, drawn in pencil, and peppered with cryptic symbols. Each symbol represented either a hole filled with barrels of chemical waste or a body that Pellacini's organization had buried here. He wasn't keen on digging up either one, so Vince and his cronies kept thorough but mysterious notes, taking care no one could attach the schematic to them.

He started into the yard and stopped. *Forgot the mask*, he thought. He reached back into the trunk and yanked out a gas mask. Vince didn't plan on being here long enough to need it, but Pellacini was too cheap to get two separate lots for his dirty little dealings and the less he breathed of the yard's air, the better.

Vince froze. Without raising his head, he craned his neck to listen around the open trunk lid. Were those keys he heard jangling? The hit man pulled his pistol as quietly as he could, and crept behind the car. He peered through the windows of the stolen Caddy and scanned the dark horizon, the weapon's suppressor frozen in midair.

Ordinarily, there wasn't much to see: a few tall mounds of dirt, a couple of abandoned cars, the chain link fence enclosing the yard. The place had a funny smell and a bad reputation, which kept kids and teens from playing or parking here. Without that sort of tourism, there shouldn't be anyone else around.

Then he saw it: the bulk of another car. A small vehicle sat with its rear end hanging out from behind a gravel heap. He had pulled the gate closed after he'd entered, but hadn't locked it, and someone managed to cruise in silently while he was heaving Arnold's fat ass out of the trunk. Vince dropped the mask, readied his weapon, and took several loping strides across the dirt toward the car, using his intimate knowledge of the lot to avoid as much loose debris as he could.

A distinct footstep from behind the towering gravel pile stiffened the hit man, and he swung his gun around the obstruction an instant before he followed it. When he did, he found his pistol leveled at the head of another man whose own weapon targeted Vince in return. They stood and glared dispassionately at each other, their aims rock-still. Vince's black eyes met the stranger's, one brown and one green. This personal trait called up some background.

"Felipe Perez," Vince breathed. "'The Gaze.'"

"Vincent Fontaine," his opponent observed, inclining his neck curiously. It was the first movement either man had made. "'The Grocer.' Forgive me my smile; I've never understood the reasoning behind many of the nicknames given to the members of American organized crime. Are we going to go John Woo on each other, or shall we call a truce?" Perez's cultured voice was silky and went down like good liquor.

Both men dropped their gun arms like the strings holding them up had been cut, but continued to stare at one another. Perez was a Puerto Rican with a trim build, slender features, and a perfectly coifed little stack of dark hair atop his head. Perez looked Vince over as well, and Vince was pretty sure he didn't cut nearly as slick a figure. He, too, was trim, but his face was thick and his hair black and heavy. *And sweaty*, he reminded himself. Aloud he wondered, "Man, don't tell me you know my rep."

"Don't sell yourself short, my friend. No one would be in Pellacini's yard unless he had permission and a reason. Who but a hit man would have need of such a foul playground?" Perez asked with a vague sweep of his gun. "And from that select roster, who but the Grocer is in possession of such skill to *almost* catch me unaware?" His casual attitude, even with a weapon in his hand, bespoke his class and confidence.

This guy gets all the chicks, Vince thought. "What're you doing here?" he asked, noting with a glance that the newcomer's vehicle was a Honda Civic. *Small and quiet.*

"Señor Pellacini and I have an . . . arrangement. He is kind enough to allow me access to his property, and I pay him a handsome sum."

"How do I know that?"

"How much would my life be worth if I were caught in so flagrant a transgression?" he purred.

This could just be how he schmoozes his way out of jams, Vince thought, but as he considered it, he was also inclined to believe Perez. Anyone who thought they could get one past Pellacini had only to look here. They'd be under this lot soon enough. And Perez's reputation spoke for itself. He was a Puerto Rican that even the Mob respected. . . .

Perez holstered his weapon and opened the trunk of his car. He had a cargo like Vince's, only his was wrapped in burlap. Like Vince's, the mass proved difficult for its proprietor to move. Unlike Vince's, Perez's payload was squirming.

"What, you're gonna bury the guy alive?" Vince blurted. He was cold—anyone in this line of work had to be—but he never went so far as to leave them alive for the interment. Perez, however, seemed puzzled as well.

"If I must, but . . ."

"There's a 'but'?"

"He should be dead. This man, I killed him not one hour ago."

Vince knew that meant strangulation, if the stories were to be believed. Such calculated passion for his work made it all the more improbable that Perez's next act would be to take a shovel and hammer the sack mercilessly, but that's exactly what he did. Vince recoiled reflexively from the sudden violent outburst, and stared with renewed admiration at his companion. *Guy knows how to get the job done. . . .*

The sack was still for a moment, then began shifting again. "Allow me," Vince interjected, helping himself to the exhausted man's shovel. He stepped up to the plate and delivered a single, cruel blow to what he assumed was the victim's head, and the movement stopped.

"Thank you," Perez said, wiping his brow with a glossy kerchief. "Most peculiar. When I kill a man, traditionally he remains dead."

"Well, lots of weird stuff happens with a dead body," Vince replied breezily, trying to sound relaxed and clever at the same time. "Had one guy who, my hand to God, must've lost a fourth of his skull and still called my mother names for a full minute before he ate carpet." He shook his head with the memory.

Perez withdrew a silver cigarette case and offered one to Vince. He started to take it, then pulled back. Perez smiled. "You do not wish to leave cigarette butts at the scene."

Vince smiled sheepishly. "Missing a chance to have a smoke with the Gaze, I gotta be crazy. But there's DNA . . ."

"You are not crazy, you are prudent. You will last a long time in this business, my friend." Perez pulled at the cigarette, heedless of his own cautions. "O. J. Simpson was lucky. Men such as us, we cannot afford to depend on the whims of Fortune." The cigarette finished, Perez extinguished it and placed it in his pocket.

"You were serious about knowing me?"

"I was. I am."

"Well, that's saying something. I hardly get any respect in my own damn town. What do you know about me?" Both men leaned against the Civic as if waiting for a bus.

"Uses a Glock 9mm. Prefers three shots—one each in the head, chest, and stomach," Perez quoted from memory as though he were reading from a dossier.

"The map ain't the territory. Pellacini, he's got a weird sense of humor about him. I try for the three-shot combo, figure no one's coming back when the bullets get passed out so, uh, democratically, you know? But Pellacini—for him, every killing's a message to somebody. Guy skims from him, Pellacini wants I should skim the flesh off his hands."

"Once killed eight armed men in a warehouse single-handedly," Perez continued.

"Yeah," Vince said, pride swelling his chest. "Only got paid for one of 'em."

"A tragedy," Perez noted, waving his hand dismissively. "They were associates in league with the target and his operations, yes?" Vince nodded. "But when you strike a deal, you abide by it." Vince smiled; it sounded so dignified coming from the dark man beside him.

There was a scraping noise from the yard, and a witness would have sworn he never saw either man move to draw his gun—in a heartbeat, the weapons were simply *there*. Armed and alert, they whirled out from behind their cover, Vince in a crouch, Perez towering above him. They peered into the darkness for a moment before the lower man growled, "I do not fucking believe this."

The plastic bag behind Vince's Caddy was moving. It wasn't going anywhere, but it constricted in the middle, fell over, went slack, and repeated the process. The two men watched this inchworm motion in astonishment for several moments. Somewhere nearby, a barge drawled its dirge. The sound broke the hold the strange sight had on the assassins. They looked at each other, then slowly approached the bag, Vince with his gun and Perez now holding his shovel.

Vince poked at the bulk with his toe, then put away his gun and retrieved his own shovel. The two men wordlessly took up a staccato rhythm as they beat the bag with the shovels, but were finding it just as hard to put this one down as the last.

When the package lay still, both men stood panting over it. Perez asked, "Three shots? Head, chest, stomach?"

Vince paused. "No. Pellacini wanted him to take it in the stomach. Three guesses why." He mimed Arnold's bulging belly with his hands. "Not like the son of a bitch needed it. Opening a phone book would have given him a coronary. Probably why he went to the Feds. Wanted to live out the last fifteen minutes of his life feeding on the government's dime."

"Are you thinking the same thing I am thinking?" Perez asked after an uncomfortable silence.

"That two heartless, professional bastards in the same line of work ain't gonna screw up the same job, the same way, the same night?"

Perez nodded. "There is something most unusual about the customs followed by your corpses here in the States."

"Hey, Felipe, I'm an old-fashioned guy," Vince said, looking up to assure him. "This ain't par for my course, either. This is messed up, so I say we—"

In one fluid motion, as if the two men were controlled by the same mind, Vince drew his pistol and Perez dropped to the ground. Three shots, each with a high-pitched *vip*, slapped into a man who had appeared behind Perez. The new arrival looked stunned, dropped to his knees, then fell face forward into a puddle. Vince offered his hand to his counterpart.

Perez's tensed fingers fell away from the butt of his pistol as he stood up. The Gaze then rolled the dead man over with the tip of one of the most expensive boots Vince had ever seen. Even in the darkness, the assassins could see the fallen man was yellow and his skin looked tight.

"Who is this man?" Perez asked.

"Where are my manners?" Vince responded, stricken. "This is Paolo Domingues. He's a mule for a local gang—or he was, until I killed him *six fucking months ago.*"

"I was going to ask 'Where did he come from?' but I will forego that."

"And this is Benny Pagani," Vince continued, voice rising, "who ran numbers for Pellacini." Perez watched as Pagani introduced himself. The numbers man offered his hand—both of them, in fact, and both squirmed with maggots—but Perez chose not to shake and drew his pistol instead. Benny opened a loose and cavernous mouth to greet the killer. For a reply, Perez blew the top of Benny's head off.

"He never was big on conversation," Vince said weakly.

"You are saying these men are your victims?" Perez glanced from the corpse on the ground to the man standing next to him. Vince could only nod.

More scraping and shuffling from the ring of darkness surrounding them forced the pair into a defensive stance, back-to-back. Shapes took on a harder edge as they crept toward the duo, passing from the anonymity of the blackness to the cold light of recognition. All had their arms outstretched. Their legs wobbled uncertainly beneath them, and their clothes hung loosely from decayed flesh. A weaselly man with a soiled bow tie and thin mustache fixed his vacant eyes on the pair.

"This guy I do not know," Vince announced firmly.

"Galveston," Perez said. "Competing counterfeiter working against an acquaintance of mine in Missouri. I eliminated him—oh, five months ago." Perez then repeated the service with the silent pop of his gun. The dark, dry line encircling Galveston's throat like a necklace was now complemented by a bloodless black hole in his forehead. He fell over noiselessly.

"Phew," Vince gasped. "That smell. I know that smell. These things've been soaking in that damn chemical bath Pellacini has going under the dirt here." Both men looked uncertainly at the rough soil beneath their feet, then back at the shambling throng. Where there were four shapes before, now there were eight.

"The chemicals—you believe they have brought about this unusually . . . healthy . . . reaction?" Perez spastically flapped his hand to dispel the foul odor. "I am inclined to agree." His pistol barked, louder now as the suppressor began to wear.

Vince watched a Korean man collapse at his feet. "Guess I owe you a cut of the bounty for helping me with Ling there."

"Think nothing of it," Perez sniffed. "By the way, your aim is all your reputation suggests."

"Thanks," Vince said. He put a bullet into a man's midsection experimentally. There was no effect, so he put another slug into the chest cavity. Not until he hit the brain did he receive favorable results. "Head shots. Gotta destroy the brain."

Perez did as the other man suggested, nodding appreciatively at the outcome. "So one must."

"Hah! I knew it!" the Italian declared triumphantly, pointing at the next figure to approach. "You did kill Salvatore Marcos."

Perez glanced back at the reanimated Marcos. "Yes, I did."

"Rudy owes me twenty bucks," Vince grumbled.

Slowly the two men, still back-to-back, moved toward one of the debris piles. The eight creatures had doubled their number, and when the hit men had put those down, there were twice that number again, crowding forward, raw hands reaching needfully.

"This is looking most grim," Perez observed.

"Yeah, this is turning into a piss-poor night all right," Vince agreed, stumbling over thick slabs of stacked and broken concrete. He grabbed a length of rebar with his free hand and used it to drive back a mass of dead flesh as it half-climbed, half-crawled up the heap after them. "I knew this job was gonna come back to bite me in the ass one day." The torso of an arsonist named Wendel Friedman clutched at Vince's ankles, getting a knee to the jaw for its struggles.

"As I think of it," Perez offered, "certain members of OPEC, who shall remain unnamed, asked that I thank whoever killed financier Gregory Fitzsimmons, should I ever meet him." Perez fired again, and Fitzsimmons' forehead became as ragged as his ratty Armani suit. The Puerto Rican could not help but notice Vince had buried the banker complete with his Rolex watch.

"They're welcome," Vince said, watching Fitzsimmons collapse again. *This guy's done wetwork for OPEC?* he marveled to himself. *Criminy, he's* international. . . .

The suppressors on their guns were completely worn through now, though neither man seemed worried that the deafening reports might draw the attention of the authorities.

"I am almost out," Perez said quietly. He paused to check his clip as several new targets took up position on the rubble. He popped the clip back in. "One bullet left."

Vince took a moment to examine his own clip, even though both he and his companion knew without looking how many shots were left. "Two," he said, pulling his sleeve across his sweaty brow. "And the rebar." He swung the heavy metal rod and teeth flew from a gun dealer's mouth as his body spun to the back of the line.

"I would like you to know that it has been a pleasure meeting you," Perez said, offering his hand. Vince took it in his own.

"Working with you's a privilege. Lonely job, you know. Only takes one guy most days." They surveyed the pressing mob of undead, each man wondering how many more were even then climbing from their shallow graves.

"Although I share some of your employer's delight in poetic justice, I have no desire to end up like these poor souls," Perez sighed. "If souls they have."

Vince nodded. "Okay. I got a spare slug, though. Anyone in particular you don't like?"

Perez kicked a kiddie-porn dealer sharply in the nose, and the skull cracked audibly. "I have always held that personal feelings have no place in this business. Emotions, allowed free reign, will be the death of you." He looked at Vince, who met his eyes. The Puerto Rican pointed to a corpse who, even in the half-light, appeared to have once had olive skin, now running to yellow. "But if I were to be completely honest with myself, I always felt Santos Alamar was an irredeemable asshole."

Alamar fell at the feet of his fellows.

"You have lifted a weight from my mind," Perez quipped. "Shall we?"

"You bet," Vince replied, inwardly lamenting his lack of sophistication. "You think we can pull it off?"

"Events earlier in the evening suggested yes. My experience since then has only cemented this opinion."

The two killers swung their guns swiftly, with mechanical grace, and leveled them at each other, just as they had done when first they'd met. Neither saw the other's barrel, only the other man's eyes. The guns cracked with one sound, the bodies fell with one motion.

They were just that good.

THE SECRET IN THE CELLAR

ED GREENWOOD

Jeremy Sturbrant came awake shivering in the dark. His fingers felt like needles of sharp, stabbing pain.

He did not need light to know what had caused that pain, or what it was that his fingers were streaking with blood. He'd been clawing at the bolts of his cellar door.

Again.

✛ ✛ ✛

As always, the framed photograph of Jeremy Sturbrant on the wall smiled breezily back at the real man.

And why not? The world had been his oyster. Keen eyes, deft hands, and the finest training wealthy parents could buy had made Sturbrant one of the country's top surgeons. He didn't mind hard work, and developed a knack for befriending colleagues. Crusty old doctors saw him as a capable assistant, eager and honored to learn from them, not a young hotshot.

Eager and honored he'd truly been, too. He'd done brains and hearts, livers and eyes. Snipped bowels, delicately hollowed out fat, removed moles . . . and he'd kept his mouth shut about whose insides he'd seen. Not a slip, nary a dispute. Success after success.

With success had come cash and laughing ladies, fine wine, fast cars. "Smiling Jerry" had played hard, and shrugged off his ailing liver and the slow creep of his right eye into occasional and then less-than-occasional "lazy" blurred vision.

What Sturbrant couldn't ignore was his first heart attack. It had happened when he was cutting into a patient—and the woman had died on the table.

His colleagues had hushed it up, put Sturbrant into three months of enforced rest—morose boredom they'd tried to make bearable by frequent gifts of Glen Morald, a thirty-year-old single malt, and even better liquids of its ilk. He could taste them all still.

They'd warned Sturbrant to take it easy. No more cream sauces and thick crusts of melted cheese on everything—between days of not much more than coffee and steaks grilled alone in the wee hours. No more ten-operation days. After all, there'd never be a shortage of patients, and they couldn't *all* be rescued by the skilled hands of Jeremy Sturbrant.

He'd chafed under the lighter regime for a year, bored by tennis and even more by golf—what fun was *that*, trying to guess just how some sadistic designer had tilted a distant, invisible green to make his ball do strange things?—and then slowly drifted back into a swifter, heavier workload.

His second heart attack had been worse, but at least it had come in private, at the wheel of his car on a lonely road in the hills. The crash cost him the deftness of his left hand, so lacerated that he'd risked losing fingers. They'd never been free of stiffness and aches since.

Jeremy Sturbrant's days of brilliant surgery were over. Sliding along on oceans of Glen Morald, he'd sat alone for days, read some books, talked to many colleagues . . . and finally faced it: His body was failing him. He still had his looks, but his liver was going—and his third heart attack was a full-blackout, awaken-in-hospital-days-later affair. Which was when he discovered stiffness had come to both hands.

Reluctant to leave behind power, prestige, and adoring nurses, Sturbrant had quietly retired from daily cutting at the hospital department he headed, and took up promoting younger doctors, guiding and training with such enthusiasm that he attracted the notice of a rich patient, who lured him away to the Company with an obscenely large salary.

"The Company" was all anyone who worked there, except lawyers and the shareholders' recording secretary, ever called it, but its proper name was "Moote-Darneth-Eon Integrated Omnisystems." To reporters, and therefore the general public, it was "Moodereo." It was a large and mysterious firm—the public would have been shocked to learn just *how* large and mysterious—that had something to do with drugs, and medical systems, and manufacturing diagnostic and patient care devices.

A true octopus, the Company was active in thirty-eight states and a dozen countries—that Sturbrant knew of—and regularly set some of its many-eyed tentacles to watching over its other tentacles. Part of his huge pay packet, he'd been told very firmly, was to buy his utter silence and cooperation.

How *utter* he soon saw. A scientist whose office was a few doors down from his, Ashton Vrooman, developed telefactoring equipment that allowed the user to operate on himself or carry out other exacting tasks while remaining conscious, because the rig electronically isolated the wearer against shock, nausea, and pain. It had been understood that the Company would eventually—and very quietly—sell the telefactoring project to the military, but in the meantime Vrooman wanted to perfect it by making it available, on an "assume all risks" experimental basis, to search-and-rescue and underwater salvage concerns. Someone higher up in the Company had other ideas—specifically, selling access to the rig to the richest and most secretive bidders. It didn't matter if they implanted drug-smuggling bags, weaponry, and replacement black-market organs into themselves, so long as they paid.

When Vrooman objected, there'd been an unfortunate "accident"—a fiery crash caused by all four wheels somehow coming off the scientist's car at once. The tragedy was grimly foreshadowed, in a cold little lesson to other employees, by company security men posting a regretful notice about its occurrence while Vrooman's car was still in the noon lineup to get out through the security gates.

Of course what was developed on Company time, with Company resources, belonged to the Company—but it seemed that Moodereo would go to all lengths to keep firm control over all uses of what was theirs. On the other hand, there weren't many jobs outside the classroom for a still-handsome surgeon with stiffening hands who'd suffered three heart attacks, each worse than the last.

Still, Vrooman's fate had made Sturbrant more aware of the legions of Company "marketing liaisons," and how close a watch some of them kept over his phone calls, trips to stores and banks, and even his rare visits to movie theaters. *Why not play God, if we can?* was the unofficial motto of the officially nameless Company department to which Sturbrant belonged, and it seemed that the faceless men who made Moodereo's guiding decisions followed it wholeheartedly.

How much so became clear with Herb Wilmarth.

Wilmarth was an old researcher, a kindly man who'd been with the Company since its earliest days. In recent weeks, though, he'd taken to muttering in staff meetings about the ethics of organ transplants. Eventually, he began to state his objections more forcefully. "We are all making a huge mistake in pursuing these things," he shouted at one meeting about some new anti-rejection fluid. "Certain body parts have a life of their own. I can prove it. In the lab, they seem to want to get back together with the bodies they came from!"

Crazy, of course. Someone had muttered, "Whoooo, we are all zombies," near Sturbrant's ear, and someone else had raised both arms straight out, in mimicry of the Hollywood "mummy walk." Sturbrant and the others had carefully avoided looking at each other as the meeting broke up. He never saw Wilmarth again.

Moodereo's on-site human resources manager suggested kindly old Herbert take some rest from the considerable strain of his groundbreaking projects and visit a famous psychiatrist in Boston—at Company expense, of course. But there'd been another unfortunate accident on the way to Boston, involving Wilmarth's car and—by the strangest of coincidences—a Moodereo delivery truck. Again, notification of the regrettable fatality had been posted, it turned out, almost an hour before the crash actually occurred.

Sturbrant was careful to play the model employee from then on, even if he secretly sought ways to rebel against the Company, just as he had with the regimens forced upon him by his heart attacks. In public, he politely turned aside even casual questions as to his line of work, in case the questioner proved to be a Company snoop. Most Moodereo marketing liaisons were simply spies, he realized. We are all zombies, indeed.

In private, Jeremy Sturbrant did all that he could to maintain his independence, his identity, even while reaping the benefits of his employer's largesse.

His research team was developing infection inhibitors, fluids that could be brushed or squirted onto wounds, breaks, and severed body parts to prevent exposure to air, water, insects, and the contaminants they carried. Such a miracle fluid should both seal and anesthetize . . . and was taking years to perfect. The team was currently working with three promising substances left from an initial eight.

Under the constant scrutiny of security cameras, Sturbrant ran his experiments and kept careful notes in accordance with both his own working style and Company policy. However, he'd always been blessed with a swift and prodigious memory—and on the late night of lone laboratory work when he discovered what he would later call his "wonder broth," he oh-so-casually noted conclusions in the Company log that bore little resemblance to his actual observations.

Sturbrant, however, remembered the true findings quite clearly. Working in his cellar to foil any Company cameras that might have been stealthily installed in his home lab, he was able to replicate the compound upon which he'd stumbled: wonder broth, a nutrient fluid that caused rapid growth of nerves, bone, cartilage, sinew, veins, arteries, and flesh—the works. He hid his discovery well, in a box buried under the cellar's dirt floor, and never so much as hinted at it as he continued his Company work.

✜ ✜ ✜

Sturbrant knew very well what lay on the other side of the blood-smeared door: a sturdy stair made of thick old boards descending into a large, labyrinthine cellar. Once it had been a low-beamed, filthy, cobwebbed place, choked with broken furniture, lit only by a few bare lightbulbs dangling here and there above its uneven dirt floor. The sort of dank, littered underworld a child might be frightened to enter.

That old, dirty cellar had outlasted the rest of the sagging farmhouse above it by a few years, as Sturbrant's sprawling new mansion took shape, but the sort of money a brilliant surgeon like Jeremy Sturbrant made can transform a dozen cellars in a season. And with the sort of money the Company paid for his researches, he could buy counties full of cellars, new and old. A much-enlarged, deepened cellar lay on the other side of that door now.

So why, whenever he fell asleep—just these last few nights, all of a sudden—was he desperate to get through that door, desperate enough to bloody his hands clawing at it?

What was down there, calling to him?

✜ ✜ ✜

After the wonder broth discovery, Jeremy Sturbrant took a keen interest in what the other teams at the Moodereo site were doing—at the usual meetings only, of course, never betraying his boldness in any way that might arouse suspicion. When another research team thought they'd hit on something that ensured rejectionless grafting of lab-grown tissues or donated organs into living bodies, Sturbrant proposed that the two teams combine their work. Suggesting a complex battery of tests to determine the feasibility of his suggestion, Sturbrant generously surrendered control of the combined project to the head of the other team.

That man promptly handed him back the donkey work of refining the tests in light of the precise chemical formula of 94-0434, the "rejectionless squirt" the second team had developed, and Sturbrant toiled away at that until a superior, Dr. Whateley Ward, quashed the idea. Ward no doubt reasoned that, if the Company could sell two expensive anti-rejection fluids, they could make far more money than if they sold one. Even if Sturbrant's team appeared stalled, better to have him go on alone, at least for now.

It was Sturbrant himself who calmly proposed to Ward that all the test regimens he'd completed on 94-0434 be destroyed "for best security." This was soberly approved and done. But, of course, by then Sturbrant had gathered all the information he needed and had carried it home, without detection, inside his head.

"Why not play God, if we can?" Sturbrant found himself chuckling aloud, alone in his cellar. "Why not, indeed!"

He "developed" more heart trouble, adding regular visits to cardiologists to his limited schedule of personal errands, until Company watchers tired of following him to specialists' offices in increasingly distant cities. While inside these medical buildings, it was simplicity itself to order certain chemicals and medical supplies from businesses housed therein, to be sent to the last dusty warehouse of Thanatos Importing.

Sturbrant had been the youngest of a dozen surgeons who'd set up Thanatos years earlier, for the sole purpose of bringing Glen Morald and similar little luxuries into their hands without the ruinous prices demanded by specialty shops. Time had done its work, and Jeremy Sturbrant was now the last living partner, though he'd never gotten around to formally shutting down the business.

The traffic through the Thanatos warehouse had returned to normal a few days before a minor disaster struck the Moodereo site: an explosion and fire. No one had been hurt, and—literally—after the smoke had cleared, the damage was found to be minimal, though the aging sprinkler system had shorted out the security cameras in half the complex. The security boss loudly and profanely observed as much, early on, and promptly followed his curses with an all-hands order to vacate the premises for the day. After helping secure his section, Jeremy Sturbrant obediently complied—driving out past the distracted security checker with two of Vrooman's prototype telefactoring rigs, stored and forgotten since later— and smaller—models had been adopted for oh-so-profitable Moodereo use.

Over the next few months, Sturbrant carefully gathered information and stole tiny lenses, screws, and the like, things that would be easy to pilfer and hard to acquire without attracting notice out in the real world. And before long, he was almost ready to live forever.

Well, not precisely *forever*. Death comes to us all, of course, but if Sturbrant was correct, he'd found a way to keep age at bay for a long time—twenty years at least, if luck and skill were both with him.

It was time to retire from Moodereo. Another heart attack, though quite minor, gave him both urgency and means. In its wake, Sturbrant feigned memory loss, telling his superior with quiet anguish that he could no longer recall most of his past work for the Company. He saw Whateley Ward's cold eyes flicker, and knew his ruse had worked. He'd given Moodereo an excuse to retire him—and do so without the fear he might reveal all he knew to their competitors or the press. Or the police.

The Company assigned a marketing liaison to watch Sturbrant, of course, to make certain he didn't undertake business dealings indicating a return of his memory and a willingness to use Moodereo-acquired knowledge in any ventures they didn't own and from which they would not profit.

He'd taken very good care of the Company snoop, making sure the Moodereo man saw him borrowing lots of Westerns and historical novels from the town library, trudging to his car with a cane, and carrying out any number of small, daily errands with the same slow feebleness. And whenever the snoop went off to investigate someone else on his long, long list of "probably unimportant" surveillance targets, Jeremy Sturbrant struck again.

The idea had first come to him the day after he'd successfully combined his wonder broth and the anti-rejection serum. Trotting out to his barn after lunch, he found a pair of young, vigorous hikers pilfering tools and fittings from his bench. He was so angry—and so frightened when their response to his angry shout was to wheel around and laughingly threaten him—that Sturbrant had drawn the Glock Model 18 he'd bought years before and shot them both dead, surprising himself almost as much as the hikers. Almost.

He'd bundled the bodies into his huge specimens freezer, afraid someone would happen along before he got them hidden. And then, as he panted hard over a full glass of whiskey, an idea came to him.

Sturbrant mixed a fresh batch of his improved wonder broth, lugged one of the bodies into his lab after dark, and did a little midnight surgery. A heart that should replace his own ailing one was soon floating in the broth. While he was at it, he harvested the man's right eye to substitute for his own lazy one. He took the same organs from the other hiker, just in case. And, because his own member had always been on the small side and the second hiker's penis impressed him, he took that, too, then buried the bodies back in the woods.

The penis became his first self-surgery experiment. After all, if something went wrong and he ended up with a uselessly dangling member—or worse—he could always urinate into a bag, via tube, if need be.

However, things went without a hitch, aside from an irritating tendency of the new part to itch, all by itself, from time to time.

Then came the car crash, right outside his door. A logging truck had rolled over on the road below his cliff-top home, spilling the terrified driver and loader before it burned. Sturbrant had raced out to help, and found the loader messily dead on the road, but the driver more hysterical than hurt. He helped the man into his car for the drive to the hospital in Rowley—and then a better idea had occurred to him. After explaining that he was a doctor and lived quite close by, Sturbrant drove back up to his own house, where he gave the man a sedative.

The truck and its load were a fierce pillar of flame that would soon attract the curious. Eventually, the police would come looking for the driver's body, too. Sturbrant ran to where he'd buried the hikers.

A foraging beast had dug up and gnawed the remains. Sturbrant salvaged what bones he could and threw them, in a sack weighted with stones, over the cliff and into the heart of the blaze. Only then did he reach for the phone.

✢ ✢ ✢

He'd been so cool and calm about everything. After all, he'd cut into countless living and dead bodies in operating rooms, and he didn't know any of the people he had harvested since starting his experiments. None of it bothered him, particularly.

So why, for the past three night, had he taken to sleep-walking?

And why did all his walks end *here*?

✢ ✢ ✢

Sturbrant's donation of a new heart and eyeball to the unwilling logging truck driver was a complete success—so much so that it took almost his entire supply of sedatives to keep the logger from harming him or escaping, even from the manacles he'd put together. Eventually Sturbrant gave the man a doubled dose and put him in the freezer to let the cold and the lack of air make an end of him.

Then began the long, exacting process of preparing to operate on himself. Sturbrant started his generators to guard against power failures, set up and tested the telefactoring equipment and the intravenous plasma and wonder broth hookups, and then cut himself up.

He'd never sweated so much in his life, nor felt so icy inside and yet hot on his skin. But otherwise, he found it astonishingly easy to give himself the other hiker's heart and right eye.

From then on, it was a simple matter of patience, exercise—he had to keep himself strong enough to carry the dead weight of a body—and caution. He took longer and longer drives to find victims, employing a Moodereo doctor's full array of drugs to subdue the men he found, until he had an ample supply of spare parts, immersed in wonder broth, to replace anything of his own that showed signs of failing. His most important take was a very skilled surgeon, whose hands—first the left, then the right—replaced his own. He buried the leftovers in the cellar so that neither his handyman, Bert Mason, nor any bold intruders would find something suspicious.

As time went on, he decided to be more active in discouraging possible trespassers. Sure, the Company's spies had given up all but the most perfunctory surveillance long ago, but you never knew when they might decide to come nosing around again.

All it took was the covert sale of a few body parts to a certain sickly and very wealthy individual from the Company's telefactoring client list. The cash funded one final sweep for Moodereo cameras and the beginnings of the Sturbrant fortress. All that remained was to spread tales for the ears of the Company's snoops—stories, abetted by a few appearances in appropriate makeup, about the unfortunate disfiguring disease Jeremy Sturbrant had developed, and his bitter decision to wall himself away from the world in his mansion and keep all ridicule out in his last, lingering years.

✛　✛　✛

Jeremy Sturbrant panted for breath, on his knees in the darkness, forehead against a door.

The cellar door. Of course.

His throat was raw; he must have been screaming. With a sudden shudder, he threw himself away from the blood-streaked door, clambered to his feet, and stumbled to the elevator. As he entered the part of the house reserved for the laboratory, the lights came on around him automatically.

"Damn," he hissed at the lit elevator button. "Am I losing my mind?"

The elevator calmly opened its doors by way of answer. With one knuckle he pushed the button for the topmost floor and sagged back against the burnished metal wall. The doors obediently closed, and the muted thunder of the elevator motor surrounded him.

Well, at least he didn't have to worry about someone investigating any screams. Built to his exacting designs, the house around him was most certainly secure. Thick windows, thicker walls, built to keep the nosy world out . . . and him in.

Shut in with whatever was waiting for him in the cellar.

Sturbrant shook his head. He'd never felt like this before, never been afraid of living alone, never looked over his shoulder for one instant. What was *happening* to him?

Was he becoming addicted to his nutrient broth? No, surely not. But, well, what else could be calling him down there? The place was enlarged and well lit, most of it new—and he could list quite precisely every last thing that was down there. Damn it, it was *his* cellar.

He needed a drink. Bandages and a wash first—but before both, some Glen Morald.

The doors rolled open. Sturbrant lurched down the dark, deeply carpeted hall to his bedroom, slammed its door shut behind him, and plucked out the false book from the crammed bookshelf. With fumbling fingers, he dug inside its shallow tray of keys until he found the right ones.

The bedroom door had a deadbolt and a passage lock in its doorknob; both could be locked from either side. Sturbrant secured both, locking himself inside his suite—bedroom, dressing room, and bathroom—and went in search of whiskey.

Stars glittered in the night sky over the wooded hills outside his bedroom window. Sturbrant gazed at their cold, distant twinklings as he sipped. Then he sighed, shook his head, and slid aside another bookshelf to reveal his bedroom safe. It was the work of a few impatient moments to lock the door keys inside it, slam its door, drain his glass, and get back into bed.

He lay there in the darkness, sweating and scared . . . but exhausted, too. It wasn't long before the dark fingers of sleep dragged him down again.

✛ ✛ ✛

He came awake suddenly, knees stiff, in the bright morning sunlight. He was kneeling in front of the safe, bandaged fingers on its knob. He'd been trying to dial the right numbers in his sleep.

"Jesus," Sturbrant growled, snatching his hands away as if the safe could bite him.

"Jesus bleeding *Christ*," he added in a snarl as he started the coffeemaker, raided the bar fridge for leftover pizza, and headed for the shower.

"I am appalled," he announced a shade more calmly to his steamed-over bathroom mirror, wiping it ineffectually with one hand to stare at a blotchy, fuzzy version of himself. "Thoroughly appalled."

He waved his razor angrily. "And Jeremy Sturbrant doesn't get 'thoroughly appalled.' Or crazed out of his mind, either." Snatching up a towel, he padded toward the snorkeling sound of the coffee making itself.

Beside the coffeemaker stood the whiskey bottle from last night. Sturbrant gave it a considering glare, then drank a swig. The coffee was still drizzling into the carafe, so he ran his tongue around the whiskey taste in his mouth and went looking for clothes.

Work rags, nothing showy; cellar time awaited him. He glanced out the bedroom window at the wooded hills again. A few white wisps of cloud hung in a bright blue sky, above the frowning concrete of his walls.

He wasn't scared, and he certainly wasn't going crazy. He was just . . . just . . .

His head held no words to end that sentence.

Thinking empty thoughts, Sturbrant stared at the phone. The phone! He reached for it as he poured his coffee.

His handyman answered on the third ring. "Morning, Mr. Sturbrant. What can I do for you today?"

"Could you meet me at the back gate in, say, ten minutes? Bring a flashlight and . . . your tools. I may need some help in the cellar."

"Oh?" Bert Mason's voice was flat and calm.

Half the county thought Jeremy Sturbrant was some sort of scar-faced recluse up to God-alone-knew-what behind his high walls, but at least he was a *rich* scarred recluse, who always donated to local drives and charities, and refrained from using his wealth to force his will and whims on his neighbors. Rich enough to give his handyman a rent-free house just outside his fortress walls—a house far grander than most of the weathered homesteads in the hills.

Sturbrant had no idea what Mason really thought of him, but the man was an attentive gardener and capable handyman who earned his generous salary, kept his mouth shut about his employer's lack of scar tissue, and refrained from prying. He'd never even invited Mason inside the main house before.

"It might be nothing at all," Sturbrant said into the phone. "On the other hand, it might be a big mess it'll take the two of us to set right. I heard something huge fall over late last night, under the floor, in the cellar. The crash sounded big enough that I doubt I can get whatever it is upright again without help. But I haven't checked yet to see what fell. Probably a heating duct or something like that."

"Back gate in ten minutes, sir," Mason replied calmly, and hung up.

Sturbrant scalded his mouth on too-hot coffee. With a growl of exasperation and pain, he snatched up two of his emergency flashlights, sliding both into deep pockets of his coveralls.

He'd seen plenty of movies and read enough horror stories wherein people—doomed people—were haunted by ghosts or *things* in their cellar. But he'd be damned and blasted if any such tale had a shred of truth to it!

Nevertheless, he didn't want to explore his cellar alone. Unlocking the bedroom door and returning the keys to the fake book, Sturbrant selected a larger book from a higher shelf and pocketed what it kept hidden from the world: his Glock, heavy with a full thirty-three-round magazine. Then he went to the dressing room closet. There, behind his ready tool chest, was a pair of rubber boots—and sticking up out of them was a crowbar.

Sturbrant hefted the bar in his hand as the elevator took him down to let the handyman in. He'd forgotten to wash the bloodstains off the cellar door, but Mason's face stayed expressionless as Sturbrant shot back its three large bolts, snapped on the large kitchen flashlight with his bandaged fingers, and swung the door open.

Nothing was waiting on the stairs to lunge out at them. Nothing seemed out of place or unusual at the bottom of the steps, either. Sturbrant snapped a light switch, and light flooded the cellar. Face set, he led the way down the stairs.

They explored, walking together. It didn't take long. The wine cellar, the shelves of neatly boxed, labeled oddments . . . everything was ablaze with light. Nothing looked damaged or out of place as they peered into every corner, behind the monster oil tanks and furnace on their massive concrete pad, installed a few years ago to heat Sturbrant's luxurious new home. A small patch of dirt floor survived around the furnace pad and in one far alcove—the one that still held what anyone living in these hills would expect to find in a cellar: a dusty tangle of old, disused furniture.

Mason's face remained carefully expressionless as he accepted his employer's thanks and departed. Resetting the expensive security system as the monstrous doors of the back gate closed, Sturbrant reflected wryly that the futile little foray into the cellar might convince the tight-lipped handyman his boss was indeed as crazy as the rumors said, if he didn't believe them already.

He opened another bottle of whiskey, sipped it straight, and went into the library to gaze down at one of his favorite possessions: the huge old state map inlaid into the tabletop, with its wandering lines of roads reaching spiderlike through the hills.

If the locals knew what Sturbrant really did here, it wouldn't be just vandals, casual thieves, and annoying solicitors that his walls would have to keep out. They'd come to kill him, for sure.

He glanced at his reflection in an ornate mirror and flexed his bandaged hands thoughtfully. He'd dip them in a fresh batch of wonder broth this evening.

Sturbrant raised the bottle again—and then set it down without drinking. He had to drive into town, and policemen didn't let drunken drivers off with warnings these days.

There was a new home improvement store in Rowley, one of those super hardware barns belonging to a large national chain. He'd marked the catalog that had come in the mail, circling padlocks, hasps, and bolts, some of the latter lockable. These were the things he'd need to keep the cellar door closed no matter what he did when sleepwalking.

Applying his makeup and taking his cane in case the Company snoop was watching—though he'd not seen the man for several months now—Jeremy Sturbrant went to the garage.

✛ ✛ ✛

It had been an exhausting day. For most of the afternoon he'd drilled and sawed and driven safety screws, covering their heads with metal plates. When he was done, a dozen new bolts were in place within and across the face of the massive old cellar door. He stowed most of his tools in the cellar—which was quiet and serenely undisturbed—then locked everything up, shutting the various new keys in his bedroom safe.

Sturbrant prepared and ate an elaborate solitary dinner, listened to soothing music as he read the daily paper, and went to bed with a favorite hilarious novel. For good measure, he locked himself into his bedroom.

He was chuckling sleepily at the same paragraph for the third time as oblivion claimed him, and he fell asleep with the lights on and the book in his hand.

✛ ✛ ✛

The stumble awakened him. Jeremy Sturbrant came awake, shivering in the dark, as he slammed into the cold, rough wall. *Rough?* That could only mean—

He smelled damp earth, ever so faintly, and flailed out wildly with his hands until he found the stair-rail. Yes. He was halfway down the cellar stairs, in the dark.

All remembrance of the nightmare that had been tormenting him was swept away in an icy instant. Somehow, in his sleep, he'd opened the safe, got out all the keys, and opened his bedroom door—and then the cellar door, despite all his precautions.

"Oh, *God*," Sturbrant wailed, whirling around on the step and racing up the stairs. He charged through his darkened house, crashing into things without slowing, as if all the clutching, nameless things his mind was now conjuring really were clawing at his back.

He fled, naked, to his car, in which he promptly squealed out of the garage. The automated gate barely had time to rise and let him out before he was tearing away from the grounds at top speed. He turned onto the road faster than was safe, the tires protesting shrilly, and roared off toward Rowley—and beyond.

With each mile, Sturbrant grew more calm, and as he calmed, he let the car fall back to a safe speed. Nothing could be following him after that exit, not even the Company spy. Still, he looped around the back streets several times before taking an unfamiliar road out of town, in what direction he wasn't certain.

Sturbrant drove aimlessly through the darkened countryside, until weariness came creeping back. When his eyes started to close for the third time and his yawns came faster and faster, he found an isolated dirt lane, pulled off onto a grass verge, killed the engine, and fell asleep.

✛ ✛ ✛

Birdsong and bright morning sun on his face awakened him. He was . . . God knew where, naked, slouched behind the wheel. Thankfully, the lane was deserted.

There was a blanket and an oil-stained pair of coveralls in the trunk. Sturbrant laid the blanket over the expensive leather of the front seat, pulled on the overalls, checked the gas—thankfully, he kept all his vehicles full, so he still had plenty—then started driving. He turned always onto larger and more important roads, until he found a sign that told him where he was, which was not as far from home as he'd feared.

Back in his mansion, Sturbrant grimly explored the cellar again. Finding nothing amiss, he locked and bolted every fastening on the cellar door, returned the keys to his bedroom safe, and went to the phone.

Several frustrating hours later, he tracked down a security company that would install the type of timed locks he wanted. But the earliest appointment he could make—even when he agreed to pay cash for a system so expensive that the salesman on the other end of the line gasped in surprise—was two days hence. The men would be happy to come right away, but they just didn't have the hardware at hand.

Slamming down the phone, Sturbrant reached for the bottle of Glen Morald.

+ + +

He was too drunk to drive, and the thought of what he might do in a cab or at a movie theater, if he tried to get away from the cellar that way, made Sturbrant giggle. No, if he went out in public now, he'd make the headlines for certain. Or maybe right to the sanitarium. And he'd be there forever, once they did a little digging. . . .

Shuddering, Jeremy Sturbrant tried to get hold of himself long enough to check and secure the house locks, inside and out, before going to sleep. He finally crawled into bed, which was a large, heavy Colonial affair. Aside from removing his shoes, he did not undress—and instead added an unusual fashion accessory: a pair of handcuffs he'd acquired to keep victims secured on drives home to the mansion. He put an empty juice can by the bed to urinate into if the need arose, injected himself with a strong sedative, and handcuffed himself by one wrist to his bed. He was locked into his bedroom suite now, and he'd figure out how he was going to get free in the morning.

Turning out the light, he tossed his keys away into the darkness, hard.

The last thing he heard was them smacking against the wall and dropping to the floor.

+ + +

Nightmares again, of whispering voices full of cold menace, voices accompanied by hands that clawed and clutched at him—foes he could not see when he whirled to confront them.

Jeremy Sturbrant came awake at last, drenched in cold sweat. In the darkness, of course. And stooped over a . . . a shovel . . . in a place that smelled of damp earth.

He was in his cellar.

Sturbrant had a sudden, wild urge to flee, a sense that something was lurking right behind him. He swung the shovel in a vicious blow that clanged off the furnace and sent the blade rebounding into his face. He was in a corner of the dirt floor behind the furnace pad, where he'd buried the remnants of his victims.

Sturbrant flung the shovel down and ran, so precipitously that he tripped over the tool's bouncing handle. Staggering on without slowing, he slammed into the end of the stair rail, breaking something in his hand, and clawed his way up the stairs and out into parts of the mansion where the lights came on automatically.

He did not stop to close the cellar door, or do anything but claw open the connecting door to the garage and drive. He almost went over the cliff in his haste, but slowed almost immediately when the house was out of sight. From there he drove mechanically, letting the car take him on into the endless night as he focused on what had happened.

The shovel was his, fetched in his sleep from the locked barn. Somehow, despite the drugs—still whispering their deadening song to him, not loud but insistent—he'd retrieved all the necessary keys, gotten the cuffs and all the locks and bolts undone, gone out to the barn and back, and . . .

Shaking his head, Jeremy Sturbrant stopped at an all-night fast food restaurant. Blinking under the garish lights, he bought food he barely tasted but did not like—and soon tossed out the window as he drove aimlessly along. When utter weariness overcame him, he parked at the roadside and threw the car keys out into the night.

✢ ✢ ✢

Around noon the next day, Sturbrant came awake. The hand he'd banged the night before was stiff and sore. It took him a while to find his keys, submerged in a few inches of water in a roadside ditch. Then he drove himself home, feeling almost numb. Numb and desperate.

Resolutely he explored the cellar, tramping smooth the small mess he'd made with the shovel before returning the tool to the barn. As Sturbrant drank too-hot, too-strong coffee, the security company salesman assured him on the phone that the appointment was still on for the next day. When the salesman noted that Sturbrant sounded stressed, he thanked the man bitterly and hung up. Collecting his handcuffs and all the supplies he'd need to give himself injections, he locked up the house and went for a long drive.

Not long before sunset, in a distant city, he took a motel room. He gave his car keys and house keys to the desk clerk—a bored young man with earrings who'd dyed his hair an almost luminous green—and insisted they be locked in the motel safe until the morning. Then Jeremy Sturbrant treated himself to a nice meal at a low-lamps, black tie restaurant a short walk away. Though he could very much have used a drink, he declined the wine list, not wanting to do anything that might alter the effects of the double-strength sedative he was going to give himself back in his room.

When he'd drugged himself, he lay down on the bed without undressing and handcuffed both ankles and one of his wrists to the old metal-framed bed. Despite the drugs, sleep was a long time coming. Sturbrant stared at the ceiling.

We are all zombies, but some of us are more zombies than others. . . . When playing God, it's not whether you win or lose, but . . .

✢   ✢   ✢

No nightmares, just a deep and endless fall. At some point, it became a drifting rather than a descent, until quite suddenly Jeremy Sturbrant was awake.

In bright light, not darkness. In his own cellar. He'd just propped the shovel neatly against the scratched furnace and was reaching down into the hole he'd dug.

His hands were sticky with drying blood—blood that didn't feel as if it were his own. Blood in which were stuck, here and there, hairs of an almost luminous green.

As if they belonged to someone else, his hands were moving against his shocked, awakening bidding. They were closing on a dirt-covered, slimy ball. The surgeon's head.

"No!" Sturbrant screamed, or tried to, as his body turned—despite his wild inward tuggings to the contrary—and marched across the cellar to a table that held a large stainless steel vat.

A vat of freshly mixed wonder broth. The nutrient fluid bubbled eagerly as his traitorous hands gently lowered the head into it.

Helpless, Jeremy Sturbrant watched the ghastly bobbing thing grin up at him . . . as his own hands went to a scalpel on the table beside the vat, and raised the blade to his own throat.

FAMILIAR EYES

BARRY HOLLANDER

Whenever she returned, he killed her.

She lurched from the woods again. By the time he grabbed his aluminum bat, she was fumbling with the back gate. By the time he slipped out the front door and rounded the house, she had given up on the gate and crawled over the chain link fence, leaving behind scraps of rotting cloth and pale flesh. He hid behind an overgrown azalea, watched for something familiar in those eyes.

All he saw was a zombie's empty stare.

Her next challenge: the wooden steps leading up to the deck and sunroom door. With a foot on the first step, she hesitated, as if considering the daunting nature of the task she faced. He held his breath, hopeful. Maybe this time. Maybe she would recognize the house, the deck where she spent so much of her time coaxing plants to life, where she loved to sit in a chair at the end of a long day, sipping tea and reading some trashy romance novel. He'd seen hints, no matter what the experts said, hints that she was more than a walking piece of dead meat.

Another step, then her hand gripped the rail, almost caressed it in recognition. Blank eyes scanned the yard. She knew. Somehow she realized he had moved from inside the house to where he now stood, sensed that he hid nearby. Tired of the game, he stepped from behind the bush, bat concealed behind his back. He didn't want to use the thing, not again, not unless he absolutely had to.

"Hello, Margaret."

Vacant eyes met his, orbs offering no spark of recognition, only the mindless hunger of a zombie.

His zombie.

The deck forgotten, she made an awkward, stumbling fall off the steps, arms outstretched for a deadly embrace. He danced back, tried again.

"Margaret. It's me. . . ."

She took another step, and he backed away farther.

"It's John. . . ."

She gathered momentum, her legs finding their pace, their rhythm.

Avoiding tree roots, he kept a safe distance between them.

"Please, Margaret. I know you're in there. You have to remember."

Fingers clutched empty air. He ducked a second swipe of her broken, dirty nails. He didn't want to feel that cold touch. Not again.

"Please." He almost choked on the words. "I can't keep doing this."

Another sweep. Icy fingers brushed his cheek, and his skin crawled at her touch. He thought of the flower garden, angled that way, but she cut him off and forced his back against the fence. It was too late. As she staggered forward, fingers clawing for his face, he brought the bat from behind his back, felt its weight seem to grow into an anvil's as he realized what had to be done. With a shift left to draw her off balance, he swung the bat in a wide arc to meet her head. The impact made a dull metallic *thump*.

She crumpled into the dew-washed grass, face upturned to the sky. Her mouth continued to work, as if chewing his skin and bones. In that movement, he thought he heard the whisper of his name. He bent closer.

"Margaret? God, I'm sorry. . . ."

Eyes focused, then were overtaken by a blank, indifferent stare.

✢ ✢ ✢

John pulled a dripping beer from the ice chest and handed it to Frank as the man joined him on the front porch step. The summer evening turned purple, fireflies winking in the shadows. A bat flitted across the cul-de-sac as a streetlight sputtered to life, luring insects to the feast. Frank popped open the can, took a long, hard drag, then another, and wiped his mouth with an arm.

"She came again, didn't she? Third time? Fourth?"

"Third." He watched the Georgia night come slow and sweet, hurting all the more to be out with a beer on such an evening, him alive and alone, Margaret's body covered by a plastic sheet in the backyard. They stared at the darkening sky, drank quietly.

Frank sighed. "Dealt with the body?"

"No." A cat crossed the street and disappear into a line of shrubs. "I'll bury her tomorrow. In the morning."

Frank shook his head. "It's your business. I've told you that before, and I'm not going to report you or anything, but it's a hell of a risk. You sure about this?"

John answered with a long drink, letting the beer dull the ache inside. He knew what Frank meant, even if he didn't want to come out and say it.

Fire.

Douse her with gas, toss a match, sit and watch her skin bubble and blacken until there's nothing left but ash and charred bones. Grind the bones to dust and scatter them as far as you can manage. People did that with their zombie, if the zombie didn't get them first. John shuddered, reached for another can. He popped the top, a misty spray wetting the grass.

"She can wait until morning," he said.

Frank rolled the can in his big hands, searching for wisdom on the warning label.

John looked at him. "I can't do it."

"Bury her?" His friend shrugged. "I'll do it. Won't like it, but I'll do it. I know you're not one of those nuts on TV, the ones who think the zombies have come to take us with them—what is it? Oh yeah, to a 'higher plane of existence.'" He snorted, then put out a hand. "Sorry."

"I understand. No, it's not that." John took a breath, let it out slowly. "I just can't burn her . . . not like that bastard Willard."

The old man lived on the next street. His wife had come back for him, as had one of his grown children, and he'd burned both in front of the whole neighborhood. John still couldn't believe either woman would return for such a fool, that he mattered so much to them. That he mattered to anyone. "Fried and forgotten," Willard had said, grinning while what remained of his wife smoldered in the yard, the sweet stench of cooked flesh filling the air.

"Willard might be a bastard, but he's no fool," Frank said. "Burning's the only way. If the cops find out, they'll come and do it whether you like it or not, then probably cart your ass off to jail for good measure. You know the law."

"Screw the law and screw Willard." John stood. "I can't burn her. Not yet, at least." He let his reasons hang in the air, unsaid.

His neighbor hadn't moved, just looked up at him from the porch step. "Not everyone uses fire. Shirley Martin didn't."

A few weeks after her husband Sam died, Shirley Martin lucked into spotting him as he reeled toward the house. She got in a lucky blow to the head—that always dropped the zombies cold for reasons scientists couldn't begin to explain—and stuffed him into an old wire dog cage they kept in the garage.

The best anyone could figure, she'd hoped to talk sense into the man, if only she could force him to sit still and listen, as if being a zombie were no different than him coming home after a few too many beers. That night, as she slept, Sam pried apart the metal bars with his bare fingers.

He didn't eat her all at once. Zombies never did.

Later, some neighborhood kids spotted a bloated Sam wallowing in the street like a snake after a big meal. Where he would have gone next was anyone's guess. John knew you could never tell with zombies. After killing their most important loved one, some went after a second, but others just called it quits and clawed their way back into the hole from which they'd come, dragging a thin blanket of dirt back on top of them as if they were embarrassed by what they'd done. The late-night TV shows were full of gags on the subject: the zombie husband who ignored his wife and killed women from his various affairs, or the wife who chased her zombie husband in hopes of being the one he wanted, or the bachelor who rose from the grave only to find himself with no one to kill, not even his mother. He just sat there, body parts falling off while he tried to come up with someone, anyone, he loved well enough to eat. Sick stuff, but no worse than the industries that had popped up around the zombies' emergence. If religious beliefs didn't allow burning, you could, for a hefty price tag, bury the dear departed in a high-security cemetery. Crematories, of course, were now almost as plentiful as McDonald's.

Burning. It always came back to burning.

The neighborhood teenagers chased Sam down with bats and rocks, beat his body to a mushy pulp, and started a bonfire in the middle of the street. They danced around what was left of him as he burned.

Frank crushed his can, sat it with the other empties. "Thanks for the beer."

"I'm sorry, Frank." John put a hand on the man's shoulder. "You did what you had to do with Kelly. I understand that. I'm just not ready. Not yet."

Frank nodded. "It's your call, but it's not her, John. Not any more. No matter what she looks like or sounds like, even if she manages to mumble a few words like they sometimes do." His bones creaked as he stood and stretched. "Just get her in the ground as quick as you can, like you've done before. You know what can happen if you don't."

"Yeah, I know."

✛ ✛ ✛

He couldn't sleep. He ended up in the sunroom, staring out the window at the dark lump in the yard. The sheet was a waste of time, but he couldn't stand the thought of her out there, exposed to the night like some pile of dirt. She deserved better.

Kelly and Margaret had died together when a drunken jerk in an SUV ignored a red light and plowed into Kelly's compact car, killing both women. The drunk walked away with a few bruises and long list of criminal charges. After the funerals, he and Frank had spent the next few weeks plotting ways of torturing the guy, once he got out of prison, eventually settling on a plan to strap him into a compact car out at the junkyard and slowly crush it.

It had to be slow. On that much they agreed. The man had to scream.

The zombie risings had only just started, though no one could explain why. No comets had blazed across the sky. No weapons of mass destruction had erupted in a third world country. There was no reason at all for the resurrections that anyone could identify, though several religious sects claimed responsibility once it became clear what was happening. A few dead people crawled out of the ground, then more, and after a short time, people figured out that the zombies tracked the person they loved the most in life. Get in its way and a zombie on the hunt might take a swing or two, maybe give you an infectious scratch, but that was often the worst of it. So long as you weren't the loved one of choice, that is. The dead seemed eager to take those special few back to the grave with them.

The government ordered everyone to report zombie sightings, and special units armed with flame throwers patrolled the larger cemeteries. Backhoes dug up graves, and the disinterred corpses were piled and burned. At night, the fires glowed in the distance and with the breeze came the smell of burning meat. Later, people learned that a blow to the head would stun the zombies, but it didn't keep them down. Zombies reburied after being stunned often rose up again a short time later.

Leave the body out too long in the open air, they also discovered, and the zombies became almost impossible to destroy, even with fire.

At the time of Margaret's death, John hadn't cared one way or the other about the undead plague, he missed her so much. They'd never had children of their own, couldn't have them because of Margaret's childhood illness. Friends had kids, watched them grow and go off to the college, and through it all he and Margaret had smiled and quietly promised that they would always have each other. No matter what else, they would have each other. John never considered that she would come back, not as a zombie. Not her.

Until she did.

He remembered how he woke early that morning, before sunrise, made coffee, happened to glance out the kitchen window and see a shape moving among the trees. Margaret, wearing the dress she had been buried in, worked from tree to tree, hugging each for support as she neared the house. Without a thought, he rushed out the back door, calling her name. The moon had dropped beneath the pines, yet some of its ivory light leaked through the needles and branches. She turned to him, eyes like black buttons. Again he called her name, tried to reach the woman behind the blank face. Instead, she groped her way toward him and he quickly found himself with his back pressed against the deck, his dead wife moving closer.

He'd seen the news, the video of zombies as they roamed the landscape—but Margaret? She reached out, grabbed his arm, sent ice into his veins. He ducked a sweep of her hand, pulled her along with him across the yard, aiming for nowhere in particular, just trying to get away and stay close at the same time. He jerked free, stumbled his way into the flower garden grown wild, the weeds now competing with blooms for space—another sign of her being gone. Backing into the tangled growth, he tripped on a shovel and fell. He grabbed the wooden handle on impulse.

Dead eyes took in the garden and, for a moment, John thought she connected somehow with that place she had spent so much time tending. The world stopped: The morning birds fell silent in the trees, the low hum of traffic from the highway a half-mile away quieted.

"Margaret?"

She looked nothing like the woman who'd driven away that afternoon, laughing with her friend, nothing like the woman in the casket, solemn yet at peace. Her clothes were stained red by the Georgia clay. A clump of grass and leaves hung in her hair. A vacant stare greeted him now. Her starved mouth moved as if chewing him in advance.

And even now, when he thought back to her first return, he remembered the sudden, shameful relief he felt.

"At least you came for me," he remembered whispering as she gathered herself, pushed through the flowers, groping for his flesh. For him, not the man from her first marriage, who'd left her for a younger woman, one able to bear children. "At least I have that."

She did not acknowledge his words. Instead, she reached for him hungrily.

"Please," he begged. "Don't make me do this."

Fingers clawed at his face. He jerked left, saw the way she responded, noted that she stumbled a half-step in that direction. He tested it again to the right, saw the same response. Slow, to be sure, but every move he made she countered, trying to cut off his escape. He stepped left, brought the shovel swinging from the opposite side, felt the dull thud as it struck her cheek.

Later that morning, Frank came to see him.

"God, I never thought it would happen to her." Frank put his hands in his jeans pockets, glanced back over his shoulder at his own empty yard. "Do you think. . . ?" He let his voice trail off.

All John could do was shrug. He had spent the morning in tears.

Frank sat next to him. "You have to destroy the body. That's what they are saying. Do it fast." He waited for an answer. "John, either destroy the body or report it to the cops so they can do the job. I know it's hard, but that's not Margaret."

Maybe it wasn't, he remembered thinking.

Maybe it was.

Let her come back, he decided. He'd bury her, but at least then she'd be able to come back. There had to be something of her left inside, the real Margaret. And they'd have each other again. She'd promised that, after all. And she had recognized something about the garden, he was sure of it, no matter what the experts said about the way the dead perceived things.

He dragged her out to the woods behind the house, that first time. Her mouth moved once, but nothing came out. It was the eyes, the cold eyes, that hurt the most.

Those he covered first.

✢   ✢   ✢

A week after Margaret's first appearance, Kelly came looking for Frank and almost got him.

A deep sleeper, he woke just in time to see his dead wife bouncing wall-to-wall down his hallway. He had a gun at his bedside and put six shots into her before she made it to his bedroom door. She staggered back a few steps as if slapped, the bullets doing little more than create a few holes and slow her momentum, but it bought him enough time to grab a bat from behind the bed and take care of the rest. He telephoned, asked John to come over. By the time he'd arrived, Frank had dragged Kelly's body into the backyard. A gallon of gasoline waited nearby.

Frank handed him a beer as he approached. "Drink," he said.

Frank tossed his own can into a pile of empties. "I'm not going to make her go through this again," he said. "*I'm* not going through this again."

John hadn't said anything. What could he say? Even then, he knew that they saw things differently. Frank and Kelly had three grown children, a couple of grandkids. He had someone else.

So he stood silently by as Frank filled the air with the sharp smell of gasoline, lit a piece of paper with his cigarette lighter, and dropped the flame onto his dead wife's body. John looked away, but he stood next to his friend and they choked together on the stinking smoke that seemed to shift in their direction no matter where they moved, as if Kelly were insisting upon one last, horrible memory of her passing.

✜   ✜   ✜

After Margaret's first appearance, John had spent hours on the Internet, researching what people knew—or thought they knew—about the zombies. Some experts argued that there was a pattern in the appearances and wanted to study it further, but the government, pushed by religious leaders, clamped down on any such proposal. State and federal law required the destruction of any zombie, regardless of who they were or where they were spotted. John read what little he could find on patterns, tried to reason out the truth from what scientists and New Age nuts and Goth gurus offered to a frightened public. A warped mythology dominated most discussions, a strange mix of hard fact and Revelations-inspired fear. One woman on CNN had insisted the dead followed a biological cycle of rebirth, that they only wanted to return to those they loved and shepherd them to a new level of existence. When the newscaster pointed out that the zombies also wanted to eat their loved ones, she sniffed and explained that consumption was their only method of incorporating "the other" into themselves, into the lives they now enjoyed.

"It's all about love," she said, her voice calm and serious. "It's all about return and renewal."

Her interview had been followed by the story of a young mother who'd come back and eaten her own children.

A few fringe groups claimed that, given enough time, the "returned" could be brought back to actual life. They had loaded up their dead and taken them to compounds designed to allow the zombies to rise. Then they would "put them down" as gently as possible and let them rise again, in a continuous series of deaths and resurrections. Police raided a few such places on public safety grounds, dragging out a jumble of kooks and, in those instances where a zombie had slipped out unnoticed and found its target, half-eaten bodies.

"I'm not one of those kooks," John told himself every time he came across such a story. "I'm not."

But he was becoming more and more convinced that, just maybe, he could reach Margaret. Maybe the crazy people were on to something that the Feds didn't want known.

Armed with baseball bats and all the information he'd been able to gather, he waited for Margaret to return a second time. Now, he'd be ready. There was a motion detector near her new grave, out behind his house, with a wire that ran back to the sunroom. It was there that he slept, on the creaky couch she'd always threatened to throw away.

A beeping seeped into his skull.

He made it to the grave as she was still scraping away the soil, trying to free herself from the sticky clay. His teeth chattered despite the warm night. It was Margaret, he told himself, not some monster.

Her eyes searched the darkness, found his.

He stepped clear of the tree behind which he'd been crouching. He called her name, tried to explain what was happening, even as she stumbled forward like some creature from an awful late-night horror movie. He kept the tree between them, begging and dodging, allowing her to get close enough once to grab his shoulder and send the cold of the grave through the shirt and into his bones. Then he fell over a root, and crawled through briars and pine straw until he made it to the open gate to his backyard. Always in his mind lingered the idea that she would recognize something, anything, of the place she loved so well. That, he hoped, would bring her back to him.

He never had the chance to test his theory.

Margaret knocked him down halfway into the yard, fingers tearing at his clothes to rip them free and expose what lay beneath. He kicked her off, felt her hand grab an ankle as he stood, fell hard again. She came up on one knee, began to reach for his face, so he swung the bat sooner than he had hoped would be necessary. It slammed into the side of her face.

She fell, tried to rise.

"Stay down," he sobbed. She pushed herself to stand, so he hit her again—then listened, hoping to hear his name, to hear anything at all. She lay there, quiet.

In the morning he woke, dragged her to the same hole from which she'd crawled a few hours earlier. Before he could roll her into the grave, her mouth formed a word. Some said zombies could talk, a word or two at most, but the skill never lasted and their utterances never qualified as real conversation. They spat out random sounds, usually, at best phrases spewed from the depths of their calcified brain like an animal twitching even after it was dead.

Still, John risked the danger of putting his ear to her open, drooling mouth. But he heard nothing. She did not speak again. He waited as the sun climbed over the trees, waited as long as he dared, then rolled her into the grave and covered her face with dirt.

✛   ✛   ✛

And now, she had come a third time.

John drank coffee, ate a piece of dry toast, then walked into the yard and pulled the plastic sheet back from his dead wife's body. He waited for her to speak, of course, and heard nothing at all. Maybe Frank was right. Maybe they all were right—the government types who said zombies were nothing more than animated meat. He was fooling himself.

He grabbed her arms and dragged her out the back gate, across the ravine that ran like a spine through the neighborhood, up the slope, and into the scattering of pine and oak where the hole, the same hole, gaped ready. His shovel leaned against a tree, as it had since after her first appearance. He dropped her arms, leaned on the shovel, and listened to the day: the birds and the traffic, the quiet of his neighborhood. Some people had left, had moved to safer, gated communities that promised zombie-free living. But the promises never panned out. Whatever invisible tether existed between the zombie and their loved one could not be broken so easily.

With his shovel, John cleared some of the loose dirt from the bottom of the hole, making sure it was deep enough to keep the animals away. He had just stepped out of the grave when he heard it.

"John?"

The word sounded more like "Thawn," but he knew what she meant. John closed his eyes, took a shaky breath, and steadied his grip on the shovel. Fire. In his mind, he pictured a cleansing fire.

"Hush, dear," he finally said. "I'm nearly finished."

Silence for a moment, then: "Again?"

It sounded like "Athen?"

He couldn't bring himself to reply this time, so he blinked back the tears and continued digging. He had almost finished when she spoke a third time.

"I'm trying, John."

Clear as a bell this time. He looked hopefully at her face, saw only her blank stare directed at the sky, one eye askew.

"I miss you," he said.

Silent once more, Margaret gazed through the trees, seeming to watch the few puffy clouds passing overhead. John sighed, took her by the arms, and started to roll her into the hole. Then he stopped and bent over to lift and cradle her body, so light and fragile, so like a baby's.

"Until next time," he said, gently lowering her into the grave. He straightened, took the shovel, and scooped up a spade full of red clay.

She stared up at him with familiar eyes.

Those he covered last.

CHRISTINA'S WORLD

STEVE MELISI

The pounding on Marty's door was as real as the groan it drew from him. *God*, he thought. *It's the middle of the night.*

Surely it was his friend Dolores. Had to be. No one else would dare. And no one else had really known what to do for Marty once *it* happened—once he lost Christina. It was a puzzle. Should they stay away and give him time to grieve, quietly letting it be known they were always available should he need comfort? Or should they simply barge right into his misery and offer of themselves without being asked, because it was understood that such asking would be awkward and difficult? While most of his friends opted for the former, Dolores stampeded into the latter.

She meant well, certainly. But when she inquired how he was doing, Marty's honest response of "Still the same, but doing better" was never enough. There was more he wasn't expressing, more that needed to be released. To be fair, she was right. Somehow, though, opening up to Dolores was almost as hard to deal with as the grief itself. Maybe it was because she draped herself in black clothing and surrounded herself with pentagrams and crystals and burning incense. Marty often referred to her as "a Wiccan without a cause." And he simply didn't believe that any touchy-feely, spaced-out advice from a New Ager could cure the depression he felt so deeply these days.

He hadn't heard from Dolores for almost two weeks, though. He'd even begun to think she might have finally decided to leave him alone. Then again, that two-week respite could have inspired this late-night visit, and the evident urgency in her banging. *Well*, he decided as he descended the stairs, *I'm just going to have to be firm with her.*

"Okay," he said, opening the door, "this had better be good—"

"Marty," said the woman in the white dress standing before him. A woman distinctly not Dolores. "Marty, it's me."

"Oh . . . my . . . God," he said, unable to believe his eyes. "Christina?"

"Oh, Marty." She threw herself into his arms. "It's so *good* to see you."

He didn't need to remind himself that Christina was dead. Had been for two months. She'd been rushed to the hospital, diagnosed with kidney failure. Complications set in, and she never regained consciousness. That was it. Dead at thirty-two.

"It's not fair," Marty had shrieked when the doctor gave him the news. How could it be? It was love they had, true love, not a doubt in anyone's mind—least of all the happy couple's— and suddenly it was gone.

Then what was this? Was this woman on his doorstep at three in the morning actually Christina? It certainly looked like her. She had the same alabaster complexion and the same flowing nut-brown hair. She moved with Christina's gentle glide as she slipped across the threshold and into his arms.

And the hug. No one but Christina hugged like that. She had a peculiar way of dropping her forehead down onto his shoulder, which always pleased him, and resting her hands on the small of his back.

It was her.

As if by instinct, Marty wrapped his arms around her the way he always did—left hand gripping his right elbow, holding her as tightly as he could.

"Mmm," Christina purred, the hum of pleasure surging through her body and into his. "Tighter," she said, as she always did.

Yes. She was back.

✛ ✛ ✛

In the morning, Marty awoke expecting Christina to be gone, vanished like the apparition she most definitely had to be. But, no. She was still there, in his arms.

As he lay with her, he wondered once more what was happening. *How could she be here?* But in reply to this question, asked over and over, he just kept saying to himself, *Marty, you shouldn't be surprised.* . . .

Christina was always a romantic. She adored old movies, especially love stories. Nothing made her happier than to see a screen couple skirting the tender edges of a wondrous new relationship, or reunited after years apart, or heading into the Happily Ever After as the fade out closed the film. Her absolute favorites were about romance taken to the extreme, movies like *Wuthering Heights* and *Smiling Through,* where love was unbounded, even by death, and could be carried on into the Great Hereafter. Now she seemed to be making that fantasy a reality. And if anyone could make art become life, Marty decided, it would be Christina.

In fact, he used to tell her that, back when they first fell in love. Since the day they met, he liked to say he lived in "Christina's world." And like the girl in the Andrew Wyeth painting, he'd be crippled without her. "How can I walk, if not for you?" he would say, holding her tight against him.

She recognized the romance in his heart when he said that, and always complemented it by replying, "How can I fly without you?"

Fly, indeed. She had flown from the grave to his arms. But how? In truth, Marty didn't want to know. She was here. And he was happy again.

✣ ✣ ✣

When Marty called in sick to the office four days in a row, it wasn't looked upon as a man ducking his duties. The sympathy for him was strong, and it was assumed that he was still suffering, that he had come back to work too soon, had taken things on again too fast. There was no timetable to be put upon the grieving process, and his friends and co-workers knew that it would catch up to him every so often. They just needed to cut him some slack when it did. Surely this was the case now: He was still having trouble getting over Christina.

What they didn't know was that Marty was over Christina, and under Christina, and on top of Christina, and behind and beside and curled up tightly with Christina. The only thing "sick" related to him calling in was that, to all the world, Christina was dead, and so Marty might be considered a necrophiliac. Well, to those who frowned upon him Marty might say, "Let them eat cake," because Christina was alive and well, and she had come back, and there was nothing to keep them from continuing the love they'd once had.

✣ ✣ ✣

The outside world concerned them little those first few days. Their hunger for each other, made ravenous by their months apart, was the only earthly satisfaction either desired. And they ate each other up madly.

After a time, however, Marty began to notice things he thought he might have noticed sooner. Certainly the stains and tatters on her long white burial dress were easily overlooked that first night. He'd had too much else to look at to care about those. And when he noted them now, he assumed their presence was only natural, given where she'd been.

As to her appearance, he eventually admitted to himself that she had looked better. Her skin was pale—paler than it normally was—her eyes rather sunken, and her cheeks a bit hollow. She also had a few sores on her arms and legs that could use bandaging. Her whole pallor suggested sickness, reminding Marty a little of consumptives in Gothic literature. Also, she seemed to exude a frosty aura.

Her appearance didn't bother him terribly—again, she had come from the grave; a look of death was understandable—but the cold was a funny thing. With all that they had been doing the past few days, one might think she would warm up a little. A night under the covers had done nothing to improve her body temperature, and several nights almost less so. Her hands were always chilly on him, her body a deep-freeze compared to his, especially during their heaviest moments of "rein-carnal" bliss. Marty kept remembering the way it had been, the warmth he'd felt every time he touched her. Christina had once had something of the blast furnace about her when passions began to rise. Now, she sucked the warmth out of him.

If he thought about it too long, though, he made himself guilty, like he wasn't fully appreciating the miracle of her return. *You be dead for a while and see how long it takes you to get warm*, he scolded himself. Besides, the warmth of her smile more than made up for the chill of her touch.

✛ ✛ ✛

"We don't need anyone else to know," Christina cooed, taking Marty in her arms and pressing her body against his. "We don't need anyone but us." Her case was very convincing.

Marty had suggested they at least tell Dolores, since she'd been so concerned about him. Marty also figured that her intimate knowledge of things occult—a trip to her apartment was always an adventure into a realm of séances and spirit rituals—might help him to understand Christina's return from the grave.

But Christina convinced him to wait. And Marty decided that she was right. He wasn't interested in other people at the moment. Like someone newly in love, he wanted no world to orbit but the object of his affection. He would tell everyone in time—and via easy stages, to get them used to the idea.

As it was, he wasn't quite used to it himself. Not totally. He still didn't understand what could have brought her back, besides the power of love. That sounded good. Outside of the movies, though, it was hard to believe. Especially when confronted with Christina's appearance, which—as the evening of her arrival grew more and more distant—didn't seem to be any different.

No, that wasn't true. Christina's appearance had changed, but not for the better. He tried to rationalize this. If, as she had told him, she'd woken up in the grave, dug her way to freedom, and headed for his door, she was bound to have some lasting scars and would take some time to recover. Just as he himself might take a while to get reacclimated to the world after waking up from a particularly long sleep, so too would Christina, awakening from a much deeper slumber, be out of sorts for a time.

The thing was, Marty eventually did wake up and could face the world with vim and vigor. Christina had vim and vigor. What she didn't have was the appearance of being anything other than, well, dead.

She was still cold, first of all. This troubled Marty immeasurably, as the wish to be with each other in every conceivable way was still strong, particularly on her part. But the cold was frustrating. He had taken to going to bed fully clothed, which diminished greatly what fun they might have.

As to her looks, the gentle softness her cheeks had possessed in life never returned; they stayed hollow, her skin coarse and ashen. Her eyes remained sunken. When she put on clothes other than her burial dress, she did look nice—if one discounted the scaly patches and sores that never healed, no matter how much lotion or ointment she slathered on them, or how many bandages she applied.

Then there was the smell. Christina's skin had always smelled exceptional, even without perfume or toiletries. Now, her odor was something akin to the smell that clung to Marty's fingers the time he squished a beetle crawling across his keyboard. A bit woody, a bit musty. A bit more pungent than Marty preferred in a female companion.

When he suggested a shower—shower after shower, as the smell got worse—something happened that alarmed him even more than the odor. The drain clogged—not with her hair, but with a pale white substance. It was a little like plastic wrap, but thicker to the touch. Marty didn't know what to make of it. But when he looked at Christina that night, he understood. He could see, much too clearly, the roadmap of her circulatory system, and maybe even the dark shape of her bones and organs deeper down. The white stuff in the drain had been skin.

He wanted to take her to a doctor. At the very least, to a dermatologist. But she balked at the idea, saying it was just a passing thing. She would be fine eventually; it would just take time. And since she was the resident expert on all things beyond the grave, he had to take her word for it.

✛ ✛ ✛

Going out on dates, though—that was something else entirely. While Marty was growing quite content to stay at home with Christina—and yet not under the covers with her— she was suddenly acting very much like the young girl he'd first fallen for years ago. She still wanted to keep her return from her friends, but she also wanted to go places and do things, and then come back home and cuddle. But the "going out" was especially high on her list of priorities. She wanted to eat at nice restaurants and take walks and go to old movies and stroll along the beach at night, looking at the stars.

At first, Marty was happy to oblige—happy to return to the life with Christina he had always enjoyed. That life, she assured him, would eventually include others. "Right now," she said, "I just want it to be us." Marty felt good about this, but gradually, as his intoxication with having her back began to wear off, he began to wonder if anyone else would really want to see her. Her appearance was starting to be an issue. And not everyone accepted Christina in the "for better or worse" terms he had once vowed to honor.

The reactions were hard to miss. Waiters and waitresses recoiled at the sight of her, though the more mercenary forced themselves to glance at her occasionally, and not just give Marty face time, so as not to lose their tips. At the movies, people moved away from them. More than once, Marty caught a glimpse of a hand held over a nose as their owner made a hasty exodus from Christina's vicinity. And where once heads had turned whenever Christina walked by—men and women both, in admiration of her beauty and grace—now everyone looked away.

They had every reason to. Marty understood that. Even he could see that Christina was not the woman she'd once been. Not even close. And with each passing day of clogged drains and midnight Neosporin and Band-Aid runs, it seemed less likely that things would get better.

Christina's attitude only made things worse. Nothing bothered her—not her increasingly ghastly appearance, not the smell, not the reactions of others. She glossed over even the most bizarre incidents.

Like the time she accidentally cut off her finger while chop- ping vegetables. Marty found the digit in his salad that night.

"Oh," she said brightly, looking from the index finger stuck on his fork to the absence of one on her left hand. "I was wondering where that went to."

✛ ✛ ✛

What was happening?

Marty had long ago convinced himself that Christina's return was real, and not some dream from which he couldn't awaken. Yet, if there was some magic at work—art become life through the power of love—things weren't turning out like the movies at all.

Far from feeling whole again, mystically complete, he felt trapped.

All Christina cared about was being with him. Where once she'd had her family, and her friends, and the ceramics classes she'd so loved, and her job, she now had only him.

She wanted him to call in sick every day. When he did go to the office, she wanted him to arrive late, or leave early. Could he make it home for his lunch hour? Of course not, but she couldn't understand why. When finally he did come home, he inevitably found her waiting at the door, like some devoted wife out of a fifties sitcom. And the rest of the night had to be theirs, no one else's.

In a way, he felt he really was in "Christina's world," except she was now crippling him rather than allowing him to walk. He found work difficult, and dealing with others nearly impossible. He couldn't do a thing outside work that didn't include her. But he couldn't tell a soul about her either. Not simply because she didn't wish it, but because every time he thought about what he would say, he could imagine the response he would receive: incredulity, and horror should anyone actually see Christina.

It grew quite intense the night of the Clark Gable double feature. First of all, Marty couldn't enjoy the movies; he found himself wondering the entire time what Gable would have done had Carole Lombard returned to him after her fatal plane crash. On top of that, every face in the crowd turned his way and muttered something derogatory. Every face, of course, was several seats away, but Marty could see them clearly enough, even in the dark. And he could feel what they were thinking: *Look at that woman. She looks horrible. And look at the guy she's hanging all over. He must be crazy. . . .*

Maybe that was it—he was insane. Maybe the depression that had overtaken him when Christina died had never gone away and he'd simply lost his grip on reality.

That night found Marty hugging Christina even more closely than he had in all the nights since her return—afraid that he really was alone after all.

+ + +

The night at the amusement park, Marty finally admitted to himself that his life had become a nightmare. Christina loved amusement parks and insisted they go. Her pleadings didn't persuade him so much as did his revulsion at the alternative, which was to stay at home and have her hands running all over his body. Her continued loss of skin had left touching unpleasant enough—her bony fingers scraping more than caressing him—but she was still without her left index finger. Two other fingers had recently fallen off, too. That fact alone overwhelmed his fears of isolation and hostility sparked by the Clark Gable film night.

So, to the amusement park they went.

It being summer, Christina chose a tank top-and-shorts combination that, in her former life, would have made many men drool with lust for her and grumble with envy of Marty. But now, her flesh was so diminished that her bones showed through everywhere. She looked like a Dachau survivor, or a poster child for anorexia. It was horrifying. But Christina didn't care one bit.

"Ooh," she squealed when she spotted the vendors inside the front gate, "candy apples. I love them. Buy me one, please!" She hung on Marty as she pleaded, what fingers she had cutting into his arms, her happy shouts drawing more attention than she was already receiving.

"Okay," Marty said. Anything to make her stop. He pulled out some money and handed it to her, then wandered over to the next vendor to lose himself in the calming pink swirl of the cotton candy machine.

She rushed up to the candy apple vendor, who looked aghast at the horror with the five dollar bill standing in front of him. He barely looked at her as he handed her the apple on a stick, almost forgot to take her money. When he did and handed her back the change, he did it ever so gingerly, taking care not to have his flesh come in contact with hers.

"Mmm," Christina said to Marty as she took her first bite.

He had to force himself to look at her, even to witness her pleasure. Her smile reminded him of nothing so much as the perpetual grin of Yorick's skull, even if her long nut-brown hair spoiled the comparison.

After that first bite, however, Marty wished that he had been looking elsewhere. The sticky caramel coating the apple had affixed itself to her lower lip. And as she withdrew the apple from her mouth, a good portion of the skin covering her lower jaw went with it. There they were, those lips he had kissed so often—well, one of them, at least—hanging from an apple on a stick. The gums and teeth of her lower jaw were now completely exposed, and they worked feverishly to chew the mouthful of fruit she had just bitten off.

"Mmm," she said, not noticing at all that she was minus an expanse of facial flesh. Then she went in for another bite.

Marty had to turn away at last, and didn't look back again until the apple was completely gone. He wasn't sure, but he thought she'd eaten the hunk of flesh that had stuck to the apple, too. He shuddered at the thought.

Then she insisted they go to the Tunnel of Love. The idea of getting her out of the open and into a dark area was enticing enough to make him forget that he would be confined in a small boat with her for the duration of the ride, and—given her ever-present lustful state and the ride upon which they were embarking—she would want to take advantage of the dark tunnel.

And so she did. Seeing her ravaged mouth coming at him for a kiss, Marty had no other choice. He leaned over the side of the boat and let his last two meals splash into the water.

"Oh no," she said to him, her skeletal hands scraping his back in what was supposed to be a comforting rub. "You're sick. We'd better get you home."

At first, Marty felt relieved to be out of the park. But then, as the prospect of another night alone with Christina loomed before him, his stomach clenched and he let another meal go.

✦ ✦ ✦

Marty knew one thing: He wasn't crazy. If anything, he was far too sane. And this was not magical anymore. Whatever joys he had found in Christina's return were gone. He had to do something. Anything. But what? He half-thought about taking her to the shooting gallery at the amusement park and seeing if one of the faux bullets would do her in. But he knew better. A silver bullet maybe. . . .

That was when the otherworldliness of it all really struck home. Why hadn't he been thinking that way all along? Too consumed by the love surging back into his life, no doubt. But it could be denied no longer. And so, as he felt they inevitably would, his steps finally led to Dolores.

"So, what do you think?" Marty said after relating the whole saga.

Dolores sat back, very silent, looking a little worried. She had looked that way ever since Marty began his tale. At first he'd thought she didn't believe him, but he realized now that wasn't the case. She believed, and what he'd mistaken for worry and fear in her expression was something else altogether.

At last, she said, "Oh, Marty. I'm so sorry."

"Sorry?" he said. "What for? Oh, you don't think you can help, is that it?"

"No, that's not it at all. I—" She struggled to frame her words for a moment, then finally blurted it out: "I think it's all my fault."

"Huh?"

Dolores let out a heavy sigh. "I think I'm the one who made Christina come back. No—I *know* I'm the one."

"What are you talking about?"

"It was when I saw you at the funeral," she said. "You were so broken up, and you and Christina had always been so happy and in love. You know that I was always so envious of the two of you, because you were such a great couple. And there you were, just as sad as anyone could ever be. I thought that maybe a spell could put things back to the way they were. And so I . . ."

Marty shook his head, but not in disbelief. A month ago, he would have laughed, but he knew better now. "You," he sputtered. "You. . . ."

"Yes, me. I did it."

"Oh my God."

"God didn't have much to do with it," she noted softly.

Marty face flushed with anger. "What did you do?"

"I never thought it would work," she whined. "Not like this."

"Dolores, tell me what you did!"

"It was a just a wishing spell. That's all. I just wished that you could have Christina back and that she'd be in love with you again. That was it."

"Oh, no."

"I had no idea she would come back like that. Marty, if I had known, I never would have said a word."

Marty could hardly move, or think, or speak. He just sat there on Dolores' ratty couch, surrounded by her dusty stuffed animals—all black cats, of course—totally overwhelmed.

"In a way," Dolores said, "I should be happy that one of my spells finally worked."

One cold look from Marty told her that he did not share her satisfaction in her little victory, and she told him once more how sorry she was.

✢　✢　✢

Why? Marty asked himself. Why hadn't Dolores consulted him before trying anything? It was his life she was playing with, after all, as well as Christina's. But as quickly as the question popped into his head, he knew how ridiculous it was to ponder. Even if she'd told him what she was up to, he never would have believed it. Dolores often talked about spells—a particular root inhaled thrice at sunset to cause happiness, or an herb mixed with dried blood from a wound thirteen days old to bring harm to a hated enemy—but her claims were too silly to take seriously. Especially since she never seemed to profit from her command of magic. Her lackluster job, roach-infested apartment, and meager social life had not improved for years. As for a wishing spell that would raise the dead—don't be ridiculous.

Or so he would have thought. Clearly, though, she had succeeded.

Marty could not go on with Christina as she was. Surely Christina herself could not be truly happy in such a state. So there was nothing to do but break the spell.

Dolores immediately consulted her spell-casting friends. At first, they were quite dubious of her having pulled off a wishing spell, until Marty got on the phone and rather emphatically laid out the situation for them. Then Dolores got back on and explained how much in love Marty and Christina had been. "Yes," Dolores and her friends agreed, "love always makes things easier."

They advised Dolores on a course of action. It was not so much an attempt to break the wishing spell. That was fairly complex to perform and they doubted Dolores' ability to manage it. What they did provide was the formula for a substance that would kill the undead. That seemed a much simpler approach to the whole problem.

When Dolores produced the salve, Marty thought it looked like nothing more than black mud in a small decorative vial. But Dolores told him that it was a special mixture of parts of toads, lizards, sea worms, tarantulas, and human bones.

"It's pretty straightforward," she said. "We just have to rub this stuff into her skin, and I have some words that I need to say. That should do the trick."

"Well," Marty said, hardly able to believe things had come to this, "let's get started."

✣   ✣   ✣

When they opened the front door of Marty's house, Dolores reacted with a grimace. She had never smelled anything so horrible—like an animal dead in the road for several days. She covered her nose with her hand, and was shocked to see that Marty did not do the same. *I'm used to it*, his look told her.

Then she saw Christina—or what Christina had become. Her eyes widened and she gasped. The once-beautiful woman was now a walking skeleton with scraps of pulpy flesh stretched over it, gaily singing a little ditty as she watered the plants around the house. The voice was certainly as Dolores remembered it—Christina had such a pretty voice—but that was the only familiar thing about the creature Dolores could see.

"Oh. Dolores," Christina said, turning her ravaged face to Marty and his guest. Her eyeballs seemed to jiggle loosely in their sockets as she moved her head. Torn folds of skin all over her body flapped in the breeze as she came toward them. Had Marty not prepared Dolores to see just such an apparition, she might have fainted dead away. As it was, a few woozy sways nearly got the better of her.

"It's so good to see you," Christina said, taking her in a perfunctory hug. Her annoyance at the intrusion was palpable.

Dolores winced at the sharpness of bone pressing into her from all angles and the icy chill creeping into her limbs. She shuddered in fear, wanting the hug to be over right this second, and the job they had to do over just as quickly. Most of all, though, she felt sorrier than ever for putting Marty through this.

At last, when Christina let her go, Dolores exhaled and relaxed just a little. But she rapidly drew in another breath as Christina went over to Marty, saying seductively, "Saved the best for last," and wrapped her arms around him. The dead woman kissed her husband with what remained of her mouth—which was actually little more than gums and a few teeth.

I'm going to be sick, Dolores thought, looking at Marty in complete osculation with the cadaverous emaciation that had once been his wife. She wanted to look away, but that was not part of the plan. Far from it. Marty was to keep Christina occupied in this manner while Dolores produced her vial and smeared its contents onto the living corpse. He was doing his part. Now it was up to her.

Fumbling with the vial's cap, she stepped slowly toward the embracing couple. As it came loose, the cap slipped from her nervous fingers and clattered to the floor. Marty started at the sound, but Christina, oblivious to all but her lover, continued their kiss.

Dolores left the cap where it had rolled. With a trembling hand she wiped the black salve onto Christina's exposed shoulder. The feel of the dead woman's flesh beneath her fingers made Dolores shiver all the more, but she did not pull away.

Christina wriggled as the black goop melted into her bony shoulder. Marty, though, kept his grip tight—kissed Christina all the more deeply as Dolores took another helping of the salve and smeared it across the corpse's other shoulder, all while reciting the words she had committed to memory. They were Creole, a phrase that roughly translated as "Though dead you be, I set you free." Christina jerked as if the words were blows raining down on her, but Marty held her until Dolores finished the rite and gave him the all-clear sign.

At last Marty let her go, and Christina moved a step or two back from him. "I feel funny," she said, then shivered as though chills were running all up and down her quite visible spine. She looked at both of them and said, "What's going—"

Her mouth moved as though she were about to say "on," but then opened wider and wider. Skin tore and muscles snapped, and Christina's head moved backward until the top half separated and dropped to the floor, where it shattered into a blob of liquifying bone and brain. The rest of her body collapsed an instant later, imploding into a similar heap of dissolving flesh.

It was over. That quickly, that easily.

Marty couldn't believe it. He looked down at the chunks of melting bone and tissue all over his floor and waited, as though they might reform and rise again. But they didn't. The rite had worked.

He let out an uneasy sigh, and felt his whole body sag with the weight of what he had endured these past few weeks. He wanted to smile—glad the ordeal was finally over—but part of him prevented it. This had been his wife, after all. No matter what she had become, she was still his Christina. He had loved her—*still* loved her. And now she was gone.

Suddenly, Marty felt as Christina must have felt in her last moments. His body seemed to implode. His legs gave out and he collapsed, hitting the floor hard.

From what seemed like half a world away, Dolores shrieked his name. Marty lay on the floor, his useless legs splayed out at odd angles. He looked up at her. "I can't move," he said before an anguished sob choked him. "I can't. . . ."

"Oh, Marty." Dolores cradled him in her arms, rocking him gently, offering him yet again the comfort she had wanted to provide all these many months. "I'm sorry," she said softly. "I'm so sorry."

His body shook with weeping, but he let himself rest in her arms. They gripped each other tightly, there on the floor, for what seemed like hours, and Marty gradually found that he could accept her sympathy. Or maybe he simply lacked the defenses now to turn it aside. But as he let himself be comforted, he saw that he could draw strength from Dolores, from her compassion and concern, from her tender words and her deep desire to set right all the wrongs she had done, and even those she hadn't.

Maybe she understands magic after all, Marty thought, though he knew that this was not some silly spell or a secret drawn from any world but this one.

And for the first time since his wife's death, he understood that with enough time and the right help, he might learn to walk again in a world without Christina.

WHAT DEAD PEOPLE
ARE SUPPOSED TO DO

PAUL E. MARTENS

When Iris left, she said it was because "there are too damn many dead people living in this house, and I don't want to be one of them."

My dad sits in his recliner. He doesn't talk, or eat, or breathe. He watches TV. He comes home from work and he watches TV. I don't know if he knows what's on, or if he cares. We sit in the dark, and the light from the TV screen flickers on his already greenish skin, reflected light and shadows lending his face the only animation it's capable of. It looks unnatural, which, of course, it is.

But what is *natural* these days? Talking monkeys? Dogs that go shopping? Designer diseases? Crops that pick themselves? Gene-jockeys and bio-mechanics have tinkered with so many things that I've lost track. Maybe it's a good thing that there are still laws about what they can and can't do to people. People that aren't dead yet, at least.

Iris said it was wrong of me to have Dad brought back from the dead to work off his debts. But I didn't ask him to run up the balances on all those credit cards. I think a son should be entitled to inherit something from his parents. Am I wrong?

He smells funny. There's a chemical-medical smell, like that pickled frog they made you cut up in high school biology. And there's a hamburger-going-bad kind of smell. You know, like you've got some meat in your refrigerator and maybe it's okay, but maybe you'll get food poisoning, and whether or not you eat it depends on how hungry you are. Not that I ever think about eating Dad, that's just the way he smells. Actually, the odor doesn't make me want to eat much of anything.

Iris said she used to pray that she would die by spontaneous human combustion because "that's about the only thing spontaneous that could ever happen in this morgue."

I guess we are in kind of a rut. Night after night after night, we watch TV. Well, Dad's a zombie. Zombies don't roller-skate, or play the tuba, or go kayaking. They sit and stare. Iris was always after me to go out, but I can't just leave him here, all alone. Maybe he wouldn't notice, but, after all, I am the one responsible for bringing him back.

Sure, I could blame the credit card companies. They practically rule the world these days. How could they not? They get all of everyone's money. With all the politicians they own, it was no problem for them to make it legal to add a clause to their agreements giving them the right to make people pay after they're dead. But I could have paid them all off, if I'd sold Dad's house and his stocks and stuff, so it really isn't their fault. And even though Dad's beyond caring if I'm here or not, I guess I do feel kind of guilty.

Every morning I get up, go downstairs, get Dad out of his chair and make him shuffle his way to the bathroom. It was a pain in the ass getting him to lift his legs over the rim of the bathtub, so I built a ramp. Zombie speed isn't quite enough to get him up and over, and I have to give him a little push. His skin is cold and spongy. I can't help but think of that biology class frog again. I strip him down, hose him off, dry him, and put some clean clothes on him. Then I shove him out the front door. He merges with the other undead in their stiff, shambling commute down the sidewalk to their offices, directed by the computer chips in their heads.

I'm amazed by how many there are. Hundreds of them, maybe thousands. All people, or zombies that used to be people, on their way to work to pay off the bills they accumulated before they died.

I watch them for a while, then I get ready myself and drive to the same place.

I don't know how it happened. I was an okay student. I had a 2.8 in college. But what do you do with a history major? I went to work for a bank. Fifteen years later I'm a zombie wrangler, riding herd on a hundred undead bill collectors. Kind of funny, actually, having people who were brought back from the grave because they didn't pay their bills calling people who aren't paying their bills. They're really good at it, in an emotionless, monotone kind of way. They don't argue, they don't threaten, they don't get upset. They just make the calls, tell people "pay bill now," and hang up. They don't care if somebody's car needs new brakes, or if somebody's daughter needs a new kidney, or if somebody got fired. They never mention it, but just being called by a zombie makes people aware of what could happen to them if they croak with a large balance due. I'm just there to make sure everybody has enough to do and, in rare cases, take over when someone demands to speak to a live human. What the hell, it's a living.

Dad works on another floor, as a telemarketer. He talks in that flat zombie way, no inflection, no emotion. But it's not how he says it, it's what he says. Credit cards sound like free money to some people; they gobble them up. It doesn't matter to Dad. He make his calls all day and leaves at six o'clock with the other zombies on his shift. They stagger outside, and the chips in their heads send them home.

Dad gets home, sits in his chair, and watches TV. I get a beer and sit on the couch and watch with him.

And the next day we do it again.

Then one day I come home to find Dad's credit card statement in the mail.

"Hey, Dad," I say to him. "Looks like you're going to be all paid up by the end of the month."

Dad watches TV.

I watch him watch TV. Has it been two years already? It occurs to me that I'm going to miss him, even more than I miss the soft, purple armchair that Iris threw out because she thought it had gotten too ratty. I mean, he is more than just furniture. Not much more, but still. He's my dad. Granted, we weren't all that close while he was alive, but, dead, he kind of grew on me.

"Hi, Iris. It's me." She is the only person I know to call.

"What do you want, Brad? I'm going to be late for my kick boxing class. If you're just going to bother me again about coming back, you can—"

"No, no, nothing like that. I mean, I'd love it if you came home, but that's not why I called." For part of a second I fantasize about having her sitting here on the couch with me, then hurry on. "It's my dad. He's . . . well, he's just about done paying his bills. They'll take him away soon and turn him off and shove him into the ground and he'll be gone. I'll be all alone, Iris. I don't want to be alone." My voice gets very small and I have that feeling at the sides of my nose that says I'm in danger of crying.

I hear her sigh. There is the same mixture of exasperation, affection, and disgust that was in her sighs when she was still living with me. "He's dead, Brad," she says, not unkindly. "He's supposed to be in the ground. He's supposed to be gone. It's time that one of you started to do a little living."

I don't say anything. She's right. I should have seen it myself. "Thanks, Iris," I say. "I knew you would know what to do." I'm actually kind of inspired. "I'm going to make sure the next few weeks are the most exciting weeks my dad's ever had."

"Brad. That's not—" she starts to say, but I hang up. I have a lot to do.

I turn off the TV. "C'mon, Dad," I say as I grab his hand and pull him to his feet. "Let's go bowling."

He comes docilely, as he does everything else, when he does anything at all. I cram him into the car and drive to the bowling alley. This will be fun, like something we should have done when I was kid. I find an oldies station on the radio and crank it up. When I was a teenager, Dad used to yell at me to turn it down and keep my mind on driving. Now he just looks out the front window and doesn't say a word.

It turns out that bowling with the dead is not as much fun as you might think. He doesn't help me get his shoes on, and he can't seem to grasp the concept of gripping the ball. He keeps dropping it so it thuds to the floor and makes dents. His approach stinks, and he has no follow through. I move him up to the line a few times and stand behind him, helping him hold the ball, swinging his arm and lofting the ball toward the pins. It's no good, though. He throws mostly gutter balls, except for one time when he knocks down two pins. I get excited and slap him on the back. He totters a little, but his vacant stare tells me he's not impressed.

"Sorry, Dad," I say. "Let's try something else."

There's a strip joint next door. *Hey*, I think, *how's that for a bonding experience for a guy and his dad? Alcohol and naked women.*

That's no good either. And I'm pretty sure at least one of the dancers is a zombie, too. They all seem like someone programmed their moves. They look like they should be sexy, but they're just lumps of flesh. If they have minds, they're somewhere else. Their bodies are on automatic pilot. Dad stares at them the same way he stares at the TV. And it would take a lot more beer than I'm able to drink for me to get turned on by these women, either. The music is too loud, the drinks too expensive, the dancers too numb. We go home.

"Bowling and strippers—that's your idea of excitement?" Iris isn't impressed when I call her the next day. "Jesus, Brad. You're pathetic."

She's right. "You're right," I say. But I don't ask her what I should do instead. My dad, my problem. "I'm going to do better, Iris. My dad is going to have the best two weeks of his life if it kills me." I hang up, determined that Dad is going to do more than just watch TV. Iris will be proud.

A movie? No, that's just watching TV on a bigger screen.

Go-karts! Thrills and spills. The wind against your face as

you pit your nerve and skills against those of your competitors. Iris would like that sort of thing.

We get to the track, and I pay for Dad. There are three high school boys already waiting to go. They've got those tattoos that keep moving all the time, which make me seasick. One of them has fang implants. And there's a father and his twelve-year-old son joking with each other about who is going to kick whose ass. I push a helmet onto Dad's head and get him squished in behind the wheel. His knees stick up. I put his hands on the wheel—ten o'clock, two o'clock.

"Okay, Dad," I say. "Have fun." I run off the track just before the guy waves a flag to start the race. Tires squeal. The air is filled with dark gray smoke and the roar of engines that sound more powerful than they really are. But Dad just sits there, staring. He looks kind of stupid just sitting there, if you want to know the truth. I guess there's a reason why you don't see a lot of zombies driving.

The teenagers whoop it up and try to see how close they can come to Dad as they pass him. After the race, when I go to get Dad, the go-kart guy tells me, "Get that stiff out of here and don't come back." But the father stops and says, "My mom was a zombie. I think it's nice what you're doing." As he's walking away with his kid, though, I hear him say, "Stupid, but nice," and they both laugh.

There's a batting cage and miniature golf at the place, too, but what's the point?

We go home and watch TV. Maybe that's what dead people are supposed to do. But Iris said it was time he started living. At least I think that's what she said. And Iris is almost always right.

Iris could never be a zombie. For one thing, she doesn't believe in credit cards, so she'll never have to worry about paying her bills from the grave. For another, she's got too much life in her. Even if she were dead, she'd be more alive than most living people. She runs. She dances. She kick boxes. She climbs mountains. She goes scuba diving. She does volunteer work. She's got those body-sculpting bacteria that know where they should eat your body fat and where they should leave it alone. She makes me exhausted.

I love her, but I can't keep up with her. I think she loves me—or she did love me—but she needs to have more fun than she can have with me. I guess we used to have fun, but, jeez, a guy grows up, you know? I'm tired when I get home from work. Don't I have a right to just relax? Is it a crime to have a couple of shows I like to watch on TV?

A week goes by. Dad and I go to work, come home, and sit and watch TV. Only a few more days and they'll stop sending signals to the chip in Dad's head and he won't be undead, he'll just be dead. I've got to figure out something, one last shot at living before he's gone forever. Something for him to remember for eternity. A tall order, and the pressure is getting to me.

What am I going to do? What am I going to do?

Then something on TV gives me the answer. Skydiving.

Oh, yeah, I think. *A death-defying act right before death. Falling, flying, free.* And then another idea comes to me, how I can make it even better, more intense. I'm a genius. I tell Dad, but he doesn't say anything.

"Iris!" I know I'm practically shouting, but I can't help it. "I got it! I know what I'm going to do!" I picture her being proud of me, looking at me with one of those "my hero" kind of looks. "I'm going to have Dad jump out of an airplane!"

The only sound coming from her end of the phone is one of her sighs. Then she says, "Brad, you're going about this all wrong. Don't you get it? Your dad isn't the one you have to worry about. He's a zombie. He's done all the living he's going to do. You're the one who needs to wake up. You're the one who has to realize you're not a zombie, too."

This is all old stuff, the kind of thing she used to say when we still lived together. But I know I'm not a zombie. Would a zombie come up with an idea like mine? Would a zombie even try?

I have to make a few calls. I get a hold of the skydiving people. They take a little convincing, a little cash, but eventually they go along with my idea. I call Myra, the brown-haired woman in charge of zombie accounts at the bank where I work. She's short and soft, sort of cute. The timing is important—she can't turn Dad off too soon or too late. She agrees to let me call her from the airplane. She'll have her finger on the switch and throw it when I give the word.

She kind of likes my idea. She doesn't really enjoy being the one who has to take the *un* out of the undead. She says maybe we should have lunch sometime after it's all over. I say maybe we should.

Dad finishes his last day at work. His co-workers don't throw him a going away party. They probably won't notice he's gone. He comes home and sits in his chair, waiting for me to turn on the TV.

"No TV tonight, Dad," I say. I wonder if he realizes that he won't ever watch TV again. That he won't ever do anything again. My eyes fill up with tears. He's become my best friend and I'm going to miss him a lot. Who will I watch TV with? I take his hand and pull him up out of his chair. "I've got something special for you tonight."

Neither of us say anything on the way to the little grass runway that is the skydiving airport. Once or twice I swipe my sleeve across my eyes so I can see. At the airport I have to fill out all kinds of releases and waivers that say if anything goes wrong, even if it's their fault, I won't blame them. Dad and I watch as the instructor instructs us. This is how to get into the plane. This is how to get out of the plane. This is what to do when you're falling toward the ground at a hundred and twenty miles an hour. I doubt Dad is taking it in much, but he doesn't really have to.

When it's time to go, I call Myra so she'll be ready.

"I can't believe you're doing this," she tells me. Her voice has the "my hero" tone I wanted from Iris.

I call Iris.

"Brad, you're insane. Zombies don't skydive." I strain to hear a hint of admiration in her voice. "But, if you're really going to jump out of a plane, too, maybe there's hope for you after all." She pauses a second. "Maybe we can go hang gliding next weekend." Hang gliding? I wonder if she is crazy.

We get in the plane and go up about two miles. The sky is blue and cloudless. I bet we can see for a hundred miles. The instructor straps himself to me. We're doing what they call a "tandem jump." He does all the work; I'm just along for the ride. He opens the door, and suddenly there's nothing between me and the ground except Dad, who is sitting and watching.

I call Myra again. "All set," I say. I don't hang up. I've got to keep the line open; timing is everything.

I look at Dad and lean over to give him a hug, taking the instructor with me. "Bye, Dad," I say. "I love you." Did I ever tell him that before? Then I push him out of the plane. I'm not sure, but I think he gives me a look right before he disappears. Not a "thanks, this will be fun" look, more an "are you crazy, what the hell are you doing to me?" look. I'm pretty sure Dad says, "Oh, shit," as he starts falling. I'm surprised.

The skydiving guy and I rock forward, then back, then forward again—and then we're out of the plane, too. I remember to arch my back, chin up, arms out. I look down. There's Dad, arms flailing, legs kicking, like he's trying to claw his way back up into the sky. He seems to be screaming.

The instructor taps me, and I pull the ripcord. We bounce up, then start drifting slowly down toward the airfield. I look again and Dad's getting close to the ground.

"Myra?" I say into the phone.

"I'm here, Brad."

"Okay. Ready?" I wait another second. "Now!"

Dad stops thrashing. He hits the ground. It looks like it would have hurt, a lot, if he'd still been alive. It might have even hurt if he'd still been undead. But Myra turned him off in time.

"Dad," slips out of me, kind of like a sob. I hang limply in the parachute harness, ignoring the instructor as he yells at me to pull my legs up.

We hit the ground, me first. "You goddamn idiot!" says the instructor. I don't know what he's complaining about. I'm the one with the broken legs. I'm the one with the dead, squashed father.

I still have the phone, and I can hear Myra.

"Brad? Are you all right? Brad?"

"Hi, Myra. I'm okay. Except I don't think I'll be able to go to lunch for a while." I tell her about my legs. If this is living, Iris can have it. I don't think Dad cared for it much, either. "I don't think I'll be doing much besides lying around and watching TV."

"That's okay. I like watching TV. Maybe we can watch together."

If I wasn't in so much pain, I'd smile.

So Many Things Left Out

PAUL G. TREMBLAY

September 28, 1917

Momma died in childbirth thirty-seven years ago.

So it was just Daddy and I for most of those years. And he loved and raised me, his only child—a daughter—as best he could. Though I knew he wished for a son.

A writer son.

Maybe the next Mark Twain.

Daddy owned just about everything Twain published, even the early volumes that he could only order through pre-publication. And he made me read them all. Many of those books are still in my Hannibal, Missouri home, in Daddy's old bedroom.

And in the same bedroom, I store the man, the former Samuel Clemens, the one and only Mark Twain, an animate fossil as dusty and silent as the books on the shelves.

I open the bedroom door. The curtains are drawn so only a sliver of sunlight enters. Twain is a motionless shadow lying on the canopied bed Daddy built. The same bed in which Daddy spent two long years dying.

Consumption was what the local doc said. There was nothing anyone could do. And there was nothing I could do except feed him, wash and tend his failing and fading body, listen to those watery breaths sink deeper with each day, carry the weight of his increasing dementia, and care for the house.

And nobody helped this preacher's only daughter until I hired Violet.

I stand in the doorway watching Twain. No rise and fall of the chest. And no watery breaths.

I once thought I knew death.

It's damn hot. I turn and walk to the kitchen while fighting off a pair of stubborn flies, Indian Summer giving those pesky bugs a second life. And sitting on the kitchen table is a telegram and a *New York Times* that the postman delivered this morning.

I swat at the flies again and pick up the paper, finding the review buried inside.

JAP HERRON. A Novel Written from the Ouija Board. With an Introduction on the Coming of "Jap Herron." Frontispiece portrait: New York: Mitchell Kennerly. $1.50.

Yeah, his all-important *New York Times* review is in. Notice I said *his*, not *mine* or *ours*, contrary to what many folks might, or will, believe. But Twain did write *Jap Herron.*

I read the first paragraph with a bullfrog-sized lump in my throat.

> *The ouija board seems to have come to stay as a competitor of the typewriter in the production of fiction. For this is the third novel in the last few months that has claimed the authorship of some dead and gone being who, unwilling to give up human activities, has appeared to find in the ouija board a material means of expression. This last story is unequivocal in its claim of origin. Those who are responsible appear to be convinced beyond doubt that no less a spirit than that of Mark Twain guided their hands as the story was spelled out on the board. Helen Grace Emond and Violet L. Thatch, spiritualist, are the sponsors of the tale, Miss Thatch being the passive recipient whose hands upon the pointer were especially necessary.*

The review is in all right. And it ain't good. I know he's received poor reviews in the past—heck, a library group from Concord, Massachusetts famously maligned his masterpiece, *Adventures of Huckleberry Finn,* calling it "trash and suitable for only the slums."

But this book is different. Seven long, hard, painful, dirty, dark years in the making, for all involved.

> *Helen Grace Emond, who writes the introductory account of how it all happened, is from Hannibal, Mo., the home of Mark Twain's boyhood, and in her the alleged spirit of the author seems to have put much confidence. Her long description of how the story was written and of the many conversations they had with Mark Twain through the ouija board contains many quotations of his remarks that sometimes have a reminiscent flavor of the humorist's characteristic conversation.*

✛   ✛   ✛

April 24, 1910

Mark Twain died three days ago.

I'd known of his heart condition and impending death, and as a result, I was prepared. The press, often the subject of his sharp criticism, had fawned over Twain for the better part of a year, as if he were a dying prince. I suppose he was American royalty, even if he'd spent most of his life railing against society, particularly *American* society. Other than the poor and the Negroes, it seemed we were nothing but targets for his scorn. But people like my daddy ate it up because Twain left folks laughing without realizing how deeply he'd cut them.

So it was easier to not feel guilty for what I was about to do.

Sweating in my frilliest dress, I sat in the quaint but packed Presbyterian Church on the corner of Fifth Avenue in New York City. Another of the literati spoke on Twain's behalf. The casket was open, and Twain wore his legendary white suit.

Above, hiding in the aging wooden struts and support beams, lurked the foul-mouthed street urchin Violet had recruited. I couldn't see him, but I knew he was overlooking the funeral mass from his perch. After the church emptied, he was to climb down and deposit a root-bag into Twain's mouth.

I didn't listen to the haughty words from any of the men who took their turns—too eagerly for my tastes—at the pulpit. My thoughts swirled with the Haitian tales and legends that Violet had brought back from her Caribbean jaunt.

Only three days after the funeral mass, I traveled to Elmira, New York, a green place without a hint of city foulness. I thought I'd never get New York City out of my lungs. Now, the ole Mississippi had its dank days, when the smell of rot and silt clung to Hannibal like a skin, but it was nothing compared to the City stench.

I understood why Twain and his family were buried away from the City, in Elmira.

Much of the evening at the cemetery passed like a dream.

At midnight, the boy and I found Violet, on all fours, chanting and gyrating above Twain's flower-covered grave. She wore a thin, white, and billowy frock that did little to hide what was underneath. When she stopped, she ordered the boy to drop his shovel and move aside the bouquets and wreaths. While he worked, she looped a necklace around my neck. A small root-bag dangled on a chain. It smelled faintly of clove, though with a touch of the sickly sweet of rotted fruit.

"You will wear this for as long as *he* is with you," Violet said. Her pale skin reflected the moon above. "Quickly," she said to the boy.

He did as was commanded, though not without uttering vulgarities.

"How long will this take?" I whispered.

Violet pointed at the cleared site. Earth undulated beneath a fresh layer of grass. A dirt-smeared hand broke through the surface, then a shoulder, then his gray head. My view grew fuzzy until darkness absorbed me and I passed into it, without struggle . . . but I awoke soon after, and heard a sickening crunch. Violet helped me to my feet. Twain, white suit covered in soil, stood with the slack boy in his arms. Dark liquid smeared his lips, and it seemed a considerable portion of the boy's head was missing. I watched Twain dive into the boy's face with a wide mouth.

Now, Violet had told me about our servant's impending sacrifice and I'd agreed to it without much fuss. But knowing and seeing and hearing were different things all together.

I passed out again.

I awoke a considerable amount of time later, as Twain, with Violet watching like a schoolmarm, rearranged the flowers on his former grave.

Violet removed a canteen and razor from her bag. "Look at him and point at the gravestone, please."

Still groggy, I did just that. Twain sat on the stone like an obedient pet. Violet set to shaving off the earth-encrusted moustache and clipping his hair.

I stood and clutched the root-bag around my neck, thinking about the boy and the long trip back to Hannibal.

Yet, much to my shock, the journey from New York was uneventful.

With a shave, haircut, and new clothes, the most famous of Americans drew not a second glance from anyone. Twain looked like a sickly, shuffling old man. Nothing more. And truth be told, he looked a lot like my daddy.

Violet, after collecting her considerable fee—with the promise of more to come when my book was written—caught a ferry back to St. Louis as soon we returned to Hannibal. But that was all right because I didn't need her in my house. She'd told me everything I needed to know, God Bless her little-black-voodoo heart. At least, she'd told me as much as she understood herself, or could make me understand.

Now, this might sound a touch strange, like I was a farm wife who had nothing else to do but talk about how hard it

Paul G. Tremblay

was to raise her offspring, but there was no preparing for the real thing.

Violet had told me the good stuff first. And the good stuff—the best stuff—was that because Twain was freshly dead, I'd have access to everything that was in his head before he died.

It was only a matter of the getting.

But the how of the *getting* was something that I'd have to figure out on my own.

I tried just about everything to squeeze from Twain a story kernel that I could build into a novel. Something I could claim as my own. Yes, just about everything. I started with questions, which, of course, he didn't answer.

Not to say that he didn't speak to me. Lord, yes. He was a regular chatterbox if the situation was right. Mostly me saying a particular word would set him off. And I theorized that what he said was just something left over, ideas or thoughts lingering in his head from before he died. More times than not, what he uttered were words he'd written.

For example: The day after our return to Hannibal, I sat in the bedroom with ink and paper, just busting to get at him. I ordered him to sit on the edge of his bed before mumbling a joke.

"So, how's death treating you?"

"All say, 'How hard it is that we have to die'—a strange complaint to come from the mouths of people who have had to live." Toneless, gravelly voice. No inflection. Like air out of a balloon. A dead sound.

With shaking hands, I scrawled down his words. I asked more questions, but he only repeated himself. Even after I stopped talking, he kept on repeating. It was too much. I screamed at him to stop and ran from the room.

After sinking into a brandy-aided cup of tea, I realized his words were familiar and found the statement in Daddy's leather-bound copy of *The Tragedy of Pudd'n'head Wilson and the Comedy of the Extraordinary Twins.*

So I gave up asking direct questions and tried reading him his own passages, then works of other writers—including my own failed attempts. I tried showing him pictures and newspapers. I tried evening and early morning walks along the Mississippi. I tried walking him by his childhood home.

I pleaded with Violet to help, but she didn't answer my telegrams.

Finally, after a long and frustrating year, I did indeed figure it out.

At the end of my wits, I stuffed a pen into Twain's hand

and pointed at Daddy's desk, a solid oak masterpiece he'd built just before his illness. The same desk I had occupied while tending to Daddy. I used to write while Daddy rested— my scratching pen and his watery breaths weaving a strange background song I still heard at times—and then I'd read aloud to him when he was awake. He'd tell me, "It was good," but that was all. And "good" from Daddy meant *not good enough*, *never good enough*, and I would never be his *son*, and I would never be a writer, and I was only *good enough* for his and the house's caretaking. . . .

So, like a tantrumming child, I demanded Twain sit at *his* desk and write my book.

Twain didn't look at me. He didn't look at the pen or paper or the desk or the bookcases filled with his own long-dead words. With his head angled toward the ceiling, he set pen to paper and he wrote. He wrote for almost ten minutes before dropping the pen and slumping in his chair.

I had to help him to bed. His energies seemed completely drained.

I read and re-read and re-read the page of writing—coherent writing—in that famous scrawl of his. I spent the rest of the afternoon and evening scouring book after book, and another week doing the same.

I never found it. He had written something original.

Twain had written the opening to *Jap Herron*.

✛ ✛ ✛

For the next couple of weeks, I sat him at the desk with only pen and paper. And he wrote, starting each day right where he'd left off. But the duration of each session decreased until he finally stopped writing. It got to a point where even rousing him from bed was a struggle.

Another round of hurried telegrams, and I spent the next month anxiously awaiting word from Violet.

During that month, despite daily cleaning and care, Twain's body started to fail. Skin sagged and turned green in patches, emitting a most foul odor—an odor too familiar from the sickness and suffering I'd already experienced. I knew the Lord was punishing me, making me relive Daddy's long death. Soon I was drowning in the same feelings of inevitability and futility.

That was, until I received a short, handwritten letter from Violet.

And within the note was something all those docs had never found for my first ailing patient: a cure.

Dear Helen,

　　His "creating" fiction is an unforeseen drain upon his energies. I'm afraid that for him to continue to function in the manner you described, he'll need sustenance.

Yours,
Violet

I set to curing my patient that same night.

✣　✣　✣

We walked off the riverboat and onto a sleepy dock that hovered above the murky waters of the Mississippi. The stranger I'd met onboard had my left arm hooked within his, feigning to be the gentleman he wasn't. He joked and I laughed, but otherwise, I remained silent, imagining each house we passed harbored a nocturnal spy.

I wondered if anyone would miss him, a practically anonymous man from New Orleans, just one of a river filled with his ilk—gamblers and conmen. Men who lived without the forward thinking to see past the next hand of poker. Men who had no ambition, no desire of greatness. Men so different from Twain. Men so different from myself.

This man seemed harmless enough—and *harmless* meant that I was confident I'd arrive home without a slit throat. I made it a point not to remember his name.

While making our way across the wooden dock, I wondered if I might have married, had I not spent all those years alone with a dying man. And now, a dead one.

Once away from the dock, my stowed carriage took us to the farmhouse. On the ride I allowed his wandering hands on my body, if only to enhance his state of pliant intoxication.

It was all too easy.

And I wondered what Daddy would've thought of this man.

We ran like giddy children beneath a moonless but starlit sky, and across my yard toward the back entrance. Dressed in white, I imagined myself as a blithe spirit, a siren, leading this man toward his fate. Only I never believed in fate. I believed in doing-for-yourself.

And I believed in death.

We ran into the kitchen. I sat at the large oak table and he approached like a wolf. "Oh, be a dear," I said while unfastening two buttons on my blouse. "Get us a bottle of wine from the cellar. An occasion such as this requires it."

With lantern in hand, he opened the cellar door. The darkened stairwell swallowed his light. As he descended, he said something that I didn't hear. And before the screaming—and there was a horrendous and awful amount of screaming, and tearing, and other sounds—it occurred to me that I had already forgotten what the stranger looked like.

But the aftermath of his visit—that would not be gone from memory so soon. . . .

Twain had seemed so weak, I hadn't anticipated the violence or the volume of the occurrence in my cellar. That was a mistake I wouldn't repeat.

Shaking like a runt kitten, I sat in the dark kitchen and called Twain. He came. I couldn't see the color of stain on his face and hands and clothes, but it had a smell. Still in the dark, I led him toward my washing room, stripped and bathed him in cold water that had been sitting in the tub since that afternoon.

"There isn't anybody that will miss him," I said under my breath.

Without emotion or inflection, a bloody mouth replaying a lost idea, Twain said, "Everyone is a moon, and has a dark side which he never shows anybody."

I slapped his cold face and growled through gritted teeth, "You are going to write my book."

"Well, my book is written—let it go. But if it were only to write over again there wouldn't be so many things left out. They burn in me; and they keep multiplying; but now they can't ever be used. And besides, they would require a library— and a pen warmed up in Hell."

I cried and for the first time thought of using Daddy's shotgun.

He did not speak again that night.

The next morning, Twain's skin had a healthier glow than mine.

✣ ✣ ✣

As the months passed into years, we honed a routine.

Change of clothes, morning bath, dress and stitch any wounds or skin fissures, writing session, an assortment of house chores, sew shirts and trousers for the parishioners of Daddy's church—a side-job that was really nothing more than a show for the denizens of Hannibal; I didn't need the money, since Twain wasn't the only one living off the riverboat wanderers the Mississippi provided—stroll around the farm to try to keep our muscles in working order, and, at night, type transcriptions of what he had written.

Some days I made a game of speaking to him. I'd throw him a question or phrase and try to guess what his reply would be. If he happened to quote a familiar work, I'd try to find the words amongst Daddy's Twain collection.

Some days I let him roam the farm by himself and I watched from the kitchen window. I could almost believe that he was alive, that he was a man sharing my home, sharing my life.

Some days I avoided him and walked along the shores of the river, debating whether or not it was better to dump him—or myself—into the dark waters. But we'd done too much and gone too far to stop.

Yes, this book he was writing had taken over my existence.

Notice the *writer*'s choice of word—*existence*. What I had certainly could not be considered a *life*.

But most days, I gave myself to the routine. Just like with Daddy.

And, Lord help me, it was comfortable.

Five years passed in such comfort. I had hoped to be done with him, at the very least so that I didn't have to keep killing. I didn't rationalize my involvement, shuck off responsibility for the deaths at Twain's hand, for the fueling of his machine.

Twain was nothing but a typewriter, a tool. Or a weapon.

And I used him.

But the *how* had changed.

My intention to squeeze a story idea from him and write a book from it myself didn't happen. I had every intention of being a writer. I had every intention of achieving my own greatness, after a gentle push to get me started.

I needed to be on Daddy's bookcase.

I tried and I tried and I *tried* to continue what Twain had started, to go off in my own direction, but I failed each time. Yes, I was tired from his constant care, and trying to write seemed like another chore on the endless list of chores. But I know a true writer, a great writer, needs soul, and I'd poured most of mine into Daddy and sold the rest for Twain.

As for Twain, he was writing, very slowly, a complete novel. And it was too good. Living characters with plot and symbol and meaning and a style that was undeniably his. I wouldn't be able to put my name on this book. I considered tweaking the manuscript, to change its style and tone. But I couldn't do that without gutting the essence of what made it literature, of what made it great.

As Twain was close to finishing *Jap Herron*, I telegrammed Violet and told her of my predicament. She admitted to expecting a quick payment of the rest of the money owed her. To that end, she insisted I publish the book as soon as possible—with no delay for revisions.

In order to help me get through the last few weeks, and to watch over her investment, Violet temporarily relocated to Hannibal from St. Louis. She set up a curio shop downtown, advertising her fortune telling and ouija board prowess.

And Twain finished his book.

✛ ✛ ✛

"Shoo, now. Go on with you." The flies land on the *Times* and I flick my wrist. There has been no shortage of the filth-ridden little creatures in my home since Twain finished his writing.

In an effort to settle my churning stomach, I swallow a quick shot of brandy. I look at his closed bedroom door before going back to the review.

The story itself, a long novelette, is scened in a Missouri town and tells how a lad born to poverty and shiftlessness, by the help of a fine-souled and high-minded man and woman, grew into a noble and useful manhood and helped to regenerate his town. There is evident a rather striking knowledge of the conditions of life and the peculiarities of character in a Missouri town, the dialect is true, and the picture has, in general, many features that will seem familiar to those who know their "Tom Sawyer" and "Huckleberry Finn."

If this book had been published when he was alive, would it be getting this review?

Is it possible that *Jap Herron* just isn't that good?

Had it become so important to me that I could not tell?

The humor impresses as a feeble attempt at imitation.

Oh, irony of ironies.

Now, I'm no fool, and I sure as hell expected a healthy skepticism with the book's publishing. But I thought it was so authentic, so *him*, folks would come around to believing—to realizing—he wrote it.

Looks like I was wrong.

Just like I was wrong in thinking I knew death.

If this is the best that "Mark Twain" can do by reaching across the barrier, the army of admirers that his works have won for him will all hope that he will hereafter respect that boundary.

The flies are gone. I put down the paper and add more brandy to my tea. Beneath the pile of newsprint is a yellow telegram. I almost forgot about it. I read. . . .

It's from Clara Clemens—Twain's daughter—and Harper and Brothers publishers. They are serving me notice that they're going to court to cease publication of *Jap Herron*.

I throw both newspaper and telegram into my wood stove. Walking to my bedroom, I sit at my cluttered desk.

I write a quick note:

> *Violet,*
> *I am certain you've received the news of the impending lawsuit. It is my decision to withdraw the book and destroy any remaining copies—and its author. I hope the splitting of the advance monies will suffice for your payment.*
>
> > *Be well,*
> > *Emily*

After sealing the envelope, I stare at the reflection in my bedroom mirror. The woman that stares back is older than I expected. Worry lines and sagging features have replaced any promise of youth. I know that I've thrown away seven years.

More than seven years and so many things left out.

Daddy's shotgun hasn't been fired in over a decade. I take it out and load both barrels, just like he taught me before he was sick, a lifetime ago. I hope it still works.

Regardless, my life will change today.

I remove my root-bag necklace and put it on my desk. It shrivels and emits a plume of dust. Now a dark lump, a black heart, it falls to the floor and I grind it under my heel.

There is a stirring in his room, and I hear his door open.

But I am not afraid. Those filled with regret don't know any other emotion.

Twain stumbles out, tongue lolling from his mouth, limbs twitching with want.

"You have more than earned your rest," I say.

He stops and stares. Though I do not expect otherwise, there is no gleam or hint of recognition in his eyes. The look is the only one that has been mine to receive for two lifetimes.

"The report of my death was greatly exaggerated," he says.

Twain lunges toward me.

Aiming the shotgun, I know this is something I should have done for my first dead man.

SHOUTING DOWN THE MOON

MYKE COLE

Mumbi's hands were on him, and she was beautiful, beautiful, and beautiful. He filled his hands with her and she called out his name as softly as she could.

When they were finished, Nkosi rose and picked up his spear. He looked at her for a long time, memorizing the contours of her face.

"What if you don't come back to me?" she asked.

Nkosi smiled. He plucked a flower from a nearby sugarbush, stringing it to her necklace. "I will come back."

Mumbi sniffed the blossom. "They will kill you."

Nkosi's smile did not waver. "Ah, my love. I will still come back."

✛   ✛   ✛

When Nkosi opened his eyes, he was alive again.

No, not alive, but standing and seeing. A quick glance at his body and he wished that were not so. His skin was pitted and withered like rotting tree bark. Moss hung from the gaping spear wound that had killed him.

"It isn't pretty, I know." It was a harsh whisper.

At first, Nkosi thought the speaker was a ghost. He was tall and robed in black. Gold bangles wreathed his thin arms. The ash paste on his skin glowed white in the firelight.

The man snatched a burning twig from the fire and thrust it into Nkosi's belly. It hissed out a tendril of gray smoke.

Nkosi felt nothing. The man grinned. "It has its advantages, my *makeri*. You can't feel pain."

Nkosi shuddered. *Makeri*, a walking corpse. The man was a sorcerer. Nkosi tried to reach out for him, but could not move his arms. He shook and groaned.

The sorcerer's face was painted with the same dotted pattern worn by the Kaonde warrior who had driven the spear into Nkosi's side.

"You'll move when I decide. How do you like that, *makeri*?" the sorcerer asked. "Now you fight for the Kaonde."

Nkosi found he could turn his head. Beyond the crackling campfire, he could make out the small jumble of fetishes the sorcerer had used to pull him from the graveworld: a decapitated bird, some rattles, a bundle of small bones. Farther out, the black waters of the Uele raced along, stripping away the soil and laying bare veins of gold. Though he could not see them from here, Nkosi knew his fellow Zande tribesmen sifted the earth for the gold quietly, casting wary eyes about for roving bands of ravenous *biloko*. The sorcerer must have dragged his body from the banks of the Uele to raise him here.

Nkosi tried to speak. It sounded strangled. "Piss on you, Kaonde."

The sorcerer laughed. "Piss on you, Zande. You should be happy. You're going to see your beloved tribe again."

The sorcerer couldn't know that Mumbi was among the Zande. If Nkosi's heart still beat, it would have quickened at the thought of her. He turned his head again. The Zande fires could still be seen a little way off, along the banks; the tribe hadn't yet moved. That meant he had not been dead more than a fortnight.

The sorcerer leaned in close, wrinkling his nose at Nkosi's rotted face. "I don't think your Zande brothers are going to like you very much now."

✢   ✢   ✢

Mumbi scratched in the ground, filling the basket with roots as quietly as she could. The *biloko* combed the savannah, blending in with the tall grasses, eating all in their path. Mumbi hadn't believed that the monsters were more than legend—until she saw them for herself. The size of a leopard, they had round bodies that were mostly mouth. Stubby claws propelled them through the savannah faster than any man could run. That speed was used in the hunt that consumed their every waking hour. No man had even seen a *biloko* sleep. Even the Kaonde feared them.

Since they'd arrived, the Zande worked day and night without pause, sleeping in shifts, the faster to be away from the *biloko* runs and out of harm's way.

The silence was as complete as the darkness blanketing the plain, broken only by the muffled ringing of a cloth-wrapped shovel scraping the earth and the soft glow of the hooded candles lighting the ground.

Standing beside her, Njanu nervously hefted his spear and sniffed the night wind. The air smelled clean to Mumbi. Filling her lungs with it helped shake off some of the fatigue of their work's breakneck pace. The quicker in and out, the quicker they would have the gold home—gold that would buy metal for spearheads. Gold that would hire Chokwe mercenaries.

Gold that would save them from the Kaonde.

She glanced at Njanu. The tall warrior looked strained, his dark skin waxy in the moonlight. She hadn't seen him sleep since they'd arrived on the Uele. He'd been either digging or guarding the entire time. She took another deep breath before standing and picking up the basket.

She stopped. Another smell rode the air now. The breeze felt thick.

She whispered a warning to Njanu, but he was already moving cautiously out into the darkness, waving her back with a callused hand.

Despite his fatigue, Njanu moved carefully, his powerful legs parting the tall grasses. Mumbi caught a glimpse of the lion pelt draped about his waist before he vanished into the night.

Mumbi froze. With Njanu gone, and the rest of the Zande back panning gold, she was alone. The darkness swallowed her. Only the dim light of the moon and the feel of the basket at her hip reminded her that she had not fallen into the graveworld.

She took a step backward.

The smell grew stronger, cloying. She heard the tall grasses rustle.

A tide of relief washed over her. Njanu was returning. But the relief soon curdled in her gut. No man moved that swiftly.

The moonlight revealed the *biloko* driving arrow-straight toward her. The low form was bent, and plains grass sprouted from its hide, blending it seamlessly into the surrounding savannah.

The only indicators of its presence were lines of movement, eyes, and row upon row of teeth.

The mouth was horrendous.

And the smell . . . even at this distance, the stench was stifling.

Mumbi began to walk backward, not daring to shriek and risk bringing more *biloko* down upon them. She bit her tongue until the copper taste of blood filled her mouth.

The *biloko* picked up speed. The mouth snapped once, experimentally. The sound was lightning rending a tree.

Mumbi threw her load at it. Another lightning crack, and she watched as basket, roots and all, disappeared into the giant mouth. The creature darted forward, the stink locking out all her senses.

Mumbi stopped moving backward. It could not be outrun.

She kicked at it, once, but the *biloko* knocked her foot aside with a quick swipe of a stubby claw. The mouth opened wide.

Then Njanu was upon it, leaping on the creature's back and sinking his spear deep into the gaping maw. The *biloko* let out a strangled cough and clamped its jaw shut, snapping the spear shaft in two and throwing Njanu off. It ran in tight circles and clawed at its throat. It flexed its jaw once, twice, trying to howl. Each time, the spear point protruded farther from the wound and all the beast managed was a hissing choke.

Mumbi snatched up a rock and hammered on the monster. Njanu stood stunned for a moment before he joined her. The *biloko* slowed under the rain of blows. Finally it stopped, twitched once, and collapsed.

Mumbi and Njanu stood completely still, barely daring to breathe, waiting. The night wind whispered in the long grass. Somewhere in the distance, a sunbird let out a mournful call.

Nothing.

Njanu let out his breath. "It must have sniffed out your basket of food, or perhaps this—" He patted his lion pelt. "We are fortunate it foraged alone."

Mumbi nodded. She looked back to Njanu, his strong frame ropy with muscle. He was as strong a warrior as any could hope for, but she would not feel safe until her Nkosi returned. Njanu returned her glance and she felt the heat of his eyes. Mumbi almost went to him, but he was not Nkosi. It would do no good. The moment would pass and her trembling would subside, and he would still not be Nkosi. Nkosi would still be out on the Uele, fighting the Kaonde scouts who had come to sniff out the gold for themselves.

A few more nights here and the carts would be loaded with enough gold to make the Kaonde the smallest of worries. In the meantime, there were men to feed, water to be drawn, carts to be loaded.

There were *biloko* to hide from, and a lover to pine for.

Nkosi would come back to her. Mumbi stroked the dried sugarbush blossom she wore around her neck. Even after all this time, it emitted a faint scent of mountainsides far from *biloko*, Kaonde, and suffering.

Nkosi had sworn that even death couldn't keep them apart.

Mumbi believed him.

✢ ✢ ✢

There were few Kaonde after all. The sorcerer had hired Chokwe mercenaries to do his work. They crouched in the grass, the Uele dark and brooding at their backs. Some clustered around Nkosi where he stood with two other *makeri*, both Zande warriors killed along the river. Rare was the man who had seen a *makeri*. One of the Chokwe came close to Nkosi and lifted his beaded mask. "Does it hurt?" he asked.

"I feel nothing." Nkosi's answer was mumbled, his lips thick.

The Chokwe repeated the answer to his fellows in their own dialect. Nkosi thought it sounded like the croaking of frogs. The Chokwe leaned into one another, whispering through their masks and leaning on their spears. After the hushed conference, they asked him what the graveworld was like.

"The sky is the bottom of a thousand graves," Nkosi said, "and the rest is cold vastness." He did not tell them about the wandering, calling out Mumbi's name, scrambling for an exit back to her.

"Did you see your father? Your mother?" the Chokwe asked.

"No. You know they are there, but it is dark and there are many voices crying out. You cannot find anyone."

Nkosi had been completely alone. Faintly, he had smelled the dried petals of a sugarbush blossom and had nearly gone mad running after it. But he had always known that it was beyond the graveworld—and his reach.

Another round of whispers, and Nkosi suffered them thrusting their spear points into him until the sorcerer shooed them away. The other Kaonde came forward with him, distributing ankle rattles, drums, wooden whistles. The Chokwe took them, muttering about warriors reduced to playing music.

"Why waste your lives in a battle you can have the *biloko* fight for you?" the sorcerer asked. The Chokwe fell silent at the mention of the monsters. "Make certain that you upset the ore carts; leave the Zande no way to move the gold. Most importantly, drum and cry out! Shout down the very moon! Bring the *biloko* down upon them."

Nkosi turned to the Chokwe beside him. "They will kill you, too. The *biloko* do not care who they take."

The Chokwe shrugged. "They aren't hyenas, *makeri*. They won't touch dead flesh. You have nothing to fear."

"And as long as you are with us," one of the Kaonde cut in, "we have nothing to fear either. You will protect us, won't you, *makeri*?"

Nkosi could feel the Chokwe smiling behind his mask. The Kaonde paid in gold. For a Chokwe, gold was second only to a woman in its power to make men brave.

The sorcerer ushered them into reed boats assembled along the rocky riverbed, prows tossing gently in the rippling water. A Kaonde warrior led each party, a host of Chokwe behind him and a *makeri* at his side. The sorcerer stood on the bank as they pushed off, gesturing encouragement. "Remember the noise," he whispered as loudly as he dared. "Shout down the very moon!"

Nkosi had seen the *biloko* at work when his people had first come to the Uele. One of the men had gone gathering grass for his belt and had barely made it back to the caravan before a lone *biloko* caught up with him. They had killed the creature, but not before it had a chance to take a single bite.

A single bite had been more than enough.

Nkosi gazed in horror as the Chokwe shook the rattles experimentally. He turned to the Kaonde next to him, hoping his rotting face could convey the hatred that burned in his dead heart.

The Kaonde smiled, showing white teeth. "You hate it now, *makeri*? Wait until we make you fight."

Nkosi reached for him, but the painted patterns on the Kaonde's face seemed to swirl and spread, and at once the strength fled from his arms. The Kaonde laughed again.

Nkosi felt a sob rise in his throat, but he could not bring it out. So he stood silently as the Chokwe pushed against the river, poling the boats off shore until the current took them.

+ + +

Mumbi pressed the sugarbush blossom to her nostrils and inhaled. Amidst the dry smell of the savannah grasses and the faint odor of the *biloko*, it was an oasis of sweet air.

The Zande smelled like fear. It was a sharp, intense odor borne on the sweat running in rivulets down their straining backs. They cast nervous glances over their shoulders, searching the horizon for *biloko* with each toss of their muffled shovels.

The smell threatened to overwhelm her. Mumbi brushed her lips with the dried blossom and again thought of Nkosi. He had been many things—impetuous, bull-headed, sometimes even childish.

But he had never been frightened.

And so she hadn't been either.

Her need for him was a needle in her belly. Njanu could hold her, but he could not be Nkosi.

One of the scouts came trotting in, his cloak woven with long grass to blend him with the savannah. The light of the hooded work candles shone dully on his chest. Njanu raised a hand in greeting, and the scout stepped lightly over to them, shaking his head to show that he had seen no *biloko* on his

patrol. The less words the better. Every breath carried poten-
tially death-dealing noise.

In the short time she had been on the Uele, Mumbi had
learned to speak without words, keeping the silence that had
become almost sacred over the last weeks. She made her eyes
large and fixed the scout hard with them.

He looked at her and shook his head again. Once. Firmly.

No sign of the Uele party or of her Nkosi. Mumbi recognized the shame the scout felt in telling her, and put out a
hand on his arm to steady him.

The scout looked at her, his eyes pools of sympathy. Then
the pools abruptly emptied, his eyes rolled up in his head, and
he collapsed.

A brightly painted spear protruded from his back.

The silence split apart in a thunderclap of beating drums
and shrieking reed whistles. The sudden din washed over the
Zande, a wave of confusion and alarm. For a moment the
whole camp could do nothing but stare in disbelief.

The grass about them rustled into life. Dozens of Chokwe
stood in a line of throbbing sound. Their masks dripped beads
and stringed shells as they beat their instruments and threw
back their heads, shouting down the moon. Three Kaonde
warriors ran out before them. Beside each was a black and
shriveled form that could not possibly be a man.

The Zande were desperately silent as they advanced to
meet them.

Mumbi covered her ears as if shutting the sound from her
hearing could shut it from the world. It did no good.

The Zande ignored the quieter Kaonde and made for the
drum-wielding Chokwe. But the mercenaries made no attempt
to fight; they faded backward into the tall grasses, blowing
their whistles for all they were worth. Njanu and a few others
realized they could not catch them, and turned their attention
to the Kaonde.

As they did, the Chokwe concealed in the grass suddenly
ceased their harsh music. A few took off running toward the
Uele. A small group broke off, as if only then remembering
their mission, and made for the gold-heavy ore carts.

Mumbi watched Odiambo, her tribesman, engage one of
the black, shuffling things protecting the Kaonde. It shambled
forward, swatting at him as if he were a troublesome insect.
Odiambo leaped at it, burying his spade deep in the thing's
chest. It merely shrugged and slapped at him again.

"*Makeri!*" Njanu called to Odiambo. "Leave it and come
on!" But Odiambo, desperate to keep a weapon in his hands,

pulled on the spade's handle, trying to wrench it free. The creature grasped the spade with one hand and Odiambo's throat with the other.

Mumbi looked away as Odiambo emitted a choked gurgle.

Njanu scrambled after the Chokwe, hoping to protect the carts. He darted wide and herded them against one another, feinting and waving his spear when they made to move past him. A few of the other Zande—those not dueling with the *makeri*—took up the chase. But there were not enough to shield the carts for long. Too many of their fellow tribesmen had run off into the night, thinking it better to take their chances with the *biloko* than the raiders and their dead servants.

Seeing the terrible price the dead things exacted upon the Zande made Mumbi wonder if the others had been right to flee. The few tribesmen battling the Chokwe for the carts were bloody, but still standing. Those who attacked the Kaonde and their *makeri* fell one by one, until their corpses ringed their enemies. No warrior could stand against the dead men; they shrugged off spear thrusts and brushed away deadly blows from even the heaviest of picks. The *makeri* were slow, but they were tireless. The initial desperation of the Zande soon dwindled to resignation, until Mumbi thought the warriors resembled tired dancers, going through the motions of combat for the benefit of some expectant audience.

Mumbi cursed the withered plain as she crushed the sugarbush blossom to her breast. As if responding to this, one of the *makeri* looked up, sniffed the air, and began to move toward her. The Zande leaped on the undefended Kaonde warrior, hammering him with their pans and shovels. He called after the creature, his voice shrill and desperate until it was cut short by a shovel's edge.

Mumbi watched the *makeri* close the distance between them, each unsteady step throwing its rotten body forward. She opened her mouth to call for help, but found it suddenly dry.

The *makeri* reached forward, dead lips working silently. A sound escaped its ruptured throat—an almost musical groan of longing.

Mumbi's ears filled with the buzzing of terror. The wind, the shouting, the crooning of the *makeri* were all reduced to the same low hum. The scent of sugarbush rose in her nostrils.

Through the hum, she could hear Njanu call her name. The warrior was charging toward the *makeri*, but he would not reach the dead thing before it reached her. Mumbi retrieved the spear from the fallen scout; she would have to defend herself.

The *makeri* groaned again and lurched forward. As it neared, the smeared remains of the war paint on its dead face came clear.

They were Zande patterns.

Mumbi could remember painting them.

The spear became heavy in her hands; she could barely raise the point toward the walking corpse. It reached for her throat, fetid hands brushing the flower that hung there.

Njanu howled and let fly his own spear. It arced gracefully and buried itself, haft deep, in the *makeri*'s shoulder.

Mumbi continued to stare into the empty eyes. A rank stench replaced the smell of sugarbush, bullying the lighter fragrance from her nostrils.

The *makeri* turned as the tall grasses about them seemed to dance and grow—and finally erupted into scores of charging *biloko*.

The few remaining Chokwe abandoned their assault on the ore carts and fled for the Uele. A dozen or so *biloko* chased them. The rest plunged among the Zande, their massive jaws working feverishly. They came low, snapping up running legs, grass, earth, and stone—everything in their path.

The *makeri* worked to protect their Kaonde masters, buying them time to join the Chokwe in flying for the river.

Most of the Zande ran, as well, but a few men recalled that a *biloko* could outrun a frightened antelope. Those men turned to fight.

Mumbi could see there were too many. The *biloko* crashed over the camp, scores of darting, snapping mouths. Though the *makeri* struck at them, the *biloko* ignored the dead men in favor of warmer flesh. The *biloko* were hunters, not scavengers. Mumbi heard a low cry and the sound of splintering wood as they fell upon the oxen, gulping down their harness and most of the carts in their frenzy.

One of the *biloko* separated itself from the pack and charged toward her, only to be intercepted by the *makeri*, which snatched the creature up in its arms and flung it away. Mumbi again heard Njanu calling her name as he struck about him with a fallen shovel at the snarling *biloko*. The shovel rose and fell, rose and fell, each time more slowly, as the circle of creatures about the warrior grew. Before long, there were only *biloko* and she could not see Njanu or his shovel at all.

Two of the monsters raced toward Mumbi. The *makeri* tackled one, wrestling it to the ground and driving its clawlike hands into the beast's side. The other neatly sidestepped the dead man and leaped at Mumbi. She threw herself to her right, striking the creature's back with the spear's butt and sending it sprawling. She leaped to her feet and threw her weight behind the weapon. The head tore clean through the *biloko* and into the earth beneath it. The beast howled, then fell still. Mumbi tugged on the spear, but she could not pull it free.

A shriek rose in the back of her throat as she wrenched at the shaft, hauling it back and forth, cursing the hated tree from which it had been carved. She only succeeded in shifting the *biloko*'s corpse.

It was then she noticed how silent the plain had become.

No drums, no whistles, no screaming. There was only a faint rustling of wind, the distant murmur of the river.

Mumbi looked up from the spear shaft and met the eyes of dozens of *biloko*.

She was completely surrounded. Only the three *makeri* stood, black sticks in a sea of monsters and gently shifting grass.

The *biloko* moved slowly forward. They examined her, relishing her fear, lightly snapping their huge mouths as if her terror were a thing to be eaten.

She backed up, turned around. The *biloko* had formed a ring. Horrible, piggish eyes stared at her from all sides.

Mumbi raised the dried blossom to her face and breathed deeply. The smell calmed her, the sweet tendrils of scent reaching into her lungs and gentling her heart.

Defiantly Mumbi threw back her head and cried out, longer and louder than she ever had before. She sang out to her Nkosi, letting him know that she loved him, that she was sorry, that she would miss him terribly.

But it wasn't Nkosi who answered. It was the *biloko*. They howled and gnashed their jaws, eating up her screams.

Then they were upon her.

✢ ✢ ✢

Nkosi threw the *biloko* aside, but it didn't matter. Seeing that there was nothing left to eat, they scattered, streaming out of the camp.

They had even eaten the bones. There was nothing left but mud, broken shovels, and piles of crude gold scattered amidst the splintered remains of ox carts.

There was no sign of Mumbi at all. Not a scrap of cloth, not a spot of blood.

Nkosi shifted and moved toward where he believed she had last been. A passing *biloko* paused at the movement and sniffed at him. Finding nothing worth eating, it moved on to join the rest of the departing pack.

As quickly as they had come, they were gone, and the camp was left to the dead.

The other *makeri* stood still, looking at their feet, waiting for word from their Kaonde commanders.

A cry rose in Nkosi's throat. The sound welling within him was one to rival Mumbi's defiant final shout, which still echoed in his ears, but nothing would come out. He stood like the other *makeri*, looking at the ground.

The heavy stench of the *biloko* was gone. The night breeze swept it away, replacing it with the clean smells of the Uele and the shifting dust of the plain.

And something else.

The faint wisp of a sugarbush flower, petals dried and broken by time and wear.

Nkosi lifted his head. He sniffed the air experimentally.

There was no doubting it. The smell was faint, barely perceptible, but it was there. It danced on the wind and tickled his upper lip.

He turned his head this way and that, seeking the blossom. The *biloko* had devoured it along with every other shred of his lost love, yet its fragrance rose from everywhere at once, whispering on the wind.

Nkosi found his voice. "Mumbi," he rasped.

The air around him vibrated. At the edge of his hearing, a gentle voice sighed his name. The voice came from somewhere in a dark emptiness, beneath a sky of graves.

There was a thud. Nkosi turned to see one of the *makeri* drop. His task complete, the magic binding his soul to his corpse was broken.

Nkosi sniffed the sweet air once more—and smiled.

The other *makeri* closed his eyes, then fell backward into the grass.

Nkosi could no longer move his arms. His body had begun to feel like an old cloak, in need of replacement.

The corners of his mouth curled further.

The graveworld was vast beyond counting. It was dark, and millions of voices screamed in fear and wonder. It was impossible to find another soul in the midst of that maelstrom.

Unless you had a trail to follow.

Nkosi sniffed the air again, filling his dead lungs with the scent of the blossom, and went into the void with a glad heart.

Seven Brains, Ten Minutes

CHRISTINE MORGAN

The brain was in front of me, pink-gray and pulsing in the sun.

I could see the edge of the skull, sheared off so neatly by the cranial saw. The bony rim of nature's bowl, with its contents bulging up out of it like an extra-large scoop of ice cream. Or maybe gelatin. Hadn't they even, in the dim and gone days before the world ended, made gelatin molds shaped like brains?

If I pretended that's what this was . . .

No. It might quiver. It might shimmer. It might have the same gelatinous quality. But I knew better. I knew that the temperature would be all wrong. Warm. Body temperature, it'd be.

Of course it would. And why not? The body was still alive.

The guy the brain belonged to was in shock. He'd be dead—and probably glad of it—within minutes. Sooner, if I did what I was up here to do. What I had to do.

I couldn't.

Not even for Val.

Did she even know? Did she even recognize me? Or had fear taken her beyond all that?

The sun beat down. A rusty haze of dust filled the air. I could hear the flap of canvas and the sounds of the crowd. I could hear the Fat Man's laughter from above and behind me.

That's where Val would be. Up there in the bed of the customized pickup truck. With the Fat Man. Naked. Chained. A blue ribbon wrapped around her waist.

The others in the line to either side of me were straining against the iron bar, teeth bared, foamy drool on what was left of their lips. We had our hands tied behind us and number placards strung on ropes around our necks.

The bell rang.

The bar dropped.

"And theeeeeyyyyyy're off!" the Fat Man bellowed.

✛ ✛ ✛

We picked up Patty just outside of Bakersfield.

I didn't want to. I would have roared on past and left her in a whirl of grit and soot. But when Patty waved, Jess said we should stop.

"We can't take care of everybody," I said. "We've got to look out for ourselves."

"Don't be a jerk, Scotty," Val said. "Stop the car."

"Don't call me 'Scotty.' You know I hate it."

"Scotty, Scotty, Scotty," she sneered.

The end of the world hadn't done a thing to Val's looks or her attitude. It hadn't put a shake in her hands or purple circles under her eyes or anything.

Gorgeous.

But a bitch.

"I think we should stop," Rick said as he checked out the thin blonde. He was Val's brother but didn't have any of her good looks. Skinny, pimply, a loser from the word *go*.

Two of a kind, that was me and Rick.

"We *are* a girl short," Jess said, putting his arm around Sharon. She only rocked in her seat and hugged the dog. "Us, you and Val, and poor Rick left over."

"Oh, puh-lease." Val's laugh was a snort. "Me and Scotty? Don't make me sick."

I hated her.

I wanted her so much it burned.

When everything started, with the deadies and all, Rick and I were the first ones to figure out what would happen, how it would all go down. We read comic books and horror novels and watched all those old movies. We knew.

Everyone else went around in denial. First they said it was nothing but rumors, urban legends, hoaxes. Then, when the stories were proved real, they said it would blow over. Then that the government would take care of it. Then that scientists would find a cure. Then . . .

And by *then*, well, there wasn't much of anyone left who wasn't taking bites out of people.

✜   ✜   ✜

The crowd roared. Deadies lunged with jaws gaping and putrescent tongues snaking out. They went face-first into the opened domes of the skulls and commenced a smacking, slurping, munching feast.

I shook so hard my teeth clattered. Someone threw a crumpled-up aluminum can at me. It bounced off the filthy rags I'd draped over my chest.

Couldn't do it.

Wouldn't do it.

They'd kill me, though, if I didn't. If they found out.

It had seemed like such a good idea at the time.

No, that's a lie. It had seemed a stupid, gross, inhuman idea from the get-go. But the *only* idea. The only way to get out of this hell, let alone the only way to save Val.

I turned my head. The mud and gunk with which I'd coated my face cracked and flaked off in places, but that was okay. It made me look authentic, like I was losing skin in the dry, desert heat. My disguise fooled the livies, and somehow it fooled the deadies, too.

That was the part I'd been most worried about. Rick said that they could sense us, that they homed in on the signals our brains gave off or something. I didn't know if the ones in the contest were decomposed beyond that, or if the Fat Man just had them so well-trained that the only time they'd chow on a livie was when it was part of a competition or a prize.

Either way, my ruse had gotten me in. Fooling the livies had turned out to be the easy part. Whenever a livie died, rather than burn the corpse, the guards moved it over to the corral before it could reanimate. They weren't exactly diligent about checking for vital signs, either. I'd made like I had been hiding a wound all along, played dead, and *voila*. In among the deadies penned up for the contest.

Maneuvering to be one of the contestants had been a little trickier, but it had worked. Here I was, competing for a tempting prize.

I could see Val in the flabby circle of the Fat Man's arm. He was feeling her up, squashing her against his blubbery side.

Val looked on the verge of tears and that decided me. I had to do it no matter how sick it was. For her. Then she'd finally look at me and *see* me—see and appreciate the real Scott Driscoll.

The deadie beside me was gnawing on the side of a hollowed-out head, trying to peel off a flap of scalp. One of the handlers was there to inspect the empty hole of the cranium.

"Done!" the handler shouted, thrusting his fist in the air.

More people hustled forward. With movements born of practice and efficiency, the contest wranglers unlatched the empty, popped in the refill, and scrambled out of the way as the deadie dove in for the next course.

The stock of a gun rammed into my back. I barely stifled a cry. *They* didn't feel pain. I had to remember not to react.

"What's the matter with you?" the gun-wielder snarled. "Eat up."

"Done down here!" came another cry.

The crowd was clapping rhythmically. On my right, the female deadie struggled to get the last tasty morsels from the bottom. The deadie popped up, triumphant, with the medulla oblongata hanging out of its mouth, and jerked its head like a bird, gulping it down.

I was losing. I wasn't even on the board yet.

Liver. I'd eaten liver before. Once, on a hunting trip, I'd even had deer liver raw and dripping from the carcass.

If I'd done that, I could do this. For Val.

The handler jabbed me in the back again, and this time I bent forward, toward the rippled folds of brain tissue.

✦ ✦ ✦

My dad had given me the crappy old family station wagon for graduation. When the deadies started ambling, we stashed guns and other supplies in the wagon. Canned food, camping gear, blankets.

Everybody laughed at us, you bet they did. Even Val had, at first. But she'd stopped in a hurry when her mom came home from the beauty shop one day and tried to open her head with freshly manicured acrylic nails.

No one was laughing now. There weren't enough people left to laugh.

The station wagon had held up like a trooper during our entire crazy escape and flight south. Now, as I pulled over to the side of the road, its engine let out a sort of weary rattle. The tires sent up a huge plume of dust and soot.

The girl came running up to the car. "Thank you, oh, thank you, I thought you were going to drive by and leave me. Thank God you stopped."

She was giving me big, adoring, "my hero" eyes. I thought for a minute she was going to hug me, maybe even give me a big "my hero" kiss to go with that look. If she'd been a babe, enough to make Val jealous, I would have been all for it.

The others had climbed out of the car and were looking around nervously. Jess had the shotgun, and pushed his glasses up, squinting. Sharon clung to the bandanna collar on her dog. The girl introduced herself as Patty.

"You'll be safe with us," Rick told Patty, puffing up his chest.

It was kind of funny to see him trying to act all manly. I mean, he's been my friend since grade school, but I'd never had any delusions about either of us. Smart, okay. Jocks, we were not.

"Let's not stand around all day," Jess called. "I don't see anything moving, but . . ."

"Yeah, 'but.' Back in the car," I said.

✛ ✛ ✛

The smell was acrid and meaty and awful. I hadn't been aware of it before, not with the stale stink rising off the dead-ies and the rancid sweat of the crowd.

I could even smell the fine-ground bone dust and the charred, cauterized skin left by the bone saw. The inner membrane—I hadn't even known there was such a thing, but I'd seen them snip through it with kitchen shears—was peeled to the sides in neat folds.

Drying blood streaked the surface of the exposed brain. It had been wet, glistening, when they first clamped the livie into place before me. The desert sun was baking it.

If I waited too long, it would get tough to chew.

My eyes closed. My mouth opened.

I thought of liver. Of oysters. And, of course, I thought of gelatin. "There's always room for Jell-O!" Wasn't that how the old ads went?

A curved, quaking surface touched my lips. I skinned them back from my teeth, which had never needed fillings or braces. That had to give me an edge on the average deadie, whose teeth were chipped or broken from chewing on bone.

For Val.

I took a big, slippery bite.

✛ ✛ ✛

I steered in and out of traffic jams, cars and trucks that had been abandoned, overturned, smashed into scrap. Heaps of rot-ting food spilled from produce trucks dotted the sides of the highway. The only movement besides ours was that of count-less scavenger birds and animals, feasting with impunity.

That, and the windfarms. Talk about creepy. Miles and miles of posts with spinning pinwheel blades, whirring around and around. Generating electricity for a dead world.

The station wagon labored as it chugged up to the pass. I wasn't the only one to heave a sigh of relief when we made it over the top and started downhill.

High desert country. Home to military bases and shuttle landings, Joshua trees and borax mines. In the twilight, the desert valley was a brownish purple smear cut by the ruler-straight line of Highway 14.

We descended toward Mojave, hoping there might be something worth finding in that strip of gas stations and burger joints. Thinking about food, lulled by the hazy scenery, I didn't see the pile-up until Patty squealed a warning.

I stood on the brakes. The only reason none of us were

thrown into the dashboard was because we were packed in so tight.

Two semis had jackknifed and five cars had rammed into them, entirely blocking the road. The station wagon shuddered to a halt less than a foot from the bumper of a VW van.

"Is everybody okay?" I asked, my voice embarrassingly unsteady.

Various replies of assent reached me. I saw a turnoff to the left and a BB-pocked sign reading *Joshua Flats, 6 miles*, with an arrow.

"Can we get around?" Jess asked from the back.

"Shoulder's too soft," I said. "We'd get stuck."

"Well, think of something, brainiac," Val sneered.

✛ ✛ ✛

It squelched between my teeth. The texture was hideous, like soft-boiled eggs with striations of chewy gristle. The taste was bad, too, but the texture . . .

The man clamped into the wooden frame went stiff, then began to jitter and twitch. A fresh stink of voided bladder and bowels wafted up. I could hear his jaw clenching until bone cracked.

I took another bite. Determination drove me on. Once the initial deed was done, the first step taken, the revolting sin committed, it got easier. Don't ask me why or how. All I knew was that I'd gone this far and continuing wasn't going to make things worse. Instead, quitting would. If I quit and it was all for nothing, that would be really losing.

The noise of the crowd was louder than ever, but I ignored it. I ignored the sporadic cries of "Done!" from the handlers. None of that mattered.

Blood pooled in the bottom of the man's skull. I thrust my face in to reach the rest of his brain and wolfed it down. Something in my own brain, some switch or fuse, had blown with a snap and a sizzle.

"Done!" someone near me cried.

I straightened up, chin smeared with blood and cerebrospinal fluid and other assorted goo. They switched victims with the professional speed of an Indy 500 pit crew, and a fresh one was locked into place. I dove in, tearing out ragged, dripping chunks.

Thoughts shut off. I was an animal, a machine. I bit and swallowed, bit and swallowed, barely bothering to chew. My throat worked. My stomach hitched once, in shock maybe, then settled down.

I had the advantage, and not just because of my teeth. I had tendons that weren't withered and stretched. I had functional salivary glands. I had a whole tongue, an esophagus that wasn't riddled with decay.

Most of all, I had the motivation. I wasn't doing this out of hunger or habit. I was in this to win.

✛ ✛ ✛

We were able to push the VW van out of the way, but it didn't make quite enough room for the station wagon to get by.

Jess turned to me with a questioning look—maybe he was about to ask which car we should try to move next—and that was when the deadie reached out through the broken windshield of one of the semis and clawed the side of his face clear down to the bone.

He stood stock-still for a second, his questioning look transforming to a gape. Blood poured onto his shoulder and rained onto the blacktop.

The deadie's sticklike arms shot out again, seized Jess, and yanked. He flew backward through the shard-ringed gap and into the truck's cab. He dropped the shotgun. Sharon shrieked.

Deadies swarmed over the wrecked vehicles, and the girls screamed and the dog barked. Jess' despairing howls echoed from inside the truck.

I had time to notice how weird they were, the deadies, how different from the ones we'd seen up north. Those had been green, moldy. If you hit them in the middle, they'd belch out clouds of gas. These deadies were dry, their flesh shrunken, their skin leathery. They looked like mummies. Scarecrows. Beef jerky. The arid heat did that, I realized numbly, and then they were on us.

"The guns!" I yelled at Val. "The other guns are in the back!"

Rick panicked and went tearing off into the desert with two deadies in pursuit. The movies always showed them all shambling and slow, but these suckers were quick. Rick was moving faster than I'd ever seen him move in my life, running like he'd made the track team. Didn't matter. They caught up with him, knocked him down, started eating him alive.

A deadie woman with brittle, peroxide hair leaped on Sharon. Another lunged at me, and I danced back, tripped, and almost went down. If I had, that would have been the end. I kept my footing, though, cracked my crazybone on the side-view mirror of the station wagon, and kicked out. My foot struck the deadie in the hip and drove it back.

"The guns!" I yelled again.

Val looked at me, all big blue eyes and wide, surprised mouth. She dove into the car.

She slammed the doors and locked them.

I couldn't believe it.

"Here!" Patty cried. She shoved a stick into my hands.

A deadie in a California highway patrolman's uniform came at me, still wearing mirrored cop shades. Its mouth opened and closed in vicious snaps. I swung that stick like I was in the World Series—and missed by a mile. The effort spun me around.

I pulled Patty with me, getting our backs to the car. I hammered on the window.

"Open up! Open up, Val!"

The CHP snagged Patty's sleeve. She batted at its hand and yodeled a high-pitched cry. I brought the stick down across the deadie's forearm. Both stick and arm broke in half.

"Val, goddammit!"

Deadies were fighting over the bodies of Sharon and the dog. Others were converging on Patty and me. One snared a handful of Patty's hair. She flailed as if the clutching hand were a wayward bat. Dry fingers snapped off; they stayed tangled in her hair like grotesque barrettes. She didn't have time to pluck them out. Another deadie was heading for her with its jaws gaping wide.

A little kid deadie bit my leg. I yelled and punched down, the broken-off end of the stick still in my grasp. It pushed through the top of the kid's head. Frantic, I probed at my leg and found the heavy denim of my jeans undamaged.

Behind the dirty window, I could see Val. She wasn't doing anything useful, like maybe getting the other guns and saving our asses.

The deadies pulled Patty away from me. She was reaching out, begging for me to save her. But others had started to rock the car, trying to flip it—trying to get at Val. I shook off Patty's trailing, grasping hands and wielded my broken stick like a truncheon.

A rifle-crack split the air. A deadie pitched over, skull bursting apart to reveal a brain like a deflated football. The others froze, shoulders tucking up defensively. Patty, gasping and sobbing, scrambled to my side.

More guns went off, a chattering fusillade of them. Puffs of grit kicked up from the ground. Deadies went down in ruins of desiccated flesh.

I stared incredulously as a vehicle roared into view. It was like some sort of prop from *The Road Warrior*—an SUV painted mottled brown, desert camouflage, with spikes sticking out all over it. Guys—livies—in camo jackets and helmets stood in its makeshift turret, blasting away at the deadies.

And when they had dealt with the deadies, they leveled their guns on Patty and me.

✛ ✛ ✛

An astonished hush fell as I ate and ate and ate.

The handlers struck my rivals with batons, urged them to keep up. The deadie on my right succeeded in swallowing down another half a brain, then paused, its mummified face taking on a queer look. A moment later, the leathery skin of its belly parted and its overstuffed stomach flopped out through the slit, tore free, hit the planks of the platform, and popped.

Masticated gray matter and deadie digestive acid sprayed the front row of the crowd. A split-second later, the same thing happened to the deadie at the end of the line.

And still I ate. Blood and brain-pulp covered me to the hairline, welled in my ears. My own stomach felt hugely bloated, smooth and strained, as if it might burst, too.

"Done!" my handler shouted. "What's the score?"

"That's five," the Fat Man proclaimed from on high, where he had Val pressed against his sweaty folds. "A new record!"

"Sev-en, sev-en!" the crowd chanted. That was my number, the one they'd hung around my neck when I shuffled onto the platform with the others.

"How much time left?" my handler asked.

"Still two minutes."

"What do you say, dead boy? Got room for more?"

He didn't wait for an answer. A fresh victim was secured, the exposed brain not so neatly prepped this time. They'd run out of pre-made meals. They were grabbing people out of the crowd, doping them and sawing off the tops of their heads just to keep up with the demand.

✛ ✛ ✛

Before I could make sense of it, the guys in the armor-plated SUV had grabbed me and stuffed me in back. Two soldiers stood watch on Patty and me while the rest broke the windows and dragged Val out of the station wagon.

We tried to talk to them, livie to livie. We pointed out that we were all on the same side and should stick together and all that good stuff. Nothing helped.

They took us to the town, which had been ringed with walls and barbed wire and booby traps. At first I thought it was to keep the deadies out. But the defenses were there to keep *us* in.

The deadies were held in some sort of old barn. They gravitated to the fence of their corral, though never touched it, not after they'd gotten a couple of zaps from the electrified wires. So they just stood there, a handbreadth from the wires, staring vacantly at the activity beyond.

The town was full of livies, most of them prisoners. Some were from town. Others had been nabbed off the highway, like us. The men and women were kept separate. I hadn't seen Val or Patty since we arrived.

I got the lowdown from a local. Big Joe Callup, also known as "the Fat Man," had been Joshua Flats' chief of police until his compulsive overeating and subsequent weight gain had forced him onto disability. Fat? He was beyond obese. He was circus freak fat. He couldn't even get around on his own, so his men hauled him in the back of his customized pickup. Sort of a post-apocalyptic sedan chair.

When the world ended, Big Joe took the town hostage. He set up his own little kingdom with hand-picked soldiers and weapons from the National Guard armory. Raiding parties brought in supplies, more prisoners, and enough deadies to keep them entertained.

"Entertained how?" I asked, not really wanting to hear.

"All sorts of ways," my new acquaintance said. "He has them fight each other. He maims them, races them. Sets them on fire. Bull-riding. Rodeos. Football games. He's the emperor, they're his gladiators, and this is his private Colosseum."

"What about us? How do we figure in?"

"Us?" He smiled bitterly. "We're the prizes."

✝ ✝ ✝

The final buzzer sounded its harsh bray a millisecond after I gagged down the final hunk of my seventh brain.

Seven for lucky number seven.

"The winnah!" Big Joe exclaimed.

The livies cheered like they meant it. Anybody who didn't make a sufficient show of enthusiasm was liable to be put on the auction block for the next event.

I wasn't concerned about the next event. All that mattered was winning, getting Val, and getting out of here.

The guards had dragged Val around the outside of the electrified fence earlier that morning, their way of advertising her to the deadies as the day's first prize. In fact, they led her around twice. A shapely or muscular bod usually inspired a better effort from the contestants, and they knew they had something special with her. The deadie that won her would tear her apart, just like the steroid-popping fitness junkie I'd seen pulled to pieces by the winning team from yesterday's soccer match.

That wouldn't happen to Val. I couldn't let it.

I knew I'd only have one chance to save her and escape, before I was revealed as an imposter.

The deadie competitors struggled listlessly as the bar came back up. They were full or falling apart, but either way trained enough to know what came next. Those that were still mobile would go back to their stable. The ones who'd exploded their overstuffed guts would be taken to the edge of town and burned.

I tried to act just like them. I let my shoulders slump, my head loll, my stare go vacant. Inside, though, my pulse was skyrocketing.

I'd won. The prize—Val—was mine.

She was enough to make any deadie feel lively again, all that rosy, lush, firm flesh jiggling about.

The handlers led me toward the Fat Man's pickup truck. The routine was always the same. They herded me up to claim my reward just like they'd herded the deadie soccer team.

I tried not to let my excitement show. This was it. This was my chance.

Big Joe lolled in the truck bed like a sultan, on a layer of old sofa cushions and futons. The rig had all the comforts of home. A tarp on metal poles kept out the worst of the sun. A cord snaked through the cab's rear window, plugging the mini-fridge into the cigarette lighter. The area around him was littered with crumpled pop cans, candy wrappers, and half-empty bags of salty snacks.

He was a human behemoth in sweat pants that could have housed a family of four, and a ship's sail of a T-shirt with a beer company logo on it. Nearly lost amid the bulges and jowls was a hard, mean face that might have once been handsome.

His arm was still around Val, his greasy hand squeezing whatever he could reach. The up-close sight of him touching her almost made me lose it.

"You won a pretty piece of prime cut, here, boy," he boomed. It was more for the benefit of the crowd than for me, I hadn't a doubt. His eyes were bright and merry. Demented Santa Claus eyes.

I snatched a glance at the pickup's cab. The engine was idling to keep the battery from running down, lest the Fat Man have to suffer the misery of warm soda. The windows were down. No one was in the cab.

Deadie. Had to act like I was a deadie. I gazed at Val with an expression of slack-jawed greed, even while trying to make meaningful eye contact with her.

She wouldn't look at me.

Deadie. Deadie. I shuffled closer to the truck and let a guttural noise come out of my throat. I belched.

That was a mistake. The heavy churning weight in my stomach sent up a vile bubble, and I was tasting the brain meat all over again. My throat hitched. I suddenly knew I was going to spew a geyser.

Somehow, I held it down.

First, Val.

The Fat Man howled with laughter. "Looks like some boy's still hungry. Want your prize, sonny?"

All around me, I could hear livies crowding close, cheering, egging me on, placing bets as to what body part I'd bite first.

Out of the corner of my eye, I saw a familiar, pallid face framed in limp blond hair.

Patty.

The moment I looked at her, I saw that she recognized me. Her eyes got wide, and her mouth dropped open. She was going to screw up everything.

I caught her eye. If ever a guy had wished for telepathy, it was me and it was right then. I silently urged her to stay cool, begged her not to blow my cover.

Her chin quivered. I saw her throat work as she fought down a gag. But then she gave a slight nod. She understood.

Good girl. Smart girl.

Time to move. It was my only chance, the one I'd been waiting for.

I'd have to be quick to take them by surprise. First the handlers, while they were distracted by Val—shoulder them aside. Slam shut the tailgate with Val still in there. Then run around to the driver's door, jump in, and take off. With Val safe in the truck, and the Fat Man as a hostage, we'd get past the guards and out of town.

Next stop, anyplace but here.

I could do it, I knew I could. They weren't expecting any surprises from a deadie. The walking meat in the pens had been too well trained. They knew better than to move against the handlers, or livies not part of a contest.

"Here you go, honey bunch," Big Joe chortled. He nudged Val toward the tailgate.

She stumbled on chained ankles, fell to her knees. A hurt grunt escaped her. She looked up through a veil of hair and saw me. Really *saw* me. Just like with Patty, her mouth dropped open and my name formed on her lips.

I shook my head, trying to make it look like a nerve-jittering deadie impulse. My hungry-sounding moan was a warning.

"Uh-uh-uh," Val said, chains clanking as she trembled. She knew me. "Suh . . . skuh . . ."

No! No, oh, goddammit!

Sudden spiking fear made my stomach's heavy cargo slide and bubble. Because that was *hope* dawning on Val's face. Hope and joy and all the things I'd always wanted to see in her expression. Just not now!

Val let loose a wavering lunatic's laugh. She started to smile, started to reach out toward me.

She was ruining everything! People were looking at me more closely, seeing the solidity of my flesh—scrawny, maybe, but not dried deadie flesh.

"Shut up," I said, low but urgent, under a rising murmur from the crowd. "Shut up, Val."

Any second, suspicion would turn to certainty, and that would be all she wrote. And all because Val couldn't get with the program.

A line of phantom pain lanced around my skull. It traced the curve where the bone saw would grind and scream. Poetic justice, they'd think. I would feel the ripping of capillaries as they took the top off my head like a layer of sod.

The stupid bitch! We were so close! So close to getting out of this with our lives, and she couldn't play along for two minutes?

A glottal howl burst from me. After everything I'd done, after the horrible thing I'd done, this was the thanks I got!

"Scotty—" Val said, but her weak voice was drowned out by my furious cry. No one else could have heard.

But I did.

She called me "Scotty."

Again.

I lunged for her, shouldering the handlers aside just like in my plan. Even better than my plan, because in my surge of angry strength, I sent them flying. I seized a handful of Val's thick, dark hair and dragged her headfirst out of the pickup.

The Colosseum, my acquaintance had said. Like in the days of ancient Rome. I remembered something else they did in Rome. After a feast.

I turned my head to the side and stuck a finger down my

throat. My body heaved. A torrent of hot cerebral slush surged up my gullet and splattered everywhere.

I had to make room.

+ + +

The handlers took me to the barn. I could barely walk, my gut felt so bloated. I had consumed a lot of fresh meat. I would probably be days picking the strings of her hair out of my teeth.

I hadn't been able to get through her skull. My jaw just couldn't apply that sort of bone-cracking pressure. I'd had to go for the neck instead.

And then, once it was clear she wasn't going to talk any more and give me away, I guess I sort of went a little nuts.

They put me in with the deadies again. I was too stuffed and lethargic to worry about whether my disguise and their training would hold up. One or the other must have, because none of them made a move against me.

Or maybe, on some instinctual level, they left me alone because they recognized me as one of their own. I had never actually died, but inside, I was a deadie all the same. I had to be. No genuine livie could have done what I'd done.

A few days later, when I was finally starting to feel physically back to normal—mentally and emotionally, I was as much a deadie as ever—they brought a new one to the barn.

Thin. Limp hair that might have started out blond. Sunken cheeks and hollow eyes, and skin mottled with stains under the rags of clothes.

Not a bad disguise at all.

But then, I knew Patty was a smart girl.

She stood near me, neither of us speaking, as we stared with the deadies out through the fence at the town and waited for the next event.

THE CANNIBAL ZOMBIES OF WEST LOS ANGELES

JONATHAN PETERSEN

One thing that really bugs me is people who won't stop whining about the good old days. "Things used to be so much better," they say. "Things used to be civilized. Everybody had enough to eat. Disease didn't run rampant. There weren't raiders or post-apocalyptic bandit armies, and the Earth wasn't a devastated hellhole." Whiners. Jerks!

But name-calling is, of course, far from the only weapon in my rhetorical arsenal. I believe in rational discourse and am a firm believer in the powers of eloquence and the occasional underhanded use of anecdotal evidence. That's why when some graybeard starts going on about his Greyhound buses and potable water and MTV, I give his mopey *Weltanschauung* a verbal kick in the ass with my own pre-Apocalypse story. "You think this is bad, you ain't seen nothing," I say. "The worst group of creeps and murderers I ever saw, I saw in the year 1999, and I've got the scars to prove it."

What's that? You kids want to hear my story? This old man's nostalgic tale of times gone by, of days faded and flown away like rose petals tossed cinematically into the wind by some bullshit anime character? You warm my heart, you sweet, sweet, ugly little bastards.

✢ ✢ ✢

It took Jeffrey and me two months to find the apartment, and by then we probably would have taken it even if we had known about the zombies. We signed the contract six days before school started and moved in the next day. It was in West Los Angeles, in the part of town we now call the Smoking Lands, and it immediately appealed to my perverse side: It had a sixties, tired, bland charm to it, all smooth white steps and stucco walls and lead warnings. The place was in a complex that looked like a two-story strip mall and was big, poorly lit, and horribly insulated. The carpet was a putrid orange shag that was about seventeen years overdue for replacement. One corner smelled like cat piss. That's where we put the TV.

On our first night there, as I sat in my room eating a Twinkie, Jeffrey showed up with Annie in tow.

"You met any of the neighbors yet?" he asked.

"No," I said. "Hi, Annie!" She sneered at me in greeting.

"I just met two of them," he said. "George and Leanne from downstairs. My God, what a couple of gimps."

"They're both super-old," said Annie. "Their flesh is corrupt, and upon George hangs the smell of booze soaked into sodden skin."

"His is a moral failure," said Jeffrey.

"Huh," I said.

"I assume this isn't all of your stuff," said Jeffrey, gesturing at my card table and mattress.

"Your minimalism demonstrates strength," said Annie. "But your strength hides only weakness."

"It was getting dark when we got here, so I just stuck everything else in the garage until tomorrow," I said. "A few of my books are still at home. Oh, and I'm not getting my shotgun until next week."

"We are *not* going to have a shotgun in this home," said Jeffrey.

"Why not?" I asked.

"For the sake of the children."

"What children?"

"The children of the future," he replied, nodding sagely.

"That doesn't make a single bit of sense," I said.

"So wrong," he said, still nodding. "So wrong."

So, the next week I brought in the shotgun. I really do have to emphasize how truly impressive this is. See, these days everybody and their mutated, gangrenous grandmother has one. It's like a collapsible knife-and-fork set, or a plutonium-powered Geiger counter, or a bag full of plutonium to power the Geiger counter—essential. But back in those days, owning a firearm, especially one as outré as a shotgun, was an elite symbol of paranoid rage and psychopathy. It meant that you were a member of a rarified class of person—the type likely to open fire, with little provocation, at groups of Special Ed. children, or maybe at clusters of puppies and kittens running around, carefree, barking and mewing on a verdant field.

Anyway, I snuck it in at about three in the morning, so that Jeffrey wouldn't spot it and give me a bunch of baloney about weapon safety and accident statistics and what-all. He never did find out about it, as it turns out. I credit my powers of stealth and deception, which are considerable, for this impressive feat.

Meanwhile we were both going to UCLA, and I'll just briefly summarize that experience by saying that it sucked and I'm glad everyone who went there is dead. Also, Jeffrey and I quickly learned that we liked each other a lot more when we didn't have to see each other every fucking day. I'm still not sure why he was irked at me—as I am a mild-mannered and retiring individual—but he managed to consistently irritate me by inventively combining radical and reactionary beliefs in new and annoying ways. Take this conversation, for example, which I recount verbatim:

JEFF: Labor unions are great.

ME: Yeah, I'm down with 'em.

JEFF: I tricked you. You're a fucking idiot. They actually suck.

ME: What?

JEFF: No, I was just testing your commitment to the cause. I do like them.

ME: What cause?

JEFF: The cause that will protect the children.

ME: The children of the future?

JEFF: My friend, you are beginning to see the path. Now, if you would just abandon your die-hard commitment to labor unions, you might have something going on!

This being real life and not *Tales of the* fucking *City* or something, I studiously avoided getting to know the residents of the building, which is why George and Leanne were the only neighbors I actually met before that magical night when I gunned everybody down. I ran into them one October afternoon at the base of the stairs leading up to our apartment: a large, solid-looking old man and a similarly large and meaty old woman, staring up at our door.

"Hello there," I said, coming up behind them. "How are you guys doing today?"

They turned around, slowly. The man had sunken eyes and thin hair and reeked of bourbon, with a slightly ripe smell underneath it. The woman had brilliant and piercing blue eyes.

"Hello, soft one," said the woman in a hissing, softly ululating tone.

"Uhnnnnnnnghh," said the man.

"I am Leanne, and this is George, bound to me in ancient ritual," said the woman.

"How nice to meet you!" I said.

"Tell us," said Leanne. "Do you have a lot of *parties*? Full of young flesh and tender minds?"

"Ghhhhnnnnnnghhh," said George.

"Um, no, not really," I said. "We don't have many people over. Except Annie is over a lot. She has her own place, yet she is constantly here. She's sort of like a roommate that doesn't pay rent. Ha, ha! No, no, seriously—she's great."

Leanne stared at me ferally. Her eyes seemed to have no depth, almost to be painted onto her face.

"If you have a party we will come *over*," she said. "We will like it if you have a lot of *people*."

"Well, okay!" I said. "If we ever have a party, I'll make sure and tell you, okay?"

George moaned at me. Leanne licked her lips. "Excuse me, thanks!" I said, and went up the stairs to the apartment.

The rest of the complex's residents I saw only in glimpses, through windows. Once in a while I'd catch a flash of face or hair flitting away from sight as I turned to look at them. As far as I could tell, they never stepped outside.

✢   ✢   ✢

Late one night in early December I was sitting ramrod-straight on a wicker chair in my room, with the lights off and all the curtains closed and tightly drawn, clutching a cellophane-wrapped Twinkie in my hands, naked—which was then, as it is now, a perfectly normal thing to do. I heard Annie and Jeffrey stumble in, drunk off their gourds, no doubt on some kind of sensitive rain-dance, Earth-mother alcohol. I perked up my ears and hoped they'd have sex, because sometimes Annie would start loudly smacking Jeffrey on the ass.

"—mumble mumble oil barons mumble Che Guevara mumble Anita Bryant mumble feminazis mumble mumble of the future," I heard. Their voices thickened and clarified as they went into Jeffrey's bedroom, where the connecting walls were thin. There was a brief silence.

"He is just *so* goddamn annoying," slurred Annie.

"Shh, shh," shushed Jeffrey. "He might be awake."

"He isn't awake," she said. "God, what a fat piece of shit. He just . . . he just doesn't work for the *future* like we two, you and I."

"Yes. Let us recall the words of Kierkegaard when he wrote, 'Many men can fight jackals. Many men are jackals. In every time zone a few must rise.'"

"*Gott in Himmel,* his crimes violate all philosophy," she said.

"I mean, a) he's fat, b) he doesn't study enough, and c) he does nothing but sit around and eat Twinkies all day."

"Oh, no kidding. Did you know that he even bought that Twinkie cereal when it was out?"

"Jesus," she blasphemed.

"And a lot of the time he doesn't even finish the things, either. He leaves 'em half-eaten in the trash, or floating in the toilet. It's monstrous."

She tsked. After a brief pause, they started talking about other matters. I wiped a lone tear from my eye with my right hand, cradling the snack treat to my bosom with my left. What did they know, anyway? Sheesh.

After I'd recovered, and they'd fallen into drunken slumber, I cautiously unwrapped the Twinkie, placing the wrapper carefully on the desk, heroically maintaining my erect posture. I held the Twinkie in my lap and caressed its yellow softness. My love was greater than ever. I smiled—and penetrated to the creamy center.

✛ ✛ ✛

And now I come to the good part of my story—the part involving the obscene consumption of human flesh! You kids have waited through a lot of nonsense to get here, and for that I thank you. Of course, it's not like you have anything else to do, except scavenge for spent shotgun shells or help old Codger scrape mutant effluvia off the Land-Rover.

But first I gotta tell you something that happened around two in the afternoon, on the day of our New Year's Eve party. This event transpired far, far away—many, many moons of travel farther away than even the glassine ruins of Las Vegas, which we now call the City of the Sand King. In fact, it was over eight thousand miles away, across the great ocean.

Here's what happened in this far-away locale:

A number 99 changed into a number 00.

This caused a switch to go click.

The click had ramifications we'll get to a little down the road.

✛ ✛ ✛

Meanwhile, what was going on at our apartment was that we were having our New Year's Eve party.

I'm not sure why we did it, except that Jeffrey and Annie wanted to do it and my passive-aggressive resentment of their peers wasn't quite strong enough to motivate me to speak up. So we invited a bunch of their friends from the Cultural Appreciation department and some people we knew from our year in the dorms, and had at it. We got rolling at half-past seven—about forty-five people in all, crammed into our living room, kitchen, and the balcony overlooking the alley.

The cops came by for the first time at half-past eight.

"Okay," said a mustachioed officer to me, "you guys are going to have to keep it down, all right?"

"Bleeearrrgh," I said, directing my reply to the kitchen sink. I passed out on the linoleum for an hour, and then rejoined the fun.

It was quite a fiesta. Most of the people there were jerks, but it was better than talking to Jeffrey or Annie. I even managed to find a few people who were, apparently, unconcerned with the children of the future. Naturally, the wonder couple dissed these barbarians, leaving me to speak to them in the strange, experimental language that I invented for the evening, whose grammatical structure consisted primarily of drunken ranting and raving. Around ten o'clock, I snapped out of a five-minute blackout and found myself in the middle of a conversation with no idea how I'd gotten there or what we were talking about.

"You have to understand that fighting for the future is a noble occupation, but often a taxing one," declared Jeffrey from over by the balcony.

"What I really like about Peruvians is that, like African-Americans, they are proud to be people of the soil," opined Annie from near the fridge.

"I'm worried about the effect an event like that would have on the sociobiological/neuromathematical/contra-aesthetic matrix," worried the bespectacled girl I was talking to.

"Er," I said, and that's when the zombies attacked.

✢ ✢ ✢

Was Leanne their only leader, or were there other debased humans mixed among them?

Why would they attack such a large group of people, rather than picking off victims individually?

By what hideous method were these abominations created and maintained?

What do I look like—some kind of necro-know-it-all?

✢ ✢ ✢

It started with the yelling on the balcony. I turned my head and saw the railing go *crack* and fall into the alley.

"Jesus!" yelled Jeffrey, rushing to the edge, and when the ragged pair of hands reached around his leg and pulled him off the balcony into the darkness, it happened with such surreal

speed that nobody reacted for several seconds. Just as someone broke the silence by shouting, "Jeffrey fell off the balcony!"
two pairs of hands appeared from below, and two figures
pulled themselves slowly up into the light. Annie, frozen at the
broken railing, backed away. I barely had a chance to look at
the first figure—once a skinny, bearded white man, but now a
sallow, sunken creature with matted hair and no expression at
all—before he lurched forward, wrapped his arms around her,
then toppled backward into the alley.

Just like that, both my *de facto* and my *de jure* roommates
were eliminated, along with my chances of recovering my full
deposit when I moved out—which, at this point, I immediately
resolved to do as soon as possible.

The second figure smashed one of Jeffrey's friends in the
face and started wrestling him to the floor of the balcony. It
was at this point that the yelling began from the front door. I
spun around and saw that maybe a dozen people were crashing our party, except they weren't really people. They were
hunched, twisted, shambling husks of humanity, and they
smelled of dankness and rot. Leanne was at the rear, screech-
ing orders in a strange, gibbering tongue. George was at the
front. Moaning softly, he swung a thick fist, like a booze-
soaked ham, at Jeffrey's old roommate, James, who collapsed
with blood pouring out of one ear. Then he stepped up to a
friend of Annie's—one of the ones with horn-rimmed glasses—
and lashed out with awful, talonlike claws. As the wounded
girl retreated down the bedroom hallway, George grabbed
another bystander in a headlock and, with an apparently well-
practiced move, snapped his neck.

My hair stood on end. My jaw clenched. The partygoers
clustered in the front room started to scream, yell, hit, and
kick, all to the tune of "Brick House." I ran unsteadily for my
room. Time to meet the neighbors.

✣ ✣ ✣

I hauled the shotgun out of the closet and loaded it—*click,
click, click, click, clack*. It was the longest and blackest model I
could find, 12-gauge, semi-automatic, one shell in the chamber and three in the modified clip. I ran back to the chaos of
the living room. Leanne had vanished. Zombies were shuffling
around like crazy. There was a severed arm on the ottoman. I
saw George kneeling by the TV, his face caked in gore, yank-
ing greedily at the economy-size innards of Ethan, one of
Jeffrey's buddies from his Critical Issues in National Socialism
seminar. George was being pounded upon from behind by two

guys I didn't know. One wielded a lampshade, the other a frozen salmon. Their potence did not impress me.

"Get out of the way," I shouted, and the guys scooted. I put the shotgun to my shoulder in classic skeet-shooting pose and pulled the trigger. The ensuing blast opened up George's rib cage, created a horrific amount of gore, and caused him to slump into Ethan's open intestines. The few people who weren't already screaming and panicking got with the program and began doing so.

I turned to the left and right. By the front door, a large group of students had pounded one of the creatures to the floor. Didn't look like they needed my help. I hurried down the hall, past the kitchen, out to the balcony. The few people that weren't cowering in a corner were looking down over the edge, where the railing had been torn apart. I peered into the alley with them. The illumination was minimal, just a couple of dim yellow streetlights a hundred yards away. Dark, hunched shapes shuffled below.

"It doesn't look good for Jeffrey and Annie," said my friend Mike.

"No, it does not," I said. I fired the shotgun at two of the shapes clustered together. One froze and screeched in pain; the other shuffled out of sight down the alley. I fired my last two shells at the frozen one, and it dropped with a wet *thud*.

With Mike keeping a lookout in case the second one returned, I ran back into the living room. A guy and a girl came out of the kitchen as I passed it, each bearing a couple of cutting knives. The situation in the living room was worse. One zombie, a Thai-looking thing with bad hair and teeth, had gotten up from his beating and was throwing a partygoer across the room. And he had been joined by two of his buddies—what had formerly been a portly Hispanic woman and a skinny black guy. It was sort of a rainbow coalition of evil.

Unfortunately, I could do little at just that moment, so I ran back into the bedroom. I grabbed a half-eaten Twinkie off the table and rammed it down my throat, even as I pulled shells out of the box on the bed. I reloaded—*click, click, click, click, clack*. Then I grabbed a double handful of shells and crammed them into my pockets.

Back to the living room. The first thing I saw was the Thai zombie standing possessively on top of a pair of corpses, so I shot his head off. My dorm pal Aaron and a sharp-faced girl I didn't recognize yelled in surprise at both the loudness of the blast and the volume of bone and brain that sprayed across our milk-carton bookshelf.

Over by the front door, the skinny black zombie was throt-
tling one of Annie's irritating girlfriends. I shot him point blank
in the guts and, despite my near-toxic level of alcohol consumption, somehow skillfully missed the girl. That left just the
Hispanic woman, who shuffled to the doorway and gnawed on
my friend Gerald's neck, swinging a dismembered arm in front
of herself protectively. Dark figures lurked in the dimness
behind her, and I could see heads peering up from the stairwell. The room was beginning to smell like gunpowder.

"Hey!" yelled Mike from the balcony. I turned to see him
pulled down.

"See what you can do here," I shouted at the knife-wielders,
pointing to the zombie chewing on Gerald. They moved in as I
sprinted down the hall. But when I got out onto the balcony
there was no sign of either Mike or whatever took him. They
had crept off to the garages, maybe, or back into the complex
somewhere. It was silent below, and nothing moved. I fired
into the darkness in frustration, hitting nothing.

I went back inside, closed the slider and locked it. It
wouldn't keep anybody out, but maybe at least the breaking
glass would give us some warning. I handed a frying pan to a
nearby student—it was the one who'd been pounding on
George with the salmon—and told him to stay put. I rushed
back toward the fracas at the front door, which was not going
too well. The Hispanic zombie lay still, beaten to a pulp by a
bunch of Cultural Appreciation students, but four of her
homies had returned to the party and were making mince-
meat of our guests. I shot a wad of buckshot into a blond
European type who could have stepped out of some undead
version of a Mentos ad. The other three, sensing defeat in
whatever dim, vestigial minds they'd retained, retreated
through the door and down the steps. I slammed the door
closed and turned the deadbolt.

There was a moment of silence—except for a lot of screaming, and crying, and yelling "why God why," and vomiting, and
stuff. I guess it really wasn't that silent. Despite all this, I tried
to take stock of the situation. At least a quarter of the guests
were gone, either fled or dead or dying in the dark, and
another quarter were lying on the filthy shag carpet in various
stages of injury, up to and including dead. Maybe four minutes had passed since Jeffrey had been grabbed.

I'm going to allow you whippersnappers a peek beyond my
crusty façade and admit that the idea of my fellow students
being murdered and gnawed upon by cannibalistic monsters
didn't exactly thrill me. So, utilizing the full extent of my Cub

Scout training, I took charge of the situation. I pointed at two people and told them to get busy with calling 911 and giving first aid and all that. I pointed at the frying-pan guy and told him to hold steady at the glass slider. Then I pointed at two of the knife-wielders.

"I don't know if any of our friends are alive or not, but we're gonna get them back," I said. *Click, click, click, click, clack.*

✛   ✛   ✛

Cut to a location high in the air, some miles away from the party.

An object about the size of a whale, those we call Nomads of the Sea, hurtled toward Los Angeles.

This will have some bearing on the situation in just a couple of minutes.

✛   ✛   ✛

We grabbed a flashlight and went out into the night, locking the door behind us. Every light in the complex was broken, even the one right outside my door; the monsters had smashed them all before the attack. They probably could have found a way to just turn them off, but I guess that's zombies for you. The stars and half-moon produced only a muted illumination.

Staying on the upper level, we walked past the stairwell to the first door and kicked it open. The room beyond stank of rot and abounded in cultist paraphernalia: Scientologist E-meters, Cthulhoid symbols, Masonic neckties, a black cat, a Shriner cart, Dionysian robes, Kraftwerk records, and a few twelve-sided dice. Since I was still pretty drunk—never let anyone tell you that fear will sober you up—it's probably understandable that when the black cat screeched and leaped from the closet I accidentally shot my two companions dead with one fell blast.

I'm not afraid to tell you kids that this was a hard blow to my morale. I was weeping in frustration and trying to think of an effective way to convince two more guests to come along with me when I heard the sirens roar in. Who knew what lurked in the darkness? Better to just wait for the cavalry to arrive. I backed into a corner and kept watch.

✛   ✛   ✛

The cops came up the stairs in force. Most of them headed toward our apartment. Two came into the apartment I was in, saw the corpses and the shotgun, and immediately drew some understandable, but incorrect, conclusions.

"We're going to have to take you to the station," said the mustachioed cop.

"Get down on your fucking knees and put your hands behind your back!" said the other cop, who actually was also mustachioed.

They played good cop-bad cop for a while. The bad cop savagely beat me with his billy club. The good cop, a man of restraint, limited himself to kicking me in the ribs while helpfully informing me of my rights. Since it appeared that this treatment would soon cause me to pass out or suffer severe internal injuries, it's fortunate that, at exactly that moment, the intercontinental ballistic nuclear missile hit Los Angeles. The missile exploded with a sound louder than anything—louder than shotguns, louder than screaming. I have heard all kinds of strange sounds in my journey through life, and that was the worst, the one that causes me even now to wake up out of nightmares in a cold sweat. I had my eyes closed when the blast came, but the flash was still like having my eyes taped open and a spotlight shone at them. The floor shook. The roar finished, then echoed and echoed. The cultist paraphernalia clattered to the floor.

I opened my eyes after I finished up with my terrified shrieking. I couldn't see anything; the flash had been so bright that I was blinded for a few moments. Slowly my vision returned, which allowed me to concentrate on my total hearing loss. The cops were crumpled on the dank carpet, screaming and spasming, dying in silence. It took about thirty seconds for the massive dose of radiation poisoning to finish them off. I couldn't do anything but watch.

As my deafness gave way to a constant, clamorous whine, I stood up on shaky legs. I poked the first cop, then the second. They didn't do anything. I staggered out of the apartment.

All the lights were out, of course, and a dim, purplish glow shrouded the eastern sky. Shapes lay all around me in the dark. I walked into my place, looked around and called names. A minute later, I went downstairs. As I descended the steps, I saw Leanne huddled below, radiation burns striating her skin, a wand of bones and a strange grimoire clutched in her ancient fists. Nearby lay Mike and the zombie that had captured him, both unmoving, and the way the zombie was cradling Mike it almost looked like an embrace. I left the complex and checked out other buildings. It was no good. Everybody was deader than Dillinger. The zombies, who had become quiet flesh once again, were even deader than that.

Stinking of alcohol and gunpowder, I wandered through the streets of West Los Angeles. Every few minutes, another missile arced into the city center like a falling star.

Around the break of dawn I found myself on the corner of Westgate and Santa Monica Boulevard. Crashed cars smoldered everywhere, and about ten blocks away flames engulfed buildings on both sides of the street, a chain of burning cars between them. There were no fire alarms, only the crackling of flame punctuated by small explosions.

I wandered into the corner Mi-T-Mart and went to the snack aisle. Here I was surprised to see another living human—a chubby little kid tucking into a box of Twinkies. At least eight wrappers were scattered around him. Comfort food. I deeply understood.

"Oh, thank God," I said as I reached into the box. The kid watched me silently as I pulled one out of the box, unwrapped it, and began chewing. He continued to watch as I ate Twinkie after Twinkie in the middle of the metropolis turned necropolis, and pretty soon he joined back in.

So why did I survive, outliving friend, peer, cultist, and zombie alike? I had no idea at the time, but it turned out that my lifelong habit of constantly consuming near-toxic pseudo-pastries loaded with obscure chemicals gave me a natural shielding against radiation. Furthermore, regularly slathering my manhood in the same lard-based chemical goo protected me from the impotence that plagued most of the other survivors. It also helped that the whole nuclear winter thing was mostly hype. I realize you kids are not versed in some of the fundamentals—physics, chemistry, the scientific method, the roundness of the Earth, and probably even the secret of fire—so just trust me when I assure you that all of this is completely plausible.

Anyway, you know the rest. We got nuked because the Russians—or whoever—didn't fix their Y2K problems in time to prevent their computers from malfunctioning, and I have to assume that we didn't get around to fixing ours either. The only people who could breed were deviant junk-food fetishists, which helps to explain why you kids tend to be sort of tubby and pasty, despite the near-constant exercise regimen imposed upon us by our semi-nomadic existence. Fortunately for all of us, a new concept of beauty has arisen, wherein the tubbiest and pastiest among us are worshiped as the acme of physical perfection.

Of course you kids know this, which makes it fairly mystifying that I am bringing it up. But I am an old man, one who has been through a nuclear holocaust and survived many subsequent, desperate battles for survival, and has often been left starving and forced to eat aluminum shavings to survive, and I do tend to ramble.

I see by the expressions on your faces—ranging from excitement to disbelief to stultified boredom—that the more inquisitive of you would like to independently verify my various claims. That's fine. I like to believe that I do everything I can to encourage a certain intellectual curiosity among the young. Unfortunately, everybody from my story is dead, my old apartment building is crumbled wreckage, and even the corpses are gone, taken from the Smoking Lands by one of the local warlords to build his Cathedral of Bones—yeah, you guys remember that.

So that's it. Sometimes I miss ol' Jeffrey and Annie, and those precious days of hanging out with idiots and being condescended to. But they live on in my heart, and every day I think of them and a smile crosses my withered lips. Is it because I think of Jeffrey's wit? His grin? How Annie's hair shone in the sunlight, or the sweet way she spent eighty-five percent of her time at our place without paying any rent?

Nope.

I smile because Jeffrey and Annie bit the dust, and I'm alive and well—and sitting here with the children of the goddamn future.

THE LAST SUPPER

SCOTT EDELMAN

Walter's mind was at one time rich with emotions other than hunger, but those feelings had long since fallen away. They'd dropped from his being like the flesh, now absent, that had once kept the wind from whistling through his cheeks.

Gone was happiness. Gone greed. Gone anger and love and joy.

Now there was but hunger, and hunger only.

As Walter, his joints as stiff as his brain, staggered through the deserted streets of what had been until recently one of the most heavily populated cities in the world, that hunger burned through him, becoming his entire reason for being.

Hunger had not been an issue for him at first. During the early weeks of his rebirth, there had been enough food for all. The streets had teemed with meat. The survivors hadn't all evacuated at once. There were always plenty of the foolish lingering, which meant that he had little competition for the hunt. Those initial weeks of his renewed time on Earth had been about as easy as that of a bear smacking salmon skyward from a boiling river during spawning season.

Those days were gone. Now, not even a faint whiff of food remained to tease him from a distance. The streets were filled with an army of the hungry, devourers who no longer had objects of desire upon which to fulfill their single purpose. For weeks, or maybe months, or perhaps even years—for Walter's sense of time had been burned away along with most of his sense of self—walking the streets was akin to wandering through a maze of mirrors and seeing reflected back nothing more than duplicates of who he was, of what he had become: a bag of soiled clothing and shredded flesh, animated by a dead, dead soul.

Staggering through a deserted square that lay in the former heart of the city, stumbling by shattered storefronts and overturned buses, he sought out flesh with a hunger grown so strong that it was less a conscious thought than a tropism born out of whatever affliction had brought him—and the rest of the human race—to this state. His senses, torn and ragged though they were, reached out in search of fresh meat, as they had every day since he had been reborn.

Nothing.

No scent filled his sunken nose, no sound his remaining ear. Yet he surged forward, sweeping the city, borne fruitlessly ahead by a bloodlust beyond thought. Until this day, when what was left of his tongue grew moist with saliva.

Blood. Somewhere out there was blood. Something with a pulse still radiated life nearby.

Whatever called to him was barely alive itself, and hidden, and quiet, but from its refuge its essence rang like a shout. Drawn by the vibrations of its life force, he turned from the square onto a broad avenue and then onto a narrow side street, knocking aside any barriers blocking the path to his blood—*his* blood now. He righted an overturned trashcan (but his promised meal was not hidden there), kicked up soot as he walked through the remnants of an ancient bonfire (but no, nothing there, either), and moved forward until he arrived at a large black car with its roof split open, flipped over on one side against a light pole.

He pushed his way through a carpet of broken glass and peered down through what remained of the driver's side door. He touched the steering wheel and a charge of energizing bloodlust coursed through him. Though the wheel's leather skin had long ago peeled away, he could feel the blood that had blossomed there right after impact, still feel the throbbing of its vanished presence. But he knew, if he could be said to know anything, that ghostly blood could not alone have sounded the call that he had heard. The tug on his attention had to be more than that. Something was here, waiting for him.

Or hiding from him.

In the back of the tilted car, a rustling came from under shredded remnants of seat stuffing. Confused eyes peered out at him. Walter filled with a surge of lust, and dropped atop the creature. A dog yelped—only a dog, and not a man, a man whose scream would strengthen him—and exploded into frantic wriggling, but there was no way the animal could escape the steel cage of Walter's hands. Seeing the nature of his victim's species, the lust vanished. There was no longer anything appealing about this prey.

But his hunger remained.

The dog whimpered as Walter shifted his fingers to surround its neck and cradle its head in his hands. Its bright eyes pleaded and teased, but Walter had learned that the promise of satiation there was pointless. He slowly tightened his grip anyway, and the animal split in two, its head popping off to drop at his feet. He held the oozing neck up to his lips, and drank.

The blood was warm. The blood was salty.

The blood was useless.

His hunger still raged, his needs unsatisfied. What he required could only be provided by the blood of human, not animal, intelligence. He let the dog fall, where it was immediately forgotten.

There had to be something more left on the face of the Earth.

Walter moved on, clumsy but determined, his hunger once more an all-consuming creature. It wasn't that he needed flesh to live. Its presence in his leaky stomach had never powered him. The strength of his desire was unrelated to any practical end.

He hungered, and so he needed to hunt. That was what he did. That was what he was.

He returned to endless days and nights spent walking the length and breadth of his island, but his prowling proved useless. Though he sniffed out the life of other dogs, and rats, and the last few surviving animals that had somehow not yet starved to death at the zoo, nothing human called to him. The city was empty.

One day, much later, he paused in the harbor and looked west toward the rest of his nation, a country that he had never seen in life. He listened for the call of something faint and distant, waited as the evidence of his senses washed over him. In an earlier time, he would have closed his eyes to focus, but his eyes no longer had lids to close.

The static of the city's life, quivering nearby, no longer rose up to distract him. There was no close cacophony muffling him from the rest of the continent, just a few remaining notes vibrating out from points west. He began to walk toward them, pulled by the memory of flesh.

He dragged his creaking body along the shoreline until he came to a bridge, and then he crossed it, picking his way past snapped cables, overturned cars, and rifts through which could be seen the raging river below. He had no map, and needed none, any more than a baby needed a map to her mother's breast or a flower needed a map to the sun.

Concrete canyons gave way to ones born of rock, and time passed, light and dark dancing to change places as they had since the beginning of time. Walter did not number the days they marked. The count did not matter. What mattered was that the sounds he heard, the stray pulsings in the distance, increased in volume as he moved.

His trek was not an easy one. He was used to concrete jungles, not the forest primeval, and yet that is where he was forced to travel, for life, if it wanted to stay alive, kept far from highways, as well. As he slipped on wet leaves and tumbled over fallen logs, he could feel an occasional beacon snuffed out, as another life was silenced, another slab of meat digested. Walter was not the only one on the prowl, and somehow he knew that if he did not hurry, the hunt would soon be over for him forever. As weeks passed, he could hear what had once been a constant chorus diminish into a plaintive solo. As Walter could pick out no other competing song, perhaps it was the final solo.

Its pull grew yet stronger, and as the flames of its sensations flickered higher, rubbing his desire raw, he moved even more quickly, stumbling lamely through a hilly forest.

Until one stumble became more than just a stumble. His ankle caught on an exposed root, and he then felt himself falling. He fell against what appeared to be a carpet of leaves, which exploded and scattered when he hit them, allowing him to fall some more.

From the bottom of a well twice his height, he looked up to a small patch of sky and saw the first face in an eternity that was, amazingly, not like looking in a mirror. The flesh of the man's face was pink and red, and as he breathed, puffs of steam came from his lips.

Then those lips, surrounded by a beard, moved, and a rough voice, grown unused to forming the sounds of human speech, said wearily, "Hello."

Walter had not heard another's voice in a long while, and that last time it had been molded in a scream.

Seeing the man up there, looking smug and seeming to feel himself safe, filled Walter with rage; it was the first time in ages anything but pure hunger had filled him. He slammed his fists wildly against the muddy walls of his hole, unconsciously seeking a handhold that could bring him to the waiting feast above, but there was nothing he could grasp. As he struggled to tear out grips with which to climb, his flesh grew flayed against sharp stones and splintered roots. Yet he did not tire. He would have gone on forever like that, a furious engine of need, had not the man above begun dropping further words to him down below. They were not frightened words or angry words or begging words—the only sorts that Walter was lately used to hearing—so their tone confused him. He wasn't sure what kind of words they were, and so he paused in his fury to listen.

"I've been waiting for you," said the man, his head and shoulders taunting Walter in the slice of sky above. "We have a lot to talk about, you and I. Well . . . actually . . . *I* have a lot to talk about. All you have to do is listen. Which is good, because I have learned from others of your kind that all you are capable of doing is listening, and barely that."

The man extended his arm over the hole. He rolled up his left sleeve, then used his right hand to remove a large knife from a scabbard strapped to one thigh.

"This should help you to listen," he said.

Walter could understand none of the words. But even he understood what happened next. The blade sliced the flesh of the man's inner forearm, and bright blood flowed across his skin, spilled into the crook of his elbow, and finally dripped in freefall. At the bottom of the pit, Walter tilted his head back like a man celebrating a spring rain, the stiff muscles in his neck creaking from the effort. He caught the short stream of drops on the back of his shredded throat.

"That's all I can spare you for now," the man said, pressing gauze against his voluntary wound and rolling his sleeve back down. "You don't like to hear that, do you?"

Walter had no idea what he liked or didn't like to hear. All he knew was the hunger. That brief taste had caused it to surge, multiplying the pain and power of his desire. He roared, flailing wildly again at the walls of his prison.

"If you can only shut up," said the man, "you'll get more. We need to come to an agreement, and then, only then, there'll be more. Can you understand that?"

Walter responded by throwing himself against the earthen walls, but this response gained him nothing. As he battered his fists against the side of the pit, three of his fingers snapped off and dropped to the uneven floor. He struggled more franticly, and those body parts were ground beneath his feet like fat worms.

"This isn't going to work," muttered the man above, who began to weep. "I must have gone mad."

He crumpled back out of Walter's field of vision. Though Walter could still sense the brimming bag of meat above, its disappearance from his line of sight lowered his rage, and he subsided slightly. His hunger still overwhelmed him, but he was no longer overtaken by the mindless urge to flail. He howled without ceasing at the changing clouds above, at the sun and at the moon, until his captor reappeared—suddenly, it seemed to him—and sat on the lip of the hole. The man let his feet dangle over the edge. Walter leaped as high as his dusty muscles would let him and tried to snatch the man's heels, but he could not reach them. He tried once again, still falling short. The man snorted. Or laughed. Or cried. Walter couldn't quite tell which.

"You can't kill me." The man peered down through his knees. "Well, you can, but you shouldn't. Because once you kill me, it might be all over. Can you understand that? It's been years since I saw another human being. Do you realize that? I may be it."

Walter growled in response and continued to batter against the sides of his prison.

"Damn," moaned the man. "What do I have to do to get your attention?"

Walter saw him bring out the knife again. The man looked at the line on his arm, which had now become a long, thin scab, and then gazed down into the pit, to where Walter's shed fingers lay crushed. The man shook his head. After a moment, he pulled his upper body back so that all Walter could see were dangling feet.

"This time," the man said, "I've got to do whatever it takes."

Walter heard a dull thud, one accompanied by a sharp intake of breath and a visible jerking of the man's legs. When the man leaned forward again, a handkerchief was wrapped around one hand. He used his good hand to dangle a bloody finger out over the pit.

"Listen to me now," the man said. Walter, frozen, stared at the offered digit. "I may be your last meal for the rest of your eternal life. I may be the last human left on Earth. Try to get that through your undead head."

The man let the finger drop.

Walter leaped and caught it in midair. He had it in his mouth before his feet hit the ground. He chewed so fiercely that he ate his lips away, and many of his teeth popped from their sockets. If the man were continuing to speak, Walter would never have known it, as the sounds of his feasting echoed deafeningly. Silence did not return until after the digit had been devoured, and only then did Walter look skyward again.

"I want to live," said the man. "I don't want this to be the end of the human race. We have to make some sort of peace, you and I. We have to reach some sort of an agreement. That's why I moved out here and filled these hills with pits like this one. I knew that your kind would eventually sweep out from the cities and find me even here in the middle of nowhere, and I wanted to be ready for you.

"You have to tell the others. You have to let them know. Know that I'm the last. That if you just pluck me off the face of the Earth, there will be nothing left, only eternal hunger. Is that something you can understand? Is that something you can communicate to the others? If so, they'll let me live. Let the human race live."

What the man said was meaningless to Walter. He knew the word *hunger*, and plucked it from the forest of words being dropped on him. But that was about it. He could not comprehend the man's message, could not possibly pass it on to others. In fact, as far as his consciousness allowed, there were no others. There was only Walter—Walter below and his food above. And the food was not getting any closer.

The man pulled his legs up from the hole, and for a moment it looked to Walter as if he were leaving, but, instead, there was another thud. Then the man poked his head into the pit, even closer this time, since he was lying on his stomach rather than sitting on the lip. The man brought his hands around to show another dangling finger. Walter leaped unsuccessfully, impatient for the flesh to be dropped.

"I can see that this is the only thing you will understand. Do you see now? If you eat me, it will all be over. Eternal hunger, with nothing more—*ever*—coming along to quench it. But if we can make a deal, I can help you feed for a long while. I can give you blood, and even some flesh from time to time."

The man dropped his finger, and this time, Walter caught it directly in his mouth. His teeth began crunching on it immediately, but, unlike before, he did not take his eyes off his captor. Walter looked up at the blood soaking through the handkerchief in the man's hand. The man noticed Walter's gaze. Loosening the cloth, he dangled his damaged hand down into the pit and shook it. The discarded handkerchief slowly and softly lofted down. Walter caught the cloth and tossed it into his mouth. He sucked on the blooming stain, the corners of the handkerchief hanging out of his mouth and down his chin.

"Do we have a deal?" asked the man. His eyes were wide, and he was so caught up in his hope that he did not immediately pull back his extended hand. Filled with lust at the sight of the wet wounds hanging there, Walter ran to the wall and leaped up toward them, wedging his feet in the damp mud before the man could yank himself back. Walter's remaining fingers intertwined with his captor's remaining fingers, and with his dead weight, Walter started pulling the man, sliding him forward so that more of his body hung over the edge.

"No! I'm the last man on Earth! You can't do this! Without me, you'll have nothing! Don't you understand?"

But Walter did not understand, not really, and the man's screaming and scrambling did little to slow his descent into the hole. Walter pulled him down mercilessly—for he had no mercy, only hunger—and at last, after far too long, the hunger was allowed to run free. Walter began with the man's lips, silencing the urgent pleas. Then he gnawed his way deep into the man's chest, cracking his ribs and burrowing into his heart. Walter's face grew slick with blood as he gorged. It had been far too long since he'd fed this well, and even though he remained trapped at the bottom of a pit, he had no concern for tomorrow, no thought of putting anything aside for another day. He savored the flesh and sucked the bones, and then . . . then it was all gone, much too soon.

Momentarily sated, Walter looked up at clouds. He sniffed out the universe, listening for the pulse of the planet—and discovered in that instant that his jailer had been correct: He had been the last man on Earth. Walter could sense no blood moving in the world. No food remained.

All that existed for Walter now were a few square feet of ground, his dirt wall, and the sky above. Time passed. Walter could not say whether it passed quickly or slowly. He only knew that the opening above him regularly darkened and lightened again. During the days, his view was occasionally altered by a bird flitting by, and at night there was the occasional flash of a falling star. Hunger returned and was his constant companion, but there was no longer any point in raging.

Mud and leaves and the detritus of time slowly filled the pit. As he paced from side to side, Walter rose a little each day, his ascension so gradual as to be almost imperceptible. He never realized what was happening, merely found himself one day high enough to peer over the lip. Only then did he pull himself up to the surface and stand, seeing the world again for the first time in ages as something other than a tunnel-vision picture of the sky . . . though the difference didn't really matter. For whether he was trapped in a hole or free to roam the land, nothing had changed. His only companion for now and forever more would be his hunger, and since he could no longer sense anything out there with which to quench it, it mattered little where he spent eternity.

Walter moved on without a destination.

Strangely, the sky now seemed filled with falling stars. And yet, they did not behave the way such things were meant to behave. Instead of vanishing quickly, as had the living human race, the bright spots crisscrossed the sky, like embers that refused to die. During the day, the stars still shone, another anomaly Walter no longer had the brain power to consider.

He wandered the world aimlessly, but only until the stars themselves were no longer wandering aimlessly. The stars were suddenly on the move in a purposeful manner, and as he gazed into the sky, he sensed where they were heading. With the flavor of the last man on Earth forever branded on his lips, he followed the path they made, moving back east across a country that was continuing to crumble, that was transforming from civilization into debris.

The bridge into the city, when he saw it again after what had been hundreds of years, had collapsed into the river. He had to pick his way over floating rubble, still bound together by cables, to move from shore to shore. He walked the city streets once more, watching the sky, until so many stars hung overhead that it seemed impossible to fit any more. Then their trajectories shifted, and they set about carving concentric circles in the sky. Walter's hunger positioned him beneath the heart of them. Others of his kind joined him.

As he watched, a single star dropped, pulling itself away from the carefully choreographed dance, becoming more than just a speck, gaining dimension as it fell. By the time it reached the buckled pavement on which Walter stood, it had grown into a globe several stories high. The fact that it floated there, sprouting legs on which it came to rest, had no effect on Walter. He sensed only dead machinery and felt nothing, not even curiosity. But when the outlines of a door appeared and then opened, that all changed. Walter could feel again the old familiar tingling that had been missing for so long.

A walkway eased its way out from the opening to touch the ground. A tall, attenuated creature walked down the ramp, followed by a hovering cylindrical machine half again as tall. The visitor, its two arms and two legs garbed in soft silver, stepped off the walkway into what, for it, was a new world. With alien eyes, it regarded Walter and his brethren.

Walter, agitated by a humanoid form stinking of the raw stuff of life, rushed forward—only to thud against the invisible wall surrounding the grounded star and its passenger. Flesh was close, so close, and Walter was enraged. He could not comprehend why his remaining teeth were not even then tearing the thing apart.

Walter roared, and his deafening anger was soon echoed by the keening of the other zombies that ringed the ship. The being removed a helmet, revealing a face that, though off in its proportions, contained all the right elements—eyes, nose, mouth—that signified humanity. This only served to fill Walter with a further fury.

The alien surveyed the crowd, looking at the crescent of the undead with all-too-human eyes. It then held a slender hand out toward Walter, who suddenly found himself able to surge forward, ahead of the others. Arms outstretched, he raced toward the flesh—*his* flesh—but stopped short in front of his meal, frozen as if encased in metal bands. Walter struggled to close that final gap, but could not.

Suddenly Walter found himself floating a few feet off the rubble. He tilted back, both alien and globe vanishing from his field of vision, to be replaced by the sky. He could see the moving stars pause in their flight. The alien stepped closer, and Walter was overcome by the need to open his mouth, to gnaw, to rend, but his body no longer followed the command of those needs. The metal cylinder, which had trailed closely behind the visitor, tilted on its side and floated to Walter's feet. It slid over Walter, engulfing him, encasing him from head to what remained of his toes. He was trapped once more. This time, he was unable to even bang against the sides of his prison.

The patch of metal before Walter's face cleared to transparency.

"Hello," the alien said, in a voice unused to forming the sounds of human speech. It leaned in close. "We have traveled a long way in search of our ancient cousins."

It waved its thin hands over the exterior of the cylinder, and sequential lights flashed, a rainbow coursing over Walter's mottled skin. He struggled to escape their glow, but, regardless of his rage, he moved in his mind only. When the colors ceased, that rage remained.

"How sad," said the alien. "Our cousins are still here, and yet . . . they are gone. They are all gone."

The words were meaningless to Walter, barely even heard over the angry urges in his head goading him to feed. Then the cylinder pulled away, and Walter found himself upright again, his muscles once more his own. He started to bound forward, but at the height of his leap, the strange creature waved its arms and Walter teleported back with the others. His momentum still carried him to complete his trajectory, and he slammed against the invisible shield.

The visitor walked back up the ramp, the cylinder floating by its side, and the metal path retracted back into the ship. The creature paused in the doorway. It was still looking toward Walter as the door closed and the force field died. Walter rushed the craft, but it rose effortlessly back into the sky before he could beat himself against its glittering sides.

The bright stars that had up until then formed circles in the sky vanished, but Walter barely noticed the emptiness above. So great was his lust for flesh that he was driven to return immediately to his hungry wandering, where he found nothing but that his hunger increased. His hunt through the rubble of humanity would prove fruitless, for his senses never again tingled to tease his immortal desire.

The sun and the moon continued to trade places, but no stars ever returned to move through the sky, and Walter's hunger, which left no room for any other emotions, never faded—at least not until, eons later, Earth's close and constant star expanded to fill his world with fire and finally erase his hunger forever.

Contributors' Notes

Kealan Patrick Burke was born and raised in Ireland. Since moving to the States in September 2001, he has had work appear in over fifty print and web-based magazines and anthologies, with many more on the way. He is currently editing *Brimstone Turnpike*, five novellas linked by a stretch of highway and the old man who watches over it (Cemetery Dance Publications) and *Taverns of the Dead*, an anthology of stories set in bars and featuring stories by Peter Straub, Ramsey Campbell, David Morrell, Neil Gaiman, Jack Cady, and others (Cemetery Dance Publications). He can be contacted at elderlemon2003@aol.com.

When **Myke Cole** isn't writing, he fences competitively in the Japanese and Korean traditions. He has short stories upcoming in *Writers of the Future XIX* and *Weird Tales*, later in 2003. He lives with his wife in Arlington, Virginia.

Kristine Dikeman was born on Long Island and lives in Manhattan, where she works as a graphic designer while pursuing a career in writing. "What Comes After" is her first published story. She is currently at work on *Panspermia*, a novel about life, love, and carnivorous plants.

Scott Edelman is currently the editor-in-chief of both *Science Fiction Weekly* (www.scifi.com/sfw), the Internet magazine of news, reviews, and interviews, and *Sci Fi*, the official magazine of the Sci Fi Channel. Prior to this, Edelman was the creator and only editor of the award-winning *Science Fiction Age* magazine. He also edited other SF media magazines, such as *Sci-Fi Universe* and *Sci-Fi Flix*. He has been published in *The Twilight Zone*, *Asimov's*, *Amazing Stories*, and numerous anthologies, including two appearances in *Best New Horror*. He was a Stoker Awards finalist for "A Plague on Both Your Houses," which can be found in his collection *These Words Are Haunted*. He has been a Hugo Award finalist for Best Editor on four occasions.

Roland J. Green was born in 1944 and currently lives in Chicago with his wife and daughter. Since he discovered C. S. Forester at the age of nine, he has devoured sea stories. When he started writing professionally, he sent his characters to sea as often as humanly possible. Or "inhumanly," in the case of his story here. But who better to work in the hellish conditions of a coal-burning boiler room than zombies, particularly when *voudun* (as might be expected of any religion that began on a seacoast and continues on islands) has a goddess of the sea?

Award-winning writer, game designer, and columnist **Ed Greenwood** is the creator of the Forgotten Realms fantasy world. He's been called the "Canadian author of the great American novel" and "an industry legend," and his one hundred-plus published books have sold millions of copies worldwide, in over a dozen languages. Ed has also produced over six hundred articles and short stories, and co-designed several bestselling computer games. His novels include Shandril's Saga, the Elminster chronicles, and the Band of Four series. In real life, Ed is a large, jolly, and bearded guy who lives in Ontario, Canada and likes reading books, books, and more books (which more than fill his farmhouse).

Barry Hollander, a former newspaper reporter, teaches journalism at the University of Georgia and may be one of the few members of both the Society of Professional Journalists and the Horror Writers Association. When not writing he helps run a MUD, an online virtual fantasy world where he gets to play god on a daily basis. His forty or so short stories have appeared in a variety of magazines, webzines, and anthologies.

Sarah de Almeida Hoyt was born in Porto, Portugal. She lives in Colorado with her husband, two kids, and four cats. Her credits include two fantasy novels, *Ill Met By Moonlight* and *All Night Awake* (Ace), which undertake a magical recreation of Shakespeare's life. The first novel was a Mythopoeic Award finalist. A third novel is expected out next fall. Sarah has also sold over two dozen pieces of short fiction. Her credits include *Weird Tales*, *Dreams of Decadence*, *Absolute Magnitude*, *Analog*, and *Asimov's*. Some of these short stories have been collected into a book, *Crawling Between Heaven and Earth* (Dark Regions Press, 2002).

James Lowder has worked extensively in fantasy and horror publishing, on both sides of the editorial blotter. He's authored several bestselling fantasy and dark fantasy novels, including *Prince of Lies* and *Knight of the Black Rose*; short fiction for such diverse anthologies as *Historical Hauntings*, *Truth Until Paradox*, and the forthcoming *Shadows Over Baker Street*; and a large number of film and book reviews, feature articles, and even the occasional comic book script. His credits as anthologist include *Realms of Valor*, *The Doom of Camelot*, *Legends of the Pendragon*, and Eden Studios' first two zombie anthologies, *The Book of All Flesh* and *The Book of More Flesh*.

Pete D. Manison lives in Houston, Texas, where he is currently at work on a novel, teaching himself charcoal drawing, and searching for a full-time job that will leave him time to write. His short fiction has been published in two Writers of the Future anthologies, *Marion Zimmer Bradley's Sword & Sorceress*, and in such magazines as *Analog*, *Dragon*, *Science Fiction Age*, *Altair*, *Amazing Stories*, *Tomorrow SF*, and *Space & Time*. His first zombie story, "The Cold, Gray Fingers of My Love," appeared in *The Book of All Flesh*. Pete is forty-two and lives with his significant others: a Labrador retriever who won't retrieve and a suspected spectral entity.

Paul E. Martens is under the care of a wife and son, neither of whom are to blame for any of his actions. He was a first place winner in the Writers of the Future Contest, with stories in *Writers of the Future XVI*, *3SF Magazine*, *Speculon*, *On Spec*, *Future Orbits*, and other print and online magazines. "Miles Away," published in *Deep Outside*, received an honorable mention in the 2001 Best of Soft SF Contest. Paul will have stories in two other upcoming anthologies: *Low Port*, edited by Sharon Lee and Steve Miller, and *I, Alien*, edited by Mike Resnick.

Mark McLaughlin's fiction, articles, and poetry have appeared in more than four hundred magazines, websites, and anthologies, including *The Book of All Flesh*, *The Book of More Flesh*, *Galaxy*, *Talebones*, *OctoberLand*, *The Best of Palace Corbie*, *The Best of HorrorFind*, *The Best of the Rest 2 and 3*, and two volumes of *The Year's Best Horror Stories* (DAW). Last year, Meisha Merlin released *The Gossamer Eye*, a three-author poetry collection by Mark, Rain Graves, and David Niall Wilson. His latest release is a solo poetry collection, *Professor LaGungo's Exotic Artifacts & Assorted Mystic Collectibles*, from Flesh and Blood Press. Forthcoming from Lone Wolf Publications is an audio CD of Mark's fiction entitled *Cryptic Doom: The CD of Forbidden Knowledge*. He is also the editor of *The Urbanite: Surreal & Lively & Bizarre*.

Sharing his birthday with the date of Custer's Last Stand (same day, different year), **Steve Melisi** has spent many of his uncounted years trying to recapture the glitter and glory of that momentous occasion. Truth be told, he's failed miserably, but at least he hasn't acquired an extensive arrowhead collection. In the meantime, he has written many short stories (some of which have seen publication) and is currently trying to elicit interest in his novel, *Before the Afterlife*. He resides in Quincy, Massachusetts and doesn't have a dog. He can be reached via e-mail at melisi_steve@hotmail.com.

Christine Morgan is a writer who can't settle on one genre, and couldn't be happier about it. She alternates between fantasy and horror, with some erotica thrown in, and has also recently begun work on a series of children's' books. A gamer since 1981, she has been pleased to have her work appear in various roleplaying game supplements and was thrilled beyond belief at seeing her previous zombie story, "Dawn of the Living-Impaired," nominated for an Origins Award. The inspiration for this current tale came from watching one too many competitive eating documentaries. Visit her web site at www.christine-morgan.net.

In the words of his favorite band, Tool, **Joe Murphy** is still right here, giving blood, keeping faith—at least as far as his writing goes. He still lives with his wife, up-and-coming watercolor artist Veleta, in Fairbanks, Alaska. His fiction has or will appear in: *Age of Wonders, Altair, 365 Scary Stories, Bones of the World, The Book of All Flesh, Clean Sheets, Chiaroscuro, Crafty Cat Crimes, Cthulhu's Heirs, Dark Terrors 6, Demon Sex, Gothic.net, Legends of the Pendragon, Low Port, Marion Zimmer Bradley's Fantasy Magazine, Silver Web, Space and Time, Strange Horizons, Talebones, TransVersions, Vestal Review*, and many others.

Joseph M. Nassise's debut novel, *Riverwatch*, was a final nominee in 2001 for both the International Horror Guild Award and the Bram Stoker Award. The mass market paperback rights for the novel sold to Pocket Books for publication in October 2003 and it has since been optioned to become a feature film. Pocket Books will also be publishing the first book in his Templar Chronicles series, *Heretic*, in 2004. Joe is the current president of the Horror Writers Association. He makes his home in Arizona with his wife and four children. More information on his writing can be found at his website, www.josephnassise.com.

Scott Nicholson's first novel, *The Red Church*, was inspired by a haunted Appalachian church near his home in the mountains of North Carolina. His next novel, *The Harvest*, will be published by Pinnacle Books in September 2003. He's published forty stories, some of which are collected in *Thank You for the Flowers*. He also had stories in Eden Studios' first two zombie anthologies, *The Book of All Flesh* and *The Book of More Flesh*. Nicholson's website, www.hauntedcomputer.com, contains writing articles, fiction, and author interviews. For the record, the song "You'll Never Walk Alone" was originally from the 1945 Rogers and Hammerstein musical *Carousel* and has since become a popular religious hymn.

Jonathan Petersen grew up in Southern California and attended UCLA. He enjoys industrial landscapes, salsa music, dogs, camping, and carnitas burritos. He plays more video games than he probably should and will likely spend his entire author's fee on Legos. He likes Twinkies but doesn't *like*-like them. This is his first published piece of fiction, zombie-related or otherwise, and was written for Joe, Ranjit, Jordan, and Aaron. Jonathan can be contacted via e-mail at enoto@earthlink.net.

Scott Reilly lives in Raleigh, North Carolina with his wonderfully supportive girlfriend, Andrea, their rescued boxer, Rocky, and their eighteen-year-old cat, Jing. By day he toils in front of a computer as a software engineer; by night he toils in front of that same computer as a writer. Yes, he works from home, but can sympathize with the bitterness of morning commuters as he has to trek downstairs to get coffee. His website is located at www.scottreilly.net. This is his first sale.

Lucien Soulban is a flight of God's fancy. He doesn't exist save as chimera and he certainly isn't speaking to you right now. Ignore him. He doesn't live in Montreal as a self-avowed bachelor and he doesn't love writing with a strange, fevered passion that belies category. At best, Lucien is a rote, grabbing random words from a dictionary and sequencing them like a form of literary eugenics. By reading his story, you merely feed into the popular delusion of his existence—that he has mass and substance. There . . . now you've done it. Are you happy? He thinks he's real.

John Sullivan is a journalist who writes fiction and roleplaying games in his spare time because he doesn't get in enough writing at work. In addition to contributions to the *Bloode Island* and *Red Dwarf* RPGs, his fiction has appeared in such markets as *Adventures of Sword & Sorcery*, *Speculon.com*, and *Year's Best Fantasy*. More information about John can be found online at www.sff.net/people/john-sullivan. He lives in Rockville, Maryland with his lovely wife, Elisa, and two reasonably attractive cats. He wrote "Relapse" because romantic comedy is woefully underrepresented in zombie fiction. . . .

Lee Thomas grew up in the Seattle area. With a background in literature, journalism, and creative writing, Lee has published numerous short stories in a variety of markets and his non-fiction articles have appeared in several national publications. Now a resident of New York City, he is working on a novel while continuing to produce short fiction.

Mr. Tremblay—as his math students know author **Paul G. Tremblay**—has a Master's degree in Mathematics, which as we all know is a prerequisite for horror writers. Recent works have appeared or will appear in *Chiaroscuro, Beyond the Dust, Fangoria, Carnival, Vivisections, Brainbox II,* and *Gothic.net*. He is also the fiction editor at *Chiaroscuro*. Fiction links and other useful tidbits are available at www.paulgtremblay.com. Other points of mild interest: His personal best of twenty-seven three-pointers in a row is considered a speculative fiction-writer record. But that and fifty cents gets him. . . . His wife, son, and Rascal the dog often make fun of him when his back is turned. He is tall. And he has no uvula.

Andy Vetromile has loved zombies ever since his parents said he couldn't watch *Night of the Living Dead*. (They later caved and gave the movie to him for Christmas—ah, Yuletide.) He has written, developed, and edited games for Steve Jackson, White Wolf, Inner City Games, Gold Rush, and Nightshift. (He's also keen on playing them.) A fan of movies and books, he reads game materials onto tape for the blind. This is his first published work of fiction, and the irony of new life in his auctorial career from writing about dead things is not lost on him.

Tim Waggoner is the author of two novels, *Dying for It* and *The Harmony Society*, as well as the short story collection *All Too Surreal*. He's published over seventy short stories in the fantasy and horror genres, and his articles on writing have appeared in *Writer's Digest, Writers' Journal, New Writer's Magazine, Ohio Writer, Speculations,* and *Teaching English in the Two-Year College*. He teaches creative writing at Sinclair Community College in Dayton, Ohio. His home page is located at www.sff.net/people/Tim.Waggoner.